747·22

AB.

THE ENGLISH HOME

By the same author

ENGLISH COSTUME
From the Second Century B.C. to 1952

Syon House, Middlesex: the ante-room (c. 1762). The coloured marbles and gilt plaster show Robert Adam in his grand manner (see p. 216)

THE ENGLISH
HOME

A Thousand Years
of Furnishing and
Decoration

Doreen Yarwood

London
B. T. BATSFORD LTD

First published, 1956
Fourth Impression, 1969

7134 0805 7

PRINTED BY OFFSET AND BOUND IN GREAT BRITAIN BY
WILLIAM CLOWES AND SONS LTD, LONDON AND
BECCLES, FOR THE PUBLISHERS
B. T. BATSFORD LTD.
4 FITZHARDINGE STREET, PORTMAN SQUARE, LONDON, W.I

TO

MY FATHER

HERMON CAWTHRA

F.R.B.S., A.R.C.A.,

IN APPRECIATION

OF HIS EXPERIENCED ASSISTANCE

AND ADVICE

PREFACE

THIS book has been written as a companion volume to my *English Costume*. It endeavours to present, under one cover, a comprehensive survey of the English home over the centuries from Anglo-Saxon to Edwardian days. There are many useful books available on interior decoration, furniture, ceramics and metalware, but most of them deal with only one of these subjects, not the home as a whole, whilst others are illustrated almost entirely by photographs. In many instances, such as H. A. Tipping's *English Homes*, published by Country Life Ltd., the photographs are of first-class quality, and give a most interesting survey of homes over the centuries, with their historical background. The great drawback, however, to such a means of illustration is that the photograph can only show the home or room as it is to-day—and this is generally a mixture of styles and periods. One can see, for instance, in one room, an Elizabethan ceiling, Stuart wall panelling, a Persian 18th-century carpet, furniture of several periods, and, if the room is still tenanted, usually 20th-century electric lighting and means of heating. It is necessary, therefore, for the student to possess considerable knowledge before he can select the items of the period which he wishes to study from the remainder in the photograph. Only by drawing can a room and home entirely of one date and time be illustrated, with interior decoration, furniture and details in keeping. This, to the author's knowledge, has not been done, particularly on a comprehensive scale, and depicting all the rooms in the home, including kitchens and bathrooms.

Owing to the general present-day disapproval of late Victorian and Edwardian building and furnishing, the author has encountered some difficulty in obtaining sufficient and accurate sources of information of this time. Nevertheless, in view of the fact that both museum exhibitions and books on the subject, almost without exception, conclude their displays and descriptions before the year A.D. 1830, or, at the latest, 1860, it is considered important to continue this work until 1914. This is not because the author has any great love for this period, but because it is essential that students should be able to study this era for themselves, and compare it with other times, and not merely accept the statements of the pundits that it was a time of ugliness and bad taste, and therefore better ignored. Within the last few years, one or two books have been published on Victorian life, including the excellent *The*

Victorian Home by Mr. Ralph Dutton, but, as yet, such books are few, and museum collections are not displayed.

It is hoped that the primary use of a book of this size will be as a work of reference. Therefore, subjects have been dealt with in the same order in each chapter, so that a student wishing to look up, for example, styles of chairs or ceramic ware, can find them readily.

For reasons of space, it is not possible to give a complete bibliography, because the scope of this book covers interior decoration, furniture, furnishings, domestic utensils, plan and lay-out, architectural design, ceramics, glassware and silverware. However, a list of books which the author has found useful and interesting is given.

The scope of this book has been limited to the interior of the English home. There are so many excellent books available on architecture—public, ecclesiastical and domestic—that this field is more adequately covered. Thus, the domestic rather than the architectural aspect of the interior of the average English home has been of concern. For this reason, where possible, middle-class homes have been chosen as examples, rather than the palaces and stately homes—the subject of several books excellently illustrated with photographs—or the houses of the very poor.

Very few of the full-page interiors shown are exact replicas of rooms existing at the present. The author has taken a ceiling from one source, wall decoration from another, and furniture from a third, etc. This is because it is considered more useful to try to illustrate as many types of design as possible. If rooms were shown just as they stand, much repetition would occur and difficulties would arise because the room would rarely be all of one date and period.

Acknowledgments to some of the most valuable sources of information are given on page xv. All the drawings show authentic work from the appropriate age: no liberties have been taken in this respect.

DOREEN YARWOOD

LONDON, 1955

CONTENTS

CONTENTS

CONTENTS

CONTENTS

xii

CONTENTS

ACKNOWLEDGMENT

IT is impossible to list, and express appreciation to, the individual sources of information for each drawing in this book. The author has been very fortunate in receiving invaluable help and advice, photographic material and permission to make drawings from a number of sources. Grateful thanks are rendered to the Victoria and Albert Museum, in particular to Mr. Ralph Edwards, Keeper of the Department of Woodwork; the Geffrye Museum, Shoreditch, for periods covering Stuart to Victorian furniture and interiors; Horniman's Museum; the London Museum, especially for the Medieval and Victorian periods; and Hampton Court Palace for the Tudor kitchen and kitchen utensils of this and later periods. Information has also been obtained from individual homes, including many of those open to the public, such as Osterley House, Ham House, Penshurst Place, etc. Mr. Clifford Musgrave, Director of the Royal Pavilion, Brighton, has kindly supplied photographs and given permission for drawings to be made from the fine Regency kitchen at the Pavilion, as depicted in Figs. 449 and 515. Mr. Jack Dove, Borough Librarian and Curator of the Hove Museum, has been most helpful in placing the decoration and furniture of the Regency and Early Victorian rooms at the author's disposal, also in supplying useful photographs. Most valued assistance and advice have been given by Messrs. B. T. Batsford Ltd., in the persons of Mr. Brian Batsford and Mr. Samuel Carr, who have spared no effort in finding suitable material for the author's use. Various librarians have also been most helpful in tracing and lending useful books: these include Mr. McColvin of the library at The Polytechnic, Regent Street, W.1, Mr. Thompson of the Newnes Public Library, S.W.15, and Miss Schlesinger of the library of the South-East Essex Technical College. Lastly, thanks are due to Mr. John Yarwood for editing the manuscript, and to Mrs. G. Allvey and Mrs. J. Bangert for typing it.

The author and publishers would like to thank the following for permission to reproduce the photographs included in this book:

The Earl of Pembroke and Montgomery, and Salisbury, South Wilts and Blackmore Museum, Salisbury, for plate IIa; Lord Fairhaven, for plate XXVIe; the Master and Fellows of Christ's College, Cambridge, for plate VII*a*; the President and Fellows of Corpus Christi College, Oxford, for plate VI*a*; the Master and Fellows of New College, Oxford, for plate VII*c*; Bracher and Sydenham, Reading, for plate XXVII*c*; Arthur Churchill Ltd., for plate XXVIII*c*; Colonel M. H. Grant, for plate XXII*b*; Wolf Mankowitz, for plates XXII*c* and *d*; Shirley Neame, for plate XXVIII*b*; Mrs. Bertha Pellatt, for plates XXVIII*d* and XXIX*a*; Brian Reade, for plate XXVIII*a*; S. J. Shrubsole Ltd., for plates XXV*a*, and XXVII*b*, *d*; the Ashmolean Museum, Oxford, for plate X*d*; the Trustees of the British Museum, for plates I*a*, *c*, *e*, II*b*, *c*, *d*, X*a*, and XIII*b*; Country Life Ltd., for plate V; the Kent Archaeological Society Collection, Maidstone Museum, for plate I*b*; the London Museum, for plates II*e*, III*a*, *b*, *c*, *d*, IV*b*, *d*, VI*b*, *c*, VIII*c*, *d*, and XI*a*; the Trustees of the Victoria and Albert Museum, for plates IV*a*, *c*, VI*d*, VII*b*, *d*, VIII*a*, *b*, IX*a*, *b*, *c*, *d*, *e*, X*b*, *c*, *d*, *e*, XII*a*, *b*, *c*, *d*, *e*, *f*, *g*, XIII*a*, *c*, *d*, XIV*a*, *b*, *c*, *d*, *e*, XV*a*, *b*, *c*, *d*, *e*, XVI*a*, *b*, *c*, *d*, XVII*a*, *b*, *c*, *d*, XVIII*a*, *b*, *c*, *d*, *e*, XIX*a*, *b*, *c*, *e*, XX*a*, *b*, *c*, *d*, *e*, *f*, XXI*a*, *b*, *c*, *d*, *e*, *f*, XXII*a*, *e*, XXIII*a*, *b*, *c*, *d*, *e*, *f*, XXIV*a*, *b*, *c*, *e*, *f*, XXV*b*, *c*, *d*, *e*, XXVI*a*, *b*, *c*, *d*, XXVII*a*, *f*, XXIX*b*, XXX*a*, *e*, XXXI*a*, *b*, *c*, XXXII*a*, *b*, *c*, *d*; Yorkshire Philosophical Society, The Yorkshire Museum, York, for plate I*d*.

Plate XXX*c* is from *A Collection of Patterns for Glass Decorators*, designed by Joseph Keller.

LIST OF ILLUSTRATIONS

COLOUR PLATES

MONOCHROME PLATES

LIST OF ILLUSTRATIONS

LIST OF ILLUSTRATIONS

LIST OF ILLUSTRATIONS

LINE DRAWINGS

LIST OF ILLUSTRATIONS

LIST OF ILLUSTRATIONS

LIST OF ILLUSTRATIONS

LIST OF ILLUSTRATIONS

LIST OF ILLUSTRATIONS

xxvii

LIST OF ILLUSTRATIONS

LIST OF ILLUSTRATIONS

I

ANGLO-SAXON AND NORMAN

7TH CENTURY TO 1154

THE various peoples who migrated from the Continent to Britain after the departure of the Romans from Western Europe in the 5th century A.D. had by the 7th century intermingled and become the Anglo-Saxon race. It is with these men and women, their background and lives, that it is proposed to commence a study of the English home. The Romans had, indeed, an influence on our mode of living, but during the Dark Ages which followed their departure from these isles almost all trace of their civilising influence on our homes was destroyed by the warring tribes, savaging, burning and looting as they came.

The Anglo-Saxons by the 7th century had built up their own mode of life, but it presented a sorry comparison to that of the Romans. They were a farming community and preferred to live in small groups rather than in towns. They made clearings in the forest, and built small groups of huts, ill-protected by surrounding earthworks or a wooden palisade. The land belonged to the community, and the people of the community were prepared to fight for it when attacked, but as they had little organisation and method in fighting, they finally had to give way in turn to the Danes and then the Normans in the 11th century. In the early 11th century, Canute, the Danish king, attempted to co-ordinate some of these small communities, and began to introduce a type of feudal system on a small scale. However, the freemen retained their land until Norman times.

Christianity had been brought to Britain by St. Augustine in A.D. 597, but Christian followers were still in a small minority. The people were pagan. They lived by farming, and fought and hunted in their leisure. They drank large quantities of liquor and were often drunk and boisterous. The small church element tried to civilise these half-savages, and did social welfare work, although, perforce, on a limited scale.

There was little **education**; this was undertaken entirely by the monastery schools. Latin literature and grammar were taught, and in the 11th century the teaching of English also began. However, this all concerned a very small section of the community.

1

1   *Anglo-Saxon Hall: a conjectural restoration (notes on page 19)*

Gradually the chief town, **London**, began to grow again after the Dark Ages. It was rebuilt on the Roman site of Londinium, a most suitable location geographically in view of the tidal river of a width which, at that point, could be spanned by a bridge. It was essential, at that time, for the capital to be in the south-east of England, because there the land was most cleared of forest and a temperate climate prevailed. London was used as a centre for trade by land and sea. The city walls, the London bridge and some roads still remained from Roman building and construction, but the rest had been destroyed by the sacking and looting of the Dark Ages. Slowly rebuilding took place, but in a haphazard, rough manner, and the new London was very small in comparison with the earlier city.

There is little left of **Saxon architecture.** Apparently the Saxons built no stone fortresses; only a few churches were in stone. The rest of the buildings were of wood, which was abundant in supply, but these have naturally suffered with the passing of time. Their general style of architecture in stone followed that in wood, and, as far as we can see, was simple, using the round arch, with crude and scanty ornament. Another reason why there is so little Saxon building left is that their lives lacked security: villages and towns were constantly being raided, so little of a permanent character was ever built.

Information about **Saxon domestic architecture** is scanty, and nothing of these wooden structures survive to-day. The illustrations in manuscripts are sometimes misleading regarding dates and places. The best way of studying the Saxon method of building is to look at some of the houses in the lands whence they came, on the Continent. There one can still see homes built in later ages, but on the same principles, though larger and by better building methods. There are also, in the country in England, trades which use huts built fairly recently on similar lines, to house men during the summer months while at work.

Both the Saxon and Danish methods of **building** were taken from their ship design and construction—at which they excelled—and the house resembled an inverted boat. It was constructed on *crucks*—two great beams or tree trunks, naturally curved, fixed in the ground so that they met at a point above. There was a pair at each end of the house, and a horizontal beam was placed across the top. The crucks were usually about 16 feet apart at the base. If a large house was needed, a third pair of crucks was added further on at the end and the ridge pole extended. Minor beams or **rafters** were placed in between crucks. The walls—which were one with the roof—were of wattle and daub (that is, branches with mud or turf to make them solid and weather-resistant). **Roofing** was of thatch. The **foundations** were often of stone.

One of the great drawbacks of this type of construction was that, having no vertical side walls, there was a lack of head-room, so later a tie beam was fixed horizontally across each pair of crucks, about a third to half-way up

3

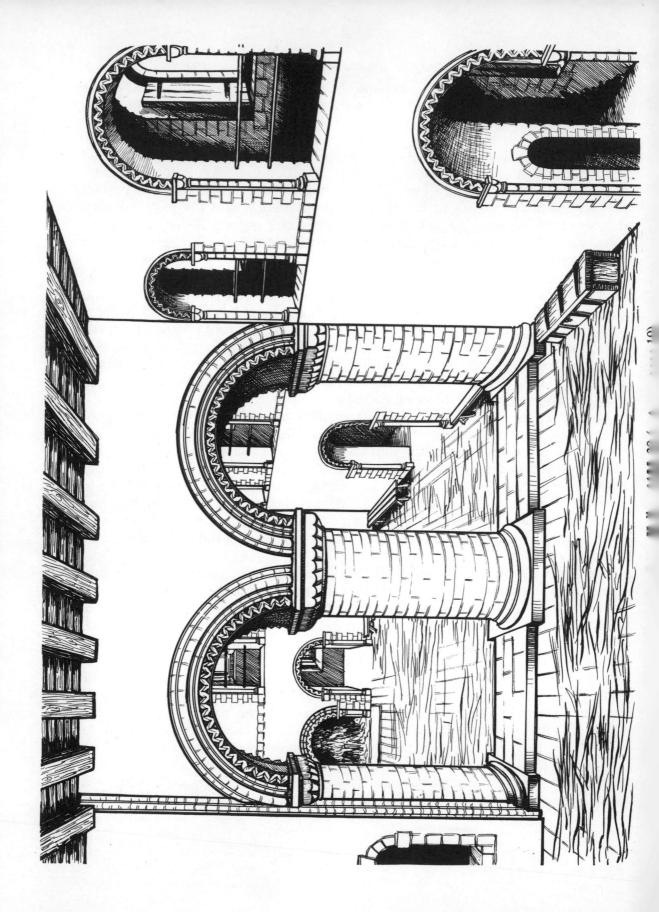

from the ground, supported on a vertical post at each side: thus low walls were provided. An example of the wall-less type of house could until recently be seen in Tea-Pot Hall, in Lincolnshire, where the crucks extended from the ground upwards and there were no vertical posts.

As the Saxon was primarily concerned in making his wealth from the land, the nobleman or chief who owned much land housed his workers and servants under his roof, together with the cattle. There was no privacy in Saxon days; everyone lived in one enormous room called the **hall**. This was built as the centre and essence of the house, and round it were kitchen, beds and cattle stalls. Life was communal; everyone ate, slept and lived in the hall. It was draughty and often leaked with rain; **windows** were tiny, being open spaces in the daytime and closed with wooden shutters at night. The **floor** was of earth or stone, covered with rushes, a fresh supply of which was added at intervals to cover up the general refuse, including food and bones thrown to the dogs. The **fire,** made of great logs, burned in the centre of the floor on a stone hearth, supported on iron dogs. The smoke escaped as best it could through the roof; sometimes a *louvre* or hole was made in the roof for this, in which case the rain and wind came in. A combination of cold air and smoke suffused the hall atmosphere. Timbers were black with smoke. This fire was also dangerous, as sparks often caught alight the roof thatch above. However, the need for warmth and dry housing made this idea of a central and communal hall desirable; lord and servant gathered together to talk, eat, warm and make merry after the day's work was done.

The **roof** was supported from inside by great vertical timbers at intervals down the length of each side of the hall, placed some feet in from the walls. The space between these and the walls was then often used for beds and/or cattle stalls, though the sleeping quarters for the nobleman and his family were sometimes in an adjoining building. The servants slept on the rushes round the fire.

The standard of life in these halls was low—there were no **drains,** no **baths,** and **wells** supplied all the water. However, in large halls there were brightly coloured woven **hangings** on the walls, and Saxon shields and arms were also hung up. The **doors** were of wood with iron bands.

Wooden **benches** were fixed round the walls for the more important members of the household and guests. The **"high seat"** or principal bench, for the lord, his family and important guests, was fixed on the north side. The lord's seat was raised (hence its name) so that he could view all the happenings in his hall. **Boards** were set up on **trestles** in front of the benches when meals were to be taken.

Small farmers lived in timber houses of similar design, though much smaller, and their cattle and other animals shared their home. **Labourers** and peasants existed in small wattle-and-daub huts, often with no windows. The fire had

no louvre, and the hut filled with smoke. Cooking was done over the same fire. The hut often had no door, only an opening and curtain, to allow a small amount of light to filter in. The family lived, ate and slept therein.

In towns, houses were also of timber, of similar type to those of the small farmers. Owing to their construction, the open fires and the fact that they were built close together, major fires broke out at frequent intervals, especially in London, and the city was at times partly destroyed. There were no drains, a polluted water supply, and dirt and vermin were everywhere.

A Saxon hall in a large home can be seen in Fig. 1. **Saxon windows** are shown in Figs. 4 and 5.

When Danish rule of England ended in A.D. 1042, the Saxons reoccupied the English throne in the person of Edward the Confessor, who reigned till A.D. 1066. During this period certain Norman laws, customs and manners were introduced, as Edward, although a Saxon, had been brought up at the Court of Normandy, while in exile from his own land. But it was not until William I, Duke of Normandy, became king in 1066 that the real Normanisation of Britain began.

As many great Saxon landowners had been killed at Senlac, William gave their lands to his own followers and nobles, while retaining some for himself. The remaining Saxon nobles, if they did not oppose him, were permitted to keep their land. He also arranged marriages between his Norman nobles and English women of high birth. After a few years, there were more Norman landowners than Saxon. William then enforced the **feudal system** in the form that existed on the Continent. The establishment of this system took many years, but it is to William I that we owe its institution in England. During the Medieval period it was a workable system, though it had its drawbacks. It did, however, bind the country together as it had never been before; it gave labour to the lords, and protection to the workers, who, in those days of violence, raiding and attack, badly needed it. Briefly, the system was that the king owned all the land and gave it out to his nobles (Saxon and Norman), while in exchange they took an oath of service to him and fought for him. At their own expense, they raised soldiers from their serfs when the king needed them. They also gave a certain number of days' service each year. The land was divided up into counties, subdivided into hundreds, and sub-divided again into manors. The manor included the demesne (the lord's own land), and the rest was given out to villeins on the same basis of services rendered as rental. The villeins had to work a certain number of days each week on the lord's land, use his mill (for which they had to pay rental) and pay tolls on hens, eggs and cattle owned. The villein was also obliged to follow his lord to war. The lord of the manor often owned several manors, and travelled between one and another, while a bailiff supervised each for him. The villeins were bound for life to the service of their lord, but on the other hand could not be deprived of their land and living. They could not leave the manor, but were not slaves; they possessed their own land to farm, and they did not starve, except in times of famine.

The **manor** was self-supporting: it had to be, as there were no proper roads. Transport was very difficult and travel dangerous. The land was farmed on the three-field system, with one field lying fallow in turn—this was necessary, as fertilisers were unknown. The manor possessed pasture for pigs and cattle, an orchard, a mill, being like a village, with the manor house where the lord lived, the houses and cottages of the rest of the inhabitants, a church, and barns and sheds for cattle. Crops were small, as drainage and irrigation schemes were unknown. Most of the cattle were slaughtered in the autumn, and used for salt meat during the winter, leaving only the breeding stock for a new start in the spring. This was because dried grass and root crops were not known. In the village, there were a carpenter, blacksmith, shepherds, miller, wheelwright and swineherds, so that all the needs of the community could be met.

A clear picture of life at this time can be seen in the Domesday survey, just as an idea of the buildings and people can be seen in the Bayeux tapestry. In 1085, for instance, it is recorded that the population was about two millions, of whom about nine thousand were clergy and landowners.

The **Normans** were a strong, capable people: they were great builders, and had made for themselves a better standard of life than the Saxons had known. They built a great number of castles, churches and monasteries—all massive and strong. The castles were necessary as centres of ruling power, in a land that for some years did not submit tamely to foreign rule. They were heavily fortified and immensely durable.

New **laws** were made, and the legal system set up by Edward the Confessor was confirmed, although to-day we should look askance at some of their methods of trial and punishment. For example, the guilt or innocence of the prisoner was often decided by the ordeal of boiling water or of fire. In the former case, the accused had to plunge his hand and arm into a pail of boiling water, to seize a stone at the bottom. The hand was then bound up, and if there was no scald after three days, he was considered innocent; if there was a blister, he was guilty. A similar method was that of lifting a red-hot iron from the fire. Some disputes were settled by "trial by combat", wherein if the prisoner gave up in exhaustion, he was hanged. The basic theme behind these methods was that God would protect the innocent, and thus declare Himself in these trials. Courts were often held in the open.

Education was still provided for a few children by the monastery schools. The custom for educating and bringing up the son of a nobleman was to send him as a page to the castle of another noble of higher rank. The boy was taught to revere his foster-father, and learnt, as he grew up, to be obedient,

Fig. 4. Saxon window

Fig. 5. Saxon window

Fig. 6. Norman window
c. 1150

Fig. 7. Norman window
early style

Fig. 8. Norman window
c. 1125-30

Fig. 9. Norman window
c. 1130-35

Fig. 10. Norman
doorway of stone-
wood & iron door
c. 1150-60

Fig. 11. Norman
doorway c. 1130-35
wood & iron door

Fig. 13. Stone capital

Fig. 12. Norman doorway
of stone - wood & iron door

4–13   *Saxon and Norman Architectural Details*

to be brave, to ride, hunt and fish, to use weapons, to swim, to sing and play, to wait at table and numerous other accomplishments. There was little academic learning in his training. Eventually he became a squire and, in due course, if he progressed well, a knight.

Great **fairs** were held from time to time in certain towns, and to these people went to buy the luxuries that could not be obtained at castle or manor, such as fine clothes, lace, spices, etc. Goods from abroad could be bought there. A fair was a great event in people's lives. Some fairs were noted for special products—for example, Nottingham, which still holds a Goose Fair. Goods could also be bought at the castle or manor from itinerant pedlars, who brought pewter ware, musical instruments and clothes.

Some **hospitals** existed—for example, St. Bartholomew's, founded in 1102. **Medical attention**, however, was rare, and often unreliable. Most people fended for themselves, by treatment with herbs, or blood-letting, or studying the phases of the moon and stars. Magic spells and witchcraft were considered potent. Fevers, plagues and leprosy were fairly common, and famines occurred at regular intervals, so that the population stayed at a low level.

Norman architecture still remaining in England to-day is chiefly in the form of castles, churches and cathedrals: it is comparatively rare to find examples of domestic architecture other than castles. The Norman style was based on the Romanesque, as typified by massive columns with cushion capitals, and round arches with heavy mouldings, decorated with chevron, billet or cable ornament. The cushion capitals were later scalloped, and ornament became richer. Walls were massive also, 10 to 15 feet thick, and ceilings were either flat and made of timber, or barrel-vaulted in simple, heavy style. The construction and design was very much the same for both secular and ecclesiastical architecture during this period.

As the **castle** was the visible symbol of Norman strength and authority in England, and served as the home for the noble lord, his family and numerous workpeople, it can be considered typical as an English home of the period. It originated on the Continental plan, and numbers of wood castles were built in the early years of Norman rule—temporary structures to defend the Normans from attack. After some years, however, permanent stone castles were slowly erected; a few in William I's time, but most of them between 1100 and 1154. These castles were fortified strongly, and were virtually self-sufficient and impregnable against attack. The **keep**—the main building— was a tall, square tower, some 70 to 150 feet high, erected on a natural or artificial hill, to command the local countryside. Around this was a moat and inner walls, and beyond these a courtyard, the villagers' cottages, stables, granaries, soldiers' quarters, workshops and other necessary buildings. Outer walls, and perhaps a moat, enclosed all these, so that the whole community was self-supporting and when attacked could retreat into the keep. The

(a) *Pottery Bottle*

(b) *Cone Beaker*

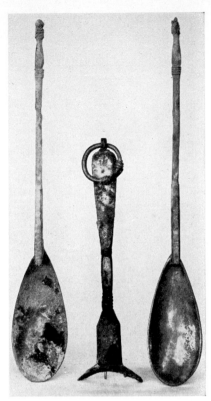

(c) *Silver Spoons*

(d) (above) *Glass Bowl*

(e) (below) *Drinking Horn*

ANGLO-SAXON UTENSILS

(a) *Bronze Hanging Bowl*

(b) *Bronze Hanging Bowl*

(c) *Silver Bowls ornamented with Equal-Armed Crosses*

(d) *Bucket with Bronze Bands*

(e) *Bronze Cooking Bowl*

ANGLO-SAXON METALWARE

stone for most of these castles was Caen stone from Normandy. Earlier castles were simply designed, but in the 12th century, as the fear of attack diminished, more elaborate patterns were evolved, including gardens, orchards, poultry yards, etc. The best-known examples of fortified castles begun in the reign of William I are the Tower of London and Colchester Castle, while later examples are Rochester and Hedingham Castles, dated about 1130.

The dwelling place for the lord, his family and retainers was the **keep,** which was massively built, on four or five floors, with walls 10 to 15 feet thick and battlements round the flat roof from where the defence was conducted. **Turrets** were usually constructed at each corner, containing a spiral stone **staircase** with a central stone newel post, which ran up through all

14 *Norman Stone Staircase*

floors. These staircases were designed so that one man at the top could defend the staircase using his sword in his right hand, while ascending men were hampered by their right arms being jammed up against the newel post (see Fig. 14). The main **entrance door** to the keep was on the first floor, while below this was the **undercroft**—a floor with only narrow slit windows or none at all and a barrel-vaulted stone roof—which was used as a storehouse. Dungeons and cellars were also on this level or lower. The primary room in the castle was, as in Saxon times, the **Great Hall,** and in here everyone ate, lived and slept. The hall occupied a complete floor of the keep, either on the entrance level or, more commonly, on the floor above. The size of the hall thus varied with that of the keep—an average castle hall was about 45 feet square and about 30 feet high. In view of this, it was difficult to obtain timbers long enough to span the ceiling, so an **arch** or arches were constructed of stone, across the centre of these large halls, to divide the room into two, but so that it could still be used as one room. The **ceiling timbers** could then span the shorter distance from wall to wall or wall to arch, whilst smaller rafters crossed these and fitted into them. A flat timber roof was thus provided, to act as ceiling and as a floor to the rooms above. The Normans were not able to use stone vaulting over such a large span as the Great Hall. The **walls** were of stone, some 10 to 15 feet in thickness, and later hung with banners and woven fabrics to provide warmth and colour. Into the thicknesses of these walls were built small rooms and *garderobes* (privies); the former served as sleeping quarters for the lord and his family. There was little privacy, however, as the only entrance to these rooms was from the hall, by way of arched doorways, which had no door, only a curtain to be drawn across at night. A **window** in the outer wall corresponded with this doorway, thus giving light to the hall and the small room. The hall windows, like the doorways, had round arches, decorated by columns, surmounted with cushion capitals, and mouldings ornamented by chevron and billet decoration. A narrower window was placed on the outer side of the wall, opposite to the hall window, as these were the means of lighting the hall. In hours of daylight cold air rushed in through the windows, also rain and snow, but at night wood shutters were fastened across the outer window. The windows were placed half-way up the walls of the hall, and a **gallery** was made between the two sets of windows, so that people could look down on the activities in the hall. Iron bars were fixed across the windows to prevent persons from accidentally falling into the hall. The **floor** was still strewn with rushes, which were added to from time to time to cover up the dirt, bones and refuse.

At meal times, **boards** were set up on **trestles** round the room, with **benches** to sit on. The lord and his guests sat at table at the upper end of the hall, sometimes raised on a daïs. Music was an essential accompaniment to meals, and a **gallery** for the musicians was sometimes built of wood, part way up the wall. At night, guests and servants slept on the hall floor round the fire, on coarse mattresses or on the rushes. It can be seen that the hall provided a place for the whole life of the people in the castle, of all ranks and stations: there was no privacy; everyone ate, slept, played and lived together.

The **fireplace** was sometimes in the middle of the floor, as in Saxon halls, or built into one of the outside walls. Large halls would have two such fireplaces. The opening was a round arch, decorated like the doorways, and the smoke escaped through a flue cut at an angle of about 45 degrees into the wall, to the outside air a few feet above. There were no proper chimneys, and the smoke often blew back again. The smoke from a central fire still escaped through the roof and windows, but filled the hall on windy days.

Illustrations of two **Norman halls** in castle keeps can be seen in Figs. 2 and 3. A **spiral staircase** is depicted in Fig. 14, and **windows** and **doorways** in Figs. 6, 7, 8, 9, 10, 11, 12 and 13.

The other floors of the castle were generally each divided into two rooms. The entrance levels of the castle sometimes contained a smaller hall, a guardroom and storage space, while the upper floors provided further sleeping quarters for important members of the household and guests. There were also a chapel, a kitchen and an armoury.

Drainage and **sanitation** were most primitive. The *garderobes* or latrines, built into the thicknesses of the walls, drained into a pit or into the castle moat. **Bathing** was rarely indulged in, being a practice limited to the upper ranks of society, and performed in a large tub, filled with hot water by servants. However, bed linen was changed fairly frequently, and washed.

The **manor house,** occupied by the lord of the manor, his family and retainers, was similar to the castle, on a smaller scale. It was equally necessary to fortify it, and as in the castle, the hall was the main room, though there

15 *Saxon Bed—cabin type, of wood, built on to wall*

would only be one or maybe two floors to the house. Some manor houses were of stone, in which case the hall was entered from a porch, reached by a few outside steps from ground level. Beneath the hall was the undercroft for storage, as in a castle. There was a passage—called the "*screens*"—at the end of the hall, to avoid draughts from the main door. Most manor houses, however, were of timber, with wattle and plaster, and were smaller than the stone ones. The **kitchen** sometimes adjoined the hall, but was often in a separate adjacent building, somewhat like a glorified shed; food was carried into the hall via the screens. The hall fire was in a central hearth, usually made with a louvre in the roof, through which the smoke could escape. An inside staircase was rare, except in large stone manor houses, where a spiral type in a turret might be constructed. Alternatively, there might be a wood ladder inside, but more often a stone or wood staircase was made on the outside of the house.

Towns began to grow after 1066; some were built around a castle, partly because it had been chosen as a good site, and partly for the protection it afforded. The streets were narrow, dirty and dark, and cattle and pigs were driven over the cobblestones; sewage ran down the centre of the street. The **houses** of fairly well-to-do people were of timber and plaster, with a thatched roof. Few remain to-day, but the "Jew's House" at Lincoln shows an example of the design. There were usually two rooms, one above the other; the lower one was used for storage, and the upper one was the hall or living room. It was open to the rafters, which were gable-shaped. Some houses had a lean-to shed, used as a kitchen, added on at the back. The **houses** of poorer people were of mud and thatch, consisting of just one room, which was shared with the cattle. Fire was still a great danger in towns, and its ravages were severe from year to year.

In the country, the **cottages** of the poor were equally miserable, or perhaps more so. Also made of mud and thatch, and consisting of one room, they had no windows in many cases, and the only light came in through the

16   *Norman Bed—wood frame, curtains on metal rods inserted in wall*

open doorway, which was covered only by a fur skin or cloth. The accommodation had not improved from that of the Saxons. This type of dwelling has not lasted at all; in fact, the huts were burnt each time an attack was made on the nearby castle or manor.

The **furniture** made and used by both Saxons and Normans was scanty in amount and crude in craftsmanship. The two essentials of life, as epitomised in advertisements for accommodation to-day, were "bed and board", only these were taken literally in earlier times. The **Saxon bed** was usually made up against the wall as a sort of bunk or cabin. A rough mattress was placed on the wood boards, together with covers; curtains were drawn across at night. In the later Saxon period, some wooden bedsteads which were wood platforms with bedding placed on them were constructed (see Fig. 15). The **Norman bedstead** was similar to this latter type, but sometimes had curtains drawn at the sides, hung from horizontal iron rails, which were attached to and projected from the wall. **Bed-clothes** consisted of sheets, pillows, quilts and fur rugs (see Fig. 16). Both these types of bed were for the well-to-do: everyone else slept on the floor of the hall, round the fire. The **"board"** was literally a board or boards, in both periods, set up on **trestles**, or tree stumps, when meals were required (see Figs. 1, 2 and 3). **Benches** to sit on were often fixed to the walls. The diners always sat with their backs to the wall, for safety and to be on guard, and food was served to them from the centre of the room. All furniture was strictly utilitarian, and either fixed to the walls or placed against them in order to leave the main part of the room free for entertainment and general activity.

Chests were another essential item of furniture; these were often only hollowed-out tree trunks, encircled by iron bands, and with iron locks to secure a lid. Later they were constructed of heavy boards, pegged together. The chest had many uses, and is one of the oldest pieces of furniture. Primarily it was to keep safe the family valuables, such as silver plate, linen and clothes. It was also used as a seat, with the addition of some fabric to make it more comfortable (see Figs. 1 and 2).

Stools were made—like a bench for one person—but chairs did not exist

14

as such, although a back and arms might be added to the lord's bench to make the "high seat".

Oak was the wood most used for making furniture, also ash and elm.

Cradles for babies were sometimes of wood, but also of rushes and cane, woven and plaited together. The babies were wrapped in linen and tied in swaddling bands.

Lighting was provided by the fire, by sputtering torches dipped in fat and stuck in iron holders in the walls, or by open bowls containing burning oil. **Candles** of beeswax were rare, and only used by the wealthy, though home-made *rushlights* were employed a good deal in Norman times. These were made from rushes, gathered in summer, dried, peeled and cut into two-foot lengths. They were then dipped in melted fat many times to provide a good coating. The burning rushlight was supported in a metal holder. Candles, when used, were held in metal **candlesticks** or on a **hanging stand** suspended from the ceiling beams. A light was obtained from the fire or from a flint and steel (see Figs. 1 and 3).

Women were busy indeed: although the noble lady had handmaidens to do her work, she made tapestry and sewed fine embroideries; she also taught girl children their manners, general behaviour and womanly crafts. When the lord was away at war or touring his manor, she deputised for him and organised the life of the castle. Less well-to-do women were responsible for spinning, weaving and making the clothes and wall-hangings for the house-hold, and country women also made the bread, looked after the dairy, and even helped in the fields. All women were responsible for providing meals, whether cooked by themselves or with the aid of servants. Each home had a spindle and whorl for spinning, and many had looms for weaving. There were also workboxes for sewing and mending, made of metal, and often hung from the girdle (see Fig. 27).

The acquiring, cooking and eating of **food** took up much of the time and energies of both Saxons and Normans. The standard and quantity of the food available increased according to rank. In castles, manors and larger houses, **meals** were served in the hall for everyone, and in the cottages food was cooked and eaten in the one room. The meals in the larger abodes were elaborately prepared and organised, with many courses and wines. The food was cooked over huge fires, and the meat roasted on a spit, turned by hand, over a fire, with a tin—called a dripping tin—placed underneath to catch the fat. Large cauldrons were used to boil food and water over another fire. Bread, pies and cakes were baked in crude stone ovens, which were heated with burning wood ash inside them; then the ashes were raked aside and the pies, etc., placed inside the oven. In cottages and small houses the central hut fire was used for all cooking and baking, which was simple and unvaried. A coarse grain mixed with water was made into bun shapes to serve instead

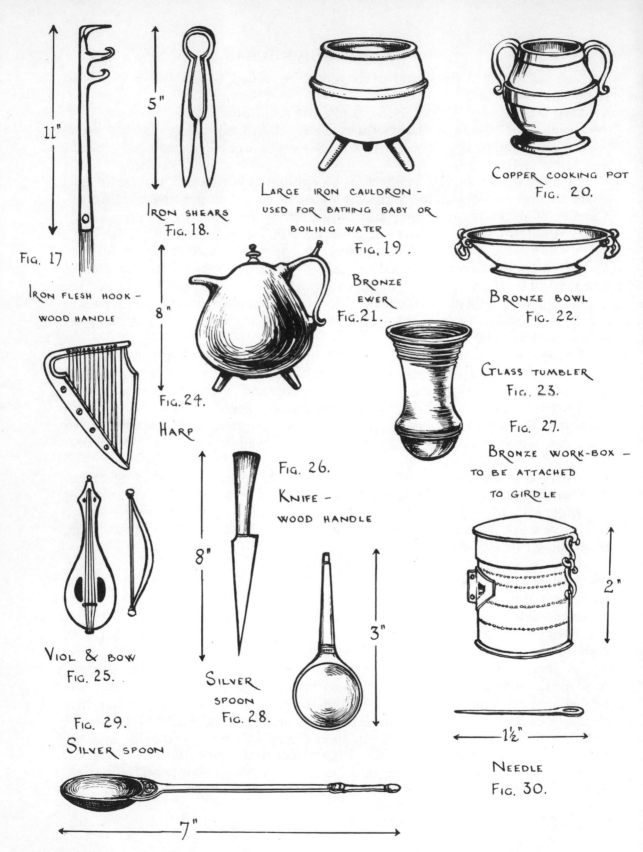

11"

5"

Iron shears
Fig. 18.

Large iron cauldron -
used for bathing baby or
boiling water
Fig. 19.

Copper cooking pot
Fig. 20.

Fig. 17

Iron flesh hook -
wood handle

8"

Bronze
ewer
Fig. 21.

Bronze bowl
Fig. 22.

Fig. 24.

Harp

Glass tumbler
Fig. 23.

Fig. 27.

Bronze work-box -
to be attached
to girdle

Fig. 26.

Knife -
wood handle

8"

3"

2"

Viol & bow
Fig. 25.

Silver
spoon
Fig. 28.

1½"

Fig. 29.
Silver spoon

Needle
Fig. 30.

7"

17–30   *Details of various Kitchen and other Utensils*

of loaves. The chief **kitchen utensils** were flesh hooks (see Fig. 17), which were used to examine and taste the food in the cauldrons—though the roasted meat was served from the spit—also roasting spits, some three to four feet in length, water buckets of wood, metal or leather, wood, metal and earthenware bowls and metal cauldrons. At least one large cauldron was possessed by every family; it was used for various purposes: boiling water, bathing the baby, washing the clothes, or for cooking purposes. Metal ewers for water were also in use. Some of these articles can be seen in Figs. 19, 20, 21 and 22. The food was stored in boxes and baskets. Chains and hooks were set up to suspend the cauldron over the fire, also trivets were used to enable cooking vessels to be stood near, or partly in, the fire. Scales were employed for weighing food.

At table, a white cloth was spread, in Norman times, but utensils were scanty in both periods. Food was served on plain wooden dishes, usually shared between two or more persons, but often the diner ate his food from a **trencher**—a thick slice of bread—again often shared with one's neighbour; trenchers were thrown to the dogs after a meal. Roast meat was served on the spits. Each person had his own knife in his belt, and used it to cut off lumps of food, which he then ate with his fingers. Gravy was mopped up with bread. In view of these methods of eating, in the castles and manor houses, pages brought round a basin, an ewer of water and a towel to each guest and member of the family to wash before a meal. A few silver spoons have been found, but these were rare.

Music was considered an essential accompaniment to a meal, both during serving and eating. A Norman lord had his own minstrels, and there were also wandering bands of minstrels who were always heartily welcomed at castle or manor house. Among musical instruments played were the viol, trumpet, flute, cymbals, lyre, bells and pipes (see Figs. 24 and 25). Other entertainers recited romances, and later, after the meal, performances were given by acrobats, tumblers, jugglers and the fool or jester. The Saxons also liked musical accompaniment to their meals, but preferred songs of war and music from a harp.

A great deal of meat and fish was eaten by the well-to-do. People liked strong flavours, and used spices in the cooking to provide them. Whale meat was considered a delicacy, and fowl, game and venison provided a relief from the inevitable salt beef of winter months. Cream and butter were scarce, and fruit was chiefly dried. There were no potatoes or root crops. Different standards of bread were baked—fine and white for the lord and his family, and coarser for the servants. Wines were drunk by the wealthy, while ale, mead and cider sufficed for everyone else. Even peasants ate a good deal of meat, though they often suffered from disease because of faulty curing methods and a shortage of salt. They also ate cheese, eggs, fruit, vegetables and coarse oatcakes.

The **pottery** of the Saxon period was crude and rough. It was made by hand, not on a potter's wheel, and it was a brownish earthenware. Decoration, if any, was provided by incised lines, uneven top edges marked by the finger, or by wood stamps or dies to make a pattern. Pottery, like the other arts, was at low ebb after the Dark Ages. Little or nothing of the Roman skill and knowledge bequeathed to Britain during their years of occupation survived the subsequent period of bloodshed and destruction. Indeed, it was not until late Tudor times, with the European Renaissance, that the arts began to flourish again. In the 12th century, a thin, uneven glaze was used on earthenware, of greenish hue, but designs were still crude and rough. Earthenware was in general use for cooking vessels in both periods, also for urns and bowls. Some work of a superior type was brought over from the Continent (see Plate Ia).

Metal ware was perhaps of more advanced craftsmanship. Celtic work had produced some fine examples in bronze and gold, decorated with enamelling. Saxon designs followed these, and included iron, bronze and brass cauldrons, pails, ewers, bowls, workboxes, and kitchen implements such as flesh hooks, knives, shears, etc. (see Figs. 17, 18, 19, 20 and 21). Silver was scarce and was used generally in the form of mounts on drinking horns, **mazers**—wood bowls of maple wood containing wine or ale—and for spoons (see Figs. 28 and 29, also Plates I and II).

When silver was used for making the complete object it was generally alloyed with copper and tin. Metal ware was decorated by enamelling, engraving, chasing, embossing and filigree work. Norman work was similar, though more Continental in style, with an Eastern influence. There was rather more plate now in large households, in the form of spoons, goblets, cups, beakers and drinking horns and mazers mounted with silver. Silver and gold were, however, still used sparingly. Other vessels of various kinds were also made, of pewter, lead, wood and leather.

It seems probable from available evidence that glass-making ceased in Britain after the departure of the Romans, and that **glassware** found after that time was of Continental origin, probably made in the glass factories of the Rhineland. The glass was only semi-transparent, and tinted green, blue or of a brownish shade. Decoration was provided by threads of glass wound round the vessel, or with dents made round the top or base. Both glass vases and tumblers existed: the latter had rounded bases which could not support the vessel. The intention was that one should drink the liquid at a draught, and set down the tumbler on its top edge (see Fig. 23 and Plate I).

Amusements and **entertainments** in Saxon and Norman times were rough and varied. Among the noisier and more energetic pastimes were cock-fighting, bear-baiting, wrestling and many forms of hunting. Jousting and tournaments were great events for both participants and spectators—the

Norman equivalent of football matches. Quieter pursuits included chess, draughts, dice, ball games, archery and skating. Children's games were similar to those of to-day, though rather rougher. They played soldiers, ball games, sat on a see-saw, walked on stilts and had dolls, tops and wooden toys. They also played "hoodman blind"—a prototype of "blind man's buff". Books were a rarity and were very expensive, as they had to be copied by hand on to vellum or parchment. Music was much appreciated, and many people could play an instrument.

NOTES ON ILLUSTRATIONS

Fig. 1. Anglo-Saxon Hall

Reconstruction from limited evidence available. Timber construction of **roof** and **walls** —stone foundations—wattle and daub in between timbers. **Thatch roof. Earth floor.** Woven and embroidered wool **hangings** on north wall behind high table. **Wood door**— iron bands. **Lighting**—torches in iron holders. **Fire**—central stone hearth—iron dogs. **Furniture**—trestle **tables** with tree-trunk supports—**benches**. Dug-out **chest**—iron bands.

Fig. 2. Great Hall. Norman. c. 1125–30

A reconstruction based on the Great Hall in the Keep of Rochester Castle. Stone construction of **walls**, pillars, etc. Wood **floor** and **ceilings**. Rushes on floor. The hall is 46 ft. square and 30 ft. in height. Room is divided in two by a centre wall which is pierced by four arches. Centre pier contains a shaft passing up every floor, with openings on each one, so that water may be drawn up from the well below. The Great Hall is on the second floor. **Fireplaces** at each end of the hall, on the outside walls. The fireplaces open out to the outside via a shaft from each one, for the escape of the smoke. Half-way up the hall walls are arches opening on to a passage which is built all round the hall in the thicknesses of the walls (12 ft. thickness). **Garderobes** and small rooms built into walls off passage. **Furniture**—chests, benches, trestle tables.

Fig. 3. Norman Hall. c. 1130

A reconstruction based on the smaller hall in Castle Hedingham Keep, on first or entrance floor. Size of hall 37 ft. × 29 ft. Height 18 ft. A stone **arch** spans centre of hall from wall to wall. Stone **walls.** Timber **ceiling.** Rushes on floor and a fur skin at the hearth. Stone **windows** with wood shutters. **Fireplace** has chevron decoration. It has a funnel-shaped flue which allows the smoke to escape through outer wall, at slightly higher level. Through wall entrance is a doorway to a small room built into thickness of wall. There are several other similar rooms round the hall. No gallery. Metal **candle-holders** and chain. **Trestle table boards** against wall.

31 *Castle Great Hall, late 12th Century (notes on page 43)*

II

EARLY MEDIEVAL, 1154–1399

HENRY II	1154–1189	EDWARD I	1272–1307
RICHARD I	1189–1199	EDWARD II	1307–1327
JOHN	1199–1216	EDWARD III	1327–1377
HENRY III	1216–1272	RICHARD II	1377–1399

LIFE, for the majority of people, continued in much the same way as in Norman times until the 14th century. For the privileged classes, a higher standard of living was slowly approaching; the arts, especially architecture, were flourishing under the patronage and domination of Church and Throne; lords and nobles began to pay money to the king in lieu of service, and villeins were able, to some extent, to buy their freedom from their masters. With the money acquired in this way the lords built fine homes and furnished them with luxuries from abroad—rich hangings, carvings and clothes. The 13th century saw the rise of Oxford and Cambridge **Universities,** where lectures were given, notes were taken on wax tablets and discussions held. The principal subjects taught were Latin grammar and literature, logic, astronomy, music and mathematics. Later, law, medicine and theology were studied there. Most **schools** were still attached to the Church, but there were more of these now. St. Paul's, the famous London school, was founded in the 13th century—pupils were called "Paul's pigeons" because of the preponderance of these birds in the neighbourhood. A grammar school was also attached to each university. The pupils of these schools came chiefly from the well-to-do merchant families. Poorer children had no education, and few people could read or write. Noblemen's sons were still educated as in Norman times, by sending them to the castle of a noble of higher rank as a page. Girls of all classes received such education as they were given at home.

However, greater freedom for the individual was evolving slowly. In 1215, the signing of the Magna Carta by King John marked the respecting of the rights of freemen, villeins and merchants. By the 14th century the appalling devastation and loss in human life from the recurrent plagues, particularly the Black Death of 1348 and the Great Plagues of 1361 and 1369, caused a

32   *Great Hall*, 1230–40 (*notes on page 43*)

great shortage of labour, and the **feudal system**, as initiated by the Normans, largely broke down. There were not sufficient villeins to work the lords' land, and the peasant began to realise that he held an important asset in the giving of his labour. Villeins were then allowed to purchase their freedom, and many went to work in towns in a trade such as that of a tailor, blacksmith, carpenter, tanner, silversmith, etc. Others rented land from their lord and reared sheep on much of it, largely because they lacked sufficient labour to raise abundant crops. There thus arose a new class of men: yeomen farmers. The lords also turned much of their land over to pasture for sheep, for the same reason. After the Peasants' Revolt near the end of the century, villeinage slowly disappeared. Apart from this gradual freeing of men, in regard to agricultural work, **manors** were organised in much the same way as in Norman times. They were, of necessity, largely self-supporting for food because travel was still very difficult and dangerous, as roads were few and bad. Much of the land lay fallow each year and, owing to the lack of fertilisers and manures, crops were small. Cattle were killed off each autumn, since there were still no root crops. Wheat, barley, rye, oats, beans and peas were the chief crops. Famines occurred at fairly regular intervals, due to failure of the harvest; a poor crop was always a disaster, as little was ever saved from a previous year's yield, even if it were abundant. Plagues and famines together kept the population at a steady two-and-a-quarter millions.

The improved **legislation** of Henry II's rule in the latter half of the 12th century brought in the origins of "trial by jury", and by the 14th century this method of trial had largely replaced the earlier custom of "trial by combat". The latter was only adopted then by men of rank. "Trial by ordeal" of fire, water, etc., died out in the 13th century. However, legal punishments were still, to our present-day way of thinking, brutal. Witches were still burnt at the stake; hanging was a common punishment for various offences, primarily theft, and lesser crimes merited certain mutilations or the stocks.

There were as yet few **doctors,** and most people could not afford their services. Instead they coped with their own ailments, or, if in need, visited the barber, who dealt with most cases. The usual treatment was bleeding or the use of herbs. Witchcraft and sorcery were believed to be a potent evil in causing illness and death. Superstition was rife, and it was considered important to say the correct charm if the treatment was to be successful. There were a few hospitals, chiefly for the insane, the poor, the blind and for leprosy. One of the many cures for the last dreaded affliction was "an adder boiled in leeks". Some surgery was performed, but it was crude indeed. Many of the patients died from shock, pain or subsequent infection. To submit to the operation, in these days before the use of anaesthetics, the patient was knocked out by sandbagging, then tied down securely; he was often drunk—and no wonder—by the time the operation was due to begin.

33 *Manor-house Hall, 1230–80 (notes on page 43)*

Britain had several thriving **industries** in these times. The wool and cloth trade was flourishing; it had been given particular impetus by Edward III's scheme for bringing over Flemish weavers to teach their methods to the English workers. Mining and quarrying were extensively practised, producing lead, tin, iron and copper; also various stones and marbles. There was a good deal of fishing round our coasts.

London, the Medieval capital, was growing steadily in size and importance. A new stone bridge replaced the old wooden London Bridge, and more houses were built. There was still danger from fire, but after a law had been passed in 1189 making it compulsory to build at least the lower parts of the house walls of stone, conflagrations became less numerous and dangerous. There was a moat all round the town for defence. Streets were rarely paved: they were narrow and dark, and an open drain ran down the centre. Refuse of all kinds was everywhere, and cattle, sheep and pigs wandered at will through the streets. Water was supplied from wells and the river—both sources were polluted. There were more shops now: in general these were situated in groups of one kind. Thus the fishmongers were in one area, bakers in another, etc. The following figures will give some idea of the cost of living in those days. A labourer earned 7s. 6d. per year plus some food. Masons earned 5d. a day, smiths 6d. a day, and carpenters $4\frac{1}{2}d$. A fair-sized goose would cost 6d., a hen 4d., a gallon of ale 1d. and a gallon of wine 3d. One could buy 25 eels for 2d. Wheat and flour varied in price, but were generally expensive. London merchants and those of other towns were becoming wealthy and important. They elected the first Lord Mayor of London in 1191.

With the second half of the 12th century came the introduction of **Gothic architecture.** All over Western Europe this new style began to replace the Norman one. In the latter part of the 12th century, the designs were chiefly **Transitional**—that is, a combination of the new Gothic style with Norman architecture. While the columns became slenderer and foliage replaced the cushion capitals, the arch usually remained round, though often, in the case of windows, encompassing two lights. Sometimes the round and pointed arch were used simultaneously in the same building. By the 13th century, Gothic architecture was established in the **Early English** style. Its chief characteristics were the pointed arch, narrow **lancet** windows—singly or in groups of three, five or seven, with the tallest in the centre—clustered piers, all much slenderer than hitherto, and ribbed vaulting. Later in the century, window tracery was evolved, with two or three lights in one arch, divided by a stone column or moulding, and the top part above these lights was pierced, at first with a circle, later with more elaborate patterns. The earlier types, in the second part of the century, were in **plate tracery** styles, the later ones chiefly in **bar tracery.** In **ornament,** foliage was used extensively, still based on the acanthus leaf. As the 13th century progressed, however, new leaf motifs replaced this. The leaves grew out of arches or columns and were formalised in design. Dog-tooth and diaper ornament were used in mouldings.

At the end of the 13th century, the **Decorated** period in Gothic architecture superseded the Early English. The arch became wider and window tracery was more elaborate, with three or five lights, and the bar tracery in complicated curved circular and ogee patterns, hence the alternative name for the period: **Curvilinear**. **Ornament** became more naturalistic and free, using floral motifs, especially vine, oak and maple, and also more complicated in design. Towards the end of the 14th century, the last phase of Gothic architecture, the **Perpendicular** style, began in turn to supersede the Decorated, but as this is predominantly a 15th-century style, a full description will be found in Chapter III. In general, in the whole Gothic period, **domestic architecture** followed closely upon ecclesiastical styles, though the former was usually less refined, simpler in interpretation and less ornamented. However, there are a great number of ecclesiastical examples which have survived to the present day, whereas there are few domestic buildings remaining undamaged. Nevertheless, a study of our great Gothic churches and cathedrals gives a good understanding of the methods of construction and design of the 13th and 14th centuries, and thus provides a knowledge of the domestic scene.

The **castle** and the **manor house** continued to be the homes of the ruling class. Both, but particularly the former, were still heavily fortified against attack, but with the advent of the 14th century, and a more peaceful existence at home, the castles and manor houses became larger, more elaborate in layout, with more rooms and less fortification. Both were designed on a similar plan, though the castle was generally much larger, and in many cases dominated a fortified town, the walls of which were an extension of the castle walls. Caernarvon Castle and the Tower of London are examples. Within the walls, the village or town was self-supporting, with a large courtyard, cultivated fields, houses, a church, stables, a lake, gardens, orchards and the buildings of important, necessary trades; for example, bakehouses, carpenters' shops, a smithy, falconry, etc. In the 14th century, consequent upon the interminable war with France, successful lords returned home with ransom from their captives, and with this wealth built large castles, often showing French influence in architectural design. Inside the **castle** the hall remained the centre of all activity and the main living room. It was on the first or second floor, leaving the ground and lower floors for storage. With the later more elaborate designs, the lord and his family had a withdrawing room called a *solar*, in which to sleep or receive friends. Bedchambers were also built on upper floors, or in the thicknesses of the still massive walls.

The **manor house** of the late 12th and 13th centuries was rather smaller than most castles, but was also fortified with a moat round the house, a drawbridge, and walls round the accompanying village or manor. A courtyard

(a) *Buff-ware Jug* (13th century)

(b) *Jug of Light Red Ware*
(14th century)

(c) *Buff-ware Jug* (13th century)

(d) *Vase of Netherlands Maiolica*
(early 16th century)

(a) *Mazer Bowl, mounted in Silver Gilt*
(late 14th century)

(b) *Bronze Cooking Vessel*
(14th century)

(c) *Silver "Maidenhead" Spoons*
(14th–16th centuries)

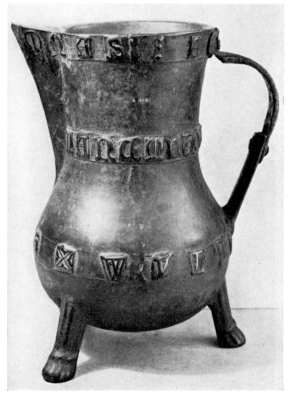

(d) *Cast Bronze Ewer (c. 1400)*

34   *Manor-house Hall, mid-14th century (notes on page 43)*

was made in front of the house. The main floor of the house was, as in the castle, above ground level, and one ascended steps up to the front door and entrance porch. The accommodation below this was used for storage. After entering the front door, one stepped into the hall—the principal room, and much the largest in the house, usually 40 to 50 feet in length, and lofty, as it extended to the roof timbers above. On the left-hand side of the hall, proceeding from the front door, was the lord's solar, a chapel and washing accommodation. On the right-hand side, or in a separate building, was the kitchen with cellar beneath. The 14th-century manor house was, in general, larger, with a greater number of rooms. Privacy was beginning to be regarded as of more importance; at the same time fortification became less necessary. The hall still occupied the main part of the house and was entered from the front door, but the solar was usually next to it, on the first floor, over the cellar. From outside, the house seemed to consist of two houses joined together, as the solar and the hall roofs were of different heights, the former being a small room and the latter extending to the roof as before. A large bedchamber for important guests was added in this century, also on the first floor, on the other side of the hall and over the pantry and buttery. Next to these was the kitchen, still a long way from the hall in which the meals were served. Some kitchens were even yet in a separate building. One room was still set aside for a chapel. Both manor houses and castles were generally of stone construction, though some of the former were still made of timber and plaster. It is due to this that so many examples of these buildings remain to us to-day, while smaller town and country dwellings have not stood the test of time, being chiefly of timber.

As the **hall** was the main living room in all Medieval homes, large and small, it is proposed to describe fully the hall of a manor house or castle. The student must then realise that windows, doors, roofs, etc., in other rooms in these dwellings were of similar design, though smaller and less pretentious. Following the Norman custom, everyone lived, ate and enjoyed themselves in the 13th-century hall, even though some privacy was now sought by the lord and his family. The room was still spacious and lofty, but at the same time draughty. The stone **walls** were now thinly plastered, with the stone construction partly visible through the plaster. Colour was of paramount importance in Medieval life, and the gay colours of tunic and hose were echoed in painted patterns on the walls. These were often geometrical, or alternatively showed scenes with human figures, animals and flowers. Wooden wainscoting often surrounded the room, but was not panelled at this stage. The hall was rectangular, and at the upper end was a low daïs on which the lord, his family and guests sat at table to dine. At the other end of the hall were the "*screens*". These consisted of a carved wooden partition or screen which cut off a narrow section of the hall and enclosed a passageway, into

35 *Typical 14th-century Hall, c. 1340–50 (notes on page 43)*

which the front porch gave ingress (see Fig. 34). The idea was to prevent the draughts from the front door and other doorways from kitchen, etc., reaching the hall, and also to provide a covered route for food to be carried from the kitchen to the dining tables. There was often a gallery above the "screens", approached by a ladder, and later a staircase. The **floor** was still strewn with rushes, which were supplemented at intervals.

The **timber roofs** of the Medieval period provide a monument to the skill and ingenuity of the carpenter. Domestic roofs closely followed ecclesiastical patterns. Most roofs were pitched, that is with gable ends, pointed up to the centre, though the pitch varied considerably. A large beam, running the length of the hall roof at the apex of the gable, was called the *ridge-purlin*, and others, named *purlins*, ran parallel to it at intervals down the gable sides. Into these and across them were attached numbers of beams, called *common rafters*, fixed from the top of the walls to the ridge purlin; larger ones placed at intervals to add strength were *principal rafters*. To provide greater strength and stability, *tie beams* were placed across from wall to wall, and these were braced by curved beams which were extended part way down the wall and supported on stone *corbels*. Alternatively, shorter beams were fixed across the hall from purlin to purlin: these were called *collar beams*. As a further support a vertical post was often erected from the centre of the collar beam to the ridge purlin. This was referred to as a *king post*. If two or more were used, from the collar beam to the principals, they were termed *queen posts*. Examples of these roofs in the 12th and 13th centuries, showing variations in construction, can be seen in Figs. 31, 32 and 33.

Doorways were of stone, in Transitional or Early English style, with heavy oak doors, close boarded, and decorated with ornamental ironwork (see Figs. 31, 32, 40 and 42).

Windows, also in the Gothic style applicable to the period, were still fairly narrow, set at intervals down each side of the hall. There was sometimes also a smaller one above the "screens" at the end of the hall, and a larger one at the upper end, over the daïs. Glass was not yet in use for domestic architecture; wood shutters were affixed to the lower part of the window, with iron bars between the tracery (see Figs. 31, 32, 33, 36, 37, 38 and 39). A tiny window, or squint, was placed in the upper end of the hall so that the lord could view the happenings in his hall from his solar after retiring for the night (see Fig. 32). There was much noise, singing, laughing and talking at night, as most of the people living in the house still slept in the hall round the fire—privacy was rare at this time. However, everyone was used to this, and the lord liked to keep in touch with his people even after he had retired.

By the **14th century, windows** were placed lower in the wall, and were larger, in the **Decorated** style of tracery. Many had lead frames with horn panes, and the rare but coloured glass in the top lights. These began to

FIG.36. STONE LANCET WINDOW-
IRON BARS - UNGLAZED - MANOR
HOUSE TYPE - c.1220-30 FIG.37.

STONE CASTLE WINDOW - IRON BARS -
UNGLAZED - 2ND ½ 13TH CENTURY
FIG.41.

STONE FIREPLACE -

c.1180-1200

FIG. 38.
TRANSITIONAL
STYLE OF
STONE WINDOW
FROM MANOR
HOUSE - IRON
BARS - UNGLAZED

c.1170-80

FIG.39. STONE CASTLE
WINDOW - IRON BARS -
UNGLAZED - c.1230-40

FIG. 40.
STONE DOORWAY -DOOR
OPENS INSIDE - LATE 13TH CENTURY

FIG. 42.
STONE DOORWAY -
CARVED OAK DOOR -
LATE 13TH CENTURY

7'6"

36–42 *Details of Transitional and Early English Period, 1154–1300*

replace wood shutters in this century (see Figs. 34, 35, 43, 44 and 45). **Door-ways** also followed the new Gothic style (see Figs. 35, 47 and 49). The **timber roof** was more complicated and elaborate, though basically of the same construction as before (see Figs. 34 and 35). Many **walls** were now hung with rich **hangings** of silk, velvet, wool or brocade, embroidered in bright colours. **Tapestries** were also much in use later in the century: they became very popular, and everyone of importance possessed tapestries from Arras or Paris. These hangings made the hall much warmer, and were carried about the country, when necessary, in great chests (see Fig. 35). Rugs, brought from abroad, also began to make their appearance in this century, and replaced the rushes on the floors. Many **floors** were tiled now.

The **fireplace** was still often a central hearth of stone, with iron fire dogs, against which the great logs were stacked. The smoke then escaped through an ornamental louvre in the roof (see Fig. 35). The advantage of this type of fire was that everyone could gather round it at night and keep warm, but the great disadvantage lay in the fact that the smoke filled the hall on windy days. Because of this, as time passed, more fireplaces on first-floor halls were built in an outside wall. A stone hood was constructed over the top of these fireplaces, to direct the smoke up the flue, which in the 13th century usually had its outlet to the outside air only a few feet above the fireplace. By the 14th century, some houses were constructed with proper chimneys. The fires in all these fireplaces were never allowed to go out, and were built up on the ashes which remained there. Turf, wood and charcoal were used (see Figs. 33, 41, 46 and 48).

Illustrations of 12th- and 13th-century halls can be seen in Figs. 31, 32 and 33, and 14th-century types in Figs. 34 and 35.

In the 13th century the withdrawing room, or *solar*, was used only as a bedroom by the lord and his family, who still dined and lived in the hall, except when ill. This room was on the first floor in a manor house, and was reached by an outside stone or wood staircase, which led to a door partway up the house. It was a much smaller room than the hall, but windows, doors, fireplace and furnishings were of similar type. By the 14th century, as the desire for privacy grew, the lord and his family spent more time in the solar: they dined there often, and received their friends in it. Sometimes a wood indoor ladder or staircase led up to it now from the end of the hall.

There were few **bedchambers** till the 14th century. They were built into the thicknesses of castle walls, and were dark, small and draughty. After 1300, however, as more rooms were added to castle or manor house, guest bedchambers or bedrooms for important servitors were designed. These again were similarly planned to the solar with regard to architecture and furnishings.

In castles, **staircases** were still of spiral type, made of stone and built into

FIG. 44.
MANOR HOUSE
WINDOW - IRON BARS -
UN-GLAZED - c. 1370 - 1400

FIG. 43. CASTLE WINDOW c. 1390-1400 -
IRON BARS - UN-GLAZED

FIG. 45.

FIG. 46.
STONE FIREPLACE -
IRON FIRE-DOGS -
MID - 14TH
CENTURY

MANOR HOUSE WINDOW WITH
WINDOW SEATS - TOP LIGHT
HAS LEAD FRAMES WITH HORN -
IRON BARS IN LOWER LIGHTS -
c. 1330 - 50

FIG. 47.
STONE DOORWAY -
OAK DOOR - IRONWORK DECORATION -
MID - 14TH CENTURY

FIG. 48. STONE
FIREPLACE - IRON
FIRE-DOGS - MID-14TH
CENTURY

FIG. 49. STONE
DOORWAY -
c. 1340 - 50.

43–49 *Details of Decorated Period—14th century*

the turrets which were at each corner of the keep. In manor houses, 13th-century staircases were almost invariably outside, made of stone or wood. The few inside ones were merely ladders. By the 14th century, these indoor wood ladders became more usual, and later indoor wood staircases were constructed, particularly from the hall to upstairs adjacent rooms, or to the gallery above the "screens". There were also indoor stone spiral staircases in some manor houses (see Figs. 50 and 51).

Stone vaulting for roofs was comparatively rare in domestic architecture. It was found chiefly in the ground or lower ground floors of castles or manor houses. This part was commonly called the **undercroft**, and was used for storage. It had a low ceiling and tiny slit windows. Simple forms of vaulting, modelled on ecclesiastical designs, were used (see Fig. 52).

Sanitation was still very primitive. Privies were built into the thicknesses of castle walls, and drained into the moat or by conduits to outside. **Washing** was not indulged in to excess. It was done in small basins, and baths were taken from wooden tubs (see Fig. 53). Ablutions were performed in company; no one felt privacy to be necessary for these operations.

Because of the risk of fire from cooking in open fireplaces within timber houses, the **kitchen** of a castle, manor house or large town house before the 14th century was frequently housed in a separate building, often connected to the main house by a covered way. However, after 1300, when greater numbers of the large houses were built of stone, or partly so, the kitchen was more and more to be found inside the house, to one side of it. It was situated so that the kitchen was a one-storey building with a louvre in the roof, through which smells, steam and smoke could depart. The roof was generally stone-vaulted, and in shape the room was rectangular or octagonal. There were several narrow windows, in the same architectural style as the rest of the building. Methods of cooking were much the same as those described in Chapter I, and the essential furniture consisted of large trestle tables, racks and hooks. Sides of bacon, hams, dried fish, herbs and salt beef were hung from the ceiling. The great **spits** were turned by a boy or man who was known as a turnspit (see Fig. 57). In smaller houses and farms the cooking was done in the main hall or room, over the central fire as before, or outside in a shack or shed. Essential **kitchen utensils** listed in contemporary writings of the 13th and 14th centuries include cauldrons (metal or earthenware), pots, saucepans, frying pan, kettles, skillets,[1] platters, spits, gridiron, dressing board and knife, gobard or bread-grater for making breadcrumbs, flesh hooks, scummer, ladles, pot sticks, slice (for turning meat), pot hooks, mortar and pestle, pepper quern and saucers.[2] Some of these articles can be seen illus-

[1] These were small cauldrons standing on three legs and having a handle on each side. They were used for boiling and stewing.

[2] These were, oddly enough, used for making sauce.

trated in Figs. 55, 56, 58, 61 and 63, also in Plate IV. A Medieval kitchen is depicted in Chapter III in Fig. 81.

Town houses improved very slowly, if at all, in this period. Only those belonging to rich merchants and well-to-do people set a higher standard. However, after the law of 1189 insisting on stone party walls[1] of a minimum of 3 feet in thickness and 16 feet in height, the risk of fire diminished. In the majority of houses the remainder of the building was of timber and plaster; brick was almost unknown. Roofs were of thatch still, though by the 14th century this was frequently replaced by slate, tiles and lead. Chimneys were only constructed on large town houses; for the majority, a central hearth with a louvre in the roof sufficed; alternatively, there was a short flue to the outside wall from a wall fireplace. The plan was similar to that of a manor house, though generally on a smaller scale. The word "hall" was applied to the main living room, however small the house. In general, the layout provided a hall—the largest room on ground or first floor—a solar over it, reaching up to the gables, a kitchen, usually in a separate shed, and cellars beneath the hall. The average price of one of these houses was about £10. Windows were larger than the Norman styles, and were of Early English or Decorated Gothic design.

Though the town houses only improved slowly in this period, the poor in the towns were still better off than their compatriots in the country. Whatever improvements had been made in town life did not reach the country peasants in this period. The average poor country family still lived in a **mud-and-wattle hut** with thatched roof. The beams were often rotten and the walls in a state of collapse. There was only one room, with straw-covered, earth floor, and a central fire over which all cooking was done. Everyone in the family lived, ate and slept in this room, which had an opening, but often no door or window. In the 14th century, some of these cottages were made partly of timber. Possessions were kept in baskets and boxes; there was little or no furniture.

Furniture in this period was still somewhat rough and scanty. However, as time passed, the craftsmanship improved, and carved designs, based on Early English and Decorated Gothic patterns, were used; in large houses more items were seen. But throughout this time only essential pieces of furniture were made and bought. Everything had one or more uses—nothing was just ornamental; each piece was placed round the walls, leaving the centre of the room free. The chief materials used in making furniture were wood —oak, poplar and other native woods—leather, iron bands and scroll work, and fabrics for bed-hangings, quilts and to soften chests for seating purposes.

The **chest** or **coffer** was much the most common item of furniture. Most households would have at least one, however crudely made, for it served

---

[1] The walls which separated the houses.

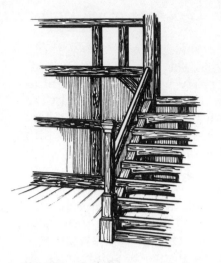

50 *Wood Ladder-type Indoor Staircase—leading from Hall to Solar. 14th century*

several purposes—notably as a safe storage place for linen, plate and clothes, and a seat for dining or resting. A bride usually possessed a dower chest in which her belongings were taken to her new home. Until 1300, most chests were plain, made of solid heavy boards with hinged lids and iron locks. Iron bands often bound them at intervals. Some had rounded tops like trunks. Dug-out tree-trunk types were still seen. In the 14th century the carved wood chests generally superseded the iron-bound ones, and those showing French influence from the Hundred Years' War were richly decorated with Gothic carving, which was often painted in gay colours. Some had doors in front, to open as cupboards; these were called hutches. Increasing numbers of chests have survived for us to see from these later periods, some of which are illustrated in Figs. 31, 32, 34, 35, 65, 68, 69 and 70.

In the 14th century, various types of **cupboard** evolved from the hutch style of chest. These were referred to as *aumbries*, or *dole* or *livery cupboards*, according to their contents and purpose. There are very few domestic examples extant from this century, as the talent and energy of the carpenter and carver went primarily into ecclesiastical work. Some, however, are depicted in Figs. 33 and 35.

Chairs were still very rare. Even the large houses usually possessed only one, for the lord at his high table. The importance attached to being seated in a chair can be seen in the derivative word "chairman", as applied to a board or meeting. In Medieval days only a man of importance possessed a chair. Also in those times of danger and unrest, most men preferred to sit on a chest or bench with their backs to the wall, where they were in a key position. There appeared to be two types of chair: the solid box style, later carved in Decorated Gothic designs, and one with wood turned legs and supports, a wood seat and wicker back. This latter type has not survived, being of weaker construction, but it is depicted in relief

51 *Spiral or Newel Stone Indoor Staircase—manor-house type. Late 13th century*

36

sculpture and in illuminated manuscripts (see Figs. 32, 35, 66 and 71).

Tables were still of trestle type. That on the daïs or those for guests were usually made solidly, but the others were still boards set up on trestles for the meal, then taken down and stacked against the wall afterwards to provide more room in the hall. **Benches** accompanied these tables: that at the high table often had a carved back to it (see Figs. 32, 33 and 35). **Stools,** like benches for one person, were still used.

Other smaller items of furniture included cradles, fire-screens, and racks against the wall for hanging clothes and armour (see Fig. 67).

52 *Manor-house Ground Floor on Undercroft—vaulted ceiling.   Late 12th century*

The fairly well-to-do members of the population had feather beds on wooden boards, raised off the ground on a carved wooden **bedstead**. The cold and draughts—fires in bedrooms were rare as yet—made bed-hangings essential. These hung on rings from curtain rails which were attached to the wall behind. A canopy or **tester** was later suspended overhead by cords from the beams above. There were bolsters, pillows and cushions, rich quilts of silk or fur, sheets and covers. By the 14th century, when **bedchambers** were becoming more usual, walls were gaily painted, floors were tiled, and there might be a rug. Even tapestries were hung, and a large chest was set at the foot of the bed to contain clothes and linen. A page would bring an ewer of water and a basin for washing. Less fortunate people would still sleep on a straw mattress round the fire (see Fig. 72). A bedchamber is depicted in Chapter III in Fig. 80.

The commonest form of **lighting** was provided by the oil-burning **cresset lamp**, made of stone or pottery, and hung from the ceiling. Most poorer people used home-made **rushlights**, or the light of the fire, but as few could read or write it was little hardship. They mostly lived their days according to the hours of sunlight. In large houses and in the churches, fine wax **candles** burned in **candlesticks** or in **hanging candlestands.** The former were of bronze or other metal, generally of the pricket type, with the candle impaled on a spike, and stood on three legs (see Fig. 60). The latter hung from the beams by chains or ropes and were of wood or metal construction. They could be lowered for trimming by a rope and pulley (see Figs. 33 and 35). Metal **lanterns** were also in use: these were hung from beams or stood on window seats or tables. They were cylindrical and contained a candle on a pricket spike. The lantern had a door attached by a hinge; this might have a horn panel (see Fig. 59).

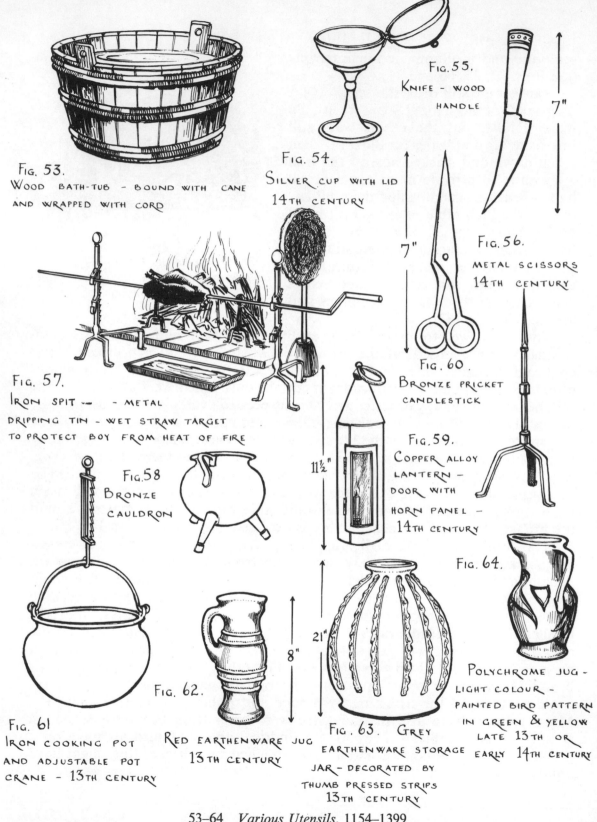

Fig. 53.
WOOD BATH-TUB - BOUND WITH CANE
AND WRAPPED WITH CORD

Fig. 54.
SILVER CUP WITH LID
14TH CENTURY

Fig. 55.
KNIFE - WOOD
HANDLE

7"

Fig. 56.
METAL SCISSORS
14TH CENTURY

7"

Fig. 57.
IRON SPIT -- - METAL
DRIPPING TIN - WET STRAW TARGET
TO PROTECT BOY FROM HEAT OF FIRE

Fig. 60.
BRONZE PRICKET
CANDLESTICK

Fig.58
BRONZE
CAULDRON

11½"

Fig. 59.
COPPER ALLOY
LANTERN -
DOOR WITH
HORN PANEL -
14TH CENTURY

Fig. 64.

Fig. 61
IRON COOKING POT
AND ADJUSTABLE POT
CRANE - 13TH CENTURY

8"

Fig. 62.
RED EARTHENWARE JUG
13TH CENTURY

21"

Fig. 63. GREY
EARTHENWARE STORAGE
JAR - DECORATED BY
THUMB PRESSED STRIPS
13TH CENTURY

POLYCHROME JUG -
LIGHT COLOUR -
PAINTED BIRD PATTERN
IN GREEN & YELLOW
LATE 13TH OR
EARLY 14TH CENTURY

53–64 *Various Utensils, 1154–1399*

The **diet** for middle-class and well-to-do people was varied and adequate; a great deal of meat was eaten—venison, beef, mutton, veal, pork, wild boar, poultry and the great delicacies of roast swan and peacock. Game, pigeon and waterfowl were also enjoyed. These provided variety from the monotony of salt meat in winter months. Fish, shell fish, eels and eggs were in demand, so the protein content of the diet was not neglected, although of course this was not considered, only the probably more important aspect of the enjoyment of good food. A variety of vegetables were grown now, but still no root crops. The best-known vegetables were cabbage, beans, peas, onions, leeks, lettuce and watercress. Oysters were cheap, and most people enjoyed them. There was no sugar yet; bees were kept to provide honey for sweetening. Poorer people ate chiefly porridge and milk, coarse oatcakes, eggs, cheese, some meat, bacon and vegetables. Coarser parts of game were made into pies called "umbles"—an expression later appearing as "humble pie". Butter and cream were still scarce, and fruit was largely dried. The well-to-do drank wine, often from France; others drank ale, cider and mead.

Meals were taken early in the day compared with present-day ideas, in order to utilise the best hours of daylight. In an important household a light breakfast was taken at 7 a.m., followed by dinner at 9–11 a.m. The next meal, supper, was about 5 p.m., and light refreshments might be served later. Dinner and supper were formal meals, taken by everyone in the hall. In smaller households, breakfast was at 8 a.m., dinner at 12 noon, and the last meal, supper, at about 6 p.m.

Formal meals taken in the hall were, in large establishments, imposing affairs, the setting being composed of strangely contrasting elements of dirt and magnificence. The floors were filthy, with bones and refuse among the rushes, while the nobility sat in gloriously rich apparel, eating from silver and gold plate. Only a few items of the latter were possessed as yet, and these only by rich houses. Candles and flaring torches lit the scene. Several white tablecloths covered the important tables. There were, as yet, few utensils; men used their own knives, and ate with their fingers from wood platters and trenchers of bread—one shared between two. Serving dishes were of wood, silver or pewter. Few silver spoons exist to-day from this period, but it is thought that horn or wood ones were in use at the time. Grace was said before meals, music was provided by the minstrels between courses, and after the meal acrobats, jugglers, story-tellers and dancers entertained the company.

From the 13th century onwards, sufficient **pottery** has been found to reveal a national style of work made in England, and the remains of many Medieval kilns have been discovered, notably at Cheam in Surrey, Nottingham, Hastings and North Devon. These kilns were obviously built near the sources of clay. The type of work became more elaborate and less crude as time passed.

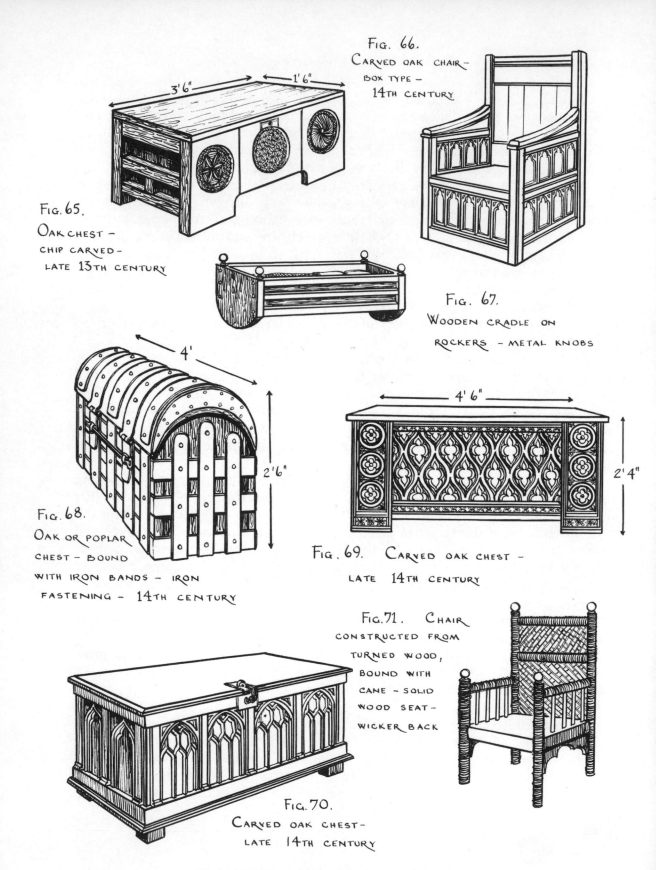

FIG. 66.
CARVED OAK CHAIR –
BOX TYPE –
14TH CENTURY

FIG. 65.
OAK CHEST –
CHIP CARVED –
LATE 13TH CENTURY

FIG. 67.
WOODEN CRADLE ON
ROCKERS – METAL KNOBS

FIG. 68.
OAK OR POPLAR
CHEST – BOUND
WITH IRON BANDS – IRON
FASTENING – 14TH CENTURY

FIG. 69. CARVED OAK CHEST –
LATE 14TH CENTURY

FIG. 71. CHAIR
CONSTRUCTED FROM
TURNED WOOD,
BOUND WITH
CANE – SOLID
WOOD SEAT –
WICKER BACK

FIG. 70.
CARVED OAK CHEST –
LATE 14TH CENTURY

65–71 *Early Medieval Furniture, 1154–1399*

72   *Bedchamber, late 14th century: wood bedstead—silk cover, bolster and cushion—canopy suspended by cords from ceiling beams—side and back curtains on rings and rails—wood stool— painted wall—tiled floor*

13th-century pottery was often undecorated, grey or buff **earthenware**, with a thin, imperfect green lead glaze. Stripes or studs of clay were sometimes used to make a pattern, also incised lines were made. Motifs were based on rosettes, stars, shells and birds. In the 14th century there was more decoration in relief work with coloured clays, even crude animals and heraldic devices.[1] **Polychrome ware** of 14th-century date has been found, chiefly in the London area, but is thought to be too fine to be of local make, and was probably imported from France. It is nearly white in colour, and has painted decorations of animals, birds and heraldic devices in colour. A transparent glaze was added afterwards. The chief **items of pottery** in this period were jugs and

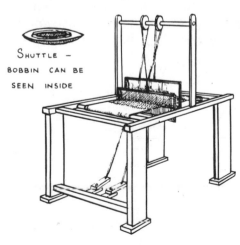

SHUTTLE – BOBBIN CAN BE SEEN INSIDE

73   *Treadle Type of Loom*

[1] This echoed the contemporary popularity for heraldic motifs in dress.

41

pitchers, bowls and cooking vessels, although in the 14th century metal cauldrons and skillets largely replaced the latter (see Figs. 62, 63, and 64, and Plate III).

Wood vessels were in common use in this period, but few have survived to the present day.

Glass-blowing as a craft at this time was still in its infancy in England. It was carried on in areas where sand and wood were in good supply, chiefly in Kent, Surrey and Sussex, where also were the centres of civilisation. The glass was greenish in hue and was made either for window glass in ecclesiastical buildings, or for beakers, lamps, bottles and tumblers. Bowls and cups were made in the 14th century. Finer glass work was imported for the nobleman's home from Venice, which city founded at this time its later great reputation for glass-making.

In **metal ware,** bronze was the common material, and was used extensively for the manufacture of cauldrons, bowls, jugs, ewers, buckets and cooking vessels. Pewter and copper were also in use (see Plate IV). **Silver** and **gold plate** was still comparatively rare, especially the latter. Maple mazers were still mounted with silver, and standing cups of silver in Gothic design were made. Other items were candlesticks, spoons, dishes for salt or sweets, flagons and ewers. All this work, however, was only for the rich and well-to-do, and particularly for the Church (see Plate IV).

There were as yet few **books**: women did fine **needlework** and embroidery, also spun, carded and wove wool; men learned the **arts of war,** to use a sword and mace, and to take part in jousts and tournaments. Favourite **pastimes** were dances, picnics, wrestling and skating. Cockfights, bull- and bear-baiting were among the cruel but popular **sports** of the day. There were many card and ball games, and chess and draughts were much enjoyed. Travelling Punch and Judy shows amused the population. Most well-to-do men and women were proficient at playing at least one **musical instrument**. These were numerous by this time and included the viol, the harp, pipes, the recorder, the trumpet and the cornetto.

74   *Medieval Spinning Wheel*

NOTES ON ILLUSTRATIONS

Fig. 31. *Castle Great Hall. Late* 12*th Century*

A ground-floor hall. Stone **walls** thinly covered with plaster. Stone **columns**—architecture of capitals, arches, doorways and windows of Transitional style. **Windows**—stone—iron bars—wood shutters. Stone window seats. Wood **doors.** Stone doorways. Iron bands on doors. Rushes on **floor.** Timber **roof,** gable shape. Horizontal beams span inner walls, which are supported on columns. **Furniture**—Oak **chests** with iron bands. Oak **benches.**

Fig. 32. *Great Hall.* 1230–40

Timber **roof**—has upper and lower collar beams. Principals supported on stone corbels on walls. Stone **walls**—covered thinly with plaster. Lower part painted in gay colours. Stone **windows**—Early English style. Wood shutters. "**Squints**" in end wall from solar. Stone **doorway**—wood **door.** Rushes on **floor**—daïs at upper end. **Furniture**—Trestle **table, benches** and "**high seat**" or lord's chair. Oak **chest** with iron scrollwork decoration.

Fig. 33. *Manor-house Hall.* 1230–80

First-floor hall. Stone **walls**—lightly plastered. Timber **roof**—nearly flat. Horizontal heavy beams supported on vertical posts, which terminate in stone corbels on side walls. **Windows**—stone. Early English style. Iron bars, wood shutters. Stone window seats. **Fireplace**—stone, on side wall. Smoke escapes through flue to outside wall a few feet above. **Furniture**—Trestle **table** of wood. Wood **benches.** Box-type **chair** of oak. Early English carved decoration. **Armoire** or cupboard oak, iron bars and locks. Cloth and earthenware jug. **Lighting**—candles in iron hanging stand, hung from chains. **Rushes on floor,** also fur rug.

Fig. 34. *Manor-house Hall. Mid-*14*th Century*

Ground-floor room. View of lower end of hall. Stone **walls.** Timber **roof**—collar-braced type. Decorated-style **windows** and **doors.** Oak carved **screen.** Oak **chest**—iron bands and lock. 3 ft. 6 in. long, 1 ft. 6 in. in width.

Fig. 35. *Typical* 14*th-Century Hall. c.* 1340–50

Timber **roof**—with collar beams. Stone **walls**—lightly plastered, hung with tapestries and rich cloths. **Floor**—tiled. Stone slab daïs. **Windows**—stone. Decorated-type tracery. Iron bars, lead frames, with horn panes. **Fireplace**—central hearth, heavy andirons. Smoke escapes through ornamental louvre in roof. **Lighting**—by candles in hanging wood stands, and metal holders in walls. **Furniture**—**Chests** in window bays. **Tables**—some large, 27 ft. long, on heavy supports. Those for less important people were still of trestle type. **Forms** and **stools. High seat** has carved back and sides—Decorated style. **Armoire** or aumbry—on each side of the daïs. Six cupboards in each. Iron locks and bands.

75　*Manor-house Hall, c. 1465–70 (notes on page 62)*

III

LATER MEDIEVAL AND EARLY TUDOR, 1399–1509

HENRY IV	1399–1413	EDWARD IV	1461–1483
HENRY V	1413–1422	EDWARD V	1483
HENRY VI	1422–1461	RICHARD III	1483–1485
	HENRY VII	1485–1509	

WITH the onset of the 15th century, feudalism was dying out: a new prosperity attended the freemen and yeomen farmers, and more villeins were free. At the same time towns were becoming larger, and British industry was expanding; mining produced coal, lead and iron, quarrying was carried out for marble and stone, and other industries included the making of pewter, tiles, glass and cloth. Bronze foundries were active; so also were brewers. Working hours were long, from dawn to dusk in town and country alike.

The 15th century was an unsettled time, with intermittent, but apparently unending, war, first with France, then the civil war of the White versus the Red Rose. It was a lawless age, though chivalry still held sway. However, at the end of the century, when Henry VII defeated Richard III at Bosworth Field, ascended the English throne, and founded the House of Tudor, a new age began for Britain. Slowly there appeared security, peace and a new lawfulness; the feeling of the Renaissance began to penetrate from the Continent. With this came new riches, larger and more impressive homes, and, at the same time, the gap between rich and poor widened—poverty was much in evidence.

More **schools** and **colleges** were founded; among these was Eton. More children went to school, but girls were still usually educated at home.

Much of the English **cloth** was still made in the home by the womenfolk. The fleece was washed, scoured and dyed, then teased and carded. It was later spun with distaff and spindle, and finally woven on a treadle loom.

Gothic architecture had entered its final phase towards the end of the 14th century with the **Perpendicular** style; this formed the foundation of both

45

76　*Great Hall, c.* 1480 (*notes on page* 62)

77   *Great Hall, c.* 1450–80 (*notes on page* 62)

ecclesiastical and domestic designs throughout the 15th century, although some buildings showed an early Tudor influence after 1485. Much fine ecclesiastical architecture was constructed in this century, from the magnificence of York Minster and Gloucester Cathedral to the village churches which provided small variations on the same theme. The chief characteristics of the Perpendicular Gothic style were the windows, with elaborate but fine tracery, emphasising the vertical line—whence comes the name Perpendicular —and illustrating a more restrained design than the earlier, more flamboyant Decorated windows, the wider, four-centred arch, the lofty, slender columns, and, perhaps the most typical and distinctive feature, the delicately traced fan-vaulted roofs, constructed from radiating spokes in the shape of a fan. The supreme example of this can be seen in Henry VII's Chapel in Westminster Abbey. **Domestic architecture**, as before, was much simpler and less ostentatious in design, but the same features predominated as in ecclesiastical building. Windows were smaller and less elaborate, and fan vaulting was sparingly used. It was chiefly seen in the interior roof of the oriel window, which became a feature of this period, in first-floor rooms of large manor or town houses. A French influence could be seen in English domestic architecture in this century; this was largely due to noblemen returning from the war with France, to build castles and manor houses on the French pattern. Examples of this can be seen in Bodiam Castle in Sussex, also at Hurstmonceaux, in the same county. Other noble houses of this period include Buckden, and Oxburgh Hall.

Ornament was more formal now, though the same motifs of vine and other floral designs were in use. Birds and animals were often introduced.

There were fewer **castles** built in the 15th century than previously as the country slowly became more settled, though some were erected, particularly in the north. Large **manor houses** were the typical homes of the wealthy landowners in the country, and similar houses were built for the equivalent town-dweller. Such houses were generally made of stone—brick came into limited use at the end of the century—and some were of timber and plaster with stone foundations. Smaller houses in town and country were built for less well-to-do citizens, and these were usually of timber and plaster with stone foundations. The rooms had low ceilings and the upper floors overhung. This practice was general in towns, in order to provide the maximum possible space in the upper rooms. The streets were in consequence narrow, dark and crooked; they were also still very dirty.

There was now much more available accommodation in the large **manor** or **town house**, and therefore more privacy for the family. The hall was still the largest room in the house, occupying two floors, and was entered from the main door and porch, but it was by now kept primarily for entertaining and feasting. The majority of the household still lived, ate and slept there, but

78   *Manor-house Solar, c. 1475–85* (notes on page 62)

the owner of the house and his family only attended there for important dinners and for entertaining friends and celebrated guests. They lived for much of the time in their private rooms, of which there were now a greater number. The more important servants now also had bedchambers or alternative sleeping accommodation.

The general **plan** of such homes placed the entrance porch in the approximate centre of the front of the building, and this led from the courtyard, as before, into the "screens" at one end of the hall. The hall was now either on the ground floor or one entered up steps to the porch, and the hall floor was raised as hitherto. There were several other rooms on the hall floor, on either side or behind it: a cellar, buttery, bakehouse, and perhaps the kitchen, although this was still sometimes in a separate, adjoining building. On the first floor there was the solar—the hall still occupied two floors—and other rooms which included bedchambers and another private room or parlour. In a large house there would by this time often be two indoor **staircases**, either of the stone newel type, or a wood newel or straight style (see Figs. 82 and 83). Some staircases were still indoor wood ladders or outside stone steps.

Large houses were by now designed primarily for comfort and spaciousness, rather than defence, as hitherto. Thus, windows were larger, and often undefended, giving more light to the rooms. Chimneys, of stone, were more common than before. A chapel was still built into larger homes.

Smaller houses in town and country, for middle-class and poorer people, were still made of timber and plaster and had few rooms. These were low-ceilinged and rather dark. The hall still provided the central feature and living room, but there would be perhaps a bedchamber and shed for a kitchen. Cottages for the very poor were more or less unaltered from those of earlier centuries.

There was an abundance of gay **colour** in all homes; walls, furniture and wood-carving were painted. Stained glass appeared in the windows of well-to-do houses, also tiled floors with rugs, and wall tapestries completed the rich effect. These features provided a suitable background to the colourful costume of the day, and helped to conceal any defects in comfort which still existed.

The average **hall** was a lofty apartment, still occupying two floors and dividing the house into two parts. The **roof** was of timber and plaster and, in large halls, very elaborate in design. The most usual style was the *hammer-beam roof*, wherein the **tie beams** of the older type were cut away in the centre, leaving the **hammer beams** projecting on each side from the wall tops into the room. Curved struts or braces supported these beams on a stone corbel attached to the wall. A vertical post, called a **hammer post,** helped to support the roof from the hammer beam, and both these posts and the beams were

V *Westminster Hall, London. The Timber Roof was designed by Hugh Herland
and built c. 1395*

(a) (left) *Silver-gilt Salt* (*c.* 1500)

(b) (centre) *Bronze Cooking Vessel*
(*c.* 1500)

(c) (right) *Buff-ware Jug*
(15*th century*)

(d) *Silver-Gilt Mazer Bowl* (*early* 15*th century*)

often elaborately carved into figures or animals (see Plate V of Westminster Hall). There were also **false hammerbeam roofs** wherein the hammer post was tenoned into the end of the hammer beam, giving a weaker construction than when it was supported on top of it (see Fig. 76). Simple roof styles with **tie beams, collar beams**, and **king** or **queen posts** were still constructed, especially in smaller halls (see Figs. 75 and 77). Much of this woodwork and carving was painted in bright colours. Oil or tempera was used, on a basis of whiting and size. Gilt was also used in palaces and very large homes.

The **walls** could now be decorated in a variety of ways: some were of stone, thinly covered with plaster, then painted with rich colours depicting biblical scenes, or in floral patterns; others were simply of timber and plaster (see Figs. 75 and 77); **tapestry** was hung to window level in many halls—it was more usual now and many beautifully made tapestries displayed all kinds of scenes and subjects in rich colour (see Fig. 76). Hangings were of brocade, gold and silver cloth, velvet or wool; these helped to keep the large halls warm. Tapestries were made in many places now, though they were still also imported from Arras, their town of origin; Norwich and London became centres in England for making them. Towards the end of the 15th century, a new method of wall furnishing—the use of **wood panelling**—became very popular. At first the walls were only wainscoted up to a certain level, and the style consisted of narrow vertical boards overlapping one another, as in a clinker-built boat. Following this simple method came panels with plain wood frames, mortised and tenoned. Then, at the end of the century, appeared the linenfold panel, with plain frames. This was carved in vertical folds to resemble folded material, though there were many varieties of imitation linenfold that are vertical mouldings with carved ends (see Figs. 86 and 87).[1] These types of wood panelling had been in use in ecclesiastical buildings for a long time, but only appeared in domestic architecture in the late 15th century, and then generally only in smaller rooms. In the hall, the large tapestry was the usual wall furnishing in a well-to-do home, while smaller halls had timber and plaster, painted walls and small wool hangings.

The **hall floor** was either of wood or was tiled, the latter method being reserved for larger houses. Beaten earth was still usual in very small homes.

Windows were of Perpendicular Gothic style and were now much larger. The four-point arch was wider and flatter, admitting a greater number of lights. The tracery was sometimes elaborate, but was dignified, and always emphasised the perpendicular line. A large **bay window** was usual at one side of the top of the hall, and the floor here might be raised a little. The daïs end was now often not raised at all from the hall floor. The bay window usually occupied the wall from the top near the roof almost to the floor (see Figs. 75 and 89). Glass was in fairly general use by now, sometimes with

[1] The term "linenfold" was apparently given to this type of panelling in much more recent times.

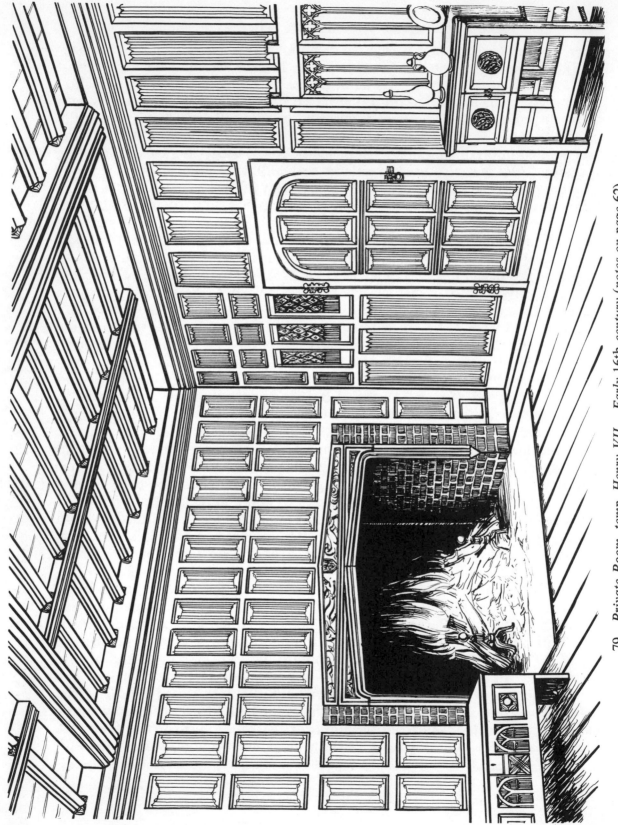

79 *Private Room, temp. Henry VII. Early 16th century (notes on page 62)*

80 *15th-century Bedroom, temp. Henry VI (notes on page 63)*

stained designs in heraldic or historical patterns (see Fig. 75), giving more colour to the room when the sun shone through the glass. In small halls, wood shutters and horn panes were still used instead of glass.

Hall doors were of heavy wood design with a wood or stone Perpendicular arched doorway. By the end of the century, panelled doors could be seen. Most doors were about 8 to 9 feet in height, although in smaller houses 6 feet was more usual (see Figs. 77, 84 and 88).

The **hall fireplace** was still sometimes on a central hearth, with the louvre above in the roof (see Fig. 77). However, the wall fireplace, with proper flue and chimney, was more general by this time; it had a stone Perpendicular arch, and perhaps a carved oak chimney beam. The fire was open, of wood logs supported on iron fire-dogs as before.

Illustrations of three 15th-century halls can be seen in Figs. 75, 76 and 77.

The **solar** was, by now, the second most important room in a fairly large house. Its function was still to act as a withdrawing room for the owner and his family, and was usually a living room where the ladies worked at their spinning and weaving, the children played, and the men indulged in cards or chess. The **roof** was of timber and plaster, with tie or collar beams, and the **floor** was generally of wood. The most attractive feature of the room was the *oriel window*—a typical 15th-century innovation and design. This type of window was like a bay window with many sides, but was on first-floor level, and was either supported from the ground or on stone corbels attached to the outside wall. The oriel window had a Perpendicular arch and its roof was generally fan-vaulted in stone tracery. The floor was often raised a little above the solar floor, and the bay was used to sit in (see Figs. 78 and 85). The **walls** were plastered, and usually covered with tapestry or hangings up to a high level. There was a **wall fireplace.** A manor-house solar of the 15th century can be seen in Fig. 78.

There was, by this century, in larger houses, a **parlour** or additional withdrawing room, used generally for the taking of meals by the family—perhaps a prototype of our dining room. It was much like a smaller version of the solar, without the oriel window, but by the end of the century was typically wood-panelled all over the **walls,** and had a flat wood **ceiling** with horizontal beams and smaller cross beams. The room had a brick or stone **wall fireplace**, with carved oak chimney beams. The **door** panelling would match that of the walls. A general example of this type of room can be seen in Fig. 79.

Prior to the 15th century, **bedchambers** had been regarded as necessities only for the well-to-do owner of a house, his family and principal guests. After 1400, however, there were several bedchambers in a larger home, and although some of these were very small, they gave greater privacy than the communal arrangements in the hall. There was, though, little comfort in these rooms until after 1450: they were cold, often damp and very cheerless.

81 *Late-Medieval Kitchen (notes on page 63)*

82 *Manor-House Stone Newel Staircase*

After mid-15th century an attempt was made to enliven such rooms: the plaster **walls** were gaily painted in floral patterns, or in richer houses hung with tapestry. The **floor** was tiled instead of being covered with dirty rushes as hitherto, and the **ceiling** was of horizontal beams, like that of the parlour. A **wall fireplace** was added, of stone or brick, and a fire burnt cheerily in cold weather. There might be a rug on the floor.

The **bed** itself was large, with a wooden bedstead, which had wood boards on which to rest the mattress, but these gave place at the end of the century to a rope-mesh support. To keep out draughts, bed curtains hung all round the bed from metal rails fixed in the wall behind, and a canopy or tester was supported above by cords from the ceiling beams. The well-to-do citizen had a feather mattress and pillows, and fine covers of embroidered fabric, with white sheets. Poorer people had wool woven covers and slept on boards. A bedchamber is depicted in Fig. 80.

Although **kitchens** were by now regarded as a more important part of the home, and were therefore built in a part of the house or, if separate, in a more solidly constructed and larger building than hitherto, the methods of cooking and serving remained unaltered. A large kitchen would have at least three fireplaces: one for the spits, hand-turned, to roast meat; one for boiling water and food; and a third for the ovens. Such a kitchen is shown in Fig. 81.

There was still a minimum of **furniture**, even in large homes, and the examples which existed were strictly utilitarian, heavy and large in design. Oak remained the principal wood, although carving was more in evidence now, and this was generally painted and/or gilded. Ironwork and leather were used as fastenings and for decoration. The **chest** continued to be the most essential item of furniture, and was seen in all rooms as a seat and as a receptacle. In the early 15th century, the

83 *Castle Stone Newel Staircase*

sides, top and back of chests were still made of large boards, whilst the front board was generally carved with a Perpendicular Gothic or floral design. Towards the end of the century, panelled chests, often carved with linenfold pattern, were in use. In this century most chests had legs and hinged lids, and some had back-rests to make them more comfortable for sitting. Examples of chests can be seen illustrated in Figs. 76, 79, 80, 90, 94 and 95.

Various types of **cupboards** existed by the 15th century. There were **plate cupboards**—also called dressoirs—which were made to display the plate on a fine cloth. These had a carved back and canopy of wood, and in the lower part was a cupboard with doors, and a shelf near the ground for jugs and ewers (see Figs. 75, 79 and 81). There were also simple **cupboards** with a flat top—on which a cloth and utensils were often placed—which were capacious for their size, and **aumbries** or food cupboards, which had perforated, Gothic carved designs in order that the air might have access to the food (see Figs. 77, 78, 97 and 98).

Tables were sometimes solidly constructed, and very large examples were seen in halls—for instance, 27 feet in length and 3 feet in width. The supports were of solid carved oak, and the tops usually of elm. There would be a support at each end and one in the centre (see Figs. 75, 76 and 77). **Trestle tables,** to fold up and leave against the wall, were still in general use, especially in smaller houses and in kitchens (see Fig. 81). **Benches** and **stools** were used in conjunction with all tables: these were still solidly and simply constructed (see Figs. 76, 77, 92 and 96). A carved Perpendicular Gothic oak back was added to the high seat (see Figs. 75 and 77).

Chairs were still rare: only well-to-do people possessed them, and then in limited number. The carved oak box type prevailed, with Perpendicular Gothic design. There might be one or two examples in a large hall, and perhaps one in the main bedchamber and in the solar and the parlour (see Figs. 78, 80 and 91).

Other items of necessary furniture included **cradles**, made of carved oak on rockers, or turned wood bound with cane; also racks, wash-tubs and draught-proof **screens** (see Figs. 80 and 93).

Lighting was by the same methods as in the 14th century. Well-to-do homes had a supply of candles, made of mutton fat or beeswax, and these were set in a wood or iron support which hung from the ceiling beams and was operated by a pulley. The hanging stands were sometimes called **candle-beams** (see Figs. 77 & 78). Alternatively, candles were placed in **candlesticks,** which could be set on a piece of furniture. These were of pricket or socket type now, and were made of silver, brass or iron, on a tripod or solid round base. Towards the end of the century, tall **candlestands**, made of ironwork, to hold a number of candles, came into use for large halls and rooms (see Fig. 76). Copper and brass **lanterns**, which held a candle and had a horn or

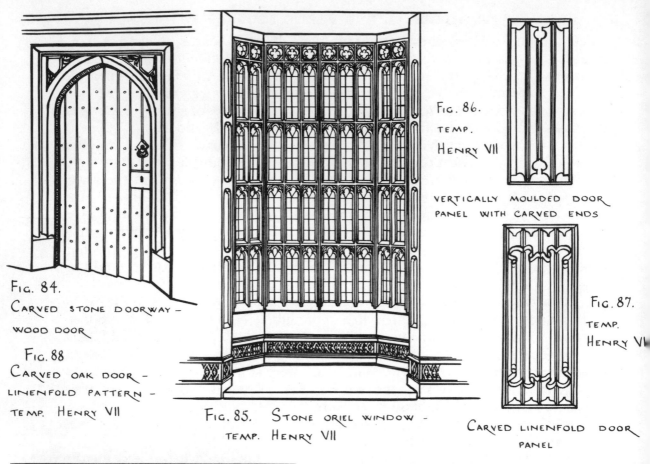

FIG. 84.
CARVED STONE DOORWAY —
WOOD DOOR

FIG. 88
CARVED OAK DOOR —
LINENFOLD PATTERN —
TEMP. HENRY VII

FIG. 85. STONE ORIEL WINDOW —
TEMP. HENRY VII

FIG. 86.
TEMP.
HENRY VII

VERTICALLY MOULDED DOOR
PANEL WITH CARVED ENDS

FIG. 87.
TEMP.
HENRY VII

CARVED LINENFOLD DOOR
PANEL

10' 6"

FIG. 89.
STONE
BAY
WINDOW
OF HALL

TEMP. HENRY VII —
BAY ROOF OF WOOD BOARDING WITH
WOOD MOULDINGS

84–89   *Details of Doors and Windows in the 15th Century, 1399–1509*

3' 10"

Fig. 91.

Carved oak

box chair

1450-90

3'6"

Fig. 90.

Carved oak chest -

late fifteenth century

Fig. 93

Carved oak cradle -

second half of

fifteenth century

Fig. 92.

Oak stool - late fifteenth century

Fig. 95.

Heavy oak chest

4'

Fig. 94.

Carved oak chest -

c.1500

Fig. 96.

Oak form -

first half of fifteenth century

3' 6"

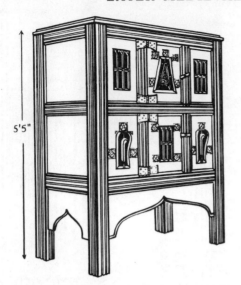

97 *Standing Aumbry, c. 1500 (food cupboard). Carved and painted wood—pierced design*

glass-panelled hinged door, were hung from beams or set on the furniture (see Fig. 105). Smaller homes still used tallow or resin **torches**, or home-made **rushlights**, dipped in fat, and secured in a rushlight holder.

The serving of **food,** table manners, meal-times and the type of food eaten were much the same as described in Chapter II. There was still little cutlery; forks did not exist, though more spoons were available, made of silver, pewter, wood, horn or bone, according to wealth and position. Each man carried his own hunting knife (see Figs 100, 101, and 102, also Plate IVc).

The majority of **cooking vessels** were by this time made of metal—except in poorer-class homes, where the cheaper earthenware utensils prevailed. Bronze, pewter and iron were the principal metals, and were made into cooking pots, jugs, ewers, skillets and pans. Wooden vessels were still used by country people and poor townsfolk (see Figs. 99, 104 and 106, also Plate VI).

A higher standard and greater variety of **pottery** was now produced in England, particularly in London and the south. More items were patterned with coloured clays added in strips, also painted designs and incised and relief work. Glazes were still poor, and generally of a greenish hue. Jugs and bowls were made more than any other articles (see Plate VI). By the end of the century, some maiolica ware was imported from Italy; this was tin-enamelled earthenware, using browns, yellow and red. Gothic, heraldic floral and animal motifs were paramount in both British and Continental ware at this time (see Plate III).

Glassware and **silverware** were made in similar quality and design to those of the 14th century (see Plates VI and VII).

Energetic outdoor **sports** were still the usual pursuits, particularly for men and boys. Hunting and hawking were supreme amongst these, especially for

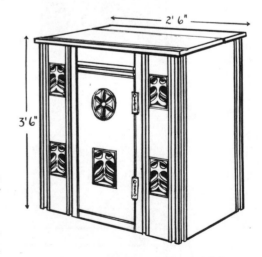

98 *Gothic Cupboard, late 15th century. Carved wood—pierced design*

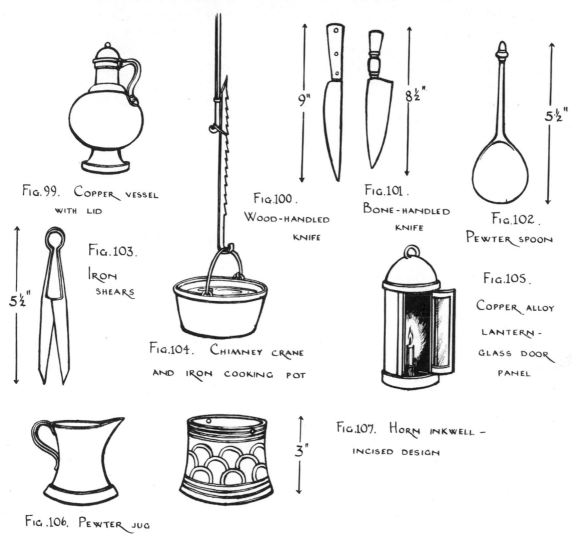

FIG. 99. COPPER VESSEL WITH LID

FIG.100. WOOD-HANDLED KNIFE

FIG.101. BONE-HANDLED KNIFE

FIG.102. PEWTER SPOON

FIG.103. IRON SHEARS

FIG.104. CHIMNEY CRANE AND IRON COOKING POT

FIG.105. COPPER ALLOY LANTERN - GLASS DOOR PANEL

FIG.107. HORN INKWELL - INCISED DESIGN

FIG.106. PEWTER JUG

99–107   *15th-century Utensils, 1399–1509*

the nobles and well-to-do country landlords.   Stag-hunting was preferred, but the pursuit of wild boar, fox, badger, hart and hare was much enjoyed, and the produce enlivened the salt-meat winter diet.   Tournaments and jousts were warmly supported and attended.   Among other popular sports were bull- and bear-baiting, cock-fighting, Morris dancing, wrestling and archery. Few could read or write as yet, but music helped to entertain and fill the dark winter hours.   People listened to the minstrels' playing, or played an instrument themselves; there was, by now, a wide variety of these, from bag-pipes to harp, and trombone to viol or cymbals.   Showmen toured the country with performing animals and puppet shows, and bands of actors gave plays and shows in the open air. There were very few **books** available yet, for although Caxton had set up his printing press at Westminster, printing was not in general use in this century. Books were still hand-written by quill pen on vellum or parchment, and were sometimes illuminated. Few people possessed them, and most books were of prayer, theology, history or law.

NOTES ON ILLUSTRATIONS

Fig. 75. Manor-house Hall. c. 1465–70

Timber **roof**—arch-braced collar-beam type. **Walls**—timber and plaster. **Floor**—wood. Tiled daïs. **Windows**—stone. **Bay window**, off daïs. Iron bars, lead frames with glass panes. Stained glass in heraldic design. **Furniture**—Oak **table** and **forms**. Carved back to daïs seat. Carved oak **plate cupboard**.

Fig. 76. Great Hall. c. 1480

Timber **roof**—false hammerbeam type. Stone **walls**—plastered. Tapestry on lower part. Carved wood **screen**. Wood **floor**. **Windows**—Perpendicular-style stone tracery. Stained glass. Lead frames. **Furniture**—Carved oak **chests**. Oak trestle **table** and **forms.** Ironwork **candlestand**.

Fig. 77. Great Hall. c. 1450–80

Timber **roof**—hammerbeam style. There is also a tie beam with king-post. **Walls**—timber and plaster. Wood **floor**—plain rug. **Side windows**, also squint in end wall, from solar. Wood **doors**—close-boarded. Central **hearth** of stone—iron fire-dogs. Louvre above. **Lighting**—hanging iron candlestand. Rope and pulley. **Furniture**—Oak trestle **tables** and **forms**. Carved oak **chests**. Carved oak **cupboard.**

Fig. 78. Manor-house Solar. c. 1475–85

Timber **roof**—arch-braced collar-beam type. Stone **walls**—tapestry on lower part. Wood **floor**—plain rug. **Oriel window**—stone tracery. Iron bars. Lead frames with glass panes. Fan vaulting. Wood **door**—stone doorway. Wood hanging **candlestands** —hung from beams. **Furniture**—Oak box **chair**. Oak **cupboard**. White linen cloth. Silver and pewter ware. Oak carved **chest**.

Fig. 79. Private Room. Temp. Henry VII. Early 16th Century

Ceiling—carved wood beams with wood rafters. **Walls**—panelled. Some panels of linenfold type. **Fireplace**—brick. Carved oak chimney beam. Stone-slab hearth. Iron fire-dogs. Wood **floor**. **Furniture**—**Chest**—carved oak, 4 ft. 6 in. in length. **Plate cupboard**—carved oak.

(b) *Silver-Gilt Cup*
(*late 15th century*)

(a) (left) *Silver-Gilt Cup and Cover* (1507)

(c) (right) *Silver-Gilt Salt* (1493)

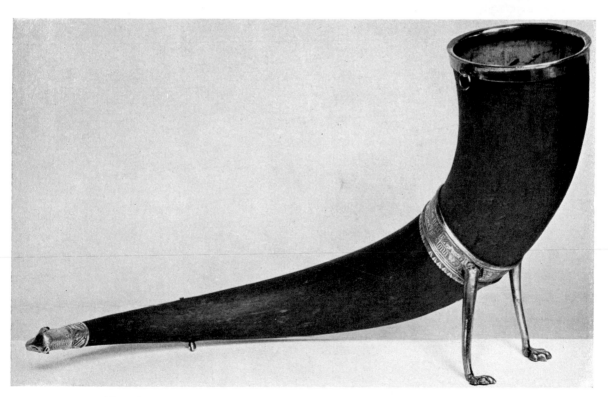

(d) *The Pusey Drinking Horn, Silver-mounted* (*early 15th century*)

LATE MEDIEVAL SILVERWARE

(a) (left) *Engraved Wine-Glass, dated* 1602

(b) (right) *Wine-Glass, engraved and dated* 1581

(c) (below) *Tudor and Stuart Pottery*

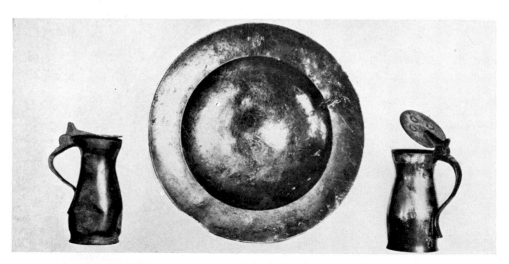

(d) *Tudor Pewter: Wine Measures and Dish*

Fig. 80. *15th-Century Bedroom. Temp. Henry VI*

Timber **ceiling**. Plaster **walls**—painted in bright colours. Tiled **floor**—stamped and plain tiles. Stone **fireplace**—iron fire-dogs. Wood **bedstead**—patterned silk curtains and tester. Canopy attached by cords to ceiling beams. Silk bed-cover. Wood and cane **cradle**. Oak **chest**. Oak **box chair**. Oak **stand** with pewter ware.

Fig. 81. *Late Medieval Kitchen of a Castle or Large House*

Ground-floor room. **Walls, roof** and **floor** of stone flags and blocks of various sizes. **Windows** at each end of the room, and in vaulted section of roof. Open, slatted **louvre** in roof. Wood **door**. Three large **fireplaces**—one for roasting meat on a spit, a second for boiling water and cooking food, and the third is adjacent to the ovens, which are built in the thickness of the wall on each side. They have iron doors. **Furniture**—Oak trestle **tables, plate cupboard**, and **racks** and **shelves** for utensils.

108   *The Great Hall, c.* 1530–40 *(notes on page 96)*

IV
TUDOR, 1509–1603

| HENRY VIII 1509–1547 | QUEEN MARY I 1553–1558 |
| EDWARD VI 1547–1553 | QUEEN ELIZABETH I 1558–1603 |

THE dawn of the 16th century heralded a new age for Britain. New life was awakening, and the old ways of the Middle Ages were being thrust into the past. It was a century of adventure; the exploits of the Tudor seamen in sailing uncharted seas, the building of a navy and the wars against Spain aroused intense national feeling in Britain. Greater luxuries such as furs, jewels and better furnishing and decorations in their homes were available to the well-to-do, an improved standard that extended, to some degree, even to the less wealthy members of the community.

The Renaissance—that rekindling of the torch of learning, set alight originally in Greece, handed on to Rome, then lost in Europe in the barbarism of the Dark Ages that followed the eclipse of Rome—showed itself in Italy with a rebirth and a re-acquired knowledge of the arts in the fifteenth century. This is seen in the work of Leonardo da Vinci, Michelangelo, Raphael, Cellini and many other famous artists. Slowly this new learning in art, architecture and craftsmanship of all kinds spread across Europe. The beginnings of it reached England in the 16th century, though in architecture the full splendour was not seen until the 17th century.

England's **population** was growing: at the end of the century it is estimated that it was approximately four millions. The majority of these still lived on the land. There was a trend towards the towns, however, in this period owing to unemployment and poverty in the country. This was due partly to the enclosure of land for pasture and partly to the upheaval following the dissolution of the monasteries by Henry VIII, with a consequent change—often for the worse—of landlords. The increase of sheep pasture and decrease of land under the plough naturally led to less work for farm labourers.

The **law** was very severe on offenders, with hard punishments for even trivial offences. Prison conditions were appallingly bad; moreover, the unfortunate culprit often had to languish in jail for months without ever being brought to trial. Consequently, even painful punishment was usually

65

109 *Elizabethan Hall, c. 1570–80 (notes on page 96)*

110 *Tudor Parlour, c. 1530 (notes on page 97)*

preferred to imprisonment. Beggary had become so common because of much unemployment, particularly amongst soldiers returning from campaigns, that new laws had to be made against vagabonds. Punishment for begging ended in death after three convictions. For other minor misdeeds, the pillory or stocks were the result, but other forms of punishment for more serious offences included hanging, burning, boiling, branding and tortures—including the rack.

Tudor England enjoyed pageantry and pomp, under the auspices of its monarchs, particularly Henry VIII and Elizabeth. There were colour, furs, jewels and fine clothes, but the extreme contrast between rich and poor had never been greater. The people had courage and daring, but were intensely superstitious; they were often intolerant, and their manners were rough and crude.

At the opening of the century the **Church** was still powerful, in education, politics and many secular affairs, but the dissolution of the monasteries at the order of Henry VIII brought a great change. The dissolution was thorough: many ecclesiastical buildings were largely destroyed, and their occupants killed or expelled to fend for themselves elsewhere. This had a profound and, initially, adverse effect on education, because up to that time the monks and nuns had carried out a large part of the teaching of the community, and the Church had founded the principal schools. However, later in the century many fine schools were founded, or set on their feet again to prosper once more. Among these were Christ's Hospital, St. Paul's, Westminster, Rugby and Uppingham. With the Renaissance, a great desire for learning began amongst the people, and books became more numerous with the advent of printing. Paper was still fairly expensive, but, as time passed, became more plentiful and somewhat cheaper, so that more books were made. The majority of people were still illiterate, but more boys received a good education at the grammar schools, and many went on to the universities, which flourished later in the century under Elizabeth.

The knowledge of **medicine** was improving; many doctors studied in Italy before coming home to practice. Instruments were kept a little cleaner, and methods of treatment, though rough and ready, were more sensible. However, an amputated limb was still immediately dipped in boiling pitch—an admirable antiseptic, but the patient was liable to die of shock—and bleeding was a palliative for various ills. Herbs were in general use.

Travel was a little easier now, but still dangerous. There were springless coaches by the end of the century. The rivers were used a great deal, especially the Thames, for both pleasure travel and for goods traffic.

Britain had several prosperous **industries** now, including coal-mining, cloth-making—particularly wool—quarrying, and mining of tin, lead and copper. Wood was still the usual fuel for domestic purposes, though coal was used more and more in industry.

111 *Elizabethan Main Chamber, c. 1575–80 (notes on page 97)*

Wages and **prices** varied a good deal. An unskilled man or woman on the land or in the home would earn from 16*s.* to £1 per year, while a skilled agricultural labourer received up to £2 or £2 10*s.* a year. A cook, on the other hand, was considered most valuable and might earn as much as £4. These wages sound meagre, but of course prices were in keeping with the scale; for example, beef was ½*d.* per lb., and a hen could be bought for 3*d.*

London was said by travellers to be the cleanest city in Europe, but by 20th-century standards would have been considered filthy. The stench from the open sewers, still running down the centre of the streets, from slaughter-houses and from refuse littered all around was overpowering. Plagues in the towns were recurrent, as they had always been, exacted a heavy death toll, and increased superstition. London grew larger as the century progressed and by 1600 was very large compared to Continental cities, having nearly 200,000 inhabitants. The city was still walled, with its famous gates—now just districts to us—Aldersgate, Cripplegate, Bishopsgate, Oldgate, Moorgate, Newgate, Billingsgate. All these were named after various factors: a hospital, a market, a bog, a prison, etc., as can readily be seen. The stone London Bridge was decorated by traitors' heads impaled on the spikes of the tower—there were generally about thirty, left to dehydrate slowly. The remainder of the bridge was occupied by houses.

Provincial towns were even filthier, and though smaller, suffered equally from plague. They had more space, however, and contained pleasant gardens and orchards. The larger towns included York and Bristol.

The 16th century was a time of **domestic building**—the Middle Ages had seen all the best of craftsmanship in wood and stonework put into ecclesiastical building, while homes had taken second place. By Henry VIII's reign there was an emphasis on domestic building, and this continued with increased momentum in the Elizabethan period. At first the Gothic style of architecture, in the form of "perpendicular" work, was paramount. Then Henry VIII, interested to hear of the new Renaissance styles in Italy, encouraged artists and craftsmen to come from there to his Court. The best known of these was **Pietro Torrigiano**, an Italian sculptor who, among other works, was responsible for the design of the tomb of Henry VII, erected by 1518 in Westminster Abbey by Henry VIII. The majority of these Italian artists and craftsmen, however, worked in the field of decoration, in stucco, paint, metalwork, etc., and their influence, therefore, was primarily of a decorative nature, and did not greatly affect the architectural style as a whole, at this time. With the breakaway from the Catholic Church in Rome, Henry discontinued his relations with Italy, and for many years the Renaissance influence made no further entry into Britain, except indirectly through the Low Countries.

Among the best examples of Perpendicular Gothic work in England in the early 16th century is **St. George's Chapel** at **Windsor**. The best-known example of domestic architecture of the period, however, is probably **Hampton Court Palace** (Tudor portion). It was built for Cardinal Wolsey, and some of the building of his time still exists, in particular the panelled room known as "Wolsey's Closet". This shows the early classical influence in ceiling and frieze. Henry VIII took over the Palace in 1525, and made considerable alterations; he had the Great Hall built, where can still be seen to-day the Gothic-style hammerbeam roof and "perpendicular" windows. Other fine examples of domestic architecture of this period include Hengrave Hall, Suffolk, Christ Church, Oxford, Sutton Place, Surrey, Cowdray House, Sussex, and Compton Wynyates, Warwickshire.

During the latter part of Henry VIII's reign, much work was done on rebuilding and repairing ecclesiastical buildings which had been destroyed or damaged at the Dissolution, and adapting them as domestic buildings. The revenues from these estates were confiscated by Henry, and he parcelled out such estates and lands to his friends and followers. As a result, many fine houses were erected on the site of, or on the remains of, old abbeys and monasteries. **Brick** was used a great deal now for this building and rebuilding of houses, although **stone** was still in use for larger homes. In small houses, timber and plaster, with part brick, were used.

There was also a certain **Flemish influence** on domestic building in this period. Furniture, panelling and hangings were brought from the Low Countries, and Flemish workers came to England to work in English houses on decoration, chimneypieces and panelling.

With the Tudor period the country became more at peace, and this greater feeling of security is reflected in house design. The need for fortifications was waning; moats and small windows disappeared, and the house began to have the appearance of intentional pattern and design, not just various rooms put together with little heed of the exterior whole, as had been the Medieval plan. The desire for privacy increased, and as a result rooms were smaller, but more numerous. Small dining rooms and withdrawing rooms were built, leading off the hall, to supply this need. There was also a desire for greater comfort and attractiveness in the home, evidenced in more numerous hangings to keep out the draughts, curtains, large windows, and more cushions on seats. There were, nevertheless, still many draughts, and the houses would be considered very uncomfortable to-day. The **plan** of the house was still square, with a central open courtyard inside. Through the entrance porch one reached the courtyard, and opposite was the Great Hall, still often two storeys high. The "screens" were still at one end to avoid draughts, and above these, which were only one storey high, was the minstrels' gallery. Next to the "screens" were the kitchen, buttery, etc., and on the other side

112 *Elizabethan Long Gallery, c. 1590 (notes on page 97)*

113 *Tudor Bedchamber, c. 1575 (notes on page 97)*

of the hall the private rooms of the family. Passages and corridors were still almost non-existent; one room led into another. There were several staircases, still small and dark.

During **Elizabeth's reign** a great deal of **domestic building** was effected, and very little ecclesiastical. Homes were built in large numbers for all classes of the community, from palaces for the nobles to cottages for the poorer people. The style of most of these homes was set by the large estate owners, who had their houses built on the new designs. These designs contained a mixture of styles—Gothic and classical. The Gothic was a Medieval style and the classical was the result of the influence of Rome. In Italy Palladio, the leading architect, was reviving the old Roman principles, and these were brought to England via the Netherlands and Germany. The result was not pure classicism, but a Flemish classicism which lacked the purity, grace and dignity of Palladio and had a certain crudity, though also vigour and robustness. The Elizabethans took these new ideas and combined them with the older Gothic designs, paying little heed to proportions in classical orders, capitals and mouldings, but using them to suit their own ideas. The result was typically Elizabethan; it had courage, vivacity and strength, but was rough, crude in places and often over-decorated. However, it had an individual charm and interest and was suited to its age.

One of the principal themes in Palladio's interpretation of classic design in architecture was that house-building should be **symmetrical.** This theme became, in the later 16th century, of paramount importance in building design, and Elizabethan homes were no exception—indeed symmetry was their most notable feature, and was impressed upon one both in the exterior views and in the interior.

It has been mentioned that the classical influence came to England in the 16th century via Germany and the Netherlands. This was chiefly due to the strong ties which bound these countries to ourselves during the reign of Elizabeth. These were ties of religion—Protestantism against the Catholic Church of Rome; political ties—against the common enemy, Spain; and ties of trade and commerce. As a result of Spanish persecution, many Flemish artists and craftsmen came to England in this period to settle and work. They included monumental masons, sculptors, surveyors, painters, joiners and glass workers. Among the designers of the period can be particularly noted the Flemish **De Vries**, who published his designs in the 1560's, and these had a great influence on English architecture. Among British designers were **Robert Smythson,** a freemason, who was concerned in the building of Wollaton Hall, Nottinghamshire, and Hardwick Hall, Derbyshire, and **John Thorpe**, who was associated with work at Hampton Court, the Tower and Greenwich. These two men were not architects as we know the word to-day—there were as yet no architects in that sense—but they were forerunners of the architects

114 *Tudor Kitchen*

of the 17th century who followed them. In the Elizabethan period, when a client desired a house to be built, he often supplied materials and his own ideas, gleaned chiefly from pattern books and his Continental travels; his surveyor, mason and other craftsmen then carried out the work and advised him. Thus the house and its design was the product of several men's ideas, not just one man's as in later centuries. Among the best-known examples of domestic architecture of the Elizabethan period are Moreton Old Hall, Cheshire, Longleat House, Wiltshire, Wollaton Hall, Nottinghamshire, Burleigh House, Northamptonshire, and Montacute House, Somerset.

The new Elizabethan **plan** for a house was shaped like an E or an H, instead of the square building enclosing an open courtyard as before. The symmetry of the front elevation could then be seen to advantage. There was a central porch and entrance way, often in an Elizabethan interpretation of classical columns and capitals. The ground floor was raised a little and one ascended a few steps to it; the cellars were beneath this floor. The hall was still entered via the "screens", but was much smaller now. Also on this floor were various parlours, the kitchen and other offices, and the bakehouse. On the first floor were the main chamber and other bedchambers, while the long gallery—an innovation—occupied the whole of one side of the house. The main staircase was near the front door, and one or more smaller staircases existed at the other side of the house.

In large homes, various titles were given to these numerous smaller rooms which were now made to give greater privacy and comfort to everyone within. Among these were dining parlour, winter parlour, withdrawing room, library, breakfast room, servants' room, etc. Large houses also still had a chapel. Stone was used for the building of these homes, or a combination of brick and stone.

Smaller houses in both town and country changed less in appearance than the larger ones. Many small homes were still built from timber and plaster, with thatched roofs, or even with wattle-and-daub walls, though some small town houses had tiled roofs. They were usually of two storeys, and in towns the top storey overhung considerably, to give the maximum space possible to upstairs rooms. On the ground floor were situated the hall—into which the front door gave ingress—a parlour or bedroom and the kitchen, and above were two or three bedchambers.

The majority of Tudor houses had **gardens**, especially in the country, and these were carefully tended. In larger homes, the gardens were magnificent, formally laid out with small hedges of box or yew, such as those at Hampton Court Palace[1] and Nonesuch Palace. Many new plants and shrubs were incorporated into English gardens from abroad, especially fruit trees and herbs. In the Middle Ages, gardening in England was backward compared

[1] Can still be seen to-day.

to the Continent, but by the end of the 16th century English gardens had come into their own, and even small cottages had their little gardens, in particular to grow vegetables for their own tables.

The 16th century witnessed the fundamental change in the people's way of life from the Medieval fashion of having a very large **Great Hall** in which were housed and fed the majority of the household, to a more intimate idea of living in separate rooms, for dining, leisure, rest, etc. The hall, during this process of evolution, thus became smaller as time passed, until in the 17th century it was a mere vestibule. In the first half of the 16th century it remained, in fair-sized homes, a double-storeyed large room, with "screens" at one end and daïs at the other. The roof was usually open still, in gable shape, constructed of carved wood, generally in a complicated hammerbeam style. Walls were tapestry-hung or oak-panelled, and windows Perpendicular in type, with a large bay or oriel window by the daïs. The "screens" were of panelled oak, often linenfold pattern, and behind them the passage led to the kitchen, buttery, etc., as hitherto. The floor was of wood, left uncovered. One or two large fireplaces were set in the side wall, but even these were quite inadequate for the enormous room. Servants did not generally sleep in the hall now, but it was still used at meal times for the majority of the household, and also for formal dinner parties (see Fig. 108).

The **Elizabethan hall** was rather smaller in area and more frequently of one storey only, with a flat or pendant plaster ceiling. The "screens" were still there, but the carved oak of their construction was far more heavily decorated than before. Its motifs included strapwork, semi-classical columns, various decorative figures, flowers and fruit; like much of the other woodwork of the period, it was generally painted in bright colours. The chimneypiece was also far more decorated than before, in a similar manner. The floor was more frequently flagged now. Windows were of the simple Tudor style, but much larger than before, reaching nearly to the ground (see Fig. 109).

Hall furniture was still sparse, consisting generally of colossal tables and benches, on the daïs and down the sides of the hall, few, if any, chairs, some court cupboards, buffets and other cupboards for food, plate, linen, etc., and stools and chests for seating. Decoration was provided by arms and armour hung on the walls, also stags' heads and flags.

The Medieval solar for the owner of the house and his family had, by Elizabethan times, become several rooms. The largest of these was the main or **great chamber**, situated on the first floor, and functioning as a drawing room, while smaller reception rooms for the private use of the family and a small **dining room** were usual by the end of the 16th century. A **parlour** or private room of early Tudor times is featured in Fig. 110, and an **Elizabethan main chamber** in Fig. 111. These rooms all had flat plaster or wood ceilings, oak-panelled walls and wood floors. Their single fireplace was large and adequate

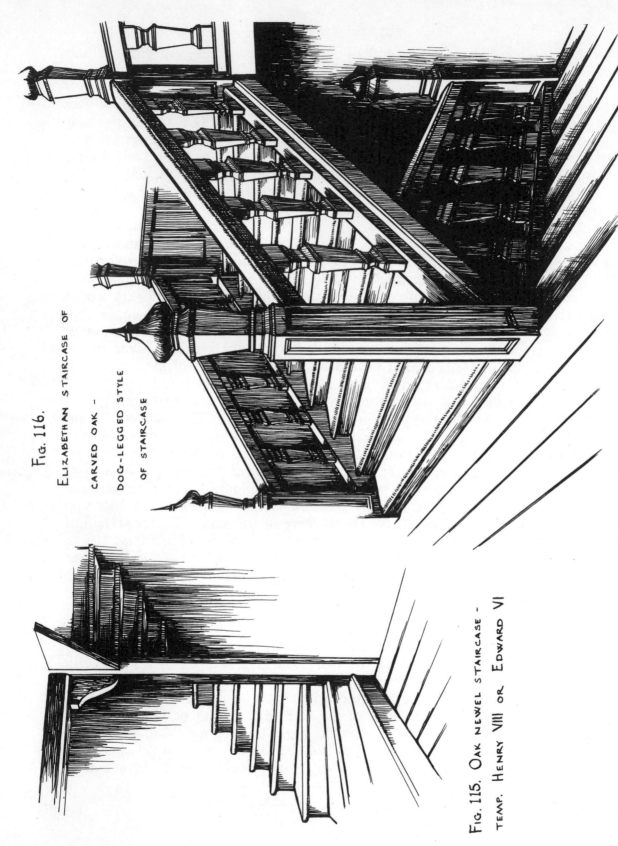

Fig. 116.

Elizabethan staircase of

carved oak –

dog-legged style

of staircase

Fig. 115. Oak newel staircase – temp. Henry VIII or Edward VI

115 and 116 *Tudor Staircases, 1509–1603*

for the smaller room. Furniture consisted of chests, a chair, stools and forms, a small table, and cupboards and/or buffets.

Although a **long gallery** did exist in a few early Tudor homes, it was, in general, an Elizabethan innovation. It generally occupied the whole of one side of a medium to large-sized house on the first or upper floor, and the outside long wall consisted in large part of window, there being more glass than wall in many cases. At the two ends were more windows and, in places, also on the fourth wall. These galleries varied a good deal in size, but some were very extensive in area; for example, two well-known galleries are respectively 166 feet in length by 22½ feet in width, and 170 feet in length by 20 feet in width. As Elizabethan women seldom went out of doors in the winter months, the gallery was used for sewing, embroidery and other feminine household pursuits, for the enjoyment of music and dancing, for children's romps and games, for lovers' strolls, for cards and other games and, in general, for leisure pursuits by the whole family. The best furniture was on view there along the walls, the best hangings at the windows, and the numerous window seats were cushioned for all to relax upon. The ceiling was of plaster and highly decorative, the walls panelled, the floor of wood, and two or more fireplaces, always kept burning in winter, were set in the long wall (see Fig. 112).

As the 16th century progressed more **bedrooms** were available in the house, and even attics for the servants, each of which housed a dozen or more occupants in cramped conditions by the end of Elizabeth's reign; nevertheless, this was preferable to the hall floor of Medieval days. Most bedchambers were small and, in reality, passage rooms; that is, narrow rooms acting as a passage way from one larger room to another, as there were few proper corridors. Ceilings, windows, floors and walls were treated as in smaller parlours. The chief item of furniture was the bedstead, and this was enormous, completely shut off inside by its heavy hangings and valance, so as to become a small room in itself when one had retired for the night. This was most necessary in view of the draughtiness of the room. Other bedroom furniture included chests for clothes and linen, perhaps a chair, a stool and a cupboard for toilet necessities, among which were numbered a ewer and basin, towels, cosmetic jars and boxes, and the inevitable chamber-pot(s). Dressing tables, chests of drawers and wardrobes were still unknown, and mirrors, if they existed, were still usually of polished metal. A large type of bedroom is depicted in Fig. 113.

The design of a **kitchen** was carefully considered in a Tudor home, as cooking and good food were thought to be of prime importance in life. No longer was the kitchen housed in a shack adjoining the house; it was a large room of stone, still often with stone vaulted roof, and having a flagged floor. It was a hive of industry, and there were many servants and retainers,

FIG. 117. CARVED OAK DOOR AND DOORWAY. LINENFOLD PANELLING ON DOOR c.1520-30

FIG. 119. CARVED OAK PANELLED DOOR c.1515-30

FIG. 118. STONE ORIEL WINDOW — FAN VAULTED CEILING c.1530-40

FIG. 121 CARVED STONE FIREPLACE c.1509-15

FIG. 120 STONE FIREPLACE — FOUR-CENTRED ARCH, SURROUNDED BY WOOD PANELLING WITH RECTANGULAR FRAMING. c.1525

117–121   *Details of the Early Tudor Period, 1509–58*

numbering, in a large home, up to eighty people. The fireplaces were enormous
—stone four-centred arches containing fires which roasted the meat on iron
spits, turned by boys or by dogs in cages. In either case the propellant was
termed a turnspit, but while the boy turned a handle, the unfortunate dog—
a short-legged variety, by necessity—had to keep padding on in his cartwheel
cage interminably, in order to retain his balance. This cage was set on the
wall. Another fire opening was in use for boiling or simmering, and enormous
cauldrons hung over the fire, supported on iron chimney cranes and a complicated system of chains. There were at least two of these fireplaces, and
often as many as four. Ovens were still of brick, most capacious, and still
heated by wood faggots, and cooking was done on the heated embers.
Smaller, daintier dishes were often cooked over braziers in tall iron baskets.
The chief items of kitchen furniture were very large wood trestle tables, store
cupboards—well stocked up to last the winter months—and racks for hanging
utensils. Adjoining the kitchen were a bakehouse, more larders, pantry and
buttery.

Kitchen utensils were made of wood, earthenware or metal, usually iron,
and included cauldrons, pots, skillets and frying pans. Other necessary items
in a kitchen were tubs, barrels, sieves, fire implements—poker, shovel, etc.—
pot and flesh hooks, ladles, skimmers, chafing dish, mortar and pestle, knives,
axes and dressing boards. A Tudor kitchen is depicted in Fig. 114, and
other kitchen implements in Figs. 148 and 152.

In the reign of Henry VIII, **staircases** continued to be built of the newel,
spiral type, of oak or stone. There were at least two of these staircases in
larger homes, because the two-storeyed Great Hall divided the house into
two parts, and a staircase was therefore necessary in each part. The treads
were of solid oak, tenoned into a central newel post, or of stone as hitherto;
the whole staircase was still narrow and ill-lit (see Fig. 115). It was in the
reign of Henry's younger daughter, however, that the possibilities of a staircase, as an item of beauty and interest in a home as well as utility, were realised.
The innovation of the long gallery on the first floor made a staircase or staircases to it essential; the new construction began in the form of short, straight
flights, broken by landings, all made in stone, with stone vaulted roof. This
type evolved, later in the reign, into the typical massive Elizabethan staircase,
made of carved oak, and of generous proportions to accommodate with ease
the Elizabethan farthingale skirts. The flights of six to ten stairs had wide
treads, an easy ascent, and were often termed "dog-legged", because each
flight returned back alongside the one immediately above and below it. An
ornately carved, massive newel post terminated each side of the top and
bottom of each flight, surmounted by a carved finial in the form of a ball and
urn, an animal or a human figure. A heavy handrail joined each newel post,
and an equivalent baulk of timber, called the string, ran parallel to this,

FIG. 122. OAK PANELLED DOOR - LATE 16TH CENTURY

FIG. 124. CARVED STONE FIREPLACE SURMOUNTED BY CARVED OAK MANTEL OR CHIMNEYPIECE - c. 1600-1603

FIG. 123. OAK CHIMNEYPIECE c. 1570-75 CARVED AND INLAID

FIG. 125. OAK PANELLED DOOR - LATE 16TH CENTURY

122–125 *Details of the Elizabethan Period, 1558–1603*

joining the staircase treads. Highly decorated carved balusters then supported the handrail on the string (see Fig. 116).

There were four principal methods of treating the **walls** of a home in the Tudor period: panelling, timber and plaster, tapestry-hanging and wall-painting. **Panelling,** or **wainscoting,** as it was usually termed, was by far the most widely used method, particularly in well-to-do homes. In Henry VIII's reign the panels were simply carved, most popularly in the linenfold pattern or an allied design. Oak was in general use for wainscoting, well seasoned in order to avoid warping. The panel framework was mortised and tenoned together and fixed with oak pins. The oak was a light golden colour in those days, although it has now darkened nearly to black in homes where the original work still exists. Colour was used a great deal on woodwork to pick out the design, chiefly in red and gold, but much of this has now worn away (see Figs. 108 and 110). Elizabethan wainscoting was more highly decorated and the carving more elaborate, though still confined in panelled frames. As there were few pictures and scanty furniture as yet, the interest was centred on the wainscoting, and intricate designs were carved; also the plain surfaces remaining were inlaid with other woods to provide colour, and holly, laburnum, bog oak and fruit woods were used for this. Colour, in the form of paint, was still applied to enrich the design. Wainscoting generally covered the walls up to three-quarters of their height, where the plaster or wood frieze then met the panelling (see Figs. 109, 111, 112 and 113).

The Medieval habit of making walls of **timber and plaster** was still seen in a number of homes in the first half of the 16th century, but the fashion died out after this, except in small houses.

The hanging of **tapestry** or velvet, brocade and silk was still in general use throughout the century. Tapestry was made in England all this time, and was still imported in considerable quantities from Flanders and France. Brilliant colours were used in all hangings, in keeping with the costume of the period. All these types of draperies were hung from the ceiling to a dado rail, which was set fairly low on the wall. Below this the wainscoting acted as covering. This method of wall decoration was in general use in halls, where the area of wall was often too large to permit complete panelling. A cheaper method of providing wall hangings was in the form of **painted cloths.** A canvas material was painted in bright colours depicting various scenes, usually mythological or biblical. This became an imitation of the more costly tapestry work. It was chiefly in use in bedchambers and smaller rooms in smaller homes. The most inexpensive method of wall decoration—often seen in poorer homes—but one which lacked the warmth of the others, was **painting** on the **plaster wall** itself. Again the scenes were largely biblical, mythological or even heraldic; alternatively, floral or geometrical patterns were used. Colours were often crude, but gave gaiety to the room.

FIG. 126. CARVED AND TURNED OAK CHAIR - LATE 16TH CENTURY

3'2"

FIG. 128. CARVED OAK CHAIR - c.1540

4'

FIG. 129.

CARVED OAK BOX CHAIR - c.1575-80 DRAWER UNDER SEAT HANDLE AT SIDE

3'9"

FIG. 130. CARVED OAK CRADLE LATE 16TH CENTURY

1'10"

FIG. 127. OAK STOOL c.1510-20

FIG. 131. CARVED OAK CHEST - LINENFOLD PANELS c.1509-1530

2'

1'6"

FIG. 132. JOINED AND TURNED OAK STOOL c.1600

FIG. 133 CARVED OAK SETTLE - TO BE FIXED AGAINST A WALL - EARLY 16TH CENTURY

5'

126–133 *Tudor Furniture, 1509–1603*

The most usual method of treating the **ceiling** in early Tudor homes was like that of the 15th century: a flat ceiling was spanned by large, carved oak beams supporting smaller ones across them, and the spaces in between were filled in by plaster and laths. In large halls the open, gable Gothic roofs remained, in carved, hammerbeam styles (see Fig. 108). The flat type of ceiling in smaller rooms was often now finished by a decorated carved oak frieze above the wainscoting (see Fig. 110). It was in Henry VIII's reign, however, that the possibilities of plaster ceilings were discovered. The Italian craftsmen whom he brought to England showed what could be done in this medium, and after their departure the method was employed. By the Elizabethan period, plaster ceilings and friezes had become general, because, provided the necessary highly skilled craftsmen were available, the method was comparatively cheap. Plaster, of course, had been used in homes as a decoration from ancient times: for example, the ancient Egyptians and the Byzantine peoples had used it, and different media had been added to the plaster to retain its setting qualities, or to aid malleability and final hardness. The Elizabethan, and later the Jacobean, craftsmen became highly skilled in this art, and added sand, quicklime, horsehair and fibre to their plaster. The Italian method was to add finely ground marble to the final coat to give a highly polished finish to the work. The actual designs of the ceiling were fairly simple at first, based on the Gothic ribbed vaulting, and consisting of narrow moulded ribs on a plain ceiling. The ribs were applied in geometrical patterns, predominantly octagons, and heraldic bosses, shields and floral motifs decorated the spaces between the ribs. Many ceilings were of the pendant type, where the ribs descended into pendants, with bosses or other decoration at the junctions. As the century progressed, ceilings became more ornate. Ribs became heavy, more complicated mouldings decorated them, and a smaller area of ceiling was left plain as the ornament gradually spread all over the surface. Motifs included strapwork, mermaids, dolphins, flowers, classical motifs, swags, scrolls and plaques, fruit and heraldic insignia. The work was also executed in high relief in the late 16th century and was by then free in treatment. Colour was used on the plaster, and became an outstanding feature of many ceilings (see Figs. 109, 111, 112 and 113).

Loose **rushes** were used on stone **floors** still for much of the 16th century, although wood floors and the floor of the hall were generally kept uncovered. According to contemporary writers, these rushes were still in an insanitary condition, being changed rarely, merely added to, and containing remains of meals, bones thrown to the dogs, spittle, vomit, beer and dogs' excrement. Erasmus considered them a source of plague and wrote indignantly on the subject. By the late 16th century, **plaited rush mats** were beginning to replace the loose rushes, and these were considerably more hygienic. Actual **carpets** were still rare, and even where referred to in inventories, were used as curtains,

Fig. 134. Carved oak buffet - linenfold panels

c. 1520-30

Fig. 135. Carved oak standing cupboard - pierced design

c. 1540-50

3'9"

5'2"

Fig. 136. Carved oak dole cupboard

c. 1525-30

2'2"

Fig. 137. Carved oak buffet

c. 1575-90

3'10"

Fig. 138. Carved oak court cupboard

c. 1595 - 1603

4'4"

134–138 *Tudor Furniture, 1509–1603*

hangings and covers for furniture and window seats—they were considered too valuable to place on a dirty floor. These carpets were imported into England from the East—Persia and Turkey—and, of course, only by wealthy people. English carpets were first made in very small numbers from *c.* 1575. Their designs were either of Elizabethan motifs or copies of Oriental specimens. "Turkey-work" was an English imitation, at this time, of Eastern carpets, and consisted of a cross-stitch on canvas, in coloured wools, cut open to make pile. English women also made embroidered carpets.

Until the late 16th century, entrance **doors** into rooms were designed to fit into the wainscoting scheme, so that when the door was closed, it was barely discernible (see Figs. 108, 117 and 119). Many rooms which opened out of a staircase or large room had an **interior porch** and double door, to avoid draughts (see Fig. 110). At the end of the century, in large houses, the door became a decorative feature of the room, and was heavily carved and often flanked by columns or pilasters which supported an ornamental panel above. Plainer doors of the late 16th century, more suitable for the average home, can be seen in Figs. 122 and 125.

Tudor **windows** were much larger than hitherto. Now that the need for defence had largely disappeared, the aim was to give as much light as possible. As a result, the large **bay and oriel windows,** first popular in the 15th century, were seen more and more in Tudor building. The bays were poly-sided or semicircular, and the window reached from the ceiling to near the floor. Window seats were made in the bay. **Curtains** were more generally used now, made of cloth, brocade or velvet, sometimes with valances. **Glass** was becoming available in larger quantities, and it was found in all medium-sized and larger houses, though poorer cottages continued to have wood shutters to keep out the cold at night in lieu of glass. Windows were made to open and close in certain parts of the structure, and had iron casements on hinges, and lead frames. Panes were still very small, owing to the size of glass available, and were of various shapes, of which the diamond pane was the most common. Stained glass was in use a good deal, representing heraldic and animal devices (see Figs. 108, 109, 111, 112, 113, 114 and 118).

The **chimneypiece** and **fireplace** of the first part of the 16th century were generally let into a wall—open central hearths disappeared even from small homes in this century, and the advent of tall chimneys for the average home was a typical Tudor innovation. The fireplace was large, with slightly raised hearth on which large logs were supported on iron dogs. A simple stone four-centred arch in Perpendicular pattern, with a little Gothic-type carving above it, was usual; alternatively, an oak lintel was sometimes made (see Figs. 110, 120 and 121). In the Elizabethan period, however, a great change was seen. The chimneypiece became the predominant ornamental feature of the room. The fire opening was now often rectangular, but at the sides of it were carved pilasters, columns of caryatid figures, male and female, which in turn supported an ornate chimneypiece or mantel, sometimes in two tiers. The Flemish influence on Elizabethan design and construction was most apparent here: the basis was a classical one, but the proportions and over-decoration ran riot, so that the classical origins were often hard to find. Some chimneypieces of this time were of vigorous design and decorative, but others were vulgar in their ostentation. Motifs were varied and extravagantly mixed with one another; they included animals, human figures, flowers, fruit, strap-work and scrollwork. The structure was made in a variety of media—wood, stone, marble or even plaster—and colour was often used. Later in the century, a few hearths were made with iron firebacks to burn coal, as wood began to be less plentiful. However, the majority of fires burnt wood till after the 16th century (see Figs. 109, 123 and 124).

Tudor **furniture** had not kept pace with the exquisite clothes, tapestries, fine wainscoting and plaster ceilings. Although in Elizabethan times there was a greater adequacy in the number of pieces in the home, the design was still primarily utilitarian, not aesthetic. Each piece was well and solidly made, constructed by panelling, mortise and tenon frame with wood pegs; and the carving, which became more profuse as time passed, was perhaps rough, but of good craftsmanship. Furniture, like clothes, reflected vividly the social position and wealth of the owner. While, by 1600, the well-to-do person owned highly carved furniture, perhaps inlaid or painted, and few pieces of walnut furniture, the poorer man made do with one or two items bought second-hand or inherited from his forbears, of 15th-century design and pattern. Most pieces of furniture were still made of oak, or perhaps partly in ash or elm, with a very few items of imported walnut. In the first half of the century, the usual decoration was panelling in linenfold pattern and carving in floral and Gothic motifs, with colour by painting and gilding to pick out the design. In the Elizabethan period, inlay was used in floral and geometrical patterns as well as carving; fruit woods, holly, laburnum and bog oak were used for this. Painting was seen less often by the end of the period, and a fine polish was made on the natural wood with beeswax and varnish. Again, at this time the Renaissance motifs began to replace the Gothic ones, and the Flemish-classical influence could also be seen here. Upholstery did not exist as yet, but more gaily coloured cushions were in use on seats and chests.

There was a greater variety of types of **cupboard** and storage space available in Tudor times than before. The **chest** or **coffer** was still in general use amongst all classes of the community, for seating accommodation was still inadequate, and a chest could be used for the two purposes. It was, in medium-sized and small houses, still considered one of the most important items of furniture. The early Tudor styles had carved front panels, usually

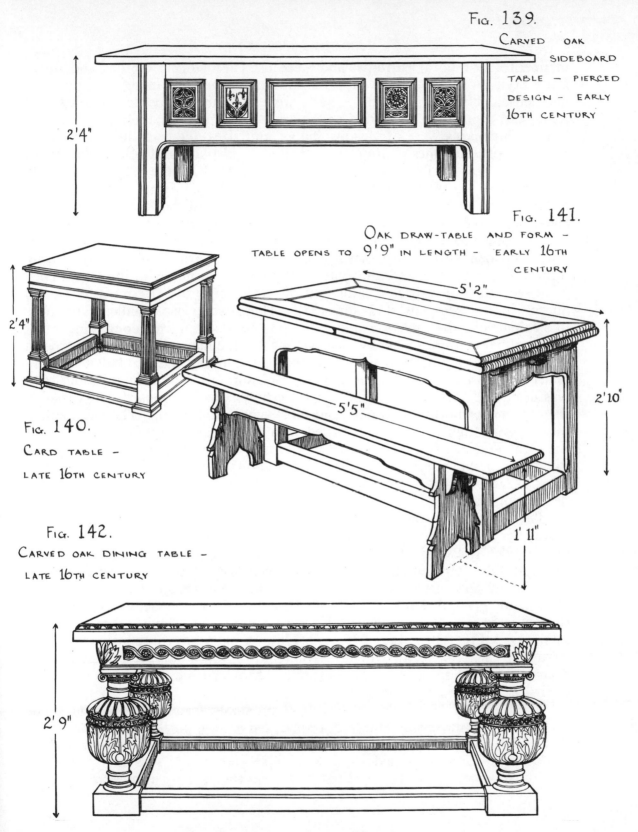

FIG. 139.

CARVED OAK
SIDEBOARD
TABLE — PIERCED
DESIGN — EARLY
16TH CENTURY

2'4"

FIG. 141.

OAK DRAW-TABLE AND FORM —
TABLE OPENS TO 9'9" IN LENGTH — EARLY 16TH
CENTURY

5'2"

2'4"

5'5"

2'10"

FIG. 140.

CARD TABLE —
LATE 16TH CENTURY

FIG. 142.

CARVED OAK DINING TABLE —
LATE 16TH CENTURY

1' 11"

2' 9"

139–142 *Tudor Furniture, 1509–1603*

in linenfold or floral patterns, and were used for storing clothes and linen. Later styles were either carved more abundantly or were inlaid in a floral or geometrical classical pattern. Chests were used in bedrooms, parlours and halls, and their contents varied accordingly (see Figs. 109, 111, 112, 113 and 131). **Cupboards** were of various shapes and sizes and had different names. Large, capacious ones contained food, linen and plate and often had carved pierced designs to let in air to keep the food fresh; these were particularly seen in early Tudor days (see Figs. 110, 135 and 136). Other large, tall types were used as wardrobes, and were called **presses**. In the later 16th century, **court cupboards** were in great demand. These were in two parts, both of which could have cupboards with panelled doors; alternatively, one half might be open with leg supports. Most court cupboards were used for storing food, linen and plate, and a display of plate could be made on the top. They were seen in long galleries, halls and dining rooms, and decoratively carved and/or inlaid (see Figs. 112 and 138). There were also smaller cupboards like **cabinets**, with drawers, made in the late 16th century for containing small personal belongings. These would be found in the main chamber or bedroom. Another item of furniture typical of the 16th century was the **buffet** or side-board. This had three shelves or tiers, each supported on four legs, and each was used to display plate or food. Some buffets had cupboard doors joining the top two or bottom two tiers, but most types were open. The Elizabethan buffets were highly decorated, carved with Renaissance motifs, such as acan-thus leaf and egg-and-dart border mouldings, while the legs of the supports, like those of the court cupboards, were bulbous in the late 16th century, and were carved, generally in acanthus-leaf pattern. Inlay was used in buffet decoration also (see Figs. 109, 112, 134 and 137).

There were few **chairs**. The box type was in general use all the century; it was very heavy, either plain or carved on the panelled back and sides, and often had a drawer in the box seat, opening at one side (see Figs. 110, 111, 113 and 129). In the second half of the century some chairs had turned or plain heavy legs instead of the box seat, and these were joined by stretchers almost at ground level. The arms usually sloped downwards and had turned supports. The panelled back was generally heavily carved and/or inlaid (see Figs. 109, 112, 126 and 128). Chairs of turned spindles with triangular seats were also in use from mid-century, but these were chiefly decorative, and distinctly uncomfortable. More cushions were available for chairs now, in lieu of upholstery.

The majority of people, however, sat on **stools, benches** and chests. The early 16th-century **stools** still had a solid, carved support at each side, a flat seat and a carved apron front and back (see Figs. 113 and 127). By mid-16th century the joint or joined stool was more common. This had four legs, slightly splayed outwards, and these were tied together by an underframe and stretchers at ground level. The legs were turned and carved (see Figs. 109, 112 and 132). Cushions were used with these stools. **Benches** and **forms** were of similar construction, and were used as window and wall seats and at table (see Fig. 110). Sometimes the benches had high, carved backs and even sides, so that they became settles, of a primitive nature. These were useful for keeping out the draughts (see Figs. 109 and 133).

The very large heavy **tables** used for dining in the Great Hall still existed in the 16th century, but their size began to diminish a little, and by the end of the century, when most families dined in their private dining rooms, the large tables tended to become obsolete. Some types were still trestle-style in the early Tudor period, particularly in smaller houses, or for servants in the Great Hall of a larger home. On the daïs of such homes and on each side of the upper part of the hall would be long, solid tables of carved oak, with elm tops, about two inches in thickness, and with four, six or eight legs, according to length. In the late Elizabethan period these legs were bulbous, and even the stretchers were carved (see Figs. 108, 109 and 142). Draw-leaf or **draw-top tables** were in use from this century. These had an extending leaf; large varieties were in use in the hall, but smaller types were useful in private dining rooms, since they could be closed up to occupy less room when not in use (see Fig. 141). **Small tables**, for cards or embroidery, were beginning to appear in late Elizabethan times. These had either square or round tops and four solid legs, classical pilaster style, with stretchers near the ground (see Fig. 140). Another innovation was the **sideboard table**—a combination of a cupboard or chest and a table. It had four solid, straight legs, but no stretchers until the late 16th century, a heavy board top, and carved front and side panels. Cupboards were contained in these, and there were doors to open in front. Food and linen could be stored inside and plate displayed on top. Such tables were chiefly in use in halls and dining rooms (see Figs. 108 and 139).

Bedsteads were considered by all classes to be the most important article in the home, and were costly items. As such, they were bequeathed in wills, as pieces of great value, to dependants and relatives. In wealthy households a bedstead might cost as much as £1,000, and even in poorer homes a much greater standard of comfort was to be expected by the latter years of the 16th century. In most homes there was one four-poster bed and often several trestle types. The bedsteads were enormous, so that when the heavy curtains were closed, the occupant(s) were enclosed in a small, draught-proof (but also somewhat airless) room. For example, the Great Bed of Ware—so called on account of its size—now in the Victoria and Albert Museum, measures nearly 11 feet square in plan, but this is, of course, unusually large. A heavy wooden carved canopy was supported on a carved bed head and posts at the head, with two further posts at the foot. The bed frame, of wood, was attached to

Fig. 143.

Carved oak bedstead c.1525 –

velvet bed curtains – silk coverlet

Fig. 144. Carved oak bedstead with painted design on

cornice and posts – c.1600 – approx: 7ft. in height –

bed curtains and coverlet in embroidered linen – design

in red, gold and white on black background

143 and 144 Tudor Furniture, 1509–1603

the bed head, and had two small posts at the foot, within the two canopy posts. The whole framework was heavy and solid, and almost the whole surface was decorated by carving. In the Elizabethan period the posts resembled classical columns, and after 1575 were often bulbous. The bed itself had a wood-board or rope-mesh foundation, and on top of this was placed one or two large feather beds, into which the occupant sank deeply. Linen sheets, blankets, pillows, bolster, coverlet and embroidered quilt completed the bedding. In comparison with other items of furniture, and indeed general living standards in a Tudor home, sleeping accommodation was luxurious. The bed curtains surrounded all the bed except over the bed head, and could be drawn back during the daytime; a valance hung all round the tester or canopy. These hangings varied in material according to the wealth of the owner, but were as rich as could be afforded, as in the case of Tudor garments. Tapestry, velvet and embroidered silks, with fringed or velvet band edges, were seen in well-to-do homes, whilst wool and cloth were used in poor ones. Tudor bedsteads are depicted in Figs. 113, 143 and 144.

The **lighting** of homes had altered little by 1603. The well-to-do used white candles bought in towns or from itinerant salesmen. These candles were made of wax or tallow and had cotton wicks. They were placed in silver or pewter candlesticks, or several of them in tall candlestands, some 10 feet high, and holding several candles, or in hanging candlestands of brass or iron, and suspended from the ceiling by pulley rope and chains. A number of these were necessary in a hall, but even so, lighting after dark was very gloomy by modern standards. In poorer homes people made their own candles from kitchen fat, or used home-made rush-lights, supported in an iron holder and set on a table or chest (see Figs. 108, 109, 112 and 146).

Washing and **bathing** were not popular pastimes in Tudor days, not surprisingly in view of their inconvenience. Most people washed in the bedchamber, using a basin and ewer; baths, when and if taken, were still in a wooden tub placed before the fire, and the water had to be carried up from the kitchen. Soap was a manufactured article from 1525, but many housewives continued to make their own scented varieties. Toothbrushes were not used; the teeth were sometimes rubbed with a cloth, and toothpicks were in daily use.

Sanitation was still very primitive. The medieval-type privy was not used now; instead, one resorted to a large pail, which was emptied out of upstairs windows into the street—the normal disposal place for all sewage—regardless of passers-by. Very large houses sometimes possessed "houses of easement", which were situated outside in the courtyard or in a cellar. These could often accommodate two persons simultaneously.

On the whole, English people ate well and—according to contemporary writers—better than on the Continent, where the standard of living, particularly

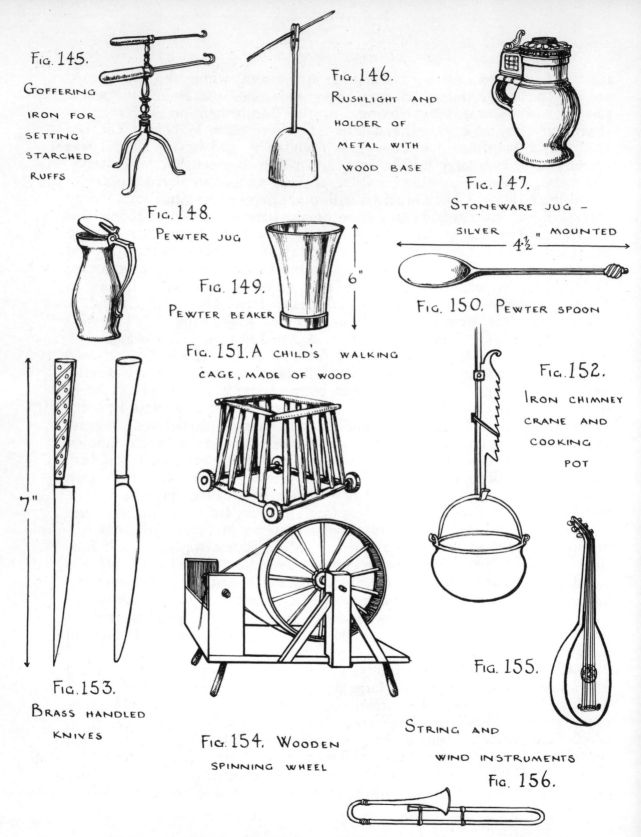

FIG. 145. GOFFERING IRON FOR SETTING STARCHED RUFFS

FIG. 146. RUSHLIGHT AND HOLDER OF METAL WITH WOOD BASE

FIG. 147. STONEWARE JUG — SILVER MOUNTED

FIG. 148. PEWTER JUG

FIG. 149. PEWTER BEAKER

6"

FIG. 150. PEWTER SPOON

4½"

FIG. 151. A CHILD'S WALKING CAGE, MADE OF WOOD

FIG. 152. IRON CHIMNEY CRANE AND COOKING POT

7"

FIG. 153. BRASS HANDLED KNIVES

FIG. 154. WOODEN SPINNING WHEEL

FIG. 155. STRING AND WIND INSTRUMENTS FIG. 156.

145–156 *Various Details of Items in the Home in Tudor Period, 1509–1603*

(a) (left) *Stoneware Jug mounted in Silver Gilt* (1580)

(b) (centre) *Standing Dish* (1564–5)

(c) (right) *Ewer* (1583–4)

(d) *Candle Snuffers* (c. 1550)

(e) *Caster and Salt* (both 1563–4)

TUDOR SILVERWARE

(a) *Gilt Cup and Cover* (1573)

(b) *Silver Spoons* (*c.* 1600)

(c) *Mother-o'-Pearl Casket, mounted in Silver Gilt*
(*c.* 1600)

(d) *Tankard, Gilt* (1574)

for the poor, was lower. In England the standard decreased gradually as the century progressed, because the price of food rose more than wages. Bread and meat were the staple diet, and a great deal of meat was eaten, even by poorer people. More vegetables were available now as root crops were grown, but these were largely utilised in soups. The diet was more varied, with the introduction of foreign fruits and other foods. For young babies, however, breast-feeding was the only possibility, and wet-nurses were used when necessary. In towns, meat, fish and butter went bad quickly, so many recipes were available for disguising this deterioration and making the food palatable. Milk could not be kept at all in towns, and had to be fetched in from the country as required. Beers and ales were drunk in great quantity by most people, and wines were imported for the well-to-do.

The main **meal** of the day was dinner, taken at 10.30 to 12 noon, and this meal, in large households, often lasted two to three hours. A light breakfast at 6.30 a.m. preceded it, consisting probably of bread and butter, a little meat, and wine or ale. Supper was about 4 to 6 p.m.—a smaller version of dinner.

There was greater refinement in English **pottery** in this century. The earthenware was still glazed a green colour or, alternatively, a brownish shade, but glazes were richer in quality. Chief items were jugs, bowls, mugs and some cups. Maiolica ware—the tin-enamelled pottery—was imported from the Continent. Much of it was made in Italy, France, Germany and the Tyrol, but there is little evidence of any English ware (see Fig. 147 and Plate VIII).

In the average home, most table and kitchen utensils were of wood or earthenware, but towards the end of Elizabeth's reign, **pewter** was seen more and more in middle-class and even poorer houses. This pewter ware was set out proudly on buffets, cupboards and chests (see Figs. 148, 149 and 150, also Plate VIII).

The wealthy possessed **silver** for their best ware, and pewter for servants' use. After the dissolution of the monasteries, silversmiths exchanged Church patronage for that of the wealthier citizens who wished to show off their affluence in a tangible form. Not only was it an age of ostentation, with the acquisition of silver, jewels and fine clothes the chief ways of showing it, but silver was regarded as a safe method of keeping wealth after the debasement of the coinage by Henry VIII. Styles in silver changed from Gothic to Renaissance, and after 1550 more items were made. These included silver andirons, cups, tankards, bowls, plates, warming pans, scent flagons, candlesticks and stands, salts, beakers, mazers, ewers, spoons, basins and snuffers. Apostle spoons became popular: there were thirteen in a set; one was the master, representing Christ. There were no forks yet, however. Posset-pots were also made in silver; these had a cover on top in order to keep the spiced night-cap hot (see Plates IX and X).

Glass articles became more plentiful. Much of the English work was in the form of window glass, but bowls, beakers and vases could also be bought. Emigrants from Lorraine came to England, and some settled to make glass for windows and vessels. This raised the standard of English work. However, the high-class work was imported from Venice. It was very expensive, but began to replace silver in popularity in the homes of the wealthy. By the late 16th century, Venetian glass was elaborate and delicate: elegant, slender-stemmed wine glasses and goblets were typical of this work (see Plate VIII).

Naturally, in the century that produced Shakespeare, Marlowe and Nash, we would expect the people to enjoy the theatre as one of their pleasures. Plays were indeed very popular in Elizabethan times, and before this masques and pageants were performed often at Court, and, on a smaller scale, in towns and villages. The people loved a show. Tournaments still drew large crowds also. Many of the other contemporary pleasures were still very cruel: the popularity of cock-fighting and of bull- and bear-baiting was undiminished. (The unfortunate animal was securely tied down, then set on by dogs, who were replaced by fresh ones as long as necessary.) Less blood-thirsty occupations included forms of tennis, hockey and golf, bowls, archery, hunting and hawking, and card and dice games. Tudor people loved music, either played by minstrels or performed themselves. They also liked to sing madrigals. Instruments were varied now, and included the viol, lute, cornet, trumpet, drum, flute and the new keyboard stringed instrument —forerunner of our own piano—the virginal. The strings were plucked to produce the sound, the instrument being played at a table. Other instruments can be seen in Figs. 155 and 156.

NOTES ON ILLUSTRATIONS

Fig. 108. *Tudor Great Hall.* *c*. 1530–40

Timber **roof—hammerbeam style**, complicated example—gilt and paint used. Stone **walls**—thinly plastered. Stone **windows**. Carved oak **screen** and **wall panelling**. Wood **floor**. **Furniture**—Oak **chests, trestle tables, forms** and **carved side-table**.

Fig. 109. *An Elizabethan Hall.* *c*. 1570–80

Plaster **ceiling**—partly painted in colours. Plaster **frieze**—partly painted in colours. Wood-panelled **walls**, doors and doorways. Stone-flagged **floor**. **Windows** on each side of the hall, in bays. **Furniture**—Carved oak **tables**, top table 13 ft. long, other tables 8–9 ft. long. Oak **benches**; the bench at the top table has a carved back. Two carved oak **buffets**, displaying plate. The nearer piece is also inlaid, height 3 ft. 9 in. Carved and inlaid oak **chair**, height 4 ft. Oak joint **stool**, height 1 ft. 9 in. Carved oak **chest**, height 2 ft. 1 in. **Lighting**—by candles, attached all round on the walls. **Decoration**—armour, arms and stags' heads.

Fig. 110. *Parlour.* *c.* 1530

Ceiling **beams**—carved oak painted. Plaster panels in between. **Frieze**—carved oak painted. **Walls**—panelled in linenfold pattern. **Interior porch** and **doors** in keeping with the walls. **Oriel window.** Oak **floor**. **Fireplace**—stone four-centred arch, brick interior, iron fire-dogs. **Furniture**—Oak box **chair**—carved panels. Oak **form**. Oak **cupboard** or aumbry—carved panels and doors—pierced decoration.

Fig. 111. *Elizabethan Main Chamber.* 1575–80

Plaster **ceiling**—fan and pendant type—different plaster, ribbed design in bay ceilings. **Walls** panelled—carved and inlaid. Two **bay windows** shown, three- and five-sided respectively. Heraldic glass. Wood **floor**. **Furniture**—Two carved oak **chests**, each approx. 4 ft. in length and 2 ft. in height. **Chair**—carved oak, box type, height 4 ft. 6 in.

Fig. 112. *Elizabethan Long Gallery.* *c.* 1590

Coved plaster **ceiling**. **Walls**—oak-panelled. **Floor**—oak. End **wall**—**window** from side to side. **Bay windows** along one side of gallery. **Ordinary windows** along other side. Stained glass in some windows. **Fireplace**—there are two fireplaces, both on the same wall: only one shows in this view of the gallery. **Furniture**—**Walnut buffet**—plate displayed, carved decoration, also inlay of holly and bog-wood, height 4 ft. **Oak court cupboard**—carved and inlay decoration, height 4 ft. **Two chests**—oak, inlaid with various woods, height 4 ft. **Two chairs**—carved oak. **Two forms**—carved oak, each form 7 ft. in length. **Oak stool**—joined and turned, height 1 ft. 6 in. **Lighting**—by candles—wall attachments.

Fig. 113. *Tudor Bedchamber.* *c.* 1575

Plaster ribbed **ceiling**. **Walls** panelled in carved oak, inlaid with various woods. Wood **floor**. Rush **mat**. **Bedstead**, *c.* 1590–95, height 7 ft. 4 in., width 5 ft. 8 in., length 8 ft. Walnut carved, and inlaid with holly and bog-wood. Silk embroidered coverlet. Hangings and flounce of velvet. **Chest**—carved oak. Oak **stool**. **Box chair** of carved oak, *c.* 1575, height 4 ft. 7 in.

167 Langham Hall, c. 1615–20 (notes at page 124)

V

STUART AND COMMONWEALTH, 1603–1660

JAMES I	1603–1625
CHARLES I	1625–1649
COMMONWEALTH	1649–1660

THE Elizabethan era had been eventful, turbulent and adventurous, led by a strong-willed, sensible monarch—for Elizabeth, despite her numerous faults, guided the state through troubled times with a steady hand, aided by her innate commonsense and deep, unerring understanding of her people. The first half of the 17th century presented, in some aspects, an anticlimax. Internal strife, rather than the external wars with Spain which had characterised the latter half of the 16th century, was the keynote of this period. Brother was set against brother, father against son, for the struggle was religious and civil. For much of this time the Church of England, as established under Elizabeth, was dominant, though the Puritan element in our life struggled constantly for recognition. Small outbursts of rebellion were evident, as instanced by the sailing of the "Mayflower" for the New World in 1620—a comparatively small event at the time, but one which had great and lasting results. From 1649 to 1660 the Puritans, under Oliver Cromwell, held for a brief spell a greater power, but extremism of any kind has always been abhorrent to the Englishman, and reaction set in after the death of Cromwell.

Bound up with this great religious problem was the struggle between King and Parliament, Royalist and Puritan. Neither James I nor his son Charles had the strength, power, commonsense and understanding of Elizabeth. They made a futile and final effort to maintain a fading monarchy—that "Divine Right of Kings" to which they were sincerely convinced they were entitled. But what had been workable in feudal days was acceptable no longer, and one error led to another until Charles found himself in an unenviable and irretrievable position. England's last civil war followed—a grim, bloody struggle, laying waste property, homes and men, setting families against one another, until, finally, Cromwell was victorious. The King was then tried and executed in Whitehall. On this occasion, Charles retained the dignity which he had

158 *Jacobean Bedchamber, c. 1610–20 (notes on page 125)*

159　*Jacobean Drawing Room, c. 1615–20 (notes on page 125)*

lost so often in his struggles with Parliament, and it is reported that he died bravely, as befitting a king, his head being severed at the first blow.

Viewing the broad picture as presented by these historical facts, the events seem largely destructive, not creative, in result. Nevertheless, much was being built in our social, parliamentary and economic structure, although a deal of it was not apparent until after the restoration of the monarchy in 1660.

Punishments for offences against the law were still heavy, particularly for theft, even of small items. Hanging was still enforced for comparatively minor misdeeds. These hangings were public and drew large crowds. Imprisonment was still dreaded, as the condition of the prisons had not improved from Tudor times, while a trial might be postponed indefinitely.

In the field of **medicine** some research work was being carried out and new discoveries were being made. Of note was William Harvey's work in connection with the circulation of the blood. Leprosy was now almost under control, but the recurrent plagues still exacted a heavy toll in large cities. The insane were regarded as a danger and menace to society and were kept in chains at Bedlam.

Education continued to expand, with more schools being founded, except during the Civil War, when much of the work was suspended. Most towns now had grammar schools, although well-to-do parents preferred a private tutor for their children, who completed their education by accompanying them on a European tour. With the exception of the privileged few, girls received little or no education beyond housecraft.

Towns continued to increase in size, though many of their houses were old and had remained untouched since Medieval times. These constituted slums, in a bad state of repair, and even in decay. Streets were still evil-smelling and dirty, with sewage flowing down open kennels in the street centre. There was much complaint of the foul atmosphere in towns, particularly London, where the coal which was burnt more and more in home fireplaces caused pollution. James I had ordered that coal must be used in order to conserve timber supplies. The concern and worry that are indicated in contemporary writings are reminiscent of similar articles to-day on "smog", and show that the problem is by no means new. Similar doubts were expressed in the 17th century concerning the effect of this atmospheric pollution on the health of the people and the damage caused to building fabric.

On the **land**, a steady improvement was apparent in agriculture: cattle were better fed, root crops were being grown, and there was a greater knowledge and use of fertilisers and manures.

In the **domestic** sphere, the average housewife of a large or medium-sized home had to be a capable woman, well versed in many crafts. Apart from general housework, she often looked after the garden and orchard, and even poultry. On a farm, she might also tend the pigs and help with sheep-

(a) *Delft Candlestick and Mug*

(b) *Child's Earthenware Mug,*
dated 1628

(c) *Wine-Cup, Gilt*
(1616–17)

(d) *Cup and*
Cover (1625–6)

(e) *Tankard, Gilt* (1607–8)

(a) *Cup* (1656–7)

(b) *Tankard* (1642–3)

(c) *Beaker* (*c.* 1640)

(d) *Cup and Cover* (1658–9)

(e) *Wine-cup*
(1650–1)

(f) *Fruit Bowl* (1649–50)

(g) *Tankard* (1657–8)

shearing. The dairy work came under her control. In the house, she would spin and weave, embroider, make wines and preserve fruit, and prepare medicine with herbs. In a large home, she had many servants, but she would have to organise the household, keep accounts and educate her daughters. Even in small cottage homes, women were busy helping in the gardens and the fields, and doing quantities of spinning and weaving, both for their families and to sell.

Rates of pay for various occupations varied a good deal, but sound most inadequate to us now. In agriculture, hop-pickers would receive 6d. or 8d. a day, and an unskilled labourer a shilling a day, while in towns a carver might receive half-a-crown. However, prices were in keeping with these scales, and 20th-century house-owners would be pleased to know that it only cost 2s. 3d. to paint a house.

Architecturally, the **Jacobean**[1] period was a continuation of the Elizabethan. As in costume, the tremendous amount of elaboration and decoration of the surfaces, so typical of late Elizabethan times, was carried to even greater excess under James I. Both outside and inside the house the whole surface was decorated—by carving, painting and inlay. The basic style of the time was Renaissance, but as in the 16th century, the proportions were incorrect according to the classical tradition, and the interpretation often vulgar and ostentatious, though the work had vitality. The Flemish influence was still clearly apparent. In the interior of the home, the plaster ceilings were decorated by ornamental strapwork all over the surface, while pendants were still seen: none of the surface was left plain. Doors and chimneypieces were the chief recipients of decorative carving, in wood, marble or plaster. Judged superficially, there appears little difference between Elizabethan and Jacobean architecture, but a distinction can be perceived upon a closer study of examples still existing. The Jacobean work is generally on a larger scale, more sumptuous, stately and lavishly decorated, with less emphasis on homeliness. The best-known examples of such homes are Audley End, Essex; Knole, Kent; Hatfield House, Hertfordshire; Blickling Hall, Norfolk; Charlton House, near Greenwich; and Aston Hall, near Birmingham.

It was in **Charles I's** reign that the Renaissance architecture began to be seen in true classical form. A lead was given by architects who designed buildings with correct classical proportions, and employed the orders and classical decorative forms as they had been used in Ancient Rome, basing their designs on those of **Andrea Palladio**[2] in contemporary Italian work.

---

[1] Considerable uncertainty appears to exist regarding the correct use of the terms **Jacobean** and **Carolean**. In this volume, the more generally used method has been adopted of employing the term "Jacobean" to denote the reign of James I, and "Caroline" (or Carolean) to cover the reign of Charles I. In Chapter VI the term "Restoration Stuart" has then been used to cover the reigns of Charles II and James II.

[2] Palladio had died in 1580, but his work, in the form of buildings and drawings, was there to study; also his followers in Italy continued the work which he had begun.

160 *Caroline Dining Room, c. 1640–5 (notes on page 125)*

161　*Commonwealth Dining Room, c. 1655* (notes on page 125)

Prominent among the architects in this new approach was **Inigo Jones** (1573–1652)—our first great English architect. Although born the son of a cloth-worker, he was always interested in architecture, and made several visits to Italy in the early 17th century to study both contemporary architecture and that of Ancient Rome. He was most impressed by Palladio's work, and studied with great care and interest his buildings and his books on architectural principles, founded on the precepts of Vitruvius. Under James I, Jones was appointed Surveyor-General of Royal Buildings. In 1619, he began work on the Banqueting Hall in Whitehall; it was completed in 1622. This building, with its pediments and deep cornice, its correct pilasters and capitals, was the first really classical example in English architecture. Inigo Jones continued in royal service under the patronage of Charles I. However, he was a Royalist, and so suffered considerably during the Civil War. In 1643 he was deprived of his offices and forced to leave London. He died in 1652. Among his best-known works are Wilton House, Wiltshire, St. Paul's, Covent Garden, and the Queen's House at Greenwich. Although the number of buildings he designed was limited, the effect of his work was far-reaching. It made a profound and lasting impression on English architecture, both in public buildings and domestic houses, in town and country alike. He had established the practice of an architect's designing the whole building, whatever its function; also that the building should be erected in true classical terms. He showed how a plain surface would set off, in contrast, a panel or area of decoration. Thus the Jacobean method of decorating the total surface area was gradually abandoned in favour of greater discretion in design of ornament.

John Webb (1611–72) followed on with the work of Inigo Jones. He was his nephew and pupil, and completed Jones's outstanding commitments on his death in 1652. Although lacking the brilliance of his master, Webb was responsible for some good works, among which are Thorpe Hall, near Peterborough, and Ashdown House in Berkshire.

From 1642 to 1660, little domestic building was carried out, in contrast to the preceding forty years in which a record amount of work had been completed. Many existing homes were stripped of their decorative features, partly to produce money and metal for the Civil War, and partly because of the Puritan influence on homes, which was to simplify and to remove all items of luxury.

Actual **building materials** were being changed in this century. Owing to the shortage of timber, which by 1603 was becoming apparent for the first time, James I issued an order forbidding the use of a great deal of timber in building houses. The greatest shortage was in south-east England, where for a thousand years and more men had felled timber for use in building, making fires, smelting iron and making glass, etc., with no thought that supplies might ever be exhausted or that trees should be planted to replace those re-moved. As a result, all homes, large and small, were made with less timber, and more stone and brick. After 1625 the actual size of the brick became standardised at its present size, $9 \times 4\frac{1}{2} \times 3$ inches. Previously bricks had varied in shape and size from one part of the country to another. However, in the countryside, wattle-and-daub cottages with timber framing continued to be made for the peasants—a style which had hardly altered from Norman times, and with little added comfort. Dried rushes and branches were held together by clay and mud. Cottages for more well-to-do labourers were, however, beginning to be constructed of brick or stone with tiled roofs instead of thatch.

A further evolution in the **plan of the house** was carried out in this century. The hall became smaller as the Jacobean period progressed, and by 1620, in the majority of cases, it had shrunk considerably; also the main door opened on to it. The dining room and drawing room took the place of the hall in importance, and were adequate for most of its functions. For the remainder of the activities which had previously taken place in the hall, other smaller rooms were designed—a study, a library, private rooms, etc. The kitchen was placed near to the dining room for convenience, or might be situated below it in the basement.

The **garden** continued its early development from Tudor times; the kitchen and flower gardens were now planned in two distinct sections, the whole being laid out formally, with small box hedges to separate the beds of flowers.

With the gradual shrinkage in size of the **Great Hall**, examples became fewer as the 17th century advanced. However, a typical Jacobean hall from a large house of the period, showing an overdecorated, Flemish-influenced screen, can be seen in Fig. 157, also in Colour Plate facing page 123. The roof, in timber and plaster, is also a fine example of the period. In these large homes, the practice of using the "screens" to keep out draughts continued into the Caroline period. The furniture in the Jacobean type of hall still comprised very large, heavy tables and forms, chests, buffets, court cupboards, stools and a chair or two.

In the 17th century, the **bedchamber** was not necessarily reserved for sleeping only; it was also employed as a sitting room or, as we might term it, a bed-sitting room. During the day a lady often received her guests there. The bedchamber, in well-to-do homes, was therefore much larger than in Elizabethan times, and possessed more furniture. The chief item was the bed, ornate as ever, and in addition there were a chest, cupboards of various types, a chair or two and stools. An illustration of a bedchamber can be seen in Fig. 158.

Drawing and **dining rooms** are also illustrated. A Jacobean version can be seen in Fig. 159, a Caroline room in Fig. 160 and a Commonwealth one in Fig. 161. The furniture in these rooms was more varied now; there were

162   *Long Gallery, temp. Charles I, c. 1635 (notes on page 125)*

also more pieces in each room. A dining table with dining chairs was usual, of smaller style than that seen earlier in the Great Hall; a settle, stools, smaller side-tables, cupboards and buffets, and perhaps a padded or upholstered chair or two. Plate was displayed on a cloth on the buffets and court cupboards, and candlesticks decorated the tables.

A **long gallery** was built on the first floor of most large homes, and was used for the same purposes as the Elizabethan examples. A Caroline version can be seen in Fig. 162. The best furniture was on display here, also the principal oil portraits, and there was a magnificent chimneypiece. Three sides were set with windows, of bay style, from the ceiling nearly to the floor.

In the average cottage and farmhouse, the **kitchen** and cooking equipment remained much the same as in Tudor times. Roasting was done on spits over an open fire in a large fireplace; so also was boiling and simmering, in huge metal cauldrons, hung from a chimney crane, with an elaborate system of chains and pulleys. In large homes, however, there were installed by the end of this period some early, and highly inconvenient, types of kitchen range, whereby the fire was confined, and ovens were adjacent. In smaller kitchens, brick ovens were still in use. Kitchen furniture was still sparse and strictly utilitarian; racks on the walls for hanging utensils, trestle tables, a cupboard or two for storage, and, by the end of the period, in large kitchens, perhaps an oak dresser to accommodate pewter and earthenware, cutlery and linen. The majority of vessels were of metal, brass, bronze and iron, with some earthenware examples. In shape and design they differed little from Medieval cooking vessels. Actual kitchen implements were similar in number and variety to those listed in Chapter IV. It has not been thought necessary to illustrate a kitchen in this chapter, as so little alteration has taken place since the Tudor one illustrated in Fig. 114, but a later Stuart kitchen can be seen in Fig. 210 in Chapter VI. Kitchen utensils, however, are illustrated in Figs. 196, 197, 200 and 201.

After 1603, in the majority of houses, **wainscoting** became more and more the general medium for wall-covering. In Jacobean days, this was often ornately carved after Elizabethan fashion, and colour was used to pick out the design, in addition to inlay patterns (see Figs. 157 and 158). After the accession of Charles I, the room was frequently designed as a whole in the form of a classical order; pilasters divided the room into bays, while chimneypieces, doors and windows were designed to fit into the scheme. The whole area might be painted, or the natural wood was left uncovered (see Figs. 159, 160, 161 and 162). Secret panels concealing small hiding places were typical of the Civil War period. Framed paintings were now becoming more common, and were hung on walls in a manner which was in keeping with the panelling scheme. Portraits in oils were the most usual. Charles I helped to popularise this idea by his patronage of Sir Anthony Van Dyck. Sculpture,

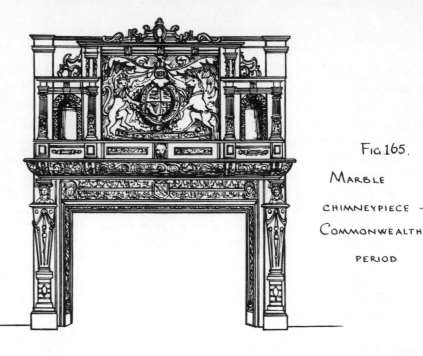

FIG. 163.

CARVED OAK
CHIMNEYPIECE WITH
CARVED STONE FIRE
OPENING — EARLY
JACOBEAN PERIOD

FIG. 165.

MARBLE
CHIMNEYPIECE —
COMMONWEALTH
PERIOD

FIG. 164.

CLASSICAL TYPE OF DOORWAY — AFTER
INIGO JONES — FLANKED BY
CORINTHIAN COLUMNS — c. 1650

163–165   *Architectural Details, Stuart Period, 1603–60*

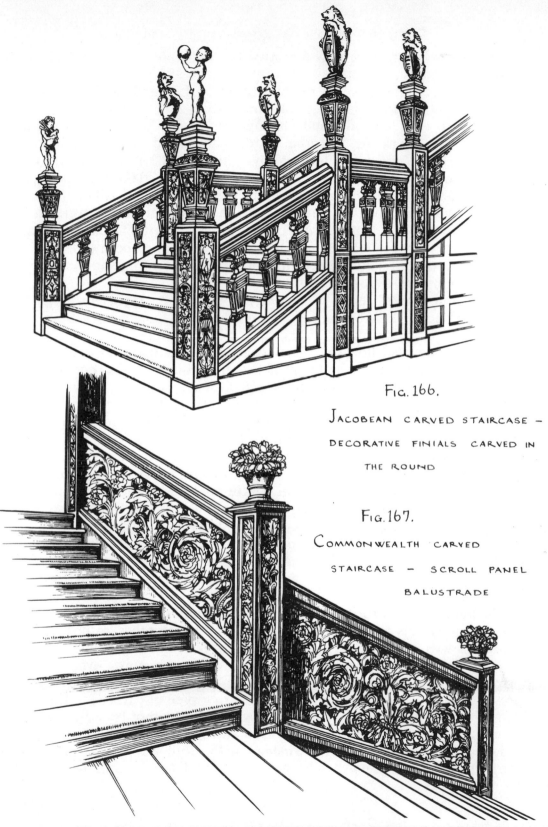

Fig. 166.

Jacobean carved staircase –
decorative finials carved in
the round

Fig. 167.

Commonwealth carved
staircase – scroll panel
balustrade

166 *and* 167   *Staircases of Stuart Period, 1603–60*

carvings and pottery were now imported by well-to-do families to adorn their important rooms.

Tapestry continued to be manufactured in England, and a factory was established by Sir Francis Crane at Mortlake in 1619, under the auspices of James I. It was a costly undertaking, but both James I and Charles I patronised the work so that the factory flourished—though the products could only be afforded by the wealthy—until the Civil War, after which it failed to continue production. The fame of the Mortlake tapestries persists to this day, and examples can be seen in the Victoria and Albert Museum in London. More inexpensive hangings, made by hand at home, were also used in a number of houses, both as wall-covering and for curtains and bed-hangings. Figure composition in allegorical subjects was typical of both types of work.

Some walls were still **painted**, in floral or figure compositions—the latter also in allegorical or biblical scenes.

Ceilings continued to be of decorated plaster: the Jacobean designs were similar to the late Elizabethan, using an all-over symmetrical pattern of geometrical basis, in strapwork. The actual straps were often in high relief, broad and decorated florally. The spaces between the strapwork were also covered by ornament, in the form of flowers, fruit, cherubs, heraldic devices and wreaths. Colour was still employed in many instances. The frieze was in keeping with the ceiling, and somewhat free in treatment (see Figs. 157, 158, 159 and 162). After 1635–40, the influence of Inigo Jones and his contemporaries was apparent in a more classical approach to ceiling design. More dignified, restrained and simple patterns were employed. Often there would be a central feature, an oval, a circle or a rectangle, in high relief, richly decorated with fruit and flowers; the centre might be plain or perhaps painted with an allegorical figure composition. The outer section of the ceiling might be divided into simple large sections by heavily moulded ribs. Classical mouldings were used, in correct proportion, with more classical motifs—the acanthus leaf and swags in particular. Commonwealth ceilings were even plainer, with all the decorative emphasis placed in the central feature (see Figs. 160 and 161).

The **floors** of most rooms were of polished wood; rushes had been generally abandoned by this time. In larger halls and some other rooms, a tiled or stone floor was still to be seen, and this might be sanded (see Fig. 157). Rugs and **carpets** were still expensive but more were seen now. Many were imported from Turkey and Persia, but home-made versions in "turkey-work" were in general use. This name was given to a type of carpet-knotting copied from Turkish methods. Floral and geometrical motifs were usual and colours rich and vivid (see Figs. 158, 160 and 162).

The large Elizabethan-style **windows** with close-set vertical **mullions** and several horizontal **transoms**, constructed of carved stone mouldings, continued

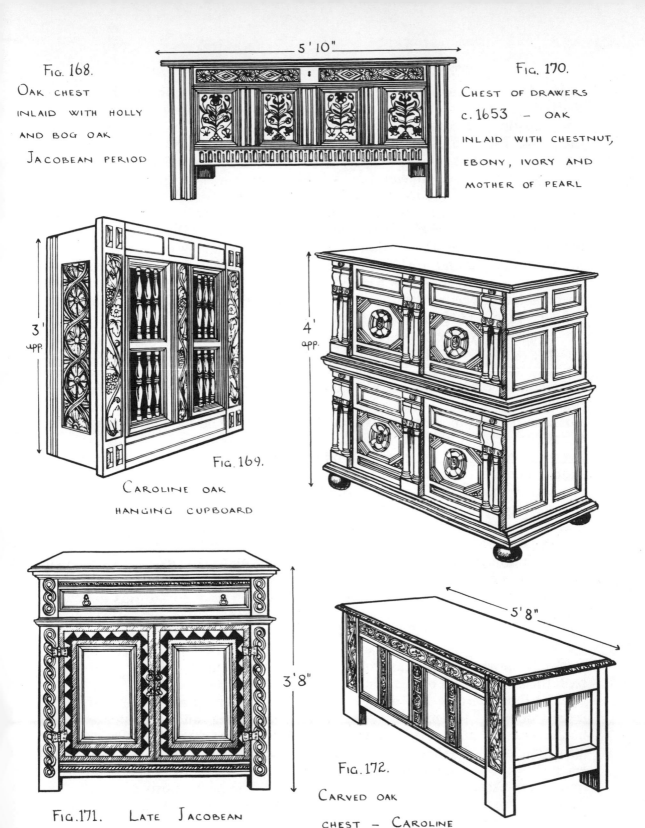

FIG. 168.
OAK CHEST
INLAID WITH HOLLY
AND BOG OAK
JACOBEAN PERIOD

5' 10"

FIG. 170.
CHEST OF DRAWERS
c. 1653 — OAK
INLAID WITH CHESTNUT,
EBONY, IVORY AND
MOTHER OF PEARL

3' app.

FIG. 169.
CAROLINE OAK
HANGING CUPBOARD

4' app.

3' 8"

FIG. 171. LATE JACOBEAN
CARVED AND INLAID CUPBOARD

5' 8"

FIG. 172.
CARVED OAK
CHEST — CAROLINE
PERIOD

168–172 *Stuart Furniture, 1603–60*

to be erected under James I (see Fig. 157). However, in the Caroline period, the tall rectangular windows were divided by fewer mullions, and usually only one transom, set nearer to the top frame in a proportion of two-thirds to one-third (see Figs. 159, 160 and 161). This method of construction gave more light to the rooms. Glass was in fairly general use by now, in rather larger rectangular panes, set in lead frames. Most windows had two or three vertical bars, and some of the lower windows were made to open casement fashion. Some stained glass was still to be seen.

The **door** and **doorway** in principal rooms were now designed as a part of the scheme for the whole room. The door panelling was carved to match the wainscoting, and, especially after 1630, the classical scheme prevailed in the doorway: the door was flanked by columns or pilasters, and above these an **entablature** was generally constructed, with perhaps a **broken pediment** on top (see Figs. 158, 159, 160, 161 and 164).

The **chimneypiece** continued to be the focal point in all rooms: the fireplace was the centre for warmth and comfort, and the chimneypiece above for decoration. **Jacobean chimneypieces** were after the Elizabethan style, but were considerably more ornate. Caryatid figures gave place to columns or pilasters—these were often in strange and unclassical proportions—and the riot of ornament included strapwork, floral, animal and human motifs, broken pediments and swags (see Figs. 157 and 163). With the classical influence from Palladian sources, in the **Caroline** period the **chimneypiece** became more stately and its ornament more restrained, if less vivid. The whole feature was in stricter classical form, with columns or pilasters as supports, and cornice above. A further tier of pilasters supported an entablature, and perhaps a broken pediment, above. A framed portrait or wood panel or even a portrait bust occupied the central position (see Figs. 161, 162 and 165). These chimneypieces were carved from sundry materials, varying in different parts of the country according to that which was easily available. Materials included marbles, stone, wood and even chalk. The open fire was in general used still, although in large houses the iron dogs sometimes supported an iron basket which, in turn, held the logs or coal. As coal began to replace timber for heating purposes, particularly in the towns, where the timber shortage was felt more keenly, cast-iron fire-backs were used. These were often patterned with floral or heraldic designs.

The oak **staircase** had developed by 1610 into the grand style seen in the large homes of the period. Among such staircases still in existence is the main stairway at Hatfield House, Hertfordshire, and that at Knole, Kent. The plan of the staircase was round the "open well", although the "dog-legged" type was still constructed in many smaller homes. The treads were broad, the ascent easy and the flights short. The newel posts were massive, generally square in plan and carved profusely; they terminated in highly decorative, tall finials of various kinds—generally of animal or human form. The handrail and string were very solid; the balusters were lavishly ornamented and carved into various shapes (see Fig. 166). After 1635–40 the balusters were often replaced by a carved, open-work panel balustrade, in strapwork and foliage designs; the finials of this period were shorter and less ornate in conception (see Fig. 167).

Although knowledge of the arts of architecture and interior decoration had increased rapidly in this period, **furniture** in these homes continued to be comparatively sparse and sometimes crude. However, there were more items of furniture than in Elizabeth's time, and the majority of homes possessed a greater number of pieces than hitherto. The workmanship is attractive, even if somewhat unpolished in character; it has vigour and interest. Oak continued to be the dominant material, particularly for furniture made in England. Walnut was used rarely, and was seen only in palaces and the homes of the rich—such furniture was usually imported, as was also much of the upholstered furniture of the period. Cedar was sometimes used as an alternative wood. Jacobean furniture was carved profusely, with Renaissance motifs, and inlay gave colour to the work, with the use of fruit woods, bog oak, and, later, even ivory and mother-of-pearl. Legs were turned, and the bulbous legs on tables and buffets continued fashionable during the reign of James I. The vase-shaped turned legs followed these. Commonwealth furniture is noted for its simplicity, leather covering to chairs, with brass studs, and the barley-sugar twist and bobbin turning to legs and stretchers.

In nearly all homes, the **bed** was considered to be the most essential and important item of furniture—it was without doubt the most comfortable. The massive poster bedstead was the valued property of well-to-do people. The two posts were in bulbous form, heavily carved, in a distorted but vital representation of classical columns. They supported a heavy carved wood tester, from the foot of the bed, while the head was supported by an ornately carved and/or inlaid head-board. Hangings, valance and bedding were similar to those of Elizabethan times (see Fig. 158.) In other homes, a wood bedstead, panelled head and foot, with rope-mesh or board base, was in use.

There were by this time a considerable variety of **cupboards** for divers uses. The antecedent of these, the **chest** or coffer, was still very much in favour, both as a seat and for storage purposes. The sides were panelled, profusely carved and inlaid, while the lid top was generally plain. The legs lifted the chest about six inches or more from the floor. In the Caroline period, some chests had a drawer constructed in them—prototypes of the chests-of-drawers which followed later (see Figs. 157, 168 and 172).

Other types of **cupboard** for storing clothes and linen existed, although the articles had to be folded, as there was no hanging space as yet. Some of these had doors and shelves, also drawers (see Fig. 171).

FIG. 174.
JACOBEAN CARVED OAK
BUFFET

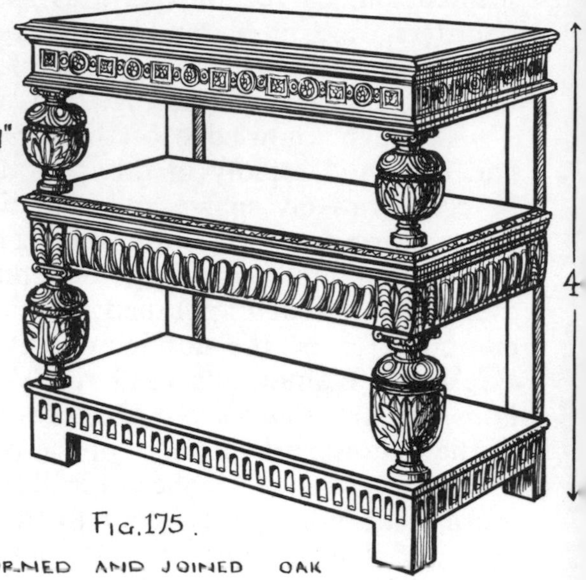

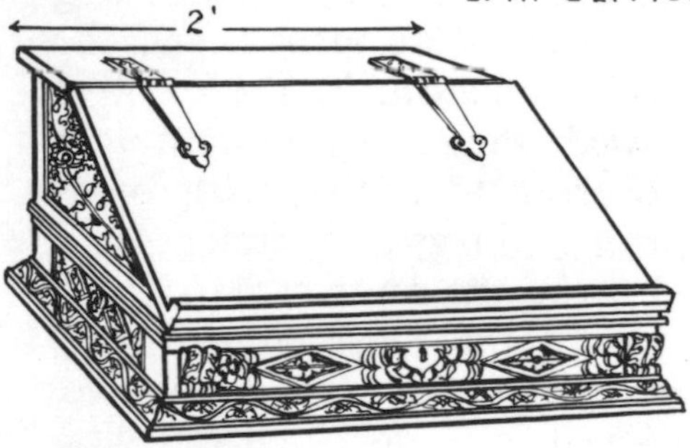

3'11"

FIG. 173.
CARVED OAK COURT
CUPBOARD — EARLY
17TH CENTURY

FIG. 175.
TURNED AND JOINED OAK
DRESSER — COMMONWEALTH STYLE — 1659

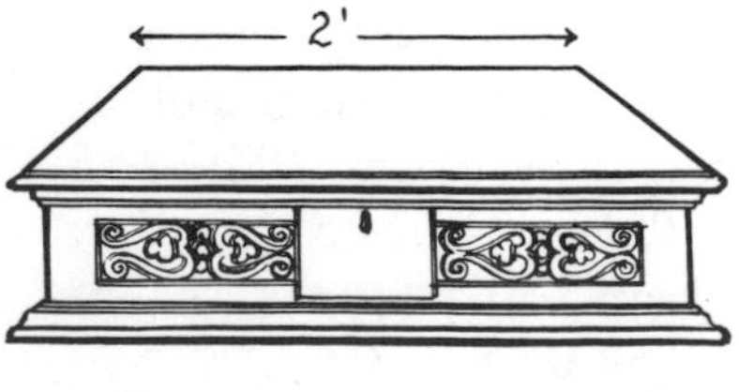

2'

FIG. 176. EARLY JACOBEAN
CARVED OAK PORTABLE DESK —
SHELF AND DRAWER INSIDE

REPENT THE LORD IS AT HAND

WATCH AND PRAY

LIVE WELL AND DIE WELL 1659

2'

FIG. 177.
CARVED OAK BAND OR RUFFLE
BOX — CAROLINE PERIOD

173–177 *Stuart Furniture, 1603–60*

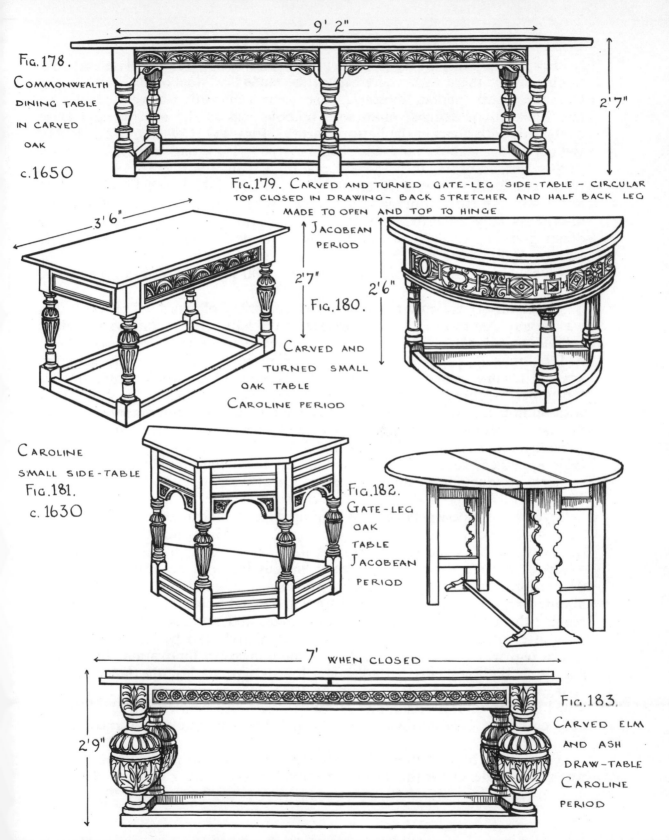

FIG. 178. COMMONWEALTH dining table IN CARVED OAK c.1650

9' 2"

2' 7"

FIG.179. CARVED AND TURNED GATE-LEG SIDE-TABLE — CIRCULAR TOP CLOSED IN DRAWING — BACK STRETCHER AND HALF BACK LEG MADE TO OPEN AND TOP TO HINGE

3' 6"

JACOBEAN PERIOD

2' 7"

FIG.180.

CARVED AND TURNED SMALL OAK TABLE CAROLINE PERIOD

2' 6"

CAROLINE SMALL SIDE-TABLE FIG.181. c.1630

FIG.182. GATE-LEG OAK TABLE JACOBEAN PERIOD

7' WHEN CLOSED

2' 9"

FIG.183. CARVED ELM AND ASH DRAW-TABLE CAROLINE PERIOD

178–183   *Stuart Furniture, 1603–60*

For use in halls, dining and drawing rooms, for displaying plate and containing linen, there were **court cupboards, buffets** or sideboards, and, by the Commonwealth period, **dressers**. The **court cupboard** was very similar to late Elizabethan designs, often with bulbous legs in the top tier and large cupboards with doors in the bottom part (see Figs. 157, 159, 160, 162 and 173). **Buffets** also resembled the Elizabethan type. They had bulbous or vase-shaped legs, according to the period, and three shelves or tiers to accommodate plate and food. They were ornately carved and inlaid (see Figs. 157, 159 and 174). An early example of a **dresser** can be seen in Fig. 175. The **chest-of-drawers** only appeared very late in this period. The top was used as a dressing-table and the commodious space inside for storage of clothes. It was generally inlaid (see Fig. 170). Another bedroom item of furniture of this type was the **livery cupboard**, which was still in use. An example can be seen in Fig. 158.

Tables also were now made in a greater variety of types. This evolution was largely due to the shrinkage in size of the hall. In the Jacobean period, very large oak tables, with elm tops, continued to be made. These usually had bulbous legs and solid stretchers near the floor. However, with the gradual decline in the use of the hall in favour of a dining room, smaller tables were adequate. Among the styles which developed was the **draw-table**, with sliding top which drew out, when required, to accommodate a larger number of people (see Fig. 183). Other **smaller tables** were of fixed size, but sometimes had six legs (see Figs. 160 and 178). Many types of small **side-table** appeared, some of which had hinged tops: these might be octagonal, circular, rectangular or square in plan. Nearly all styles had stretchers (see Figs. 161, 179, 180 and 181). The chief innovation of the period, in this field, was the **gate-leg table**: this appeared in Jacobean times, but was not fully developed until after 1650 (see Fig. 182). Most tables were made of oak, with perhaps elm tops; the sides were carved, and the legs—four or six —varied as time passed. The heavy **bulbous leg** with acanthus-leaf carved decoration was very typical of Jacobean furniture, but lasted in fashion until about 1645. The **columnar type of leg** with carved fluted decoration began to replace the bulb type in late Jacobean times, and remained in constant use until after the Restoration. A third principal style can be seen in the **vase-turned leg,** which is predominantly a Commonwealth innovation, but which also long outlasted this period. The fourth type of leg, the **bobbin-turned style**, which was introduced about 1640–45, was more suited to light chair styles than to tables. Examples of bulbous legs can be seen in Figs. 160 and 183, columnar legs in Figs. 179, 180 and 181, and the vase-turned leg in Fig. 178.

Chairs had become more common items of furniture now, although there was still a tendency for them to be reserved for important guests and the older

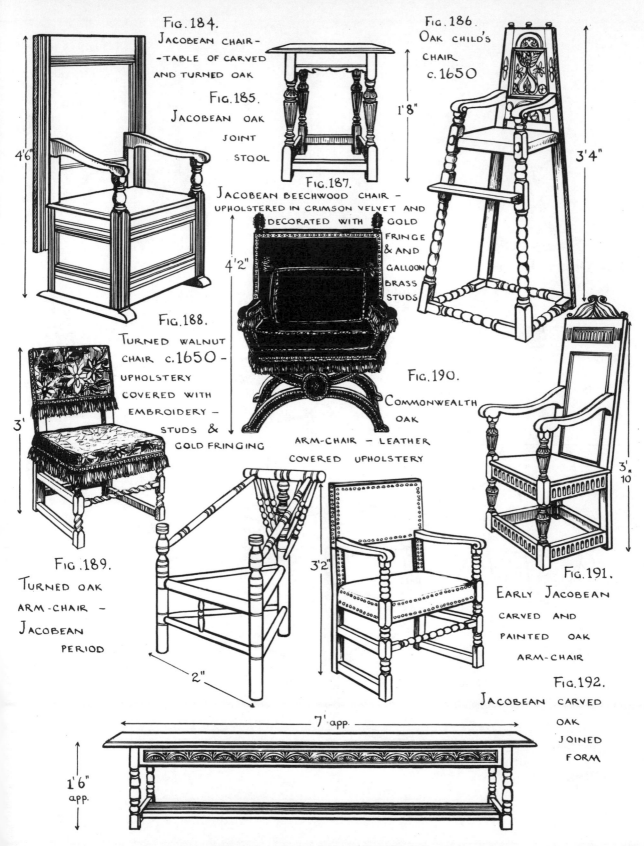

FIG. 184.
JACOBEAN CHAIR-
-TABLE OF CARVED
AND TURNED OAK

FIG. 185.
JACOBEAN OAK
JOINT
STOOL

FIG. 186.
OAK CHILD'S
CHAIR
c. 1650

1'8"

4'6"

3'4"

FIG. 187.
JACOBEAN BEECHWOOD CHAIR -
UPHOLSTERED IN CRIMSON VELVET AND
DECORATED WITH GOLD
FRINGE
& AND
GALLOON
BRASS
STUDS

4'2"

FIG. 188.
TURNED WALNUT
CHAIR c. 1650 -
UPHOLSTERY
COVERED WITH
EMBROIDERY -
STUDS &
GOLD FRINGING

FIG. 190.
COMMONWEALTH
OAK
ARM-CHAIR - LEATHER
COVERED UPHOLSTERY

3'

3'
10

FIG. 189.
TURNED OAK
ARM-CHAIR -
JACOBEAN
PERIOD

3'2"

FIG. 191.
EARLY JACOBEAN
CARVED AND
PAINTED OAK
ARM-CHAIR

2"

FIG. 192.
JACOBEAN CARVED
OAK
JOINED
FORM

7' app.

1'6"
app.

184–192 *Stuart Furniture, 1603–60*

FIG. 194.
RUSHLIGHT
AND IRON
HOLDER - WOOD
BASE

FIG. 195.
JACOBEAN
IRON ANDIRON

FIG. 193. TURNED PEARWOOD
STANDING CUP AND COVER c. 1620

FIG. 196.
BRASS SKILLET

FIG. 197.
BRONZE
COOKING VESSEL

FIG. 198.
A VIOL

FIG. 199.
WOODEN CAGE
FOR CHILD

FIG. 200.
IRON FRYING PAN

FIG. 201.
PEWTER
WINE VESSEL

193–201 *Miscellaneous Articles, Stuart Period, 1603–60*

members of the household. The chair itself was lighter in weight, and various new styles emanated from this period. The most usual type of **Jacobean chair** was still of carved oak, with panel back and solid seat. It has curved arms, turned supports and front legs; the stretchers—which were set very near to the ground—were generally plain. These chairs were often ornately carved and/or inlaid. They had rather tall backs. Some of these chairs continued to be made until well into Restoration times (see Figs. 157, 159, 162 and 191). The **chair-table** was also a popular article in the Jacobean period. The idea was to economise in space by providing two, or even three, items of furniture in one—a most useful suggestion for the small-roomed homes of to-day. The chair was of carved oak often with a box seat, for storage purposes, and the back was a hinged table top, frequently circular, which could be let down on to the chair arms, when required, to form an adequate table (see Fig. 184). **Upholstery** had been introduced by 1603, but was comparatively rare until the late 17th century. The examples which now exist are chiefly from palaces and large homes. The framework was of wood, while the back and seat were stuffed with horse-hair or wool, then covered in turkey-work, velvet or brocade. Gold-fringed edges with tassels were usual, also galloon decoration. The **X-frame** was reintroduced in Jacobean times (see Fig. 187). Among the upholstered chairs of this period were **farthingale chairs**, made of wood with an upholstered seat and half-back, but without arms. They were so called because they would easily accommodate the ladies' wheel farthingales of the late Elizabethan and Jacobean times (see Fig. 188). Yet another type of chair of **Jacobean** design was the **bobbin-turned chair**, with solid triangular or square seat. It was rather more decorative than comfortable, but continued to be made until after mid-century (see Fig. 189).

The late **Caroline** and **Commonwealth** periods produced further innovations in chair design. **Leather** as well as upholstery was often used for seat and back covering, held down by brass studs; all-wood carved chairs were also still fashionable. The design was lighter in weight, however, and the heavy turned legs had been replaced by barley-sugar twist turning and bobbin-turned shapes. This method was also used on the stretchers, which were now often placed further up the legs, away from the floor (see Figs. 160, 161, 188 and 190). Special **tall chairs** for children, of carved oak, with barley-sugar turned legs, began to be made by mid-century (see Fig. 186).

However, a majority of people sat on **stools, forms** and **chests**. Stools were, for the most part, of joint type, fairly tall, with a rectangular seat (see Figs. 159, 185 and 192). There were also cupboard stools, with box section instead of legs, and upholstered stools with fringed decoration (see Fig. 160).

By 1650, oak **settles** had also come into use for seating purposes. These had a carved panel back, curved arms, and turned supports and legs. Some

4' 3"

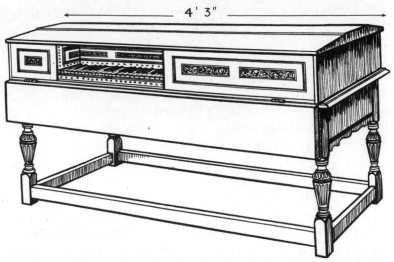

202   *A Virginal, made of oak with gilt decoration—carved oak stand, c.* 1642

examples had box seats to store linen, etc., and the back might be hinged in order to form a table (see Figs. 160 and 162).

Mirrors and looking glasses were still comparatively rare; they were small, because the knowledge of glass-making in England was still very limited. A factory was set up by **Sir Robert Mansell**, who imported some Venetian workers to instruct and assist in this craft. Much of the English production was used for small dressing glasses, while the few examples of wall mirrors were imported from Venice. Under Commonwealth rule, looking glasses were largely abolished, in view of Puritan disapproval of aids to vanity.

Homes continued to be artificially lit by **candles** and **rushlights**, according to the purse. The best candles were moulded and were made from pure wax, then perfumed; they were, however, expensive. Inferior candles were dipped many times, after the manner of rushlights. The wicks were tied to a pole, and, looking rather like a deep fringe, were dipped into the wax and hung to cool and harden. This process was repeated many times until the requisite diameter was obtained. Wax, tallow or dripping was used, and the smell when the candle was burning was, to say the least of it, unfortunate. Rushlights remained the stand-by of the majority of people. The rushes were peeled, then dipped in the same way as the candles, but were coated less thickly. Candles were set in socket **candlesticks** or **wall sconces**. These were chiefly of silver, brass or pewter. Rushlights were held by an iron grip, attached to a vertical iron rod, which was set in a wooden block base (see Figs. 160, 161 and 194). **Candle snuffers** were kept beside the candlesticks. They were of metal, and resembled scissors, with a small pan attached (see Plate XVb).

Crewe Hall, Cheshire (now destroyed): The Great Hall (1616–32). The pendant plaster ceiling, and the Flemish influence in the carved screen, are noteworthy. (See pp. 107 and 112)

Sanitation, toilet and **bathing** facilities remained much as in Elizabethan times. However, the use, by a few people, of toothbrushes is recorded by the Commonwealth period.

Meal times and the type and standard of **food** eaten were similar to those of the Tudors. The labouring classes lived chiefly on bread and cheese, beer and some meat. Well-to-do people ate very well, with a varied diet. Eggs, dairy produce and poultry were inexpensive, as the majority of people still lived on the land and kept hens. There was a plentiful supply of geese also, and swans were still served for important occasions. Sugar was now imported from the West Indies in considerable quantity, and began to replace honey for sweetening purposes. However, it was still costly—a shilling per pound, approximately, and a shilling was worth a good deal of money in the 17th century. Most people drank home-brewed ales and beer. Some of these brews were very strong, but children drank the milder varieties. Wine was imported from the Continent for the well-to-do. Spirits were known, but comparatively little was drunk. This was fortunate, because the gin, Irish whisky and brandy were very crude distillations and disastrous to the stomach. Rum was introduced into England from the West Indies sugar plantations—it was imbibed chiefly by the Navy.

17th-century **pottery** advanced considerably in technique, new methods and craftsmanship from that of the 16th century. **Slipware** was made in London and Kent from the Caroline period. In this method, coloured slip[1] was used for decoration: various colours were employed, and designs included dots, lines, animals and birds and, in the Commonwealth period in particular, quotations and scriptural texts. The ware was generally reddish or yellowish brown. Principal articles made included jugs, dishes and mugs. *Maiolica ware* was also manufactured from the early 17th century, on the south bank of the Thames near Lambeth. *Maiolica*, or tin-enamelled ware, is a method of lead glazing on low-fired earthen ware. The article is painted before firing, and the glaze is made an opaque white by the use of tin oxide. Colours were limited at first, but by 1650 became more varied. The work was influenced by similar methods on the Continent, especially in Italy. Many kinds of articles were produced, including vases, jugs, salt-cellars and even candlesticks (see Plate XI).

203 *Carved Oak Cradle, c. 1645–50*

[1] Slip is clay mixed with water to a consistency of cream, then it is applied to the pot in a similar manner to icing a cake.

Until 1640, a great deal of **silver** ware was produced. The Jacobean style was rather similar to late Elizabethan workmanship, and reflected the German influence in design. It was profusely ornamented and embossed with Renaissance motifs: acanthus leaves, flowers, fruit, animals, masks and hunting scenes. The work was rather more restrained under Charles I, and from the Civil War onwards very little was produced, and a great deal was destroyed, Quantities were sold by Charles I and his nobles to raise money for the war, and more was melted down later by the Puritans when they came to power. Silver ware under Commonwealth rule was produced in small quantities, and was very plain. Numerous items were made in silver from 1603: these included, chiefly, standing cups, tankards, apostle and other spoons, salt-cellars. bowls, posset-cups, beakers, cups and boxes. Forks were imported, but a few were made in England later (see Plates XI and XII).

Pewter was in general use by the majority of people, and all kinds of household utensils and dishes were made from it. If the home possessed little or no silver ware, the pewter was on display instead of or in addition to it (see Fig. 201).

The best **glass ware** was still imported from Venice, and some of the work was very fine. An attempt was made to restrict these imports in order to give prominence to home products, but foreign glass still came through, often via British travellers to Italy. Much of the English work was produced at Mansell's factory, including beer and wine glasses, decanter bottles and jugs. The Commonwealth gave little encouragement to glass manufacture; it was considered an unnecessary extravagance.

General **sports**, indoor and outdoor, continued in much the same way as under the Tudors. Horse and greyhound racing became popular, and there was a great deal of betting on the results. One advantage resulting from the Puritan rule and way of life was the decrease of the indulgence in cruel sports. **Music** and singing were always enjoyed, and the playing of instruments was encouraged; people met in groups to play. A virginal—antecedent to the piano—and a viol can be seen in Figs. 202 and 198.

NOTES ON ILLUSTRATIONS

Fig. 157. *Jacobean Hall.* c. 1615–20

One of the few large halls of this period—size, 60 ft. in length. **Ceiling**—carved wood structure with carved wood supports. Plaster ceiling in between wood framework. Each section contains a plaster decorative plaque. **Walls**—oak-panelled. **Screen**—carved oak, finely proportioned; heavily decorated, showing Flemish influence and interpretation of Renaissance. **Floor**—tiled. **Windows**—four of these and, in addition, a central **bay window** with 32 lights. **Chimneypiece**—carved oak with stone fire opening;

also shows Flemish-classical interpretation.   **Furniture**—Carved oak **chest**, length 5 ft. 6 in. Carved oak **court cupboard**, height 4 ft. 6 in.   Carved oak **buffet**, height 3 ft. 9 in.   Carved oak **chair**.

Fig. 158.   *Jacobean Bedchamber.   c.* 1610–20

Plaster ribbed **ceiling** and plaster decorative **frieze**.   Oak-panelled **walls** and **door**.   Oak **floor**.   Carved oak **bedstead**, height 8 ft. approx., length 7 ft. 9 in. approx., width 5 ft. 8 in.   **Curtains and valance** of dark blue velvet lined with grey silk—gold cord fringing.   **Coverlet**—white silk with gold-embroidered border.   **Livery cupboard**—carved oak, length 3 ft. 6 in., height 2 ft. 6 in.   Brightly coloured **rug**.   Oak "**farthingale chair**" —turkey-work covering, height 3 ft. approx.

Fig. 159.   *Jacobean Drawing Room.   c.* 1615–20

Plaster pendant and strapwork **ceiling**.   Oak-wainscoted **walls** and **door**.   **Window** with rectangular glass panes and lead frames.   Coloured glass upper lights.   Patterned velvet **curtains**.   Oak **floor**.   Patterned, highly coloured pile **carpet**.   Oil portraits on walls. **Furniture**—Carved oak **cupboard**, height 5 ft. 4 in., width 5 ft.   Carved oak **buffet**, height 4 ft. 2 in.   Pewter and silver plate on display.   Carved oak **chair**, height 3 ft. 2 in. approx. Oak **stool**, height 1 ft. 9 in.

Fig. 160.   *Caroline Dining Room.   c.* 1640–5

Plaster **ceiling**—oval centrepiece.   Oak-panelled **walls**—pilasters flank each doorway and window bay.   Stone-framed **window**, glass in lead frames.   Oak **floor**.   Pile **carpet**. **Lighting**—candlesticks and stands of pewter.   **Furniture**—Oak **dining table**, height 2 ft. 6 in.   Oak turned **chairs**, with leather-covered seats, height 3 ft. 1½ in.   Carved oak **settle**, height 3 ft. 4 in.   Carved oak **court cupboard**, height 4 ft. 9 in. approx.   Upholstered turned **stool**—embroidered covering.

Fig. 161.   *Commonwealth Dining Room.   c.* 1655

Plaster **ceiling**—fruit-packed oval centrepiece.   Oak **wainscoting, door** and **overmantel**. White marble **mantelpiece**.   Oil **portrait**.   Iron **fire-dogs** and **basket**.   Stone **window frame**.   Glass set in lead framework.   Oak **floor**.   Pile **carpet**.   **Furniture**—Oak **chair** with leather seat and back covering, brass studs, height 2 ft. 11 in.   Walnut **chair**, turned and joined, height 3 ft. 3 in.   Small **table** with drawer, turned legs and stretchers, height 2 ft. 3 in.

Fig. 162.   *Long Gallery.   Temp. Charles I.   c.* 1635

Plaster **ceiling** and **frieze**.   Oak-panelled **walls**.   Oak **floor**.   Coloured pile **carpet**. **Windows** now have larger frames and some windows open on a hinged frame.   Carved marble **chimneypiece**.   **Furniture**—Carved oak **settle**, length 4 ft. 6 in. approx.   Carved oak **court cupboard**, height 4 ft. 3 in.   Carved oak **buffet**, height 4 ft. 1 in.   Three carved oak **chairs**, height 3 ft. 6 in. approx.   Oak **chair** with turkey-work covering, height 3 ft. 2 in.

204 *Entrance Hall, temp. William and Mary, c. 1700 (notes on page 163)*

VI

RESTORATION STUART, 1660–1714

CHARLES II	1660–1685	WILLIAM AND MARY 1689–1702
JAMES II	1685–1689	QUEEN ANNE 1702–1714

THE restoration of the monarchy in 1660 brought back to England the extravagances and frivolities of Court life. Charles II and his nobles, with their families, had lived on the Continent during their exile, chiefly in Holland and France. In the latter country, at the court of Louis XIV, excessive expenditure on clothes, jewels, fine homes, furniture and all the comforts and luxuries of living was at its height. When they returned to England, a similar life, on a smaller scale, was embarked upon. However, despite this surface frivolity, Charles II was in many aspects serious-minded, and with the assistance of his patronage, both arts and sciences flourished. In the former field, the theatre was revived and began to resume its former glory. Under Puritan rule, theatrical art had been frowned upon, but the new Restoration theatre was rich in colour and costume, and, differing from Elizabethan productions, women now appeared on the stage. Literature also flourished: John Milton wrote his *Paradise Lost* after 1660, when he became totally blind. The period is accurately and vividly chronicled for us by such famous diarists as Samuel Pepys and Sir John Evelyn. In architecture we have the work of Sir Christopher Wren, and in music Henry Purcell. The pre-eminent figure of science of that time was Sir Isaac Newton, who, during the main part of this period, was Professor of Physics at Cambridge University. He is famed for his great work the *Principia*, published in 1687. Another famous scientist of this period was Robert Boyle, often referred to as "the father of chemistry", although his work also included studies of gases, specific gravity and electricity.

Several British **industries** were flourishing: these included coal, tin, copper and lead mining, fishing, and, still paramount, the making of cloth.

Although the roads were, on the whole, in a very bad state in most parts of the country, **travel** was becoming more general, by horse or by coach, more of the latter being now in use, both of the public and private type. The water ways provided a more reliable means of transport, and travellers were less liable to suffer robbery and violence *en route*. Sedan

205 *Small Dining or Living Room, 1686–90 (notes on page 163)*

206 *Queen Anne Dining Room, 1702–10 (notes on page 163)*

chairs were becoming more and more popular in towns for travelling short distances.

Education was slowly extending its influence, and more people were literate now: letters were written and diaries kept. The number of books was increasing, and the wealthy began to collect libraries. There were no actual newspapers, but news letters were circulated at erratic intervals.

On the **land,** experiments were being made with new crop systems, and potatoes, though not generally popular as yet, were now being grown as field crops.

The **population**, by the end of the century, numbered about five and a half million inhabitants, most of whom lived in the country. However, the towns were still growing, and London absorbed over half a million people, while Bristol and Norwich were the next largest towns, with about thirty thousand inhabitants each. The standard of **sanitation** was appallingly low everywhere, but whereas in the country this state was alleviated by the open air, and the small number of people living together, in towns, particularly London, the result was most unpleasant. In 1660 there was still no proper drainage, and the sewers were as yet open streams flowing down the street centre. Refuse and all slops and excrement were still emptied from upstairs windows, perhaps on to luckless passers-by, if they were rash enough to step out from under the comparative shelter of the overhanging top storey.

There were many slum areas of London and other cities in 1660; in the former the worst centres were to be found in Stepney, Westminster and Whitechapel, and here people were living, or rather barely existing, under very overcrowded conditions, in extreme poverty. The birthrate was very high, but this was largely offset by a heavy mortality rate, especially among infants, so that the population remained fairly static. On the reverse side of the picture, there were many fine buildings, ecclesiastical, commercial and domestic, and parts of London and other cities were well-to-do, fashionable and gay, although the stench, especially in summer, was everywhere, only partly mitigated by an excessive use of perfume.

The story of the **Great Plague** of London of 1665–66 is familiar to every schoolchild, and was chronicled vividly by Daniel Defoe and Samuel Pepys. It must be remembered, however, that although over a fifth of the population of the capital perished, the plague was not on the scale of earlier visitations, such as the Black Death of 1348 and subsequent recurrences in Medieval and Tudor times. Owing to the somewhat better living conditions, plagues had been recurring at less frequent intervals since 1550, and on a smaller scale, being not nation-wide but primarily confined to the overcrowded cities in the hot summer months where the rats abounded. The plague of 1665–66 concerned the capital chiefly, and has received great publicity, as it was the last of its kind.

The popular theory generally put forward is that it was due to the **Great**

*Humpton Court Palace, Middlesex: Wren's Great Staircase (c. 1690), embel-
lished by Tijou's ironwork and Verrio's frescoes (see pp. 140 and 144)*

Reproduced from Pyne's "Royal Residences" (1819)

Fire of London in 1666 that the plague died out and never returned to this city. Dr. G. M. Trevelyan points out,[1] however, on logical grounds that as the fire destroyed the City of London proper, from the Tower to the Temple, and was mainly confined within the City walls, it was the commercial and business centre which was burnt, while the slum areas of Stepney, Whitechapel, etc., were left more or less intact, and were apparently almost unaltered in character, even until the 18th century. Dr. Trevelyan then continues to show that, as the rebuilding of London was primarily of the commercial, residential and ecclesiastical area, this cannot be the chief reason for the plague's subsequent disappearance. He suggests that a more likely reason was the increase, as time passed, in the building of brick and stone dwellings instead of plaster and timber ones, and the decrease in the use of straw for floors and cloth wall hangings which harboured the rats. In addition, apparently after this different species of rats came to live in our cities: the newer types were not of the particular flea-bearing species which spread the plague.

Also lost in the Fire were nearly ninety churches, including **St. Paul's Cathedral**, which had for some time been used as a market, and, during the Plague, as a centre for plague victims. As in the more recent instance of a Great Fire of London, in World War II, when incendiary bombs once again set the city ablaze, a great opportunity was lost for rebuilding the city on new and better lines with an improved street plan, more hygienic conditions, with less overcrowding in the city centre, and an adequate view of London's great buildings. After the Great Fire of 1666, Christopher Wren was asked to make plans for the rebuilding of the City of London. He submitted such plans with all speed, but, owing to the obstruction of property owners, backed by legal advice, the plans were shelved, and finally abandoned, while the tortuous maze of old streets remained, many of them till they were destroyed by Hitler's bombs. Readers can draw their own mid-20th-century parallel to this example of short-sightedness, allied to a zealous guarding of personal property and rights. However, Wren did carry out the rebuilding of the churches, including his famous St. Paul's Cathedral, with its massive dome, second in size only to St. Peter's, Rome. The Cathedral was completed in Wren's lifetime, in the early 18th century, and managed to survive the bombs of two world wars, although it is only now, after the second Fire of London, that its fine silhouette can be studied, unobscured by surrounding buildings. Wren used Portland stone for his new cathedral and churches, and so popularised the quarries on the Isle of Portland, which had been little used before this. Legend has it that Wren was afraid that there would not be sufficient stone in the quarries to finish his cathedral, but he need have had no fear—Portland stone is still in use for great buildings, though it is now beginning to be supplanted by concrete and other mixtures.

[1] See *Illustrated Social History*, Vol. 2, by G. M. Trevelyan.

207 *A Saloon or large Dining Room, c. 1685–90 (notes on page 163)*

Many famous London streets and squares, still familiar to-day, were built in this period and of Portland stone. Amongst them may be numbered Berkeley Square, St. James's Square and Grosvenor Square.

With the Restoration came a time of great activity and new life in **architecture** and **building** which was all the more apparent in contrast to the scarcity of work completed during Commonwealth times, due to the Civil War and the insecurity of life which followed it.

Two important **architects** of the mid-17th century who continued their work with renewed vigour after 1660 were **John Webb,** the pupil and successor to Inigo Jones, and **Sir Roger Pratt**. The former, however, retired a few years later, after the coveted office of Surveyor-General had been given to Wren, and gave up his practice. Pratt had been studying architecture on the Continent during the Civil War, but returned to England by 1650 to design Coleshill House, Berkshire—a fine example in the classical tradition. After 1660, he was responsible for several other buildings, notably Clarendon House, Piccadilly.

The great architect of the period was, of course, **Sir Christopher Wren**, who, following on the work of Inigo Jones, established the architectural profession and consolidated the classical style of work in England, in ecclesiastical, public and domestic building, in its true Roman proportions. It is no exaggeration to describe him as a genius and the truly outstanding architect of all time in Britain. Wren was born in 1632 and early in his life showed evidence of unusual mathematical ability and inventive capacity. When he was still in his 'teens he had done valuable work on new instruments connected with astronomy; by the age of twenty-five he was a professor of astronomy and a noted mathematician, and in 1680 became President of the Royal Society. However, after 1660 he turned to architecture in place of mathematics and astronomy, and in 1666 was appointed Surveyor-General, an office which he held until the reign of George I. He was knighted in 1674, and in 1675 his designs for the new St. Paul's Cathedral were approved and the foundation stone laid. Wren had a tremendous output of work in his life of ninety-one years, but much of this was in designing churches—over fifty-two in London—and public buildings, so that, although his work had a great influence on house-building, producing a definite "Wren style", he was actually responsible for designing only a few domestic buildings. Among his most notable public works are Hampton Court Palace (Colour Plate facing page 130, Stuart section), Kensington Palace, the Royal Observatory at Greenwich and Chelsea Hospital. Most of the churches and public buildings designed by Wren were of Portland stone, but the smaller houses put up in his traditional style were of red brick, so that this medium is now associated with his work, in connection with a tiled roof and projecting cornice. Great houses of this period which show the typical work of Wren's time are Ham House in Surrey, Chatsworth at Bakewell, Derbyshire, and Marlborough House.

133

208   *Restoration Stuart Long Gallery, c. 1670–6 (notes on page 164)*

Another important architect of the Restoration period, whose work is to some extent eclipsed by that of the great Wren, is **Hugh May**, who was responsible for several fine buildings, primarily domestic, of which Eltham Lodge, near London, is a good example. Two other architects who did some fine work at the end of the 17th century were **Nicholas Hawksmoor** and **William Talman**: the former was connected with Wren in work at Kensington Palace, and was responsible for St. George's Church, Bloomsbury; the latter was responsible for the design of the great house of Chatsworth, mentioned earlier.

Another famous name of the Restoration period which is always linked with that of Wren is **Grinling Gibbons**. He was born at Rotterdam in 1648, and when he was in his early twenties, was discovered in a small cottage at Deptford by Sir John Evelyn, the diarist, who lived nearby, carving in wood his own version of Tintoretto's "Crucifixion", for the modest sum of £100. The craftsmanship and character of the work, combined with the ambition of the subject in such a medium, intrigued Evelyn, who appreciated that it was a new and more than competent approach, and also a comparatively new medium, as most decorative carving had been in plaster hitherto for walls and ceilings. Sir John introduced the young man to Wren and May, and presented him to King Charles II; as a result, he was employed in carving decoration for the great projects in which the two architects, particularly Wren, were engaged. Gibbons showed the way for a new style of decorative wood-carving: he used lime and fruit woods, especially pear, and made his designs from naturalistic motifs—birds, animals, shells, fruit and flowers—and treated them in a very free and open manner. The work was generally in high relief, with many open spaces and complicated entwinements of plant and animal form. As a result of the popularity of his work, others followed in the same style, though never quite achieving the genius of the master in their conceptions. Carved wood-panelling, chimneypiece decoration, picture and mirror frames became the decorative centres of the room, while in contrast ceilings and friezes became simpler. Much work is attributed to Gibbons which was not in fact actually carried out by him, but like Wren he initiated a style, and work after this type is referred to as in "the style of Grinling Gibbons".

The general style of **architecture** for **domestic building** became, by the end of the 17th century, completely classical in exterior lay-out, proportions and interior decoration. The **hall**, although it continued to be two storeys high in the larger houses, became smaller and less important as the century progressed, and by 1700 was a large vestibule from which the stairs ascended. It still had a large fireplace, a chimneypiece above, and a certain amount of furniture, especially chairs, a table, a long-case clock, etc., and the floor was often tiled or stone-flagged, with a coloured rug in front of the fire (see Fig. 204). Also on the ground floor would be an **anteroom**, or reception

135

209 *Restoration Stuart Bedchamber, c. 1675 (notes on page 164)*

210 *Late Stuart Kitchen, 1660–1714 (notes on page 164)*

room, and a **parlour**, while the garden could be reached at the rear. The **dining room** and **withdrawing room**, being the main reception and living rooms, were generally on the first floor and occupied the whole frontage. Also on this floor were perhaps a card room or private rooms. A Restoration Stuart **small dining room** can be seen in the illustration in Fig. 205, and a **Queen Anne dining room** in Fig. 206. A large **drawing room**—or **saloon**, as it was often called in large homes—is depicted in Fig. 207.

The **Long Gallery** was still built in very large country homes, and an example can be seen in Fig. 208.

The height of rooms varied considerably: 12 to 14 feet was usual for main rooms in an average-sized home, while in large houses a saloon or long gallery might be 20 feet in height.

Bedchambers were on the first floor or above; they were generally larger now, and in well-to-do homes no longer just passage rooms, but leading from a landing. The bedstead was still the chief item of furniture, but the remainder of the room furnishings were more comfortable by the end of the century. There was a fireplace, with a gaily coloured rug in front of it. Furniture now included a table, on which stood a dressing box with drawers, and often a hinged and sloping mirror. There were also a livery cupboard and/or a chest, chairs, stools and, by this time, a chest of drawers. A bedchamber is illustrated in Fig. 209.

Although **kitchens** were now rather more comfortable and convenient in size, the methods of cooking had altered little. The food was roasted, baked or boiled over an open fire as before, but coal was replacing wood more and more as fuel, so that a crude dog-grate with bars and iron dogs was necessary. Complicated iron chimney cranes were in use for holding the boiling and simmering pots over one fire while the spits still turned for roasting in front of another. Clockwork jacks were beginning to replace the human or animal "turnspit" in larger homes. Baking was still carried out in brick ovens. A kitchen is illustrated in Fig. 210, showing a chimney crane, clockwork jack, spit-rack, sink and general kitchen equipment. Cooking vessels were little altered in design, and were usually made from brass, bronze or earthenware.

In both town and country, **servants** were easily available and were cheap to hire. Most of them slept on the premises, the women being crowded all together in a room at the top of the house, and the boys and men in the hay loft or other outside accommodation.

Personal **washing** and bathing were still not popular pastimes. Most people washed in their own rooms, with the aid of ewer and bowl, but all water had to be carried in from an outside pump, and heated over the kitchen fire, so that convenience was only established by the aid of numerous servants. A few large houses had a "bathing house", also a "toilet", of sorts, but these were the exception rather than the rule.

FIG. 211.
CARVED LIME WOOD ORNAMENT TO SURROUND PICTURE FRAME — GRINLING GIBBONS' STYLE OF WORK. c.1675-80

FIG. 212.
OAK PANELLED DOOR AND CARVED DOORWAY c. 1688

FIG. 213.
MARBLE FIREPLACE WITH DEEP BOLECTION MOULDING — CARVING ON CHIMNEYPIECE IN LIME WOOD — GRINLING GIBBONS' STYLE OF WORK — PICTURE FRAME IN CENTRE — c. 1685-90

FIG. 214.
CARVED OAK CHIMNEYPIECE c. 1686-8

211–214 *Interior Details, Restoration Stuart Period, 1660–1714*

Small homes in town and country were being built more and more of brick, with thatched or tiled roofs, but all too many of the old wattle-and-daub huts were still existing, and the people inhabiting them had a very low standard of living.

The art of **gardening** had developed considerably in the 17th century, and a well-kept garden was now considered to be an important part of the home. In large houses where the garden covered a great area of ground, it was laid out formally by a professional man, with topiary much in evidence in trees and hedges. Trim paths and lawns, fountains and ponds were usual, with sculpture abounding on the fountains and among the glades. Smaller homes had more intimate gardens which were a blaze of colour in summer for the inhabitants to look out upon from the windows of their rooms.

Ceilings were still of decorative plaster: until 1690 the design was based upon an oval, circular or rectangular centrepiece in high relief, with a border, cornice and frieze surrounding it. The ornament was naturalistic, and, with Wren's influence, often finely proportioned; swags of fruit and flowers were most common, with other classical motifs shown also. The most impressive high-relief ceilings were reserved for the principal rooms of large homes, as can be seen in Figs. 207 and 208, while simpler versions were used in smaller rooms, as shown in Fig. 209. Towards 1700, the whole design became dignified and very restrained, except in very large homes; although a centrepiece was retained, the mouldings were often plain and in lower relief (see Figs. 204 and 206).

By the end of the 17th century **ceilings** were frequently painted in the homes of the rich. The centrepiece received the maximum decoration, and only large rooms were suitable for such treatment. The designs were on a grand scale, with allegorical, Olympian and biblical scenes. Two famous painters who carried out such work in English homes were the Italian **Verrio** and the Frenchman **Laguerre**, and later, after 1700, the Englishman **Sir John Thornhill**. Famous buildings to receive such treatment include Hampton Court Palace (grand staircase) (Colour Plate facing page 130), St. George's Hall, Windsor, the Dome of St. Paul's Cathedral and Montague House.

The most usual method of **wall covering** in England continued to be **wainscoting** or **panelling**, generally in oak, but also in cedar and fir. This method was popular because it provided the maximum warmth in our climate, and was thus not so common in the warmer parts of the Continent. The entire room was now designed as an architectural order, with the classical proportions correctly utilised: from the dado rail to the cornice represented the height of a column, with the plinth below and entablature above, while doors, windows and chimneypieces were generally flanked by pilasters or columns which fitted into the scheme. The remainder of the wall space was divided

FIG. 215.
CARVED WOOD STAIRCASE WITH "BARLEY SUGAR" TWISTED BALUSTERS SET ON A CLOSED STRING – HEAVY, CARVED HANDRAIL & NEWEL POST
c. 1670-75

FIG. 217.
CARVED WOOD STAIRCASE WITH PIERCED PANEL BALUSTRADE c. 1670-80

FIG. 216.
TURNED WOOD BALUSTERS OF VASE SHAPE. AN OPEN STRING STAIRCASE
c. 1700

FIG. 218.
STONE STAIRCASE WITH WROUGHT IRON BALUSTRADE
c. 1700-1710

215–218 *Staircases of the Restoration Stuart Period, 1660–1714*

up into large panels; those above the dado rail were vertical rectangles, and those below it were usually in the form of horizontal rectangles. The actual panels were by this period raised from the wainscot surface, in contrast to earlier in the century when they were generally sunk from the framework. **Bolection mouldings** were used to give a curved section to the raised panel, and to provide a pleasing moulding between one level and the other; these bolection mouldings were often carved with the ubiquitous acanthus pattern. Until about 1675, the panelling was often painted, in white or a light colour, but after this it was more usual to show the natural wood, treated and waxed. With the popularity of Gibbons' style of wood-carving, a great deal of decorative work was introduced into the panelling of larger rooms, particularly on the chimneybreast, to flank or frame a picture or mirror, and over the doorway (see Figs. 207, 211, 213 and 214). Various types of panelling can be seen in Figs. 204, 205, 206, 207, 208 and 209.

Tapestry was still in limited use, chiefly in great houses, and was hung from cornice to dado. Scenes were mythological, biblical or of country life, showing children, adult figures, animals and landscape backgrounds. The Mortlake factory continued to produce fine tapestries until the end of the century (see Fig. 209).

Wall paintings also had a limited vogue in England; they were carried out in a similar manner to the painted ceilings, but, owing to the panelling vogue, the area for painting was generally too small to be useful. In some instances, the whole wall was painted, but this form of decoration was confined to large homes.

The majority of **floors** were of polished oak boards, although rushes were still in use in small country homes. Some hall and downstairs rooms had stone-flagged or tiled floors, and these might be sanded (see Figs. 204 and 210). By about 1680, floors of **parquetry** were seen, the woods used being of various tones and colours to form a design: walnut and cedar were employed a great deal for this. By the time of Queen Anne, inlaid floors were very popular in well-to-do homes, geometrical designs being predominant, though occasionally more ambitious floral patterns were seen.

Small **rugs** were in fairly general use by now, though larger **carpets** were still comparatively rare, and even in a large home there might be only one or two kept for the principal rooms. The term "carpet" was still used to refer to a table or chest cover, and not necessarily to a floor covering. The majority of rugs and carpets were of "turkey-work": these were of needlework, wherein the wool was threaded through and cut afterwards. Cross-stitch carpets were also made, but involved so much laborious effort that it seems sacrilege to have walked on them. Woven carpets were still imported from the East and from other European countries, and by 1701 carpet-weaving was undertaken in England and the famous Wilton carpets began to be made (see Figs. 204,

(a) *Staffordshire Posset-pot (early 18th century)*

(b) *Stoneware Mug (c. 1680)*

(c) *Staffordshire Slipware Dish (c. 1675)*

(d) *Stoneware Mug (c. 1690)*

(a) (left) *Wine Glass* (*c.* 1710)

(b) (centre) *Mug, with Silver Rim*
(*c.* 1675)

(c) (right) *Custard Glass*
(18th century)

(d) *Table Chandelier* (*c.* 1700)

(e) *Jug* (*c.* 1675)

LATE STUART GLASS

206, 207, 208 and 209).

Windows were fairly large: at first the **casement type**, with smallish, lead-framed, rectangular panes, were still in general use (see Figs. 208 and 209), but after 1685 the **sash window** made its appearance and was used more and more. The early sash windows had to be wedged if required to remain open, but soon a system of weights and pulleys with cords was arranged, similar to that in use to-day. The panes were larger, though still rectangular; each half of the sash window was generally divided up into six panes (see Figs. 205 and 206). **Window curtains** were long and voluminous, and had a valance above. Heavy fabrics were in use, in rich colours and patterns, such as velvets, brocade, silks and damask. During the day-time, the curtains

18' approx.

219　*Temp. William and Mary.　State Bedstead with Pinewood Frame—outside of curtains in crimson velvet—inside, hung in white silk.　Decorated with crimson braid and Fringe—coverlet to match—tester and cornice of pinewood, carved, then covered in velvet and braid—cords, fringing and tassels in red and white*

were drawn up in festoons in order not to obscure the light (see Figs. 205, 206, 207, 208 and 209).

Doors had raised panels with bolection mouldings, in keeping with the remainder of the room. Two panels were usual on smaller doors, while in large rooms a double door might be in use with six panels. The architrave of the door was carved and moulded, then surmounted by a framed picture or panel, or, alternatively, a pediment: some large doors had flanking columns or pilasters. Hangings, similar to the window curtains, were common, in order to keep out the draughts (see Figs. 204, 205, 206, 207, 209 and 212).

The **chimneypiece** was still sometimes ornate, but towards the end of the century became simpler and more dignified in decoration. The fire opening was surrounded by a marble or stone moulding and a carved wood or stone framework. Deep bolection mouldings were common towards 1700. The chimneybreast was generally panelled in keeping with the rest of the room, but the panel might be decorated by a picture or a mirror. Grinling Gibbons' style of carving, in free profusion of flowers, fruit, etc., often flanked such panels. Cast-iron **firebacks** were in general use now, with floral patterns on them or the Royal Arms. Basket or **dog grates** began to supersede the iron dogs, as coal was more often used. **Andirons** were plain or highly decorative, made in silver, bronze, brass or iron (see Figs. 204, 207, 211, 213 and 214).

The Restoration Stuart **staircase** was heavy and solid, made of carved wood—usually oak, but alternatively cedar or pinewood. It was set round a rectangular well, and consisted of short, straight and broad flights, with easy ascent. The most common type of **balustrade** until about 1670 or 1675 was the **panel** type, made up from carved scrollwork, with fruit, flowers and acanthus leaves intertwined: such panel balustrades were incredibly solid and massive, and continued the fashion set for them in Commonwealth times (see Fig. 217). Also introduced in the middle of the century was the "barley-sugar" **twisted baluster**, of a heavy type, set into a massive wood string below and handrail above (see Fig. 215). Both types of staircase had weighty newel posts—usually square in plan—and ornate carved finials of fruit, flowers, cherubs, animals, etc. Towards the end of the 17th century there was a general return to balusters which were shaped either in barley-sugar twists or in **vase** shapes; these balusters were of much lighter weight than the earlier examples, and by 1690–1700 were designed for an "open string" as opposed to the earlier "closed" or solid string. In the former instance, the balusters were fixed on to the stair itself, without a heavy wooden string, and were arranged two or three to a stair. Newel posts and handrails were also lighter in weight, and either had no finials or else much simpler types (see Fig. 216). The staircase with **wrought-iron balustrade**, designed in scrollwork, also made its appearance late in the century, and was particularly in use with marble or stone staircases and galleries, and generally in larger houses (see Fig. 218).

FIG. 220.
CARVED WALNUT
ARMCHAIR –
VELVET COVERED
UPHOLSTERY
c. 1675-80

3'8"

CHARLES II

FIG. 224.
OAK CHAIR-TABLE –
TURNED LEGS & STRETCHERS
c. 1660-5   CHARLES II

2'5"

FIG. 221. TURNED WALNUT
CHAIR WITH BARLEY SUGAR
TWISTS – CANE SEAT & BACK
c. 1665   CHARLES II

3'5"

FIG. 225.
WALNUT TURNED
CHAIR WITH
LEATHER SEAT &
BACK – BRASS
NAILS –
c. 1675-80

3'4"

CHARLES II

FIG. 222. CARVED AND
TURNED OAK CHAIR –
CHARLES II
c. 1660

JAMES II

FIG. 223.
TURNED WALNUT
CHAIR FOR A CHILD
c. 1665-70

CHARLES II

2'10"

FIG. 226.
UPHOLSTERED WING OR
GRANDFATHER CHAIR
COVERED IN FLORAL BLUE
& SILVER PATTERNED SILK –
TURNED WALNUT
LEGS & STRETCH-ERS
c. 1685

FIG. 227.
CARVED & TURNED
WALNUT CHAIR –
CANE BACK
AND SEAT
c. 1675-80

3'11"

CHARLES II

FIG. 228.
BEECH-
WOOD
CHAIR –
UPHOLSTERY
COVERED IN
TAPESTRY WITH
-GROUND-PATTERNED IN PINKS, BLUE &
WHITE – c. 1710
FAWN BACK-
QUEEN ANNE

FIG. 229.
CARVED
OAK
ARMCHAIR
c. 1682

3'9"

CHARLES II

FIG. 230.
CARVED
BEECHWOOD
CHAIR –
PAINTED –
EMBROIDERED
SEAT –
c. 1690

3'9"

4'5"

WILLIAM AND MARY

FIG. 231.
CARVED WALNUT
CHAIR WITH
VELVET SEAT
COVERING –
CABRIOLE LEGS
AND VASE-SHAPED
SPLAT –
c. 1714

3'10"

QUEEN
ANNE

QUEEN
ANNE

FIG. 232.
WALNUT ARMCHAIR WITH
CABRIOLE LEGS & VASE-SHAPED SPLAT

FIG. 233.
LACQUERED
BEECHWOOD
CHAIR –
VELVET
COVERED
SEAT
c. 1710

3'3"

FIG. 234.
CARVED
BEECHWOOD CHAIR
WITH CANE BACK
& SEAT
c. 1680-85

3'9"

4'2"

CHARLES II

220–234 *Late Stuart Period Chairs, 1660–1714*

The staircase at Hampton Court Palace is a fine example (see Colour Plate facing page 130).

It is with the Restoration in 1660 that decorative **furniture** really begins its history in England. Before this time, nearly all furniture had been made of oak, carved in a bold and lively, though often crude, manner, and comparatively few pieces had been in use, even in a well-to-do home. These pieces were primarily designed as utilitarian objects, and it was not until Charles II and his followers returned from the Continent that the new ideas of furniture as a decorative item in the home, as well as a useful one, were introduced into England. From 1660 onwards until the 18th century is often referred to as the "age of walnut" in furniture, although in fact it was not until about 1680–85 that the use of walnut became fairly general. Before this, it was only fashionable, well-to-do homes, particularly those in large towns, which had walnut furniture; elsewhere, oak was still in general use. But from the time of James II, walnut replaced oak more and more, and many other methods of decoration besides carving were evolved, most of which originated on the Continent. Walnut itself was in most common use as a **veneer**, wherein a very thin layer of walnut was glued on to a "carcase" of oak or other solid wood, the "carcase" being a complete item of furniture to which the veneer was added, purely to give a decorative surface. Different parts of the tree were used to give different designs in veneer: the roots, malformations in the trunk, and the joint of a branch to the main stem all produced different and attractive designs in a thinly cut section, giving **oyster-shell** and **burl veneers**. **Inlay** was very popular as a method of decorating furniture: this was a craft wherein coloured woods were sunk into the surfaces of the item of furniture up to a depth of a quarter of an inch, in order to produce a geometrical or floral design. Bog oak and ebony were used to give black or dark shades; also, for other tones, yew, sycamore and various fruit woods.

In 1685, the Revocation of the Edict of Nantes by Louis XIV of France, which had previously given privileges to the Huguenots there, resulted in a tremendous exodus of many of these Huguenots to England in order to escape persecution for their faith; among them were skilled craftsmen in furniture-making and decoration, and it is to many of these craftsmen that we owe the introduction and spread of decorative ideas in furniture. They were particularly skilled in the art of veneer, also in a new type of decoration called **marquetry**, wherein different coloured woods were cut into thin layers and made up into a pattern in the veneer sheet, which was then glued on to the item of furniture. Marquetry is often confused with inlay, but the latter penetrates the wood far deeper, and each individual piece of wood and part of the pattern is inserted separately, while in marquetry the whole is made up in the veneer and then applied in a thin sheet. Marquetry designs were often very delicate, and generally floral or of animal derivation. **Sea-weed**

FIG. 235. WALNUT STOOL - UPHOLSTERED TOP COVERED IN DARK BLUE VELVET c.1690 -1700

16"

FIG. 236. CARVED WALNUT DAY-BED - ACANTHUS DESIGN - CANE TOP c.1685

FIG. 237. CARVED OAK SETTLE TEMP. CHARLES II

FIG. 238. WALNUT SETTEE WITH CABRIOLE LEGS - UPHOLSTERY COVERED IN WOVEN SILK FLORAL DESIGN - FRINGED EDGE - TEMP. QUEEN ANNE

FIG. 239. TURNED OAK STOOL TEMP. CHARLES II

1'7"

FIG. 240. WINGED SETTEE - UPHOLSTERY COVERED IN VELVET, WITH GOLD BRAID DECORATION - WALNUT LEGS AND STRETCHERS - TEMP. WILLIAM AND MARY

FIG. 241. WALNUT STOOL - UPHOLSTERY

1'6"

COVERED IN A FLORAL NEEDLEWORK DESIGN - FAWN BACKGROUND & FRINGE - PATTERN IN RED, LEMON, GREENS & DARK BLUE - TEMP. QUEEN ANNE

235–241 *Late Stuart Furniture, 1660–1714*

marquetry was a name given to scrollwork in this medium. Both the arts of veneer and marquetry were also practised widely in Holland, and became very popular in the time of William and Mary, with the Dutch influence in England of that period. Fruit woods were used chiefly in the art of marquetry, while laburnum was employed as an alternative to walnut as a veneer.

Two other fashionable methods of decoration in the late 17th and early 18th centuries, in addition to carving, were **japanning** and **gesso**. The former which was introduced after the Restoration as Chinese lacquer on furniture imported from the Orient, became very popular in well-to-do homes, and lacquer cabinets were often set on to excessively ornate silver-gilt stands. Towards the end of the 17th century, such cabinets were made in Holland or England. **Gesso work** had been in use in Italy, where it originated, for some time, and was introduced into England at the time of William and Mary. Gesso—the Italian word for plaster—was made from a mixture of whiting and size, which was applied to the woodwork, layer by layer, till a required thickness was reached. The surface could then be carved or incised, according to depth, and afterwards gilded. The gilt furniture acted as a foil to the background of oak panelling. The process was particularly suitable for mirror frames, tables and chests.

Upholstery was in general use now on chairs, stools and settees, making such furniture much more comfortable than hitherto. It was covered in figured or plain velvet, "turkey-work" or cross-stitch embroidery, or rich brocades, and had fringed or tasselled trimmings, often with gold braid.

In style the **furniture** became more delicate and subtle in form compared to the heavier oak furniture of the 16th and early 17th centuries. In the **William and Mary period**, nearly all furniture seemed to become tall and stately; this particularly applied to chairs and bedsteads, and echoed the tall fontange headdresses of the time. With **Queen Anne's reign** the height was reduced, though without loss of dignity, and more normal proportions prevailed. This reign also saw the establishment of the **cabriole leg** for chairs, tables and other furniture. The style had been introduced into England in the time of William and Mary, in a rather crude form, with stretchers still joining the legs, and with various terminations—usually animals' feet such as lions' paws or colts' fetlocks. By the early 18th century the claw-and-ball foot began to emerge, and the graceful curve of the cabriole leg was established, while the stretchers began to disappear as it was discovered that the legs were strong enough without them. The style of leg is said to have evolved from the hind leg of an animal, in particular that of a goat, while the term "cabriole" is derived from the French verb for "to caper" and the Italian word "cabriola". The identity of the country of origin is obscure, but the style appeared to come to England from Holland via Italy and France, while it was also known in the Orient from much earlier times. The claw-and-ball foot

FIG. 242.
WALNUT CHEST OF DRAWERS WITH ELM LID TEMP. CHARLES II

FIG. 244.
WALNUT CABINET WITH MIRROR DOORS – DECORATION BY MARQUETRY IN SYCAMORE, ASH AND MOTHER OF PEARL – TEMP. WILLIAM AND MARY

FIG. 243.
WALNUT TALL BOY OR CHEST ON CHEST TEMP. QUEEN ANNE

FIG. 245.
A DRESSING TABLE WITH MIRROR AND DESK MADE OF OAK, WALNUT AND PINE, AND VENEERED WITH BURR MAPLE, KINGWOOD AND ROSE WOOD TEMP. QUEEN ANNE

242–245 *Late Stuart Furniture, 1660–1714*

is of Oriental origin, depicting the dragon's claw clasping the precious jewel or pearl.

As in Tudor and early Stuart times, the **bedstead** was considered to be the most important item of furniture in a home, whether of rich or poor status. In the houses of the well-to-do, beds were most ornate in this period, with rich hangings of brocade, velvet or damask, with large formal, floral motifs, and fringe, tassel and gold-braid decoration. The **Restoration Stuart bedstead** was of medium height, made of carved wood, with a valance all round below the cornice, and hangings over the wooden head of the bed, arranged to draw round the whole bedstead at night as, owing to the loftier rooms and smaller fireplaces, bedchambers were still cold and draughty. The bedhangings were often made of the same material as the window and door curtains in order to complete the scheme for the room. The bedding varied according to wealth, with feather mattresses for the rich, and flock or straw for the less well-to-do. There were sheets, blankets, bolster and pillows, and rich embroidered coverlets placed on top. A bedstead of the time of Charles II can be seen in Fig. 209. In the reign of **William and Mary**, the bedsteads became very tall, though no less wide, in keeping with the loftier rooms and excessive height in other furniture and in clothes. The carved wood cornice or tester was now covered with the velvet or brocade material from which the hangings were made—it was glued to the carved wood to preserve the same decorative shapes. Hangings became more elaborate, especially over the head-board (see Fig. 219). In the time of **Queen Anne**, the **bedsteads** returned to a more average height.

From the time of Charles II, there was a great variety in the styles of **chairs** made for the home. Until 1660, chairs had been comparatively rare, only one or two being possessed by most families. However, with the Restoration, chairs became more common in most homes, and, on the whole, were designed to be far more comfortable. The typical **Charles II type of chair** was made of carved wood—usually walnut for the well-to-do and oak for the poorer homes—and had turned legs, stretchers and back supports, with a wood, leather or cane seat and back, and an ornately carved stretcher made in scrolls, crests and floral motifs. Some styles had no arms; others had curved arm supports and were designed as armchairs (see Figs. 225 and 227). Alternatively, upholstery replaced the cane or leather seat and back, and was covered in velvet, "turkey-work", cross-stitch or brocade (see Figs. 208, 209 and 220). Other Charles II chairs included the **chair-table,** still in fashion (see Fig. 224), the barley-sugar twist chair with twisted stretchers, legs and uprights (see Figs. 221 and 223), and the carved wood chair with solid back and turned legs and stretchers (see Figs. 222 and 229). In the **William and Mary period,** most chairs became very tall and dignified in design, and rather lighter in weight. Turned legs and stretchers were still used, also

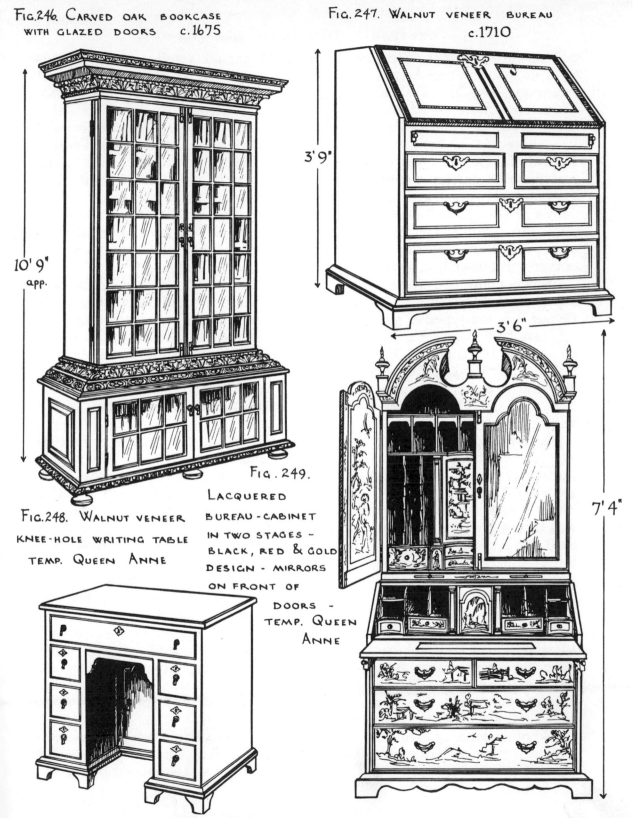

FIG. 246. CARVED OAK BOOKCASE
WITH GLAZED DOORS   c. 1675

FIG. 247. WALNUT VENEER BUREAU
c. 1710

3' 9"

10' 9"
app.

3' 6"

7' 4"

FIG. 248. WALNUT VENEER
KNEE-HOLE WRITING TABLE
TEMP. QUEEN ANNE

FIG. 249.
LACQUERED
BUREAU-CABINET
IN TWO STAGES -
BLACK, RED & GOLD
DESIGN - MIRRORS
ON FRONT OF
DOORS -
TEMP. QUEEN
ANNE

246–249 *Late Stuart Furniture, 1660–1714*

bobbin-turned backs, and the complicated carved scroll front stretchers. Such chairs were armchair or plain, and had cane, leather or upholstered seats (see Figs. 204, 205, 230 and 234). In the time of **Queen Anne**, backs were lower once more, and the single vase splat was introduced, either pierced or plain. The cabriole leg largely replaced the turned type, while stretchers were less common. Upholstery and leather were usual for seat covering, other seats were of plain wood. Arms were optional (see Figs. 231 and 232). Some chairs had plain or patterned upholstered seats and backs (see Figs. 206 and 228). Lacquer, gesso and marquetry were in use in later chairs (see Fig. 233). In James II's reign, the comfortable fireside **wing** or **grandfather chair** made its appearance, and has remained popular ever since. It was tall and upholstered, with appropriate covering, and had short carved and turned walnut legs with curved scrollwork and serpentine stretchers (see Fig. 226).

Stools continued to be used a great deal for seating purposes, and were especially convenient when, in Queen Anne's reign, hooped skirts returned to favour. Some types of stool were made wide enough for two people to sit on simultaneously. The carved and turned wood joint stool was still made in Charles II's time (see Fig. 239), but later types were more commonly upholstered, carved and decorated like the chairs, and had carved scrollwork legs and stretchers, or turned and twisted legs with serpentine stretchers (see Figs. 209 and 235). Queen Anne stools began to have cabriole legs, with or without stretchers (see Fig. 241).

A third type of seating accommodation was provided by **settles** and **settees**. The former had been in use for some time, and continued to be very popular during the remainder of the 17th century, particularly in country areas. The **settle** was a solid piece of furniture, generally made of oak, with a slightly sloping, high carved back, a plain wood seat and arms curved at the ends. It was then either designed with a box shape for the lower half, which could be used for a chest, and the seat of which was hinged and could be raised as a lid, or it had solid turned legs and stretchers. Cushions were then placed on the seat to relieve the unyielding hardness (see Fig. 237). The **settee** really evolved from the settle, and was a new item of furniture in this period. It was upholstered and covered with velvet, brocade or needlework, with braid and fringe trimming. It had loose seat cushions, and, in the William and Mary period, a very high back with wings and scroll-shaped low arms. There were then very short turned walnut legs with serpentine stretchers (see Figs. 207 and 240). The Queen Anne settee had a lower, straight back and cabriole legs; there were three of these in front and two straight legs at the rear, and, generally, no stretchers (see Fig. 238).

Another piece of furniture used for sitting and reclining was the **day-bed**— a typical item of furniture of the Restoration period, which was evolved to provide a fairly comfortable resting position, but was abandoned in the 18th

FIG. 250. A BUREAU IN TWO STAGES OF WALNUT VENEER WITH DECORATION IN MARQUETRY - MIRRORS ON DOOR - TEMP. QUEEN ANNE

FIG. 251. CABINET ON STAND - WALNUT IN OYSTER-SHELL VENEER - BARLEY-SUGAR TWIST LEGS TO STAND - TEMP. JAMES II

3'9"

4'

4'6'

FIG. 253. WALNUT VENEER BUREAU IN TWO STAGES -

MIRRORS ON DOORS TEMP. QUEEN ANNE

8'

15"

12"

FIG. 252. SMALL CABINET OF WALNUT WITH SEA-WEED MARQUETRY DECORATION - c.1700

250–253 *Late Stuart Furniture, 1660–1714*

century when upholstered sofas and settees gave greater comfort. The day-bed was, in reality, an extension of the cane-backed chairs of the time, as it had a long, narrow cane seat, with carved wood frame and a sloping back. It had six legs and elaborately carved stretchers. A number of cushions were required in order to make it comfortable (see Figs. 208 and 236).

Furniture made to contain household articles of different kinds was, by 1660, becoming various in type. The old style of **chest** or coffer continued to be made until the end of the century, but its use gradually declined, even in country districts, in favour of the more convenient cupboards. The **chest of drawers** which evolved from it became very fashionable after 1660. It was generally veneered in walnut or was inlaid or lacquered, and was usually considered to be a bedroom article of furniture, although it might also be found in other rooms (see Fig. 242). Some chests of drawers were set on a stand (see Fig. 209), while in the Queen Anne period the **tall-boy**, or chest on chest, became very fashionable (see Fig. 243). Also for bedroom use at this time was introduced the small **dressing table**, on which generally stood a small desk with a sloping lid or with a mirror attached (see Figs. 209 and 245).

Towards the end of the century there became established a wide range of **cupboards** and **cabinets**. Owing to the new popularity of tea and coffee drinking, well-to-do people began collecting porcelain—then still imported from China—which was kept in a **china cabinet** with glazed doors to display the contents (see Fig. 206). There were also small and large **corner cupboards**, some of which had glazed doors. The **bureau** appeared later in the century and had several drawers, and a sloping lid which could be let down on to pull-out slides for writing purposes (see Fig. 247). From this evolved the **bureau-cabinet** and **bureau-bookcase**. The former consisted of a bureau with another stage above, with glazed or panelled doors behind which were numerous small compartments (see Figs. 206, 249, 250 and 253). The bureau-bookcase was similar, but provided bookshelves above instead of compartments. There were now also simple **bookcases**, which had glazed doors; they were most decoratively carved, and were dignified pieces (see Fig. 246).

Many types of **cabinet** existed to contain a great variety of articles. They ranged from small desk cabinets with tiny drawers, some secret (see Fig. 252), to cabinets on stands, with barley-sugar twist legs and curved stretchers (see Figs. 208 and 251), and lacquer cabinets on ornate silver-gilt stands (see Fig. 205). There were also large cabinets with mirror doors and drawers in the lower part (see Fig. 244), and in the Queen Anne period, small **knee-hole desks** (see Fig. 248).

All these items of furniture made use of the new methods of decoration—lacquer, gesso, marquetry, veneer or inlay, and carving. Brass handles and key-holes were used.

FIG. 255.
BLACK AND GOLD LACQUER CARD TABLE
WITH CABRIOLE LEGS — QUEEN ANNE
PERIOD

2' 6"

2' 4½"

FIG. 254.
CARVED AND TURNED WALNUT
CARD TABLE WITH TWO HINGED OR GATE LEGS —
GREEN BAIZE TOP c.1700

FIG. 257.
OCTAGONAL TRIPOD TABLE
WITH TURNED CENTRE SUPPORT —
LATE RESTORATION
PERIOD c.1675-1700

2' 6"

FIG. 256.
CARVED WOOD TABLE
DECORATED WITH GILT GESSO WORK
TEMP. WILLIAM AND MARY

2' 3"

2' 4"

FIG. 258.
SMALL WALNUT
TABLE WITH TURNED LEGS AND CURVED
STRETCHERS — TEMP. WILLIAM AND MARY

254–258 *Tables—late Stuart, 1660–1714*

A few **court cupboards** and **buffets** continued to be made for a short time after 1660, but these were usually of carved oak, as hitherto.

Dressers were also made in the Restoration period, chiefly for farmhouse and country use. They had shelves above and drawers below, and, in many cases, stood on short, turned legs. They were used to display pewter and earthenware in country areas.

The large, solid oak **dining table** with four legs was still in use during the reign of Charles II, but in view of the smaller dining rooms in the majority of homes, it was generally replaced by the **gate-leg dining table**. This type became very popular in the latter half of the 17th century, especially in middle-class homes, as it could be closed up to occupy a smaller space when not in use. Gate-leg tables were made in many sizes, the larger ones measuring about 8 feet in length when open. They were generally of oak in view of the size of the top required, and had eight legs: four of these at the corners (when closed), and the other four forming two gates which could be opened to support the hinged top flaps. Heavy barley sugar twists were usual for the legs, with turned or plain stretchers (see Figs. 205 and 206).

Many types of smaller table were in use in the latter part of the 17th century: there were **card tables**, which had a great popularity in the early 18th century, when card-playing and gambling became the rage. These tables often had a hinged top, and were circular, oval or rectangular, and usually had candlestick places at the corners, and scoops for the counters or coins (see Figs. 254 and 255). There were also small **tea** and **coffee tables**, either rectangular with four legs or of the tripod type (see Figs. 208, 257 and 258). Various types of **side-table** were in use, generally made of walnut, and often with tops of marquetry or inlay in intricate patterns (see Figs. 204, 207 and 208). Tables with gesso decoration were also often seen (see Fig. 256). Most of these smaller tables had a small drawer in front.

The types of **table leg** varied during the period: the **bobbin-turned leg** was still seen in the early 1660's, but the **barley-sugar twisted leg**, the **columnar leg** and the **vase-turned leg** were all in use until the end of the century, when the **cabriole leg** began to oust all other styles from fashion. **Stretchers** were plain and straight, or turned, or of serpentine shape.

Another innovation in furniture at this period was the **clock**, which, in both its long-case form and bracket type, was seen more and more as the century progressed. The **long-case** or **grandfather clock** was an item of furniture as well as a decorative and useful article. The case was in three parts— a top or hood, the body and the base. Country versions were in oak, but in well-to-do homes beautiful marquetry or lacquer editions could be seen (see Fig. 206). **Bracket clocks** were decorated in marquetry or inlay, and had brass or silver work in them also. Many clocks of the period only had an

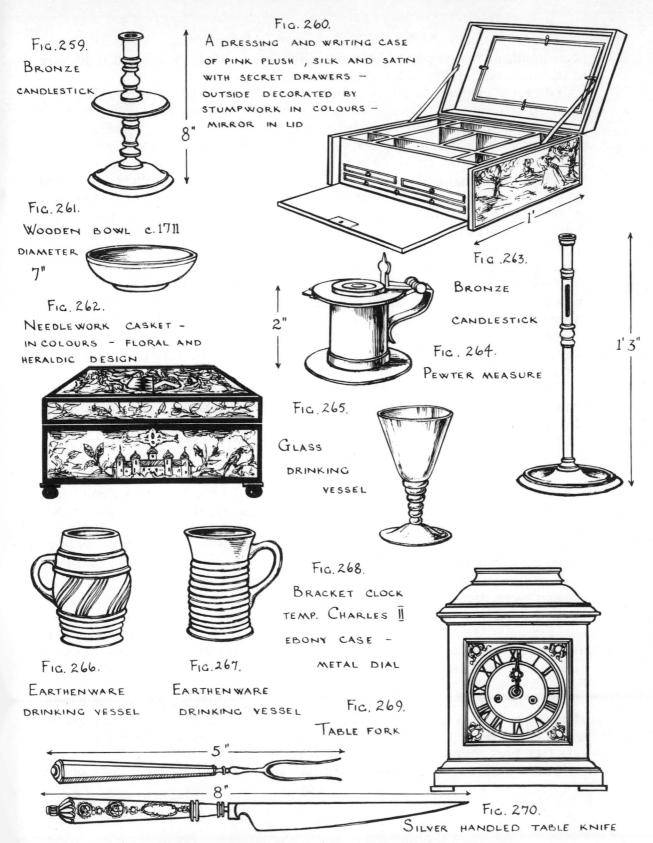

FIG. 259.
BRONZE
CANDLESTICK
8"

FIG. 260.
A DRESSING AND WRITING CASE
OF PINK PLUSH, SILK AND SATIN
WITH SECRET DRAWERS –
OUTSIDE DECORATED BY
STUMPWORK IN COLOURS –
MIRROR IN LID

FIG. 261.
WOODEN BOWL c. 1711
DIAMETER
7"

FIG. 262.
NEEDLEWORK CASKET –
IN COLOURS – FLORAL AND
HERALDIC DESIGN

FIG. 263.
BRONZE
CANDLESTICK
1' 3"

2"

FIG. 264.
PEWTER MEASURE

FIG. 265.
GLASS
DRINKING
VESSEL

FIG. 268.
BRACKET CLOCK
TEMP. CHARLES II
EBONY CASE –
METAL DIAL

FIG. 266.
EARTHENWARE
DRINKING VESSEL

FIG. 267.
EARTHENWARE
DRINKING VESSEL

FIG. 269.
TABLE FORK
5"

8"

FIG. 270.
SILVER HANDLED TABLE KNIFE

259–270   *Domestic Details of late Stuart Period, 1660–1714*

hour hand, as the minute hand mechanism was not fully developed until later in the century (see Fig. 268 and Plate XV).

Glass wall mirrors began to come into use from 1660. Prior to this, only small, costly ones had been imported from the Venetian factory where their process for silvering had been kept secret by the Guild, with the aid of a threatened death penalty for betrayal of the secret. However, about 1670, a manufactory was set up at Vauxhall, founded by Rosetti and patronised by the Duke of Buckingham. For several years it produced excellent glass, said by Evelyn in his diary of 1676 to rival the Venetian workmanship. However, in 1680 the factory was closed due to workmen's disputes, thus ending the flow of products from there for the time being. Despite this, the fashion for wall mirrors in homes grew, and culminated in the 18th-century idea of lighting and giving grace to a room by the use of numbers of them. The size of glass was still very limited in the time of Charles II, but larger types were imported and used by the end of the century. Frames were decorative: either of Grinling Gibbons' style of carving (see Fig. 205) and placed on the chimney-breast or another wall, or of marquetry decoration (see Fig. 209) or, as in the William and Mary and Queen Anne periods, of carved walnut or gilt gesso decoration (see Fig. 271).

The **lighting** of homes continued to be by candles or rushlights, according to the wealth of the household, and, as yet, the standard of illumination was still poor, even in large homes. In middle- and upper-class houses, the main rooms were lit by a central **chandelier**, while in very large rooms or galleries, several chandeliers were hung, by cord or chain. They were generally known as "hanging branches", and in the Restoration Stuart period were commonly of brass, with many S-shaped branches attached to a ball-stem design (see Figs. 207 and 208). Towards the end of the century, silver hanging branches were seen in well-to-do homes, and by 1700 the carved-wood gilded types were replacing other versions. These had fewer branches, as they were of heavier construction (see Figs. 204 and 206). To supplement the lighting in large rooms, and as the usual method of illuminating smaller ones, wall **sconces** were used, with a metal backplate of silver, brass or even of glass, later in the century. The plate reflected the candlelight back into the room (see Figs. 204, 205, 206, 207 and 208, also Plate XVIc). **Candlesticks** and **rush-light holders** were also essential, particularly to carry around in dark passages and to the bedchamber. They were of silver, brass, bronze and pottery (see Figs. 259 and 263, also Plate XIVd).

The habit of carrying the knife around in the belt or girdle was largely abandoned by this time, and many people possessed **knives**, **forks** and **spoons**, which could be kept in a "knife box", and the box was transported as necessary (see Figs. 269 and 270 and Plate XVe).

There were two main **meals** each day in middle- and upper-class house-

(a) *Clock* (*c.* 1650)

(b) *Snuffers and Stand* (1696–7)

(c) *Caster* (1692–3)

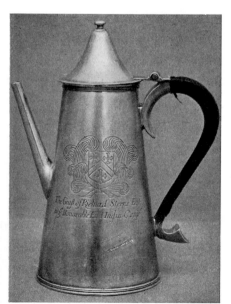

(d) (left) *Coffee Pot* (1681–2)

(e) (right) *Folding Knife, Fork and Spoon, Gilt* (*c.* 1690)

(a) *Cup and Cover, Gilt* (1669–70)

(b) *Tankard* (1701–2)

(c) *Wall-Sconce* (1703–4)

(d) *Salver* (1664–5)

XVI   QUEEN ANNE AND RESTORATION STUART SILVER

holds: breakfast merely consisted of ale or mead and bread; then dinner at 11 a.m. or noon was the chief meal, served with solemnity and care. Supper was at about 4 to 5 p.m. Cooking was considered to be an important art, and meal-times were long and much was eaten. The diet of most people contained insufficient fruit and green vegetables—leading to scurvy still—but a great deal of meat and bread. Butter was rather scorned by the well-to-do, who used it only in the kitchen, but it was enjoyed by the less wealthy folk. There were still inadequate methods of keeping food; in consequence, meat had to be salted, and was generally in varying stages of badness, especially in hot weather; fish was worse, and milk could be drunk little, but had to be made into butter or cheese. Poor people suffered a good deal at this time from malnutrition; this was partly due to the high price of corn and wheat, and partly because wood for fuel was now becoming scarce in many country areas, and coal could only be supplied to towns and places easily accessible by sea and the waterways. It was difficult, and even well-nigh impossible, to cook food in many country cottages, so the staple diet had to be ale, cheese and bread, with meat about once a week. Sugar had dropped a great deal in price by 1700, due to an opening up of trade overseas, and as a result more was used to stew fruit and make puddings and sweets.

Ale and mead were the staple **drinks** of many people; wines were imported for the well-to-do, and spirits were gaining tremendously in popularity. However, the fashion for all these basic drinks was challenged in this period by the introduction into England of tea, coffee and chocolate. These three drinks were first popularised in England by the coffee and chocolate houses opened in London in the 1650's, which became numerous in Restoration Stuart times, forming meeting places for society, business men, writers and other professional men. Gradually the fashion for these drinks spread into the home, and by 1700 tea and coffee parties were becoming fashionable, although tea was still drunk in the Oriental manner—very weak, without milk, and from handleless cups. Both tea and coffee were very expensive in the 17th century and were thus only indulged in by the wealthier classes. At first, tea was £3 to £3 10s. per pound—a truly colossal price for the 17th-century currency. This figure gradually dropped towards the end of the century, but a heavy tax was levied, and it was still 20s. per pound, so it could hardly become a general drink.

Pottery for the home was becoming more varied in design and technical methods by this time. **Slipware** was still produced in many parts of the country. There still was Metropolitan slipware, and work from Essex, Sussex, Somerset and Devon, but by the latter part of the 17th century, largely owing to its geographical position and easy access to the necessary coal, clay and water for transport, Staffordshire was beginning to assume that importance which later culminated in its supremacy in ceramic ware. The slipware of this period was varied in design: it had colour and vitality,

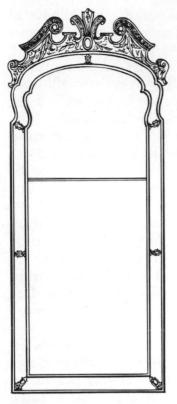

271 *Large Wall Mirror of Vauxhall Glass—gesso decoration to frame, temp. William and Mary*

and slip was used in white and many hues on dark or light backgrounds. Motifs included animals, flowers and heraldic insignia. Many items were produced, including jugs, plates, loving cups, bowls, candlestands and dishes of all kinds. **Maiolica ware** was made at Lambeth, and later in the period Bristol was famous for ware of this type. The centre for this work, however, in Western Europe became Delft in Holland, and the work was generally known as **Delftware** in consequence. It was renowned for its workmanship in blue-and-white schemes.

A new type of ware introduced into England in this period was **stoneware.** This had been known in the form of jugs imported from the Rhineland for many years previously, but it was in 1671 that **John Dwight** patented his discovery of stoneware and set up his pottery at Fulham—a pottery still proudly flourishing. The work had previously been termed Cologne ware, after its town of origin—as cream stoneware had been made near there for a long time—but later, in England, became known as stoneware. In this process, the pottery is fired at a very high temperature, in comparison with previous earthenware methods, and is glazed by means of salt being thrown into the kiln at the time of greatest temperature. A chemical reaction is produced with the pot, and the result is a thin but very hard glaze with high gloss. The ware achieved great popularity in the average home because of its great hardness and durability and also its comparative cheapness. Ginger-beer bottles are a present-day use of stoneware. There were other claimants to the process later in the century, and Dwight had to defend his patent rights in a lawsuit in 1693 against Richard Wedgwood and John and David Elers. The latter brothers had learned about stoneware in Cologne and had later worked at the Fulham Pottery. After 1693, they went up to Staffordshire and became very well known for their work at the potteries there. Elers' ware is generally associated with red and brown unglazed ware, particularly tea-pots, and marbled stoneware. Deep brown stoneware was generally produced by a high iron content in the clay, or by an iron dressing being given to the pot before firing.

Chinese **porcelain** was imported a great deal in the latter part of the 17th century, generally consisting of handleless cups for tea-drinking and various types of vases. It was, however, expensive, and consequently was only found in the homes of the well-to-do. Illustrations of pottery can be seen in Figs. 266 and 267, and in Plate XIII.

With the Restoration came a great period for making **silverware**. Following upon the Commonwealth time of destruction of plate and of little being made to replace it, there was a great demand for new silverware. At the same time, many new articles were made in silver that had hitherto been made in earthenware or other metals, and in the late 17th century there was a popular vogue for the new tea- and coffee-drinking equipment in silver. The usual motifs in decoration of Restoration silverware included the acanthus leaf, mythological scenes, flowers, birds and animals. Actual articles made varied from toilet accessories, candlesticks and sconces, bellows and fire implements, warming pans, porringers, casters, spoons and plates, to tankards, tea- and coffee-pots and tea caddies. The wealthy households owned a great deal of silverware, but the average home would possess a few pieces, to be prized greatly, such as a candlestick or two, plates, a salt and perhaps some spoons and forks. Early tea-pots were like coffee- and chocolate-pots, being cylindrical with a conical lid and, usually, a wooden handle. In Queen Anne's reign, pear-shaped tea-pots were more usual, but they were very small and needed constant refilling. A kettle was thus kept handy, and usually had a stand and lamp fitted to it to keep it hot. Some tea-pots had a similar stand and lamp. Coffee- and chocolate-pots remained tall and slender in shape. As with the skilled workers in the furniture trade, many French silversmiths came to England at the end of the 17th century, as a result of Louis XIV's revocation of the Edict of Nantes. These men gave a great deal of their skill and knowledge to English workmanship, and the effect could be seen by the early 18th century. Various items of silverware are depicted in Plates XV and XVI.

Great advances were made in the manufacture of English **glassware** at this time: from 1673, **George Ravenscroft** was carrying out research work into glass-making with a view to competing with the imported Venetian product. By 1680, his new method of making lead glass, containing oxide of lead, was well under way, and fine and brilliant glass was produced in England in the later 17th century. The ware was not as thin as Venetian glass,

272 *Carved Oak Cradle, temp. Charles II*

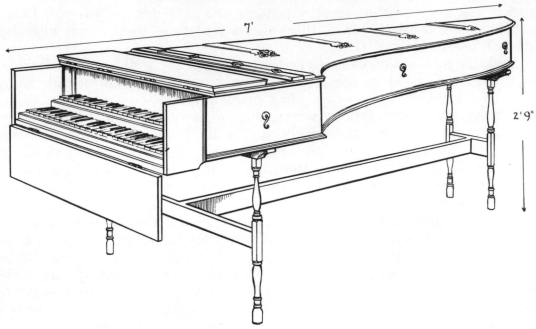

273   *A Harpsichord in a walnut case with bronze hinges and fittings, c.* 1690

but had a unique brilliance and quality.   Wine glasses were the speciality, with knopped and baluster stems, also jugs, goblets and bowls.   In addition to his Vauxhall establishment, the Duke of Buckingham also set up a glass factory at Greenwich in this period.   He employed Venetians, in the early stages.   Glassware of the Restoration time can be seen illustrated in Fig. 265 and Plate XIV.

Each home still possessed one or more **musical instruments**, and much enjoyment was gained from playing them.   In addition to earlier instruments, the **harpsichord** and **spinet** were now in vogue, descending, in turn, from the 16th-century virginal (see Figs. 205 and 273).

Other means of **entertainment** were sought in the reviving theatre, in dancing, chess and reading, as books were more common now.   Gambling gained in popularity as the century progressed—it was practised in the home in the form of dice and cards.   The coffee-houses provided centres of business and social pleasure.   In outdoor entertainment the cruel sports of the day were still paramount: bear- and bull-baiting, cock-fighting, wrestling and, most popular of all perhaps, public hangings and whippings.   Charles II encouraged the comparatively young sport of horse-racing; he patronised Newmarket, and was responsible for introducing Arab bloodstock into the runners of the day to improve the strain in speed and stamina.   In the country, the pursuit of the hare and fox were popular sports still, but these were primarily occupations for the wealthy.

NOTES ON ILLUSTRATIONS

Fig. 204.   Entrance Hall.   Temp. William and Mary.   c. 1700

Plaster **ceiling** and **cornice**—classical ornament.   Oak-panelled **walls** and **doors**—bolection mouldings and raised panels. Tiled **floor**.   Coloured **rug**.   Marble **fireplace**—also with bolection moulding. Iron **grate** and cast-iron **fire-back**. Wood **staircase**—square newel posts, barley-sugar twisted balusters set into a wooden string. Carved gilt wood **chandelier**.   Metal **sconces**.   **Furniture**—Carved and painted beechwood **chair**, cane seat and back, height 4 ft. 3 in.   Walnut **table,** top decorated by marquetry.   Chinese porcelain **vase**.

Fig. 205.   Small Dining or Living Room.   1686–90

Plaster **ceiling**.   **Walls, doors** and **window bays** panelled and carved in oak and cedar. Deep bolection mouldings to projecting panels.   Polished wood **floor** with plain **rug** of coarse material.   Green velvet **curtains**.   There would normally be a valance, but this has been omitted in order to show adjacent panelling.   **Sash windows** with wood framework and lead frames.   Pewter **sconces**.   **Wall mirror** with carved pear-wood frame in Grinling Gibbons' style.   **Furniture**—**Spinet** with oak case and stand, height 3 ft. approx. Carved and turned walnut **child's tall chair**, cane back, height 3 ft. 10 in.   **Cabinet,** lacquered in black and gold, on an ornate silver-gilt stand.   Oak **gate-leg dining table,** height 2 ft. 4 in.   Carved walnut dining **chairs**, cane backs, velvet, fringed seats, height 4 ft. 6 in.

Fig. 206.   Queen Anne Dining Room.   1702–10

Plaster **ceiling**.   Panelled **walls**—raised panels with bolection mouldings.   **Door** and **window** frames with matching mouldings.   Sash window.   Polished wood **floor**.   **Carpet** —in brightly coloured wool.   Carved and painted wood **chandelier**.   Silver **sconces**. **Furniture**—Chinese lacquer **long-case clock**, height 7 ft. 6 in.   Carved and painted wood **stand** on three legs, coloured yellow, dark red and blue, height 5 ft. 6 in. approx.   Walnut **bureau-cabinet,** in two stages, height 7 ft. 6 in. approx.; contains numerous drawers and compartments, including secret drawers.   Walnut and upholstered **chair,** covered in embroidery in silk and wool; various colours, chiefly red, gold and blue; fringe decoration; height 3 ft. 8 in.   Walnut **china cabinet**, height 4 ft. 3 in. approx.   Oak **gate-leg table,** height 2 ft. 4 in., top 5 ft. 6 in. by 4 ft. 9 in.   Dark blue velvet upholstered walnut **chair**, height 3 ft. 1 in.

Fig. 207.   A Saloon or large Drawing Room.   c. 1685–90

Plaster **ceiling** in high relief.   Plaster **frieze** with swag decoration.   **Walls** and **chimneypiece** of carved wood.   Grinling Gibbons' style of carving on chimneypiece.   **Fireplace** of carved marble.   Iron **fire basket** for burning coal and wood.   Silver **scones**.   Brass **chandelier** with tassel, hung by chain.   Casement **windows**.   Figured velvet curtains and valances in blue and grey.   Wood **floor**.   **Furniture**—Folding **side-table** of turned and carved walnut, height 2 ft. 5 in. Beechwood **armchairs**, painted and gilt; upholstered and covered in yellow satin, decorated with red cord appliqué work; height 3 ft. 8 in. Winged **settee** in carved walnut, covered in cross-stitch needlework, a crimson pattern on a gold background with black linework; braid and tasselling in blue and white. Coloured needlework **carpet**, in bright colours.

Fig. 208. *Restoration Stuart Long Gallery.* c. 1670–6

Total length of gallery is about 145–50 ft. Only about half the gallery is visible in this illustration. Plaster **ceiling** and **frieze**. Panelled **walls** with raised mouldings—bolection mouldings on window outer framework. Casement **windows**, lead frames and glass panes. Curtains and valances of plain velvet—gold fringing. Wood **floor**—several coloured rugs. **Lighting**—by brass chandeliers and silver sconces. **Furniture**—Carved and turned walnut **armchair** with cane back and seat, brocade cushion, height 4 ft. 3 in. Oak **stand** with tripod feet, height 2 ft. 2 in. Silver cup and cover. Walnut and elm **table**, top decorated by marquetry, brass handles to drawer, height 2 ft. 6 in. Carved oak **day-bed**, velvet seat and cushion for back. Walnut **cabinets on stands**, decorated by marquetry.

Fig. 209. *Restoration Stuart Bedchamber.* c. 1675

Plaster **ceiling** and **frieze**. **Walls** tapestry-covered to dado rail, then carved wainscoting to floor. Oil painting above door, with frame to match panelling. Wood polished **floor**. Woollen, knotted pile **rug**—rich colours. Casement **windows**—large rectangular panes—lead frames. Window curtains and valance to match bed-hangings. **Bedstead** of carved wood—hangings all of matching material in crimson velvet with cut and uncut pile, using other colours on a light satin ground. Fringed edges. Plain satin **coverlet** in pastel shade. The posts are hidden by bed curtains. **Other furniture**—Wall mirror, walnut frame decorated in marquetry. **Chest of drawers on stand**, made in walnut decorated in marquetry, height 4 ft. approx. **Dressing table**, turned walnut with marquetry top. **Dressing box** on table, also decorated with marquetry. **Stool**, upholstered top covered in velvet, carved wooden legs and stretchers. Upholstered **chair**, covered in cut velvet, carved wood arms, legs and stretchers.

Fig. 210. *Late Stuart Kitchen*

Stone **floor** and **walls**, the latter thinly covered with plaster. Wood beam **ceiling**. **Window** with stone frame—lead frames to glass panes. **Stone sink**—metal "taps" for water, which is pumped from outside. No regulation of flow. Wood **shelves** and **cupboards** under sink. **Smaller fireplace**, burning wood and coal—iron bars across to hold fuel, iron fire-back. **Iron basket spit** with cup dogs—turned by **clockwork jack** above. **Larger fireplace**—iron grate to burn coal and wood. Iron **chimney crane** holds metal cooking pot. Wooden **spit rack** above. **Wood table**—trestle type.

274 *Drawing Room, 1750–60 (notes on page 199)*

VII

EARLY GEORGIAN, 1714–1760

GEORGE I   1714–1727
GEORGE II   1727–1760

JUDGED by the standards of to-day, the 18th century appears a time of great contrasts. Many magnificent houses and mansions were built—indeed the period concerned in this chapter is often referred to as "the golden age of architecture"—but sanitation, hygiene and convenience were considered superfluous virtues. The sons of the rich and well-to-do travelled across Europe on the Grand Tour to enlarge their knowledge of the arts and literature, but the majority of the population received no education at all. The protagonists of medical science fought an almost losing battle against the people's strong belief in superstition, witchcraft, magic charms and patent medicines which were considered capable of curing all ills from rheumatism to venereal disease. Enormous quantities of food were eaten by the middle and upper classes, whereas the poor in the town slums were often starving. Improvements in agriculture were producing better bread, more meat and a better standard of food for the majority of people, but the colossal amounts consumed by the well-to-do caused them acute indigestion and, in many cases, shortened their lives by some years.

However, some efforts were being made to reduce the disparity between rich and poor. Housing was improving and many new cottages were being built in villages to house farm labourers; agriculture being still the chief occupation in England and Wales, whose population at the beginning of the century was only five and a half millions. Towns were spreading also, particularly London, whose wealthy inhabitants were moving westwards from the city, and building spacious new houses in the villages of Chelsea, Kensington and what is now Mayfair. London contained a tenth of the population of England and provided the greatest contrasts of all—new, elegant, well-planned squares of handsome houses, and slums of appalling filth and disease where people existed in misery and degradation.

Indeed, dirt and disease were deadly agents in the first half of the 18th century. This was partly owing to lack of sanitation—houses were drained into the streets and water was drawn from the river, while the cesspools

275　*Dining Room, c. 1730 (notes on page 199)*

276 *Interior, 1755–60 (notes on page 200)*

outside the houses often seeped through to the drinking-water supply—and to ubiquitous bugs and other vermin. Infant mortality, which, under the age of five, was reputed to be over 45 per cent, reduced the population considerably; smallpox also took a heavy toll until vaccination was established later in the century, and the heavy drinking of spirits, chiefly gin, killed many more. A person needed to be strong to survive, especially if not blessed with the wealth with which to make life safer and easier. Heavy drinking was indeed a general symptom of the times and the cheapness of gin made it accessible to all classes, although the well-to-do preferred wines and brandies. When taxes were levied on gin by mid-century, the death-rate fell considerably.

The average person of this period stayed at home a good deal, except when at work. Travel was difficult, indeed dangerous, owing to footpads and bad roads. Consequently, except in the big cities, the chief entertainments were made in the home in the form of card-playing—a very popular pastime, as gambling was rife—performances on musical instruments such as the harpischord and violin, or embroidery, needlework and letter-writing.

The tea- and coffee-houses which had sprung up in towns in the previous reign were increasingly popular. Men used them as centres for business arrangements and social intercourse, but ladies took afternoon tea with one another at home.

Many women and children worked in the home, particularly in the country, weaving cloth and spinning yarn to earn money. There was ample scope for this, as industrialisation was in its infancy, and although the great cotton and woollen industries were being established, most of the work was still done in the villages, then marketed and administered in the towns. Women had also to be capable housewives and nurses; there was cheap servant labour for the middle and upper classes, but little medical assistance in case of illness. They bore many children, a large percentage of whom died in infancy. Houses were well-kept and efficiently run despite the lack of conveniences, due to this adequacy of labour, although conditions of living for the servants were, on the whole, very bad. In rural areas, many of the homes of the labouring classes were still poor in standard. Most cottages consisted of a living room and bedroom, with low ceilings, small windows and an earth floor. Parents shared the bedroom with the children.

It was a time of creative effort in the arts, architecture and literature, but this was only by and for the few as yet. In the architectural field, the classical bent of Inigo Jones's work was continued by architects whose work has lived till this day. The **Palladian school** (named after the great Palladio, an Italian architect of note) flourished in this period, its chief exponents being **Sir John Vanbrugh**, **James Gibbs** and—under the patronage of **Lord Burlington**—**William Kent, Colin Campbell** and **Leoni**. The classical trend was still towards the Roman style, though by mid-century gradual change was apparent from

277 *Living Room, 1750–60 (notes on page 200)*

the copying of Italian classicists to a study of the original works in Italy. Some of the famous London squares are products of this time—Hanover Square, Cavendish Square, Manchester Square and George Street, while Bath also possesses fine examples of this work. Simultaneously great country mansions, and houses for the new, well-to-do middle classes, were being built in country and town. Blenheim Palace, Oxfordshire, Castle Howard, York-shire, and Houghton Hall, Norfolk, are noteworthy.

It is still possible to find many examples of English homes of this period preserved almost unaltered except for the introduction of modern conveniences in sanitation, heating, lighting and a replacement of curtains and needlework. There are perhaps more examples left in the country, as greater alterations have been made in towns to keep abreast of current fashion, but the remaining examples are a tribute to the lasting workmanship of the day.

A typical **interior** of a fairly large house of this period would be based on a rectangular plan. The living rooms, on the ground floor, lead off a large, imposing central hall. There would be a dining room, a small and a large drawing room or saloon, library, powder closets and, upstairs, the bedrooms and dressing rooms. Kitchens and the servants' quarters were deemed un-important in the planning of a house and were relegated to the basement and attics, involving the climbing of many stairs and difficulty in keeping the food hot when brought to the dining room. There was rarely a bathroom: people still bathed, if at all, in a large tin bath. Servants carried this in, together with cans of hot water—brought up many stairs—and the person sat or stood in the bath, according to its dimensions. The closet was usually outside in the garden or back yard. It consisted of a wooden seat over a pit or cesspool, and demanded cleaning out at intervals. Owing to bad drainage and organisa-tion the drinking-water supply was often contaminated by it. Water closets were still very rare and, as yet, so badly designed that the odours from them made the other type preferable.

Smaller middle-class houses were on a similar plan, though less pretentious. In this case, the dining room and parlour would be on the ground floor, and perhaps the drawing room and bedrooms above, with the kitchen in the base-ment and servants in the attics. Water supplies were inadequate, being delivered about twice a week, and drainage was poor and insanitary.

Lighting was still by means of candles. In large houses, however, **chan-deliers,** many **candelabra, sconces** and **candlestands** of gilded wood and gesso or crystal now gave adequate illumination, especially when reflected in the great gilded wall-mirrors, but they also provided yet another task for the servants who had to trim and extinguish them. Chandeliers were hanging candelabra, usually suspended from the centre of the room. In draughty places like entrance halls, covered **lanthorns** or wall **lanterns** were used. In smaller houses, owing to the cost of candles, lighting was dim; poorer people

278　*Interior, 1750–60 (notes on page 200)*

contented themselves by still using home-made candles or **rushlights**, although, on the whole, especially in the country, they ordered their lives upon the rising and setting of the sun to conserve their meagre supplies (see Figs. 274, 275, 276, 278 and 279, also Figs. 280, 281, 282, 283, 284, 285, 286 and 287, also Plates XIX and XX).

Heating was provided by open coal fires, which, in towns, produced a black pall of smoke over the houses, as although coal was expensive, it was of poor quality.

Interior decoration was based on the classical style: the heavy **baroque** ornament influenced the earlier part of the period, and the gayer, lighter French **rococo** decoration was popular from 1750 onwards. There were several methods of **wall decoration**: at first, most walls were still **panelled** in pinewood, cedar and later mahogany, carved and decorated in classical motifs, with the lower part wainscoted in oak, and the whole generally painted in light colours or white—especially after 1725–30—and perhaps gilded on the ornament (see Figs. 275 and 276). **Stucco decoration**—a plaster method— became very fashionable, particularly from 1720 to 1760, and was used for ceilings and walls as an alternative to panelling. Both methods were in use for halls, dining and drawing rooms, saloons and also staircases, but bedrooms were more often draped with velvet, silk or damask **hangings** to wainscot level (see Figs. 274, 278, 279 and 288). As the **baroque** gave way to **rococo** styles of ornament, **motifs** altered from the acanthus leaf, egg-and-dart mouldings, cherubs and classical figures to C and S scrolls, daintier shells, floral motifs and festoons taken from the French *rocaille coquille*[1] shell patterns. Gilt was lavishly used on ornament throughout the period, while the background was painted in white or light colours. **Wallpaper** provided a fourth alternative after 1740–45. It was hung from cornice to wainscot, and at first was imported from the East, being mainly of Chinese origin. It was sent in strips about four feet wide, several of which made a complete picture landscape or garden. Early English productions were painted or stencilled attempts to imitate the more expensive damask or cut velvet hangings of formal floral design. After 1754, printed patterns were in use. **John B. Jackson** of Battersea was a pioneer in this field. He published a report of his experimental work in 1754, giving information of his wood-block printing method. Many of his designs were imitations of classical sculptured figures, made in monochrome, for those who could not afford the marble realities. Later wallpaper designs were of landscapes, floral patterns and imitations of famous landscape paintings by artists such as Canaletto, Poussin and Lorraine (see Fig. 277).

Floors were of polished wood, but **carpets** and rugs were still very expensive, and were seen only in large houses or in the drawing rooms and dining

---

[1] The word *rococo* is derived from this French expression, meaning rock and shell work (mollusc, cockle, etc.).

279 *Bedchamber, 1740–50 (notes on page 201)*

CANDLESTAND - PINEWOOD DECORATED BY GILDED GESSO WORK - METAL CANDLE HOLDERS FIG. 280.

4' 3" approx.

FIG. 281. CARVED WOOD GIRANDOLE WITH GESSO DECORATION 1714-27

3' 9½"

FIG. 282. MOULDED & PAINTED TERRA COTTA STAND c. 1730

FIG. 283. MAHOGANY CANDLESTAND - CHIPPENDALE PER

2' approx.

FIG. 284. CARVED MAHOGANY, GLASS FRONTED WALL LANTERN c. 1740

18" approx.

FIG. 285. MAHOGANY & BRASS CANDLESTICK WITH GLASS SHADE

FIG. 286. SILVER CANDLESTICK c. 1750

FIG. 287. CARVED & GILT WOO SCONCE WITH MIRROR c.1 CHIPPENDALE STYLE

2 a

280–287   *Early Georgian Lighting Equipment, 1714–60*

rooms of smaller ones. Most of these carpets were imported before 1750, from the East and from France. However, needlework ones were still made in the early 18th century in England by dint of great labour and devotion. They were beautifully worked, but few now exist, as they have been worn beyond repair, or were later cut up for upholstery covering. After 1750, the art of carpet-knotting was started up again; it had fallen into disuse in England

288 *Typical Panel Wall Decoration, c. 1756–60. This section reaches from ceiling to wainscot level—wood panelling—carved, painted and gilt—candle brackets incorporated —the room has mirrors over fireplace*

in the middle of the 17th century, and was not revived again until mid-18th century, when it was thus regarded as a new venture. Several firms commenced making these carpets in the 1750's, including famous names such as Wilton, Axminster and Kidderminster. Stair-carpets were still rare, however, and carpets only covered the centre of the room (see Figs. 274, 275, 276, 277, 278 and 279).

The **drawing room** or **saloon** was the main room of the house, and was decorated and furnished in the most lavish style. It was the room for leisure

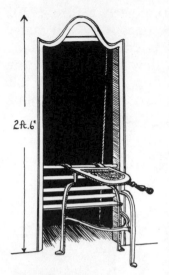

2ft.6'

289 *Fireplace of iron —copper trivet with wooden handle—brass edge to fireplace*

and entertainment and generally faced south. A massive cornice surrounded the room and a central feature of one wall was the **chimneypiece**—heavily carved, of marble, wood or stucco, gilded and/or painted, with either a large gilt-framed painting incorporated in the design or a mirror (see Figs. 275, 277 and 278). **Doors**—a six-panelled style was most usual—and **windows** were in keeping with the chimneypiece, having carved and gilded pediment and mouldings. The windows reached from cornice to wainscot, were of sash type with rectangular panes and were curtained with velvet or damask, looped up with tassels and cords (see Figs. 275 and 276). Large ornate wall-mirrors decorated the walls between doors and windows, and often had heavy gilt marble-topped console or side-tables under them. Other furniture included settees, chairs, stools, china, tea and card tables and commodes. Many pictures were hung on the walls and the wall decoration was so designed that they appeared an integral part of the scheme. Sconces provided an ornamental method of lighting.

The **dining room** was simpler and less ornate but had similar doors, windows and chimneypiece. Furniture included tables, chairs, a screen, side-table, perhaps a bureau-cabinet and wine-cooler.

Bedrooms had a large four-poster bedstead with hangings, chests of drawers and a tall-boy, dressing-table and glass, small tables, chairs, washstand, bookshelves and a wig-stand (see Fig. 279). **Firegrates** for all these rooms were of brass or steel with iron backs. Fenders, tongs and poker were of brass or steel (see Figs. 275, 277, 278, 289 and 290).

The **kitchen** was large, with plain plaster walls and ceiling—the latter often with oak beams still —and stone floor. It had one or two fireplaces, and over the fires the joint was still roasted on a spit, water was boiled and food fried or baked. A chimney-crane was fixed to the side of the fireplace, having an arm from which the kettle or pan could be hung. A stone sink was fitted. The room was well ordered, with dresser, cupboards and a larder. Also on the basement floor were the storehouse, china room, scullery and bakehouse.

290 *Steel and iron Fireplace set on veined white marble slab*

The house would have one or two **staircases**, according to size. The main staircase would be of stone if stucco decoration was used for the walls, or of wood if panelling was employed. Both types were heavily carved and turned, and barley-sugar wooden balusters were frequently used. Ironwork in scroll

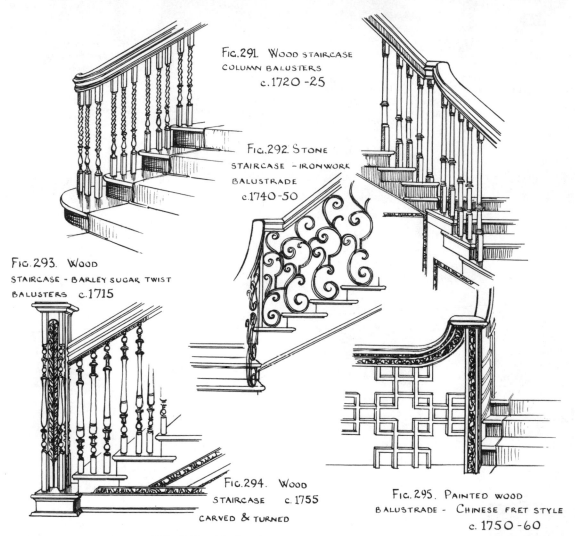

Fig. 291. Wood staircase column balusters c. 1720 -25

Fig. 292. Stone staircase – ironwork balustrade c. 1740-50

Fig. 293. Wood staircase - barley sugar twist balusters c. 1715

Fig. 294. Wood staircase c. 1755 carved & turned

Fig. 295. Painted wood balustrade - Chinese fret style c. 1750 -60

291–295 *Early Georgian Staircases, 1714–60*

designs was common with stone staircases, with a wood or stone handrail. A plain staircase for staff was constructed at the back of the house (see Figs. 291, 292, 293, 294 and 295).

An architect and designer whose name is intimately associated with the period 1723–40 is **William Kent**, a Yorkshireman born in 1684. Kent was

FIG. 296. c.1730 UPHOLSTERED SEAT - VELVET COVERED.

FIG. 297. c.1720 GILT & CARVED BEECHWOOD - CUT VELVET UPHOLSTERY

FIG. 298. TEMP. GEORGE II WILLIAM KENT STYLE - GILDED PINEWOOD - CRIMSON SILK COVERED UPHOLSTERY

FIG. 299. TEMP. GEO. II WILLIAM KENT STYLE MAHOGANY PARTLY GILDED - VELVET SEAT

FIG. 300. CHIPPENDALE CHINESE STYLE PAGODA TOP - LATTICE BACK & SIDES

FIG. 301. c.1760 CHINESE STYLE - BEECH VENEERED WITH WALNUT

FIG. 302. CHIPPENDALE GOTHIC STYLE - MAHOGANY - SILK SEAT - FRINGED EDGES.

FIG. 303. c.1755 CHIPPENDALE LADDERBACK STYLE - MAHOGANY. VELVET SEAT

FIG. 304. c.1750. GOTHIC TYPE WINDSOR ARM - CHAIR - TURNED & CARVED YEW

FIG. 305. c.1740-50 WINDSOR ARM - -CHAIR - YEW

FIG. 306. c.1750. WINDSOR ARM-CHAIR - OAK & YEW

FIG. 307. CHIPPENDALE ARM CHAIR MAHOGANY - LEATHER SEAT

FIG. 308. c.1715-20 - GRANDFATHER WING CHAIR - WALNUT LEGS - EMBROIDERED UPHOLSTERY.

FIG. 309. COUNTRY OAK CHAIR c.1750

FIG. 310. c.1730-35. SPOON-BACKED CHAIR - LEATHER SEAT

FIG. 311. READING CHAIR - MAHOGANY. LEATHER SEAT

296–311 *Early Georgian Chairs, 1714–60*

first apprenticed to a coachpainter, but ran away to London, and later received the patronage of Lord Burlington. He designed many of the great houses of the day, but was noted chiefly as one of the first architects of the time to take over the designing of the whole house, exterior, interior, furniture and furnishings down to the smallest detail. This practice was followed later by Robert Adam and others, but at this time it was a new departure. He was a versatile designer and his work was highly decorated, although thought by many to be too heavy and massive. However, if it is remembered that most of these items of furniture were designed for large mansions with enormous rooms, it is realised that they are suited to their background. He used the predominant classical motifs of the day—broken pediments, heavy festoons of flora and fruit, shaggy claw-and-ball feet, acanthus leaves and eagles, entire or just the wings and heads. Much of this ornate work was in gilded gesso, with heavy marble tops to the tables. His gilded decorative mirrors are particularly well known. He was the leader of this style during his lifetime, but by 1745–48 the newer ideas of French rococo and Chinese designs were beginning to replace the heavier gilt ornamental work in England.

The **furniture** of the reign of George I was of a heavy **baroque**[1] style. More elaborate carving was seen, using lions' heads, masks, eagles' heads and wings and the shell form, in particular. The **cabriole leg** continued in fashion, but it was more curved and of heavier shape, terminating in the shaggy claw-and-ball foot. Walnut continued to be the fashionable wood, employed both in the solid form and as a veneer, but in rural areas oak, yew, elm and beech were still more usual. Gilding over **gesso** work was extensively used on carved furniture, especially on console tables, chairs and mirrors; marble tops adorned these tables. From 1727 to about 1740, the styles of William Kent and his contemporaries were paramount: large ostentatious pieces of furniture were designed for mansions, and smaller varieties for middle-class homes, though Kent specialised in the former. Acanthus leaves, swags and festoons, flora and fauna, eagles' heads and wings, lions' heads and human masks were the chief motifs. Gilding and gesso work were at the height of their popularity, and pinewood was generally used underneath the surfacing. Marquetry, veneer and inlay were still much used, with walnut, apple, pear and holly as the most common woods employed. Mahogany became the fashionable wood for solid work about 1730–35; and after the duty on its export from the West Indies had been repealed, it remained the predominant wood of the 18th century from then onwards, owing to its suitability for intricate carving, though it was little used in rural areas, where oak and walnut were still paramount.

Lacquered furniture was seen in large quantities till about 1750. It was made in imitation of Oriental lacquer, in red, black, green and yellow; it was

[1] Grotesque, often mythological.

312   *Stool in carved gilt wood. Style of William Kent—upholstered top in velvet, c. 1730–40*

called japanning and was most popular for bedroom furniture.

Heavy items of furniture—for example, bookcases and bedsteads—reflected the architectural features of the time, in particular columns and capitals, broken pediments and architectural mouldings of acanthus leaves and egg-and-dart designs.

Upholstery on chairs and settees was covered with velvet, damask or, more frequently, needlework. Floral designs, landscapes, portraits and figures, and Eastern patterns were used, and were often carried out by the ladies of the house themselves. The upholstery was of better quality now and was much more comfortable. Other items receiving embroidered treatment were screens, bed coverlets and quilts, and some work was framed and hung in the form of pictures.

As the period of furniture design of 1727–40 was dominated by William Kent, so the time of 1740–60 is associated mainly with Chippendale. **Thomas Chippendale** was also a Yorkshireman, born in 1718, the son of a joiner. He came early to London and set up a workshop to produce furniture. By 1750 he was well known and in 1753 established his famous shop in St. Martin's Lane, and brought out the following year his even more famous *Director*. This publication—to give its full title, *The Gentleman and Cabinet Maker's Director*—was the predecessor of many others by different designers, and, unlike the work of Kent, contained designs for all kinds of domestic furniture in the three basic Chippendale styles—**Gothic, rococo** and **Chinese**. These were Chippendale's main sources of inspiration: he was a versatile creator, and some designs could only be described as "Chippendale", with no apparent outside influence, but all his designs were unmistakably English in character, whatever the source of inspiration. Many of them were never carried out, and much furniture is attributed to him which he never produced. The word "Chippendale" is applied to furniture of the type that he made, not necessarily his actual work, although the latter was prodigious in amount. His best-known contemporaries were **Robert Manwaring, William Ince** and **Thomas Mayhew**.

Mahogany is the wood inseparable from the Chippendale style of work. The popularity of the two increased together and the former provided the means with which to exploit and show off the skill of the latter. Under Chippendale, furniture designs became lighter and more delicate; carving was beautifully executed in intricate patterns, but employed in a subtle and more sparing manner. He used both a refined cabriole leg with claw-and-ball foot,

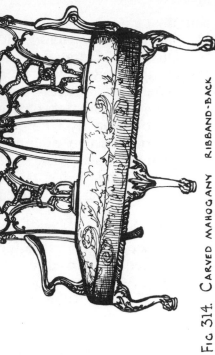

FIG. 314. CARVED MAHOGANY RIBBAND-BACK
TYPE SETTEE - EMBROIDERED SEAT - C.1755

5' 6"

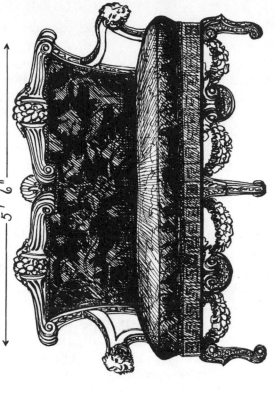

FIG. 316. CARVED, PAINTED & GILT WOOD SETTEE -
CUT VELVET UPHOLSTERY - STYLE OF
WILLIAM KENT- C.1735

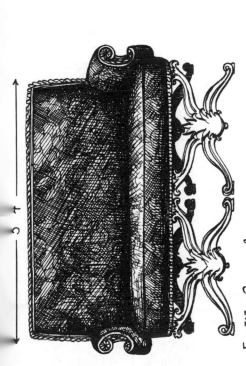

FIG. 315. CARVED & GILT WOOD SETTEE -
EMBROIDERED UPHOLSTERY - C.1740

FIG. 315. OAK SETTLE -
VELVET SEAT - C.1750-60

6'

313–316 *Early Georgian Settees, 1714–60*

and the straight leg, in the latter case reintroducing the stretcher. His motifs varied according to the type of design; in his **Gothic** work, the trefoil and quatrefoil shapes were used; in the **rococo**, the familiar shells, C and S scrolls and floral decoration; while in the **Chinese designs**, the fretted work and pagoda tops were predominant. His **ribband-back** chairs and settees—with delicate, interlaced ribbon lengths—are famous. The **tripod** style of leg support to tables, screens, candlestands, etc., was encouraged by Chippendale, usually in a delicate but strong manner. In particular, two examples of the signs of the times could be seen in the furniture of this period: the increasing popularity of tea-drinking, in the numbers of dainty tea tables designed, and the larger chair seats with wider arms to accommodate hooped skirts.

Chairs had become most varied in style by the end of this period. **George I types** were basically solid and strong-looking, with heavy cabriole legs ending in claw-and-ball feet, with seat rails and knees decorated by carved shells, lions' heads or human masks. The solid splat with carved decoration for the edge remained (see Figs. 275 and 297). From 1727 to 1740 the gilded carved styles of the **Kent type** were most favoured; acanthus leaves were popular decoration, and the cabriole leg, now very curved, and with claw-and-ball foot, was still extant. The splat was now often pierced and carved. Backs were lower and seats wider to accommodate the masculine stiffened coat skirts and feminine hoops, while **stools**, following similar patterns, were even more favoured (see Figs. 296, 298, 299 and 312). From 1740–48 to 1760 the various **Chippendale types** were most often seen. The cabriole leg remained but of slenderer silhouette, and a straight leg with stretchers became an alternative. The famous Chippendale **ribband-backs** of interlaced carving, the **Chinese fret backs** and **Gothic** arched and pointed backs were the best-known variations. Solid upholstered backs with **rococo** ornamental edges and legs were also in vogue (see Figs. 274, 276, 277, 278, 279, 300, 301, 302 and 307). In addition to these basic types, there were chairs for special use, such as writing or reading chairs, also well-known patterns still in use to-day; for example, the **ladderback** chair (see Figs. 277, 303 and 311), **grandfather** chair, **corner** chair and the **Windsor** chair. The names of some of these are self-explanatory: the grandfather chair was an upholstered wing type, with a high back and short, straight legs (see Figs. 276 and 308), and the corner chair was made to fit into a square corner (see Figs. 275 and 311). The Windsor style perhaps needs further mention. The origin of the name appears uncertain: there are several stories about this, the most common being the tale of how the King saw one in a cottage one day near Windsor and ordered some to be made for him. There are now many variations on the theme of the Windsor chair, but it was first made in the early 18th century, and by 1750 was a very popular chair, especially in the country—it was easy to make and comfortable to sit on. It was also seen in large numbers in taverns, alehouses, coffee-houses and in the famous 18th-century pleasure gardens, in the large towns. Essentially a wheel-backed chair, it had turned, vertical spindles and a solid or pierced centre splat. Legs were straight or cabriole. Gothic arch backs or flat-topped ones were also made. Arms were optional, but if present were made in one piece round the back. The seat was usually of elm, the turned spindles of beech and the bent arms and back rails of ash or yew (see Figs. 304, 305 and 306).

Settees followed chair designs to a large extent, having chiefly solid, up-holstered backs in the **baroque** period, and ribband, fret or Gothic wooden backs in the Chippendale time. Three cabriole legs were usual in front, with plain legs at the rear. Upholstery was covered with cut velvet, damask or embroidery. The settee was made to seat two or three persons, the former often being referred to as "love seats" (see Figs. 275, 313, 314, 315 and 316).

Tables were also of many types. Perhaps the most common **dining table** in use was still, as it is now, the **gate-leg table**. These usually had an oval top and two gates, though styles were also made with four gates. Barley-sugar turned legs were still popular and a drawer at each end, under the top, was usual. The only changes in style were in the more delicate types made in the Chippendale period, which were much lighter, though still strong, pieces of furniture (see Fig. 321). Other dining tables were cabriole-legged with claw-and-ball feet and a drop-leaf top. When the leaves were extended, a leg pulled out at each end to support them (see Figs. 274, 275 and 277). From about 1714 to 1740, large marble-topped **side** or **console tables**, with extravagant gilded carving and gesso work, were most fashionable, especially in large houses. Sometimes, in the Kent styles, an eagle supported the top; alternatively, swags of fruit, shells, lions' heads, etc., lavishly decorated the whole legs and top (see Figs. 318, 319, 329 and 320). Later side-tables were more delicate; they were also made to stand against the wall, but were smaller, of mahogany, and often with fret designs round the top, and with cabriole or straight, fluted legs (see Figs. 274 and 277). **Card tables**, with baize folding tops, movable fourth or fifth leg and depressed corners to hold candlesticks or guineas, were common (see Figs. 276 and 277 and 330). Tripod or four-legged dainty **tea tables**, with delicate rail tops or pie-crust edge, became increasingly popular, and the latter style was often made to fold up flat to stand against the wall when not in use (see Figs. 276, 278, 317 and 322). Small **bedside** or **worktables** were also considered necessary in the average home.

There was a marked increase in the number and size of **mirrors** seen in early Georgian times. However, the size of each piece of glass was still restricted owing to the enormous cost of production and technical difficulties which ensued. Thus large wall-mirrors were designed in complicated motifs,

Oak table for country use
1714-25
Fig. 317.

2 ft. 3"

Carved side-table - marble top - style of Kent
c.1735-40
Fig. 318.

Gilt console table - green marble top
c.1730
Fig. 320.

2 ft. 11"

Fig. 319.

Gilt console table - marble top - c.1730-40

2 ft. 4"

Fig. 321.

Gate-leg table for country use
1714-40

2 ft. 4"

Fig. 322.

Tripod table - claw & ball feet - japanned wood top -
c.1760

317-322 *Early Georgian Tables, 1714-60*

6' 2"

323 *Carved and gilt gesso mirror frame, c. 1730*

324 *Mirror—carved and gilt frame— style of William Kent, c. 1735*

3' 4"

325 *Mahogany fretted frame— Chippendale Style, c. 1750–5*

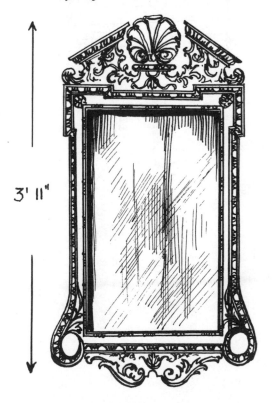

3' 11"

326 *Mirror, c. 1725—pinewood frame covered with gilt and gesso*

so that many small areas of mirror made up the whole. In large houses, mirrors—whose design included candelabra—were hung on the walls between windows and doors, and a centrepiece was provided by the mirror which was designed in one with the chimneypiece. Frames were of veneered walnut, or pinewood and gilded gesso work. By 1730 mirrors were most ornate: William Kent designed many with similar motifs to the console tables; in fact, a mirror was usually hung over the latter. Chippendale mirrors had mahogany or gilt frames, in Chinese or Gothic styles, or in simpler French scroll patterns (see Figs. 274, 278, 323, 324, 325 and 326 and 329). **Dressing glasses** were made for bedrooms: they were generally rectangular, and fitted into a swing-

327 *Oak Dresser, c. 1725. Simple style—probably country made*

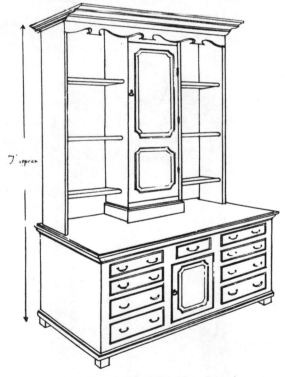

328 *Oak Dresser, c. 1750. Country Type*

back frame, hinged on to uprights, which in turn were attached to a box-like platform holding one or two drawers. This could then be placed on a chest of drawers (see Fig. 279).

The **dresser** was now more or less restricted to country use, or kept in smaller town houses. It was still a large, capacious item of furniture, having open shelves for plates and dishes or pewter and wood ware, and roomy cupboards and drawers below for storing linen and china (see Figs. 327 and 328). In more well-to-do houses, the side-table was beginning to replace the dresser, and it was in turn, later in the century, replaced by a sideboard.

188

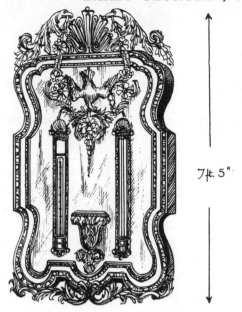

7 ft. 5"

2 ft. 9"

329 *Pinewood Mirror, c. 1730. Frame carved and gilt—with thermometer and barometer. Carved and gilt wood side-table, c. 1725. Top of scagliola in imitation of inlaid marble*

There were several other types of cupboard for storage use. **Corner cupboards** were still seen, made to fit the corner and to stand on short legs; they were generally constructed in two parts, the upper being shelved and having doors which were panelled or fitted with glass, and the lower part made into a panelled cupboard. **China cabinets** were now in great demand owing to the increase in popularity of china. These were either of a hanging type or of various sizes to stand on the floor. Most of them had glass fronts or doors to display the china (see Figs. 276, 333 and 335). The idea of glass-fronted doors and panels was still fairly new at this time. Glass was too expensive to use in large sheet form, but was split up into small panes by the design of the wood frame, usually in a Gothic tracery pattern. **Console cabinets** or **commodes** came into fashion after about 1750 (see Figs. 336 and 337).

Bacon cupboards were still seen in country homes and farmhouses. These were incorporated into another item of furniture, such as a chair, settle or cupboard. The cured hams were hung up in these cupboards near the open fireplace.

Bookcases were, on the whole, ponderous affairs, whose design was based on the architectural features of the time. Classical columns, capitals and pediments were common items of decoration and construction. Glass doors were usual in the top portion which occupied two-thirds of the height, and then the lower third had panelled doors and cupboards. The glass doors were decorated with elaborate tracery in the Chippendale period. Drawers

189

were sometimes inserted in the middle section, and the whole rested on a solid plinth (see Fig. 332).

Furniture for writing as well as storage space was provided by different types of **bureaux**. Most of these consisted of a chest of drawers, with a desk top which could be let down, when required for writing purposes, on to pull-out slides. Some had cupboards above and were thus tall pieces of furniture. They were then called **bureau-cabinets** (see Fig. 275). Some types of bureaux stood on legs, and then had fewer drawers (see Fig. 331). **Writing tables** were also in common use, having drawers on each side and a knee-hole in the centre. They were large and rectangular (see Figs. 276 and 338).

The chief item of bedroom furniture, the **bedstead**, was still massive and constructed on posts, with a high canopy and roof overhead. The posts were various in design: some were classical columns, others were carved with acanthus-leaf designs, terminating in shaggy lions' paws. They were all very high and had a carved top largely covered by the canopy and hangings, of velvet or damask with fringe and tassels, which still completely enclosed the bed when in use. Chippendale introduced Chinese and Gothic styles (see Figs. 279 and 339).

There were as yet no hanging **wardrobes**, but items of furniture called wardrobes existed, standing on short cabriole legs, and having full-length doors to open, disclosing shelves and drawers (see Figs. 340 and 341). **Tall-boys**—the chest on chest—were still used, also ordinary chests of drawers, often with curved or serpentine fronts. **Dressing glasses** were placed on top of these (see Fig. 279). Walnut and veneer were used in the early part of the period for these, but mahogany became predominant in popular taste later, and Oriental lacquer was in much demand for bedroom furniture. Chippendale's Chinese styles were also frequently seen after 1750.

Washstands came into use at this time. They were of wood, designed on a tripod stand to take a china bowl on top, and soap and bottle lower down. Basins were 9 to 10 inches in diameter (see Fig. 279). **Shaving mirrors** fitted to a small stand were seen after 1750. **Wig-stands** stood by the bed (see Fig. 279).

Miscellaneous articles include **clocks**, which were of the long-case or grandfather-clock style, or smaller types for use on the

330 *Carved Mahogany Card Table*, 1760. *Green baize top—centre fold*

190

(a) *Salt-Glaze Tea-Pot (18th century)*

(b) *Porcelain Bird. Chelsea*
(c. 1755)

(c) *Stoneware Drinking-Cup. Nottingham*
(c. 1740)

(d) *Earthenware Dish. Bristol (c. 1760)*

XVII EARLY GEORGIAN POTTERY AND PORCELAIN

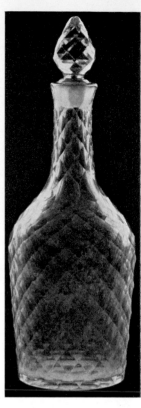

(a) *Wine-Glass* (*c*. 1700)   (b) *Wine-Bottle* (*c*. 1710)   (c) *Decanter* (*c*. 1755)

(d) *Engraved Bowl* (*c*. 1760)   (e) *Fruit Dish* (*c*. 1720)

XVIII   STUART AND GEORGIAN GLASS

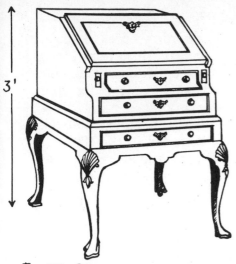

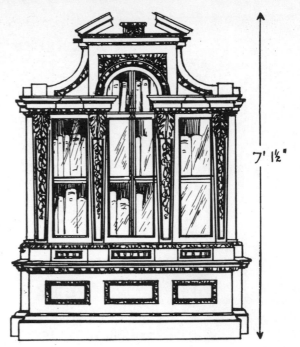

3'

7' 1½"

FIG. 331. BUREAU ON STAND -
WALNUT VENEER c. 1715

FIG. 332. BOOKCASE OF PINEWOOD c. 1730.
CARVED, PAINTED & GILDED -
STYLE OF WILLIAM KENT

FIG. 333. MAHOGANY
HANGING CHINA CABINET
GLASS WINDOWS
CHIPPENDALE STYLE

FIG. 334. CABINET c. 1740
STYLE OF WILLIAM KENT

FIG. 335. MAHOGANY CHINA CABINET -
CARVED & FRETTED - CHIPPENDALE STYLE

331–335 *Early Georgian Furniture, 1714–60*

336 *Carved Mahogany Commode Chest, c.* 1760

chimneypiece. Lacquer often decorated long-case designs, alternatively veneer or inlay work (see Fig. 274). English clocks were renowned in the 18th century and were exported in large numbers. In the early part of the period, however, some clocks were still made with the hour hand only. The **spinning wheel** was an essential part of many homes. It was made of wood, usually mahogany or rosewood and ash, with bone or ivory mounts (see Figs. 277 and 342). Most houses possessed one or more musical instruments, the chief of these being the **harpsichord** or **spinet**, which followed furniture designs of the period (see Fig. 343). Stringed instruments were also played—the violin or 'cello for instance, also the flute. **Screens** were employed a great deal for keeping out draughts (of which 18th-century people were terrified). Folding types were of painted or stamped leather and gilded. Pole screens were embroidered in pictures or floral designs, and were supported on a mahogany tripod stand, with claw-and-ball feet (see Figs. 274, 277 and 344).

In the first half of the 18th century, people were large eaters and took great pleasure in their **food**, although, to the 20th-century manner of thinking, it was often not fresh and was handled most unhygienically. Milk was taken round in open pails and meat was often

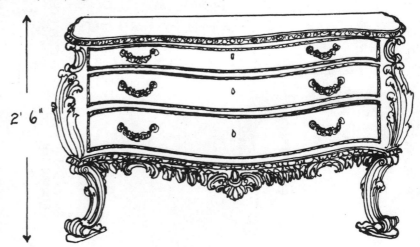

337 *Carved Mahogany Console Cabinet.*
Chippendale rococo design

338 *Carved Mahogany Library Table—Brass mounts*, 1755–60.
Chairs of carved mahogany—Chippendale style, c. 1755. *Velvet seats*

nearly bad when sold. Breakfast was a light meal, taken fairly late—10 a.m. approximately —consisting of rolls and butter, or bread and butter, tea and perhaps cold tongue. A snack or small meal about noon was followed by dinner—the main meal of the day—at 2 to 3 p.m. This meal was taken later by wealthy people, and the time became later still as the century progressed. A light supper at 6 or 7 p.m. was optional. Two typical dinner menus were: leg of mutton and caper sauce, pig's face, neck of pork and gooseberries, and a plum pudding; or roast leg of mutton and baked pudding, roast duck, meat pie, eggs and tarts, with jellies to conclude. A great deal of meat was eaten; vegetables were merely subsidiary edibles, and, according to Continental reports, badly cooked even then. Bread was of good quality, made from wheat, rye or barley, and of high standard also were the home-produced cheeses. The average labourer did not fare badly, living on bread, cheese,

339 *Mahogany Carved Bedstead, c.* 1735–50.
Dark green velvet curtains—Tassels

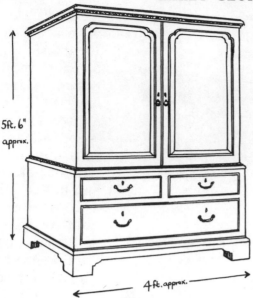

5ft. 6" approx.

4 ft. approx.

340 *Wardrobe or Press—style of Chippendale*, 1754–60. *Mahogany*

some meat, ale and vegetables. Often little cooking was done in poor cottages, owing to shortage of fuel and the inadequacy of cooking facilities, so bread, cheese and ale made the staple diet in these homes.

Ale was the national **drink**, although it was partially replaced by tea and coffee later, as these grew more popular. However, as they were expensive—tea was, even yet, as much as 9s. to 10s. a pound—the labourer kept to his ale. Wines and spirits were heavily drunk also: the more costly beverages being imbibed chiefly by the wealthier members of the community. Sugar was now more in use for tea and coffee: hitherto it had been a rarely-seen luxury.

Meat had become more plentiful as the century passed owing to the improvements in agriculture. One of these was the provision of artificial feeding stuffs for cattle. In the early part of the century, large parts of the herds had been, of necessity, slaughtered each autumn, except for the breeding stocks, and those who survived the winter were thin and small.

Meals were lengthy affairs, especially dinner, which in the houses of the middle classes and the well-to-do formed an important part of the day. It might be as late as 4 p.m. in these houses by 1750, in which case no other meal was taken after it. Tablecloths were clean, and fresh knives and forks were used for each course—these were numerous—but guests were still expected to use their fingers or their own cutlery to help themselves

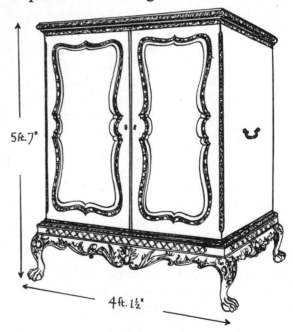

5ft. 7"

4 ft. 1½"

341 *Carved Mahogany Wardrobe*, *c.* 1750–60

194

from the main dishes; there were few serving spoons and forks. Ladies left the gentlemen to their numerous toasts after dinner for a considerable period, but rejoined them later for tea and cake.

Methods of cooking were still virtually unaltered. **Baking** was still done in a circular brick oven at the side of the fire; wood was burnt in the bottom of the oven, then the ashes were raked aside, the food put in and the iron door closed tight; the bricks retained the heat for a considerable period. Other cooking was done over the fire, on a girdle (for cakes), frying pan, pan or kettle (see Figs. 366 and 367). A turning spit was still used for roasting large joints: a dog or small boy supplied the

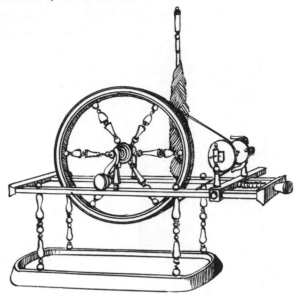

342 *Spinning Wheel—made of wood—ivory mounts—metal fittings—wood flax winder— wheel dia. 10 in.*

rotary power, by a wheel or a handle, while clockwork jacks were now more common. Meat was basted as it was cooked, and the dripping fell into a pan below—hence its name. **Kitchen utensils** were made of wood, brass or iron, earthenware or glass (see Figs. 346 to 369). **Warming pans** of brass or copper were still in use (see Fig. 370).

Clothes were **washed** at home, about once a month or once in six weeks. Women were often employed to assist in middle- and upper-class homes. The washing and ironing took three to four days. **Irons** were of brass or steel with wood handles. They were heated by the insertion of a hot lump of metal at the back under a raised slide (see Fig. 368).

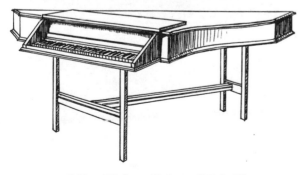

343 *Walnut Spinet,* 1714–50

Prior to the 18th century, the well-to-do homes used glass and silverware, while in the majority of houses pewter, wood and earthenware were employed. The vogue for tea- and coffee-drinking spread so greatly, however, that by 1720 **china tea services** were being imported in increasing numbers from the East, for the comparatively wealthy. These services had

Oriental designs and cups were without handles—Chinese fashion. Imports were also received later from the china and pottery centres of the Continent, from Dresden, Meissen, Sèvres and Delft. English manufacturers of china lagged behind, and it was not until the 1750's that the now famous factories sprang up **Slipware, Delftware** and **stoneware** continued to be made as in the late 17th century. Staffordshire became the main centre for this work, for stoneware in particular, due to the new ideas and methods used by the brothers **Elers** who came there from the **Fulham pottery**. White, salt-glazed stoneware—known later as **Staffordshire salt-glaze**—was made there and was in popular demand by 1725–30, in view of the fact that it was cheaper than the competing imported Oriental porcelain. **Thomas Wheildon**, working as a master potter in Staffordshire by 1740, made considerable contributions to the work, especially in the development of coloured glazes and in marbling designs. Thus, later stoneware, from about 1740 to 1750, was much thinner and more delicate, in fact, almost translucent like porcelain, and was not always glazed. It was fired at the high temperature of over 2,100° F. By 1750 nearly sixty factories were in operation in the Potteries making salt-glaze ware, and the streets of Burslem were reputed to be black with smoke from the burning salt. However, the London potteries, in particular those at **Fulham** and **Lambeth**, were

344 *Pole Screen— mahogany—petit-point embroidery,* c. 1760

also producing good work (see Plate XVII).

Porcelain—or china as it is more commonly called—was first made by the Chinese before the coming of Christ. For hundreds of years Europeans had tried to manufacture it, but could not discover the secret. Kaolin, the basis of hard-paste porcelain as

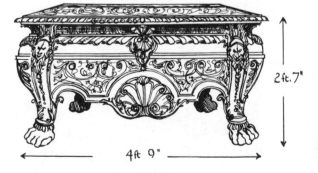

345 *Carved and Gilt Gesso Chest,* c. 1720. *Probably marriage chest*

196

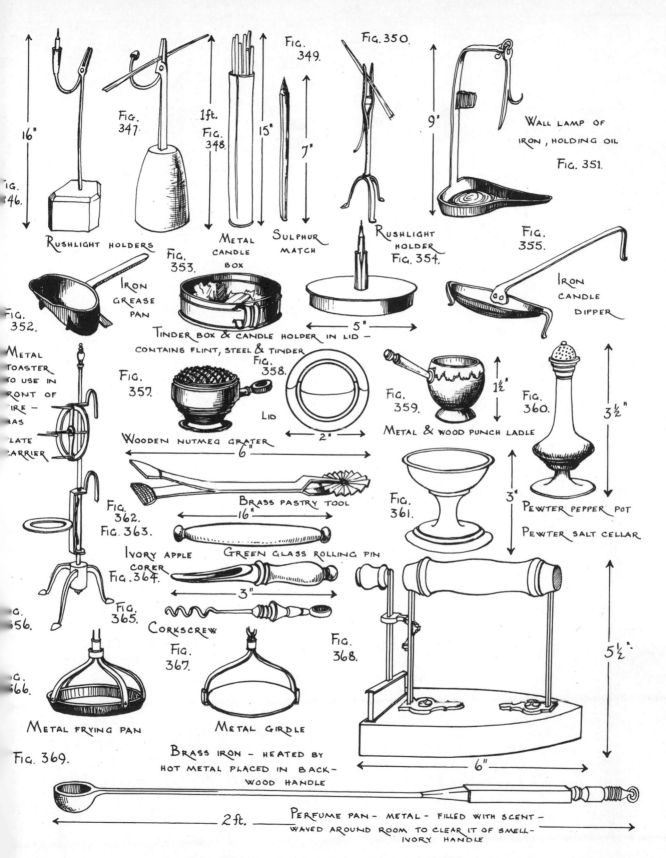

Fig. 350.

Fig. 349.

1ft.

Fig. 348.

15"

7"

16"

Fig. 347.

9"

WALL LAMP OF IRON, HOLDING OIL

FIG. 351.

FIG. 346.

RUSHLIGHT HOLDERS

METAL CANDLE BOX

SULPHUR MATCH

RUSHLIGHT HOLDER FIG. 354.

FIG. 355.

FIG. 353.

IRON GREASE PAN

IRON CANDLE DIPPER

FIG. 352.

TINDER BOX & CANDLE HOLDER IN LID — CONTAINS FLINT, STEEL & TINDER

5"

METAL TOASTER TO USE IN FRONT OF FIRE — HAS PLATE CARRIER

FIG. 357.

FIG. 358.

LID

FIG. 359.

METAL & WOOD PUNCH LADLE

FIG. 360.

1½"

3½"

WOODEN NUTMEG GRATER

6"

2"

BRASS PASTRY TOOL

FIG. 361.

PEWTER PEPPER POT

3"

PEWTER SALT CELLAR

FIG. 362. FIG. 363.

16"

IVORY APPLE CORER FIG. 364.

GREEN GLASS ROLLING PIN

FIG. 365.

3"

CORKSCREW

FIG. 356.

FIG. 367.

FIG. 368.

FIG. 366.

5½"

METAL FRYING PAN

METAL GIRDLE

BRASS IRON — HEATED BY HOT METAL PLACED IN BACK— WOOD HANDLE

6"

FIG. 369.

2 ft.

PERFUME PAN — METAL — FILLED WITH SCENT — WAVED AROUND ROOM TO CLEAR IT OF SMELL— IVORY HANDLE

346–369 *Early Georgian Utensils, 1714–60*

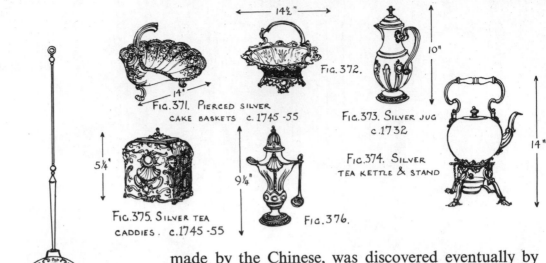

FIG. 371. PIERCED SILVER CAKE BASKETS c. 1745-55

FIG. 372.

FIG. 373. SILVER JUG c. 1732

FIG. 374. SILVER TEA KETTLE & STAND

FIG. 375. SILVER TEA CADDIES. c. 1745-55

FIG. 376.

FIG. 370. COPPER WARMING PAN.

370–376 *Early Georgian Utensils,* 1714–60

made by the Chinese, was discovered eventually by accident, on the Continent, and was used to produce the famous **Dresden** china. Soft-paste porcelain was made in England by the 1740's, but the great advances were seen after the discovery of kaolin (china clay) in Cornwall in 1755 by **William Cookworthy**. Porcelain is made by the fusion, at intense heat, of felspar glaze on to the china clay. This produces a translucent, brittle material, and is the basis of all china, as compared with pottery. Near London, **Bow** and **Chelsea** were the earliest factories: they commenced work in the 1740's. A soft paste made from clay imported from America was used in the early years, and at first the potters imitated Chinese and Continental designs in tableware; they also made the famous figures and groups. Designs were at this time in blue and white, but later in colours, painted on. In the 1750's, other factories started up at **Derby**, **Worcester**, **Liverpool**, **Bristol** and **Longton Hall**, **Staffordshire**. A method of transfer printing for the designs was in operation from 1757 at **Liverpool** and **Worcester**, whereby the pattern was transferred from an oiled copper plate to the china article via a thin paper print. Other factories later adopted the idea for mass-produced work as being quicker than painting. From 1750 to 1760, much fine-quality English porcelain was put on the market, and was eagerly bought by the well-to-do, but it was not till later that articles were made which were within reach of most people's purses, and earthenware still had a much larger sale (see Plate XVII).

This period is one of the finest for English **silverware**. The Huguenot silversmiths, who had fled to England from the wrath of Louis XIV in the late 17th century, were established by the reign of George I, and did much for the English craft. By the time of George II, the two factors—English

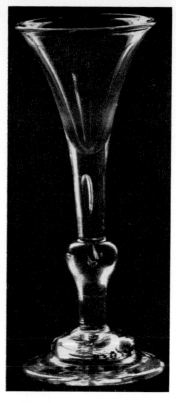

(a) *Wine-Glass* (*c.* 1725)   (b) *Wine-Glass* (*c.* 1760)   (c) *Wine-Glass* (*c.* 1760)

(d) *Candelabrum, dated* 1727   (e) *Sweetmeat Glass* (*c.* 1730)

XIX   EARLY GEORGIAN GLASS AND CANDELABRUM

(a) *Candlestick*
(1720–1)

(b) *Inkstand (1729–30)*

(c) *Caster*
(1734–5)

(d) *Tea-Caddy (1758–9)*

(e) *Tea-Kettle (1730–1)*

(f) *Chocolate Pot (1722–3)*

and French—had merged considerably, to the benefit of the English work, which was now more thorough and better finished. **Rococo** ornament was apparent at this time in the shells, fruit, flowers and mythological scenes. Pierced designs were also much in use. Most households, except the very poor, had some silver, for use on special occasions, and the vogue for tea-drinking produced many tea-pots, tea-caddies, jugs, spoons, trays and tea-kettles and stands with lamp provided. Dinner plate was well established and continued in vogue. After 1750, the new English porcelain products affected the silver market, so most of the articles made were smaller (see Plate XX).

Glassware also owes much to foreigners who fled to England for succour in the 17th century. The 18th-century work was of fine quality, chiefly made at Bristol and Birmingham. The famous Irish **Waterford** glass was manufactured after 1730. Glasses were moulded or cut, and twisted stems with opaque or coloured twists are typical of the period (see Plates XVIII and XIX).

NOTES ON ILLUSTRATIONS

Fig. 274.   *Drawing Room.*   1750–60

Sash **window**—velvet **curtains**—gold cords and tassels. Painted and stucco **walls,** gilded decoration, 1755. **Mirror,** c. 1760, Chippendale style—pinewood with gilt and gesso decoration. Wood **floor. Carpet,** embroidered in coloured wools on linen, mid-18th century. **Long-case clock,** c. 1750, oak with japanned decoration; height 7 ft. 3 in. **Side-table,** c. 1750, carved mahogany, green and white marble top; height 2 ft. 9½ in., length 4 ft. 5½ in. **Breakfast table,** Chippendale design, mahogany, fret type. **Arm-chair,** c. 1755, carved mahogany, Chippendale ribband-back style, embroidered upholstered seat; height 3 ft. 2 in. **Chair,** c. 1755, carved mahogany, Chippendale ribband-back style, embroidered upholstered seat; height 3 ft. 1½ in. **Porcelain bowl,** Chinese, mid-18th century—a Chinese scene in mauve, red, blue, green, pale blue and gold. **Silver tray,** c. 1740. **Tea-pot,** c. 1760, Staffordshire salt-glazed stoneware, Chinese design.

Fig. 275.   *Dining Room.*   c. 1730

Wealthy middle-class house. Plaster **ceiling.** Pinewood panelled **walls,** painted in olive green. Mouldings carved and gilded. **Fireplace,** marble surround, brass grate with steel basket inside. Wood **floor. Carpet,** embroidered in colours, first half of 18th century. **Chandelier,** c. 1725, carved wood, gilded. **Table,** c. 1715, walnut. **Baby cage,** turned ash and mahogany, first half of 18th century. **Chair** (left of fireplace)—writing chair, c. 1720, carved walnut, velvet seat; height 2 ft. 9 in. **Chair** (right of table), c. 1715, carved walnut, silk seat; height 3 ft. 4 in. **Settee,** c. 1720, carved walnut, embroidered upholstery. **Bureau-cabinet,** c. 1720, walnut inlaid with box and holly, gilded eagle;

height 7 ft. 11 in. **Stool**, *c.* 1720, carved walnut, patterned velvet seat. **Vase**, Chinese porcelain, blue and white, early 18th century. **Silver—tea-kettle and stand**, *c.* 1727, height 13¼ in.; **coffee-pot**, *c.* 1716, height 9½ in. **Pottery**, Staffordshire slipware, *c.* 1725.

Fig. 276. *Interior*. 1755–60

Panelled **walls** of pinewood, painted in white. **Doors** and framework of same material. **Floor** of polished wood. **Carpet**, embroidered in coloured wools on canvas, in shades of red, pink, gold, dark blue and fawn, dark grey background. **Chandelier**, Chippendale style, wood, carved and gilded. **Brackets** and **torchères**, William Kent style. **Pictures**, gilt wood frames. **China cabinet**, *c.* 1745, carved mahogany, glass panels; height 6 ft. 11 in. **Writing table**, 1751, carved mahogany, brass handles; height 2 ft. 6½ in. **Card table**, *c.* 1750, carved mahogany, folded top, one leg made to swing out; height 2 ft. 5 in. **Upright chair**, mid-18th century, walnut, needlework-covered upholstery; height 3 ft. 3 in. **Armchair** (on carpet), *c.* 1740, carved mahogany, embroidered upholstery in silk and wool—colours: dark blue background, floral design in red, gold, white and pink. **Armchair** (by wall), *c.* 1760, mahogany, embroidered upholstery in wools with dark blue-green background, and floral design in red, greens, yellow, blue and fawn. **Tea-stand**, *c.* 1760, carved mahogany, Chippendale style, height 1 ft. 11 in. **Inkstand**, mahogany, green baize interior, contains ink and sand, sliding top; length 7–8 in. **Candlesticks**, brass. **China**, Chelsea and Bow porcelain and Bristol Delft ware, *c.* 1750–60.

Fig. 277. *Living Room*. 1750–60

Walls, covered in wallpaper down to wainscot level, painted Chinese style, dated George II. **Wainscot panelling**, painted. **Overmantel**, 1760, carved and painted white on green wall. Dark green marble **fireplace**. Brass **fender** and **supports**. Steel **grate**. Wood **floor**. **Carpet**, 1757, pile, approx. 11 ft. square. **Screen**, gilt leather, stamped and painted. **Pole screen**, *c.* 1760, carved mahogany, petit-point embroidery, tripod stand; height 6 ft. **Card table** (left), *c.* 1760, carved mahogany, top folds back to open if required; height 2 ft. 4 in. **Breakfast table** (centre), 1754, Chippendale design, mahogany, folding leaves; height 2 ft. 4 in. **Occasional table** (right), *c.* 1760, Chippendale, fretwork top rail, mahogany. **Spinning wheel**, *c.* 1760, mahogany with rosewood distaff and ivory mounts. **Chair** (by table), *c.* 1760, carved mahogany, plush seat. **Chair** (by screen), *c.* 1760, ladderback style, mahogany, plush seat. **Armchair**, carved mahogany, plush seat.

Fig. 278. *Interior*. 1750–60

Pinewood-panelled **walls** with stucco ornament, painted and gilded, *c.* 1750. **Chimney-piece with mirror**, 1756, carved and painted pinewood. Marble **fireplace**. Steel **firegrate**. Wood **floor**. **Wall sconce**, wood and gilded carving. **Rug**, Turkish. **Candlestand**—pinewood carved stand, stained red and white, *c.* 1756; Chinese porcelain **vase**, 1750–56. **Stand**, *c.* 1760, carved mahogany. **Tea-table**, mid-18th century, mahogany with fretwork decoration in Chinese style; height 2 ft. 4 in. **Armchair**, *c.* 1760, carved mahogany, damask upholstery covering, Chippendale *rococo* style; height 3 ft. 6 in.

Fig. 279.   *Bedroom.*   1740–50

Walls covered with dark red silk hangings to wainscot level. Panelled wood to floor. Wood **floor.** **Rug,** early 18th century, knotted wool pile, strong colours. **Bedstead,** 1740–50, carved mahogany; hangings of damask, gold tassels and fringing; height 9 ft. 3 in., length 7 ft. 3 in. **Quilt,** embroidered, first half of 18th century. **Chest of drawers** (right), mahogany. **Dressing mirror** on top, lacquered design in black, gold and red; height 2 ft. 6 in. **Candlesticks** (pair), brass. **Chest of drawers** (left), mahogany. **Wig stand** on top, height 10 in.   **Wall mirror,** *c.* 1740, pinewood, carved and gilt, William Kent style; height 5 ft. 10 in.   **Chair,** *c.* 1750, mahogany, Chippendale style, upholstered needlework seat and back.   **Candlestand,** height 3 ft. 6 in., extending type.   **Washstand,** carved and turned mahogany, height 2 ft. 8 in.

A living-room at Osterley, 70 (taken in about 1750)

VIII

LATER GEORGIAN, 1760–1811

GEORGE III

FROM a 20th-century viewpoint, the time of George III—like that of the first half of the 18th century—presents a picture of extreme contrasts. On the one hand, the arts and architecture flourished, to reach a new high level of beauty, grace and skill. The art of living, as typified by good food, fine clothes, stately homes and cultured thought, was also practised more widely and with reverence by the well-to-do. On the other half of the picture, however, is seen overcrowding in towns—the early effects of the Industrial Revolution—extreme poverty for many, unemployment for country workers, lack of medical skill and knowledge, child labour in mines and factories, and filthy gaols. The founding of the Royal Academy of Arts and the Dilettanti Society is representative of one side of the picture, while increased numbers of people emigrating to the New World show the other.

The **population** of England and Wales increased during the 18th century by about three and a half millions to nine millions by 1801. This rise was largely due to an increased birth-rate, but was also a reflection of the benefits of **vaccination**, which had been introduced by Jenner towards the end of the century—though there was a great deal of prejudice against the idea at first. Previously, smallpox had been responsible for the deaths of an alarming number of the population of all ages. Infants were more likely to live; though a mother would still expect to lose a number of her children at birth, or before they reached the age of five years, the chance of survival had improved. Superstition still continued as a stronger force than **medicine**, and the housewife was responsible for the health and medical care of her family, only calling in professional aid in extreme circumstances. Blood-letting was the most common antidote to all ills, whilst the most usual causes of discomfort and illness were overeating and overdrinking, especially in well-to-do homes, where gout and indigestion were always present.

With new inventions, such as the spinning jenny, mechanical looms, the spinning frame and the development of steam power, the **Industrial Revolution** got under way in this period, and some of its effects, good and bad, were apparent by 1811. With a rising population to accentuate the position, the

270. The Grecian Drawing Room, 1770–5 (notes on page 256)

379 *Late Georgian Entrance Hall, 1765–70 (notes on page 256)*

trek from country to town was accelerated. In towns an unskilled worker could obtain secure, if badly paid, employment, whereas fewer workers were being used on the land because the machine was invading agriculture also. From 1760 to the outbreak of the Napoleonic Wars in 1793 was a time of great prosperity for Britain, though her working men and women gained little benefit. Such wealth went to form and keep up a new aristocracy and a growing middle class; Pitt created many new peers from professional and landowning classes. Among the British **industries** which were flourishing by the end of the century, partly due to scientific inventions and engineering developments, were the cotton and woollen trades, pottery, linen, agriculture, coal- and tin-mining, cabinet-making, ship-building, metal work and the paper industry. Whereas much work, especially in the paramount cotton and wool trades, had been done previously in the country cottage, it was now transferred to the mills and factories, and the workers had to come too, or suffer unemployment. This was particularly the case in the north of England and the Midlands, and resulted in a rash of slum building, which unfortunately was only the beginning of an evil which has not been eradicated even to-day in such towns.

With an improvement in **road** conditions, and also the opening of new **canals** to expand the old system, goods could be conveyed faster and more economically, and were distributed over areas previously neglected. Travel for the population improved also, and more coaches used the roads. It should be mentioned, though, that these roads were a travesty of present ideas on the subject—they were still mud and stone highways with large potholes full of water. Sedan chairs were used in towns for short journeys—they might be described as the forerunners of our taxi service of to-day. They were carried by two men holding poles at each end.

During the Napoleonic Wars from 1793 onwards, taxation became high, and the cost of living rose a good deal. However, the middle and upper classes weathered these increases fairly well; it was the poorer men and women who suffered badly, subsisting on starvation wages and living in warrens of slum dwellings unfit for animals, much less for human beings. Presenting a marked contrast to such a low standard of living were the truly priceless homes of the rich of this time. Their owners, as young men, had been able to make the Grand Tour before the wars with France began, and had brought back ideas and art treasures from Italy, France and the Netherlands. These included carpets, furniture, wall hangings and metal work, while the architects of the day who built and designed their homes had also studied on the Continent in their youth. The Napoleonic Wars stopped such travelling for some years, but the Continental influence still came to Britain, particularly from France, with the flow of aristocratic refugees from the guillotine and the purchasing of the contents of rich French homes in the years of chaos during

(a) *Jug and Cover.   Stafford-shire (c. 1770)*

(b) *Earthenware Punch Bowl, dated* 1809

(c) *Chestnut Bowl.   Leeds (c.* 1800)

(d) *Earthenware Plate, dated* 1760

(e) *Sauce-Tureen.   Wedgwood (late 18th century)*

(f) *Punch-Pot.   Staffordshire (c.* 1750)

XXI   LATER GEORGIAN POTTERY AND PORCELAIN

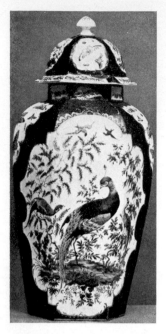

(a) *Vase. Worcester*
(c. 1770)

(b) *Vase. Wedgwood &*
Bentley. Black Basalt
(c. 1775)

(c) *Jug. Wedgwood* (1788)

(d) *Coffee Pot. Wedgwood.*
Jasper Ware (1783)

(e) *Painted Dish. Chelsea* (c. 1750)

XXII   LATER GEORGIAN POTTERY AND PORCELAIN

and after the "reign of terror" in France before Napoleon re-established order.

A beginning was made during the second half of the 18th century in the provision of free or charity **schools**. There were not many of these, however, and this new idea gained ground slowly. Unfortunately, as the staff of such schools were very poorly paid, they had to do a great deal of other work in order to subsist. Some teachers were poorly qualified, and many were habitually drunk. Private schools were of good standard on the whole, providing a fair education for a reasonable cost; science and modern languages were taught—subjects not in the curricula of public schools and grammar schools. These latter schools degenerated during this time; they provided only an out-of-date, though costly, classical education, and much of the pupils' time was wasted.

Universities also went through a bad period. Fellows were still generally compelled to take holy orders and remain single. Many of them did little or no work, and numbers of well-to-do students brought their own tutor with them. The degree examination fell into disrepute, and in some years was not held at all, though by the end of the century matters improved considerably, so that in the 19th century Oxford and Cambridge began to regain their former standards.

The boys of middle-class and well-to-do parents either had a tutor at home or began their studies this way, then attended a public, grammar or private school. Boys of poorer parentage went to a charity school, or, more frequently, had no education at all, because they could earn money for the family in factory or mine from a very early age, and this was vitally necessary in the majority of poor homes. Girls had little or no education except tuition in housewifery, sewing, painting and music. Such "ladylike" arts were encouraged by middle-class parents, who considered them to increase the chances of matrimony in an age when spinsterhood was considered a calamity. Some daughters of well-to-do parents were instructed by a governess in a little history, geography and poetry, and maybe the rudiments of French, but such learning was kept hidden as being unbecoming and likely to frighten away a possible husband. A few private schools for girls existed, teaching the same subjects, with the addition of deportment and dancing.

There were by now daily **newspapers,** costing about threepence. These had replaced the older news letters.

For **leisure** occupations people frequented the popular pleasure gardens, particularly those in London—the Vauxhall Gardens, Ranelagh Gardens and those at Kensington and Marylebone. Coffee-houses were still *à la mode*, while many famous clubs were founded in this period—Brooks's and White's in particular. People of means began to go to the seaside to enjoy the sea air and bathing, though both air and sea had to penetrate many layers of

380 *Late Georgian Dining Room, 1795–1800* (notes on page 256)

whalebone and satin. Brighton (the Brighthelmstone of the Prince of Wales's day), Margate and Weymouth were especially popular, while the spas of Harrogate, Cheltenham and Bath were much frequented later in the century. Gambling was at its height in mid-century, but was less madly indulged in by 1800.

Turning to a much less pleasant subject, that of crime and punishment, it must be admitted that here there had been little or no improvement. Very severe punishments were meted out for small offences and hanging still provided public entertainment. **Prisons** were overcrowded and in a shocking condition, even including the most recent one at Newgate. Drainage was almost non-existent, and as prisoners were fettered in irons under damp and filthy conditions, gaol fever was general. Many offenders, and even the innocent, still had to wait months for the possibility of trial.

The **London** of Stuart and early Georgian days had expanded almost out of recognition by 1811. There were now three Thames bridges, including a new one at Blackfriars and a repaired and rebuilt London Bridge. The population grew to 900,000 by 1801, and with this increase came a spreading of the city out to what had previously been country areas. The well-to-do moved to the environs as their earlier residential areas became overcrowded with both dwellings and people. The worst slum areas were still in the east, whereas new popular districts were at Finsbury, west of Bloomsbury and towards Kensington and Chelsea. There was much building at Lambeth and Southwark also. Famous London squares of this period were built on the Portman estate, which included Portman Square and Orchard Street. Later, Portland Place and Bedford Square were laid out. There was much less building after 1793 because of the Napoleonic Wars, but from 1760 to 1790 a tremendous area was covered, in the main, by fine, solid and yet graceful buildings. Portland stone was used for the larger buildings, and brick—grey or red—for smaller homes. Roofs were tiled or of slate. In the late 18th century, stucco generally covered the front elevation of buildings.

All over England this was an age of building for public, ecclesiastical and domestic purposes. New buildings were being erected and old ones modernised. For some years after 1760, the **Palladian school of architecture** persisted, based on the Roman classical style—symmetrical, solid, spacious and dignified. However, from about 1765 there was felt to be a need for something new—the Palladian style had continued almost unaltered for too long—and innovations, due chiefly to the Adam brothers, were adopted and imitated. The newer style was still classical in conception, but with a Greek and Etruscan interpretation: Roman motifs were still used, but buildings, though dignified, were in lighter vein, with less decoration, and were much more delicate in design. The heavy, gilded stucco ornament was replaced by pastel tints and white, with a touch of gilt here and there. There was a more

381 Late Georgian Private Sitting Room, 1795–1805 (notes on page 257)

382 *Late Georgian Bedchamber, c. 1775–80 (notes on page 257)*

sparing use of all motifs. This period of Greek influence on British architecture is usually referred to as the **Classic Revival**, and it lasted until the end
of the century and beyond. The French rococo styles were still seen for a
few years after 1760, but subsequently the fashion tended to die out in England.
From 1765, those who studied and were interested in the arts were much
concerned with the antique—great collections were made of original antique
sculpture, in relief form and in the round, and numerous copies were made
from them. Greek ornament was closely studied and carefully reproduced.
The egg-and-dart (life and death) moulding, the dentils, the anthemion,[1] the
honeysuckle were all used again and again. Decoration was in low relief and
small in scale to increase the apparent size of the rooms. Rooms themselves
were of varied shapes—circular, elliptical and rectangular, usually with alcoves
at each end. Curved bow windows were frequently employed.

New planning led to streets, squares and crescents being erected in many
towns. Examples are Bath, where a large area was covered with new building,
and York, Southampton, Edinburgh, Liverpool and Bristol. Later in the
century came **terrace building,** also seen in Bath and London, and especially
at seaside resorts all round the coast from Kent to Devonshire and Cornwall.
Brighton is a very fine example of such terraces. Many of the later houses
are covered with **stucco.** At first it was used as a facing to the brick, covering
the lower storey only. Then it was employed all over the façade. The idea
was to imitate stone, and the corners were cut in imitation of corner stones.
The paint was also darker than to-day, to imitate stone colour, which in
London and other towns quickly darkened further to become very dull. The
white and cream paint on such houses to-day enhances them even more than
when they were built.

In the late 18th and early 19th centuries, decoration was much more
sparingly used, in still lower relief, or even inlay, while interior colour schemes
changed from the delicate pastel shades to stronger metallic hues.

Although this period from 1760 to 1811 is, architecturally, predominantly
classical, yet the seeds of the later **Gothic Revival** were being sown. In the
1740's, Batty Langley had published some rules for Gothic architecture, but
these were not taken very seriously and were not in true sympathy with the
Gothic style. From 1750, Horace Walpole began to redesign a small building
near Twickenham in the Gothic manner. This became so well-known that
the style was referred to as "Strawberry Hill Gothic". Later, in the early
19th century, Sir John Soane produced a Gothic room. There was a small
following for the Gothic idea, but its conceptions were incorrect and found
little support as yet.

The **plan of the house** was changing also. The Great Hall had dwindled
in size to become, in most cases, merely an entrance hall, though in very large

[1] The Greek version of the earlier Egyptian lotus palmette.

383 *Late Georgian Kitchen, 1780–1805 (notes on page 257)*

homes there would be an entrance hall leading into a hall. The chief qualities admired in house design were splendour, dignity and spaciousness. Indeed, comfort and convenience were sacrificed to this end. The hall and reception rooms occupied the best part of the house on the ground and first floors, while bedrooms, private rooms and the kitchen were relegated elsewhere—to attics and basements, and even to outhouses. There was thus no smell of cooking; on the other hand, the food had to be carried along numerous cold passages, so that it must have been difficult, if not impossible, to keep it hot. Servants lived in attics and ate in the kitchens, where poor travellers were entertained.

Smaller homes had a dining room and drawing room, bedrooms, kitchen, pantry, buttery and alehouse. Farmhouses had enormous kitchens in which everyone sat and ate; a larder and scullery adjoined. In large farmhouses there would be a parlour for the family to eat and live in. Upstairs bedrooms still led off one another, without passages, as in some country cottages in Wales to-day. In the average **country cottage** the kitchen was the chief room, though there might be a parlour. Some had no sleeping accommodation, and some still had earth floors with rushes.

In the middle-and upper-class home, the method of arranging **furniture** was undergoing change. Before 1760, items of furniture had been large, comparatively few in number, and placed round the walls, leaving the centre of the room free. This continued till about 1785–90, except that designs of furniture became more delicate and there were far more pieces. This was succeeded by less formality: tables, chairs and sofas were arranged nearer the centre of the room to give a comparatively casual décor.

Gardens were still very formally laid out in lawns, lakes, shrubs and hedges, but depending on the size. It was fashionable in large gardens to erect summerhouses and fountains, and even pseudo-ruined temples and castles. After 1800, landscape gardening became less geometrical, with winding paths and more shrubs.

Outstanding among his fellow architects at this time was **Robert Adam**. A voluminous literature has been written about this man in articles, theses and several books—so much so that a reference to, say, an "Adam chimney-piece" is familiar to nearly everyone, even if they do not know what such a chimneypiece looks like. No work on the English home is complete without an account of Adam's contribution, but in view of the amount of information extant, the data considered here will be as brief as practicable. Robert Adam was born in 1728, the second son of the Scottish architect William Adam. He had three brothers, all of whom were associated with similar work. John, the eldest, took over his father's practice in Edinburgh, and as he seldom came to England, we hear little further of him. James worked a great deal with Robert, whilst William, the youngest, acted as financial and business partner and organised the firm William Adam and Co., which dealt in stucco.

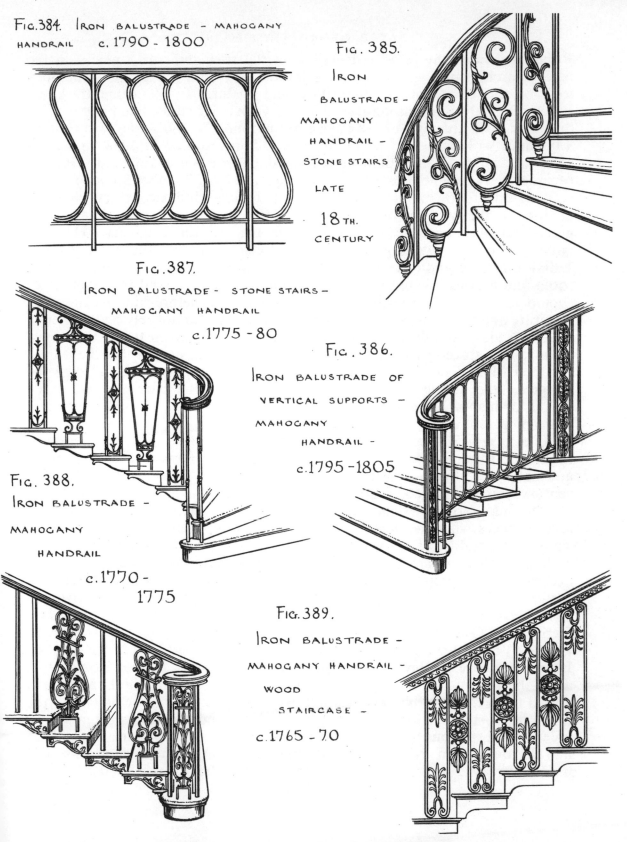

FIG. 384. IRON BALUSTRADE - MAHOGANY HANDRAIL   c. 1790 - 1800

FIG. 385. IRON BALUSTRADE - MAHOGANY HANDRAIL - STONE STAIRS LATE 18TH. CENTURY

FIG. 387. IRON BALUSTRADE - STONE STAIRS - MAHOGANY HANDRAIL   c. 1775 - 80

FIG. 386. IRON BALUSTRADE OF VERTICAL SUPPORTS - MAHOGANY HANDRAIL - c. 1795 - 1805

FIG. 388. IRON BALUSTRADE - MAHOGANY HANDRAIL   c. 1770 - 1775

FIG. 389. IRON BALUSTRADE - MAHOGANY HANDRAIL - WOOD STAIRCASE - c. 1765 - 70

384–389 *Late Georgian Staircases, 1760–1811*

Robert provided the ideas and designs of the trio, and was a genius in the field of architecture and interior decoration. In his twenties, he went on a tour of the Continent, visiting Italy and Dalmatia. He came to know Piranesi in Italy, and was influenced by his work. He studied and made many drawings of the remains of the Palace of the Emperor Diocletian (3rd century A.D.) and, with James, visited Pompeii. Adam returned in 1758, and soon after this, he and James built up a flourishing practice in England. Robert became the fashionable architect of his day, and by 1770 other architects were copying and following his work, so that it became difficult, at first sight, to distinguish the work of the originator. His work had delicacy, charm and grace, but was reproduced carefully from the classical originals. He used pastel-shaded grounds of green, lilac, pale blue, pink, very subtly graded and setting off white and/or gilt low-relief stucco decoration. He believed that a room and a house should be of one scheme throughout; and that every item should be part of that design. Like William Kent before him, he designed furniture and furnishings to go with his rooms. He did not rely on his clients' taste and ideas, but designed everything himself, even down to the fire tongs. He arranged stucco panels on the walls to enclose paintings, so that the frames for these should not clash with the scheme. His carpets often reflected the design of the ceiling and were made specially for the purpose. He made rooms of many shapes—circular, octagonal, square, etc., with the furniture in keeping.

Like other 18th-century architects, Adam's chief fault lay in that he sacrificed comfort and convenience to display. His outer façade, reception rooms and hall were all-important; the rest did not matter. However, in the 18th century, this was not considered as great a drawback as it would be to-day.

Although Robert Adam altered and redesigned many houses, there were few instances where he was given the opportunity of building a new house. Thus is the stature of his genius judged, for it is far more difficult to begin with an old-styled shell and then incorporate new ideas and methods of decoration and proportion. Indeed, it is in this very respect that some of the 19th-century Gothic Revivalists were comparatively unsuccessful. Among his most notable achievements are Syon House, Middlesex, Kedleston Hall, Derbyshire, Osterley House, Middlesex, Kenwood, Highgate, and Harewood House, Yorkshire, all of the 1760's, and, in London, Lansdowne House, Berkeley Square, Apsley House, Hyde Park Corner, and Chandos House, W.1, all of the 1770's. Of these, Syon, Osterley and Kenwood in the London area are all open to the public and are well worth a visit. Syon, belonging to the Duke of Northumberland, shows Adam at his grandest: here is magnificence indeed, with spacious halls and living rooms, a lavish but skilful use of coloured marble, decoration in vivid gilt, sculpture brilliantly executed and as brilliantly displayed (Frontispiece). Osterley, under the auspices of the Victoria

390   *Cast-iron Kitchen Range, providing cooking facilities and a boiler,*
late 18th century

and Albert Museum, has been restored to the condition and decoration that
Adam intended, and is an exquisite example of his work, but here the theme
is delicacy, walls in pastel shades and white, beautiful floors and ceilings,
superb views through gracious windows.

The three volumes of *The Works in Architecture of Robert and James Adam*
were published between 1773 and 1822, the last volume being posthumous, as
Robert died in 1792.

The brothers took out a patent for a composition of a type of stucco,
purchased from the Swiss, Liardet. It was of plaster mixed with another
substance, which could then be pressed into boxwood moulds to produce a
detailed and accurate positive. This could be applied to a surface while still
malleable, and the process was very useful to them. Adam's ornament
designs were usually of plaster, and for ceilings this was an invaluable method.

Among the contemporaries of Robert Adam whose work was at times
similar in many respects were the architects **Thomas Leverton** (1743–1824),
Henry Holland (1746–1806) and **James Wyatt** (1746–1813). Of these, **Leverton's** work resembled that of Adam most closely, especially in ornament. He
was responsible for many houses in town and country, while his best-known
achievement is probably his designs for and influence on the buildings in
Bedford Square. **Holland's** style was more restrained and solemn than that
of Adam, and he also did some work of quite a different nature. He is most
famous for his classical Royal Pavilion[1] at Brighton and the rebuilding of

_____
[1] Replaced in Regency times by the present building, designed by John Nash.

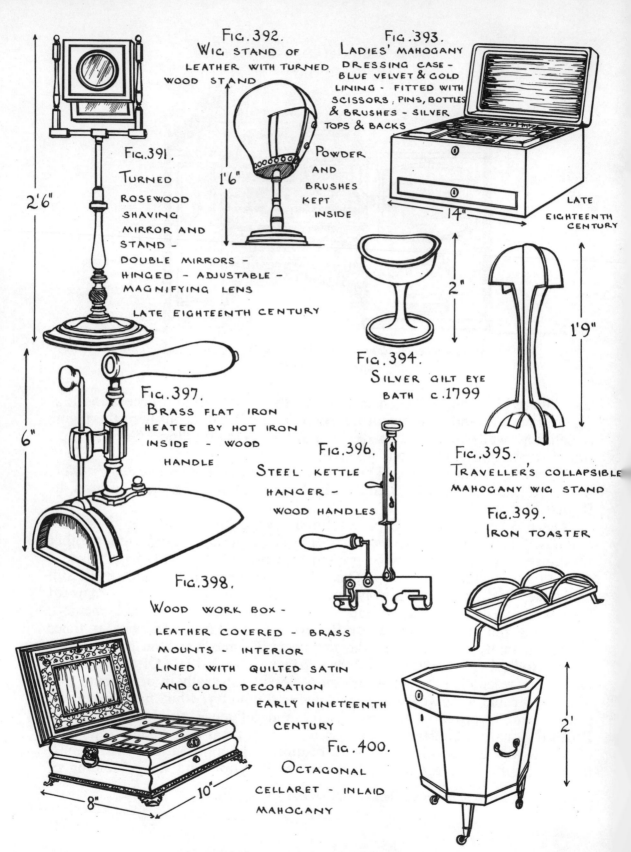

FIG. 392.
WIG STAND OF
LEATHER WITH TURNED
WOOD STAND

FIG. 393.
LADIES' MAHOGANY
DRESSING CASE -
BLUE VELVET & GOLD
LINING - FITTED WITH
SCISSORS, PINS, BOTTLES
& BRUSHES - SILVER
TOPS & BACKS

FIG. 391.
TURNED
ROSEWOOD
SHAVING
MIRROR AND
STAND -
DOUBLE MIRRORS -
HINGED - ADJUSTABLE -
MAGNIFYING LENS

LATE EIGHTEENTH CENTURY

1'6"

POWDER
AND
BRUSHES
KEPT
INSIDE

2'6"

14"

LATE
EIGHTEENTH
CENTURY

2"

FIG. 394.
SILVER GILT EYE
BATH c.1799

1'9"

FIG. 397.
BRASS FLAT IRON
HEATED BY HOT IRON
INSIDE - WOOD
HANDLE

6"

FIG. 396.
STEEL KETTLE
HANGER -
WOOD HANDLES

FIG. 395.
TRAVELLER'S COLLAPSIBLE
MAHOGANY WIG STAND

FIG. 399.
IRON TOASTER

FIG. 398.
WOOD WORK BOX -
LEATHER COVERED - BRASS
MOUNTS - INTERIOR
LINED WITH QUILTED SATIN
AND GOLD DECORATION
EARLY NINETEENTH
CENTURY

FIG. 400.
OCTAGONAL
CELLARET - INLAID
MAHOGANY

2'

8"   10"

391-400 *Later Georgian Period, 1760-1811*

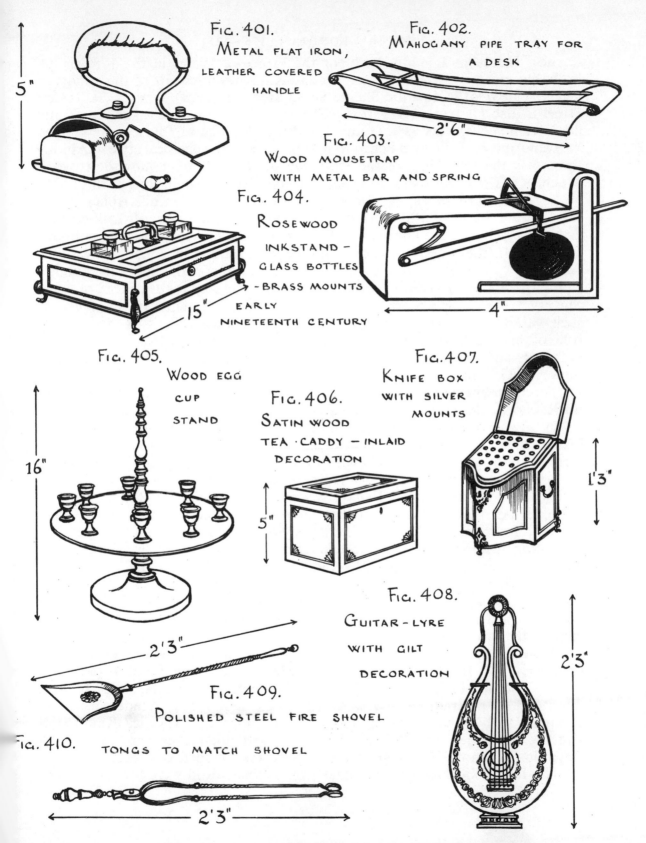

FIG. 401.
METAL FLAT IRON,
LEATHER COVERED
HANDLE

5"

FIG. 402.
MAHOGANY PIPE TRAY FOR
A DESK

2'6"

FIG. 403.
WOOD MOUSETRAP
WITH METAL BAR AND SPRING

FIG. 404.
ROSEWOOD
INKSTAND —
GLASS BOTTLES
— BRASS MOUNTS
EARLY
NINETEENTH CENTURY

15"

4"

FIG. 405.
WOOD EGG
CUP
STAND

FIG. 406.
SATIN WOOD
TEA·CADDY — INLAID
DECORATION

FIG. 407.
KNIFE BOX
WITH SILVER
MOUNTS

16"

5"

1'3"

FIG. 408.
GUITAR — LYRE
WITH GILT
DECORATION

2'3"

FIG. 409.
POLISHED STEEL FIRE SHOVEL

FIG. 410.   TONGS TO MATCH SHOVEL

2'3"

401–410 *Later Georgian Period, 1760–1811*

Carlton House in London, both for the Prince of Wales in the 1780's. Of probably greater interest to many to-day is his development of the village of Chelsea, in what is now the Sloane Street area. Brooks's Club in St. James' Street is also his work. **Wyatt** is well known both for his classical work and his later achievements as a Gothicist. From the age of fourteen he studied in Rome and on his return began to design work in the classical style. Among these was the rebuilding of the Pantheon in Oxford Street (now destroyed). Much of his work of the 1770's was very like that of Adam, but in the 1780's he began to turn to the Gothic style. His efforts at Fonthill Abbey, Wiltshire, are typical of this period: an 18th-century version of 15th-century fashions. This work, however, collapsed, due to lack of adequate support, in 1825. In the latter years of his life he was dubbed by Pugin "Wyatt the Destroyer", in reference to his wholesale restoration of cathedrals and churches (some of fine Wren-period construction), to make way for his ideas of 15th-century Gothic. His work was often successful, but that can never excuse such vandalism of any period's great achievements. This was particularly true of his work in Durham and Salisbury cathedrals. He was a prolific architect, and many examples of his work exist to-day. In 1796 he became Surveyor-General.

Three architects who were, in a sense, rivals to the Adam brothers were **Sir Robert Taylor** (1714–88), **James Paine** (1716–89), and **Sir William Chambers** (1726–96). **Sir Robert** was rather older than Adam and, though he began his career as a sculptor, devoted himself to architecture at about the age of forty. He was appointed architect to the Bank of England in 1765, and held this appointment for over twenty years, though unfortunately not a great deal of his work remains now. **Paine's** work was much like Sir Robert's, in the same period. **Sir William Chambers** provided the chief opposition to Adam, as he adhered to the Roman Palladian style of architecture, despite the later prevailing fashions. He was appointed as instructor in architecture to the young prince—later George III—and this may have been the reason why George III always preferred Palladianism to work of the Classic Revival. Somerset House is Sir William's best-known work to-day, though the results of his Far Eastern travels can be seen in the Botanical Gardens at Kew, including the famous Pagoda.

Another contributive architect of this period was **George Dance** (the younger, 1741–1825), who designed All Hallows Church, London (a victim of Nazi bombs in World War II), and Newgate Prison. He later became interested in portraiture, and was one of the first Royal Academicians, in company with Benjamin West, Thomas Gainsborough, Angelica Kauffmann and the Treasurer, Sir William Chambers, with their President, Sir Joshua Reynolds, when the Royal Academy of Arts was founded in 1768.

The famous architects of the later part of this period were **Sir John Soane**

(1753–1837) and **John Nash** (1752–1835). Both of these architects are predominantly known for their Regency work, but both did achieve success in Georgian England also, and between them they had the greatest influence on the architecture of their time. **Sir John Soane** was born in Reading and came to London in 1768. He was articled to George Dance the younger, and became a Royal Academy Gold Medallist some years later. Through Sir William Chambers, his work was recommended to George III, and he received assistance to study for three years in Rome. On returning to England in 1780, he

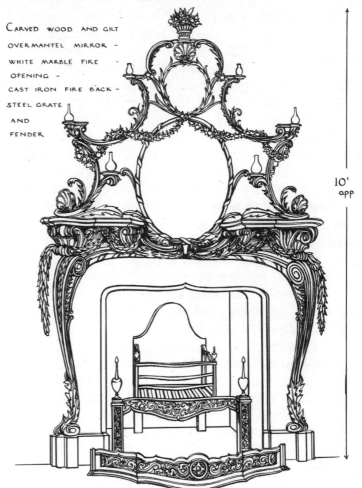

CARVED WOOD AND GILT OVERMANTEL MIRROR –
WHITE MARBLE FIRE OPENING –
CAST IRON FIRE BACK –
STEEL GRATE AND FENDER

10′ app.

411 *Carved Wood Chimneypiece, painted white, c.* 1770

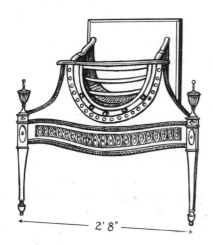

2′ 8″

412 *Steel Fire Grate, late 18th century*

began to practise as an architect. His work was classical and severe, and simple in the extreme. The curves and gaiety of Adam's work were replaced by straight lines and very low relief, or even inlay, instead of mouldings to doors, etc. His decoration was linear rather than three-dimensional. By 1788 Sir John was architect to the Bank of England, succeeding Sir Robert Taylor, and he held the position until 1823. He became a Royal Academician in 1802, and

Professor of Architecture at the Royal Academy of Arts in 1806. His best-known work in this period is Pitzhanger Manor at Ealing, completed in 1802. Although **John Nash** was an architect of the late 18th and early 19th centuries, his most famous works were of Regency times. He was a pupil of Sir Robert Taylor, and later succeeded Holland as architect to the Prince of Wales. He designed Regent's Park from 1793, but his later developments in this area were 19th-century achievements.

The 18th century, and in particular the second half, was an age of decoration by stucco and marble sculpture. In the first part of the century, most of the work was done by foreign sculptors, but by 1770 some English names were becoming known, employed by some of the architects already mentioned. **Joseph Wilton** was one of these, and notable as the only English sculptor to become a member of the original set of Royal Academicians. He had been trained in Paris and Italy, studying antique sculpture for many years. When he returned to England in 1775, he worked chiefly for Sir William Chambers, and is best known for his marble chimneypieces.

The name of **John Flaxman** (1755–1826) is the most familiar in this connection, probably because of his adoption by Wedgwood in 1775 to design classical models for friezes, bas-reliefs and portrait medallions for the famous jasper ware. This ware, with its original designs, is still sold to-day and is as popular as ever. Flaxman based his designs on Greek figures, interpreted in a simple and graceful manner. In 1787, he went to Rome to study, and after his return also designed many chimneypieces. He became a Royal Academician in 1797 and then did some fine statues of well-known figures of the time, including William Pitt and Sir Joshua Reynolds.

Among the better-known sculptors of the day were **Thomas Banks, John Bacon, William Collins** and **Nollekens**.

A variety of methods could be used to cover and decorate the interior **walls** of a home at this time: the chief of these were wallpaper, hangings, stucco and painting. Thus, from 1760, **wainscoting** was employed less often as wall covering, and was soon superseded by these means of decoration, mainly because they were generally cheaper and considered more in keeping with the lighter and gayer interiors of the period. Wainscoting, when used, was generally of deal or pine in preference to oak as hitherto; these were less expensive woods, but as the surface was then painted in a light colour, often soft greens or blues, and decorated with gilt on the carving, economy was not the motive. Carving was confined in most cases to the chimney-piece, door case and window frames, but even this was gradually replaced by stucco.

Plaster or **stucco** was in common use before 1760 as an inexpensive method of covering and decorating large wall surfaces in reception rooms, halls and staircases, especially in larger homes. It continued to be very popular, even

(a) *Tea-Pot. New Hall* (*c.* 1800)

(b) *Tea-Pot. Bristol* (*c.* 1775)

(c) *Earthenware Punch-Bowl. Liverpool* (*c.* 1790)

(d) *Vase. Worcester* (*c.* 1780)

(e) *Jug. Caughley* (*c.* 1780)

(f) *Tea-Pot. Chelsea* (*c.* 1765)

XXIII   LATER GEORGIAN POTTERY AND PORCELAIN

(a) *Ale Glass*
(*c.* 1770)

(b) *Cruet Bottle*
(*c.* 1780)

(c) *Opaque White Glass Vases*
(*c.* 1780)

(d) *Cut-Glass Chandelier* (*c.* 1770)

(e) *Sweetmeat-Glass*
(*c.* 1790)

(f) *Opaque Glass Jug*
(*c.* 1830)

FIG. 413.
CARVED
MAHOGANY
LADDERBACK
CHAIR
VELVET COVERED
SEAT. c 1775
3'1"

FIG. 414. PAINTED & GILT
SHIELD BACK CHAIR
HEPPLEWHITE
STYLE
SILK COVERED
UPHOLSTERY
c.1790
3'1"

FIG. 415. HEART SHAPED OR
INTERLACED SHIELD BACK -
MAHOGANY
HEPPLEWHITE
STYLE CHAIR
c.1780-5
3'

FIG. 416.
CARVED MAHOGANY
CHAIR - ANTHEMION
CENTRE TO SPLAT - LEATHER SEAT
c.1770
3'2"

FIG. 417.
WINDSOR CHAIR
OF YEW
c.1760-65

FIG. 418.
CARVED MAHOGANY CHAIR -
LYRE BACK
SPLAT
c.1775
3'

FIG. 419.
CARVED
MAHOGANY
CHAIR -
PRINCE OF
WALES'
FEATHERS
IN SPLAT
SHERATON
STYLE
c.1795-
1800
2'11"

FIG. 420.
PAINTED OVAL
BACK CHAIR - SILK
COVERED UPHOLSTERY
c.1785
3'2"

FIG. 421.
CHILD'S
PUNISHMENT
CHAIR -
BAMBOO
PAINTED
BLACK -
CANE SEAT -
c.1800
2'10"

FIG. 422.
CARVED AND PAINTED
WOOD HALL CHAIR
c.1770
3'2"

FIG. 423.
SATINWOOD SHIELD BACK CHAIR -
PRINCE OF
WALES'
FEATHERS
DECORATION
HEPPLEWHITE
STYLE
c.1788-90
3'

FIG. 424.
CARVED
BEECHWOOD CHAIR - GILT AND
PAINTED - SILK COVERED
UPHOLSTERY
c.1810
2'10"

FIG. 425.
BEECHWOOD & CANE CHAIR -
BLACK & GOLD JAPANNING
c.1800
2'9"

FIG. 426.
PAINTED SATINWOOD CHAIR -
CANE SEAT - LYRE BACK CHAIR
c.1790
3'1"

FIG. 427.
CARVED MAHOGANY
LYRE BACK CHAIR
METAL STRINGS
c.1775
2'10"

FIG. 428.
MAHOGANY
CHAIR WITH OVAL
BACK -
LEATHER
SEAT -
ANTHEMION
DECORATION
c.1785-90
3'2"

413–428 Late Georgian Chairs, 1760–1811

more so after the Adam brothers showed new methods of design with the old medium. The newer stucco ornament was in much lower relief than in the Palladian period architecture, more delicate in handling and more restrained in treatment. The wall surface was generally painted in a soft pastel shade, and the ornament left white or delicately gilded. It was designed to enhance the chimneypiece, doorcase and windows, and was set in panels on the plain areas of wall, or as frames to oil paintings which were incorporated in the scheme. These latter were predominantly landscapes on Italian themes, or figure compositions. Many paintings by Canaletto were bought, and many others of this master imitated, so that views of Venice became the ubiquitous theme (see Figs. 377 and 380). In the early 19th century, plain walls were more usual, ornamented with numbers of smaller paintings or prints and engravings.

Wallpaper, the newest medium, was used more and more. Chinese papers (Colour Plate facing page 256) were still imported, and many were copied in England; these usually showed scenes from Chinese life, such as the planting and cultivation of tea, or gaily decorated boats on water; others were floral, with bamboo shoots and other plants. In both cases the whole scheme was generally planned to continue unbroken round the room. Other types of wallpaper were also made in England: Jackson continued his designs at Battersea, of classical figures and reproductions of paintings by Canaletto or Lorraine, or floral all-over patterns. There were designs based on French rococo motifs, and others on Adam styles of decoration. Often wallpaper covered the whole wall from cornice to dado, all round the room, including the plain door frames, so that only a thin line showed where the door actually opened. The papers were still mounted on canvas on to a wood frame, attached to the wall by wooden wedges, so that new paper could be put up without destroying the old. The papers were more highly valued than to-day, and many have been preserved for us, as they were not subject to the damp and dirt from the walls. Wallpaper was made in small sheets until about 1800, so many sectional joins were apparent, after which it was made in longer strips.

Ceilings were almost invariably of plaster, and in this field Robert Adam made the outstanding contribution. His ceiling designs were very different from the ribbed ceilings of Palladian decoration, the ornament being in low relief and not usually covering, in unbroken fashion, the whole ceiling. His earlier designs were apt to do this, set in octagons, squares and circles, but after about 1775–80, there was generally a centrepiece and delicate decoration to connect this with a cornice of fragile appearance. The background was usually coloured in pale blues or greens, lilac, pink or cream, with white or gilded ornament. His motifs included anthemion, acanthus, dolphins, griffins and winged sphinxes, gracefully banded together with scrolls and acanthus sprays. Most of his designs had painted panels included as centres of decora-

FIG. 429. CARVED WOOD SETTEE - GILDED -
STRIPED SILK COVERED UPHOLSTERY .-

c.1780-90

FIG. 430.

CHIPPENDALE
STYLE SETTEE - FRET
TYPE OF DECORATION - BROCADE COVERED
UPHOLSTERY c.1760

FIG. 432.

HEPPLEWHITE STYLE OF SOFA - CARVED AND
TURNED MAHOGANY - SILK COVERED UPHOLSTERY

c.1788-90

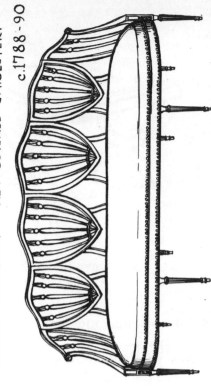

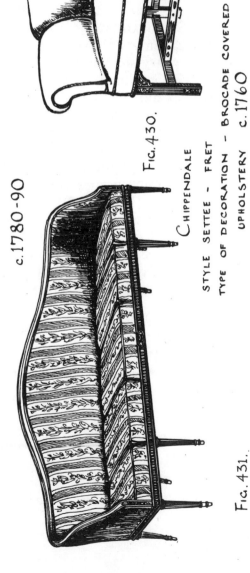

FIG. 431.

CARVED AND GILT BEECHWOOD COUCH -
CERISE COLOURED SILK COVERED UPHOLSTERY

c.1805

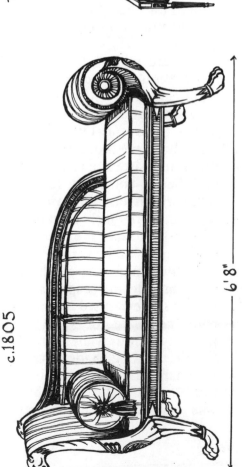

6'8"

429-432 Later Georgian Settees and Sofas, 1760-1811

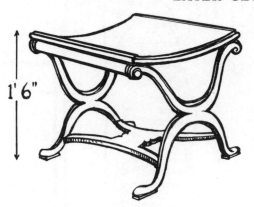

433   *Mahogany Carved Stool,*
c. 1800

tion, but these were smallish and not overpowering. They were usually set in circles, ovals or lunettes, and took the form of figure compositions from Greek mythology in most cases. Among the stucco craftsmen of the day were **John Papworth** and **Joseph Rose**. Famous painters were employed, most of whom were Italian or Swiss. The best known was probably **Angelica Kauffmann** (1741–1807), a Swiss painter who worked in London from 1766 and did a great deal of painting for Adam. She exhibited often at the Royal Academy of Arts and was one of its original members. At the end of the century she went to live in Italy with her husband, **Antonio Zucchi** (1726–95), who was an Italian painter who came to England about the same time and also did much work for Adam. Other famous Italian painters of the time who came to England and carried out painting for architects of the period included **Cipriani** and **Biagio Rebecca.**

At the end of the 18th century, ceilings became plainer, with still lower relief, though Greek motifs still predominated. Some homes even had quite plain ceilings by then (see Figs. 377, 378, 379, 380, 381 and 382).

Although **cast iron** had been used previously for utensils and implements, it was from mid-18th century that architects and decorators sought to use it for other and more ambitious purposes in the home. New methods of production assisted them; more cast iron was available in more decorative forms, and better transport facilities helped also. Adam, Nash and Soane were three architects who were noted for its use, particularly in staircase balustrades, balconies, fire grates, fireplaces, pillars and kitchen stoves.

Other materials of the period include **marble** and **scagliola**. Coloured marbles were used a great deal as columns, inlaid floors and for chimneypiece inlay into white statuary marble. Scagliola was made from gypsum, glue, isinglass and colouring to imitate marble. It could be highly polished, was very hard, and, moreover, was

434   *Painted and Gilt Wood Stool,*
c. 1775

226

cheaper and more plastic than marble for inlay work, so that it was used a great deal for columns, chimneypieces and table tops (see Frontispiece).

Floors were of polished wood, and, where possible, were partly covered by **carpets** and rugs, which were now more plentiful, but, owing to the cost, their use was still confined to middle-class and well-to-do homes. Stair-carpets were rare until the early 19th century. Many famous British carpet manufactories were producing fine carpets; these were chiefly Axminster, Kidderminster, Wilton, Moorfields and Kilmarnock. Oriental and Western designs were used, in rich colours. Eastern carpets were still imported in considerable quantities, from Turkey and Persia in particular; there were also some from India. Some architects ordered carpets to be made especially to be in keeping with their ceiling designs, and notable among these was Adam, who had several carpets made by Thomas Moore, which can now be seen at Syon and Osterley. In the late 18th century, French carpets of fine quality were also imported.

The size and plan of the **hall** and staircase varied a good deal. In medium or smaller homes, the hall was merely an entrance space and not a living room at all. The floor would be tiled or flagged, and the staircase led off this hall. In large homes, the hall was a fine reception room, and the entrance hall led off it. This entrance hall often rose to the height of the house and contained the staircase well. Where the staircase hall was left out of the scheme, smaller staircases were planned in other parts of the house (see Fig. 379).

Although wood **staircases** still existed at this time, it became the fashion as the 18th century progressed to have stone staircases based on a circular or elliptical plan, sweeping down in an unbroken line from top to bottom of the house. Each step rested on the one below; the balustrade was of iron for strength and delicacy of design, and the narrow continuous handrail was generally of mahogany. The iron was wrought or cast, and designs were made popular by Adam, Chambers and Wyatt. Such designs were graceful, though strong, and were based on S or scroll patterns, the lyre and foliated types. Towards the end of the century, balusters were plainer and just simple vertical bars or S shapes. The staircase was generally lit by a skylight above (see Figs. 384, 385, 386, 387, 388 and 389).

Against what a housewife to-day would term "heavy odds", many later Georgian housewives still made their own candles, soap and ink at home, did their own baking, brewing and preserving, and even milk-churning and butter-making. Although transport had improved in country areas, large stocks of food still had to be laid in for the winter. The average **kitchen** was little altered from several hundred years before—the benefits of the Industrial Revolution came later to the home than elsewhere. The kitchen floor had stone flags, its roof was of timber beams, and it was often set in a dark, cold basement, a great distance from the dining room (at least in large homes).

227

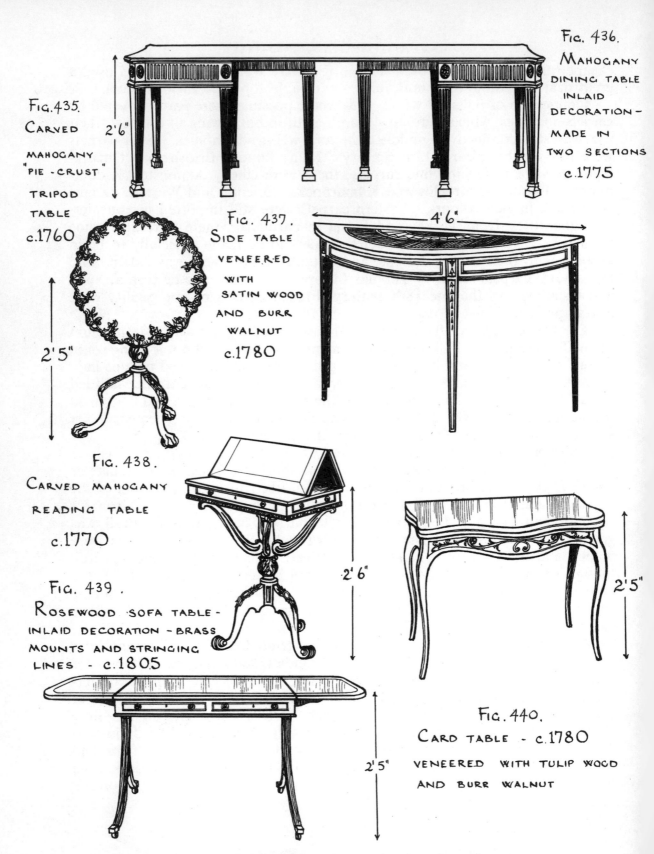

FIG. 435.
CARVED
MAHOGANY
"PIE-CRUST"
TRIPOD
TABLE
c.1760

2' 6"

FIG. 436.
MAHOGANY
DINING TABLE
INLAID
DECORATION —
MADE IN
TWO SECTIONS
c.1775

FIG. 437.
SIDE TABLE
VENEERED
WITH
SATIN WOOD
AND BURR
WALNUT
c.1780

4' 6"

2' 5"

FIG. 438.
CARVED MAHOGANY
READING TABLE
c.1770

2' 6"

FIG. 439.
ROSEWOOD SOFA TABLE —
INLAID DECORATION — BRASS
MOUNTS AND STRINGING
LINES — c.1805

2' 5"

FIG. 440.
CARD TABLE — c.1780
VENEERED WITH TULIP WOOD
AND BURR WALNUT

2' 5"

435–440 *Later Georgian Tables, 1760–1811*

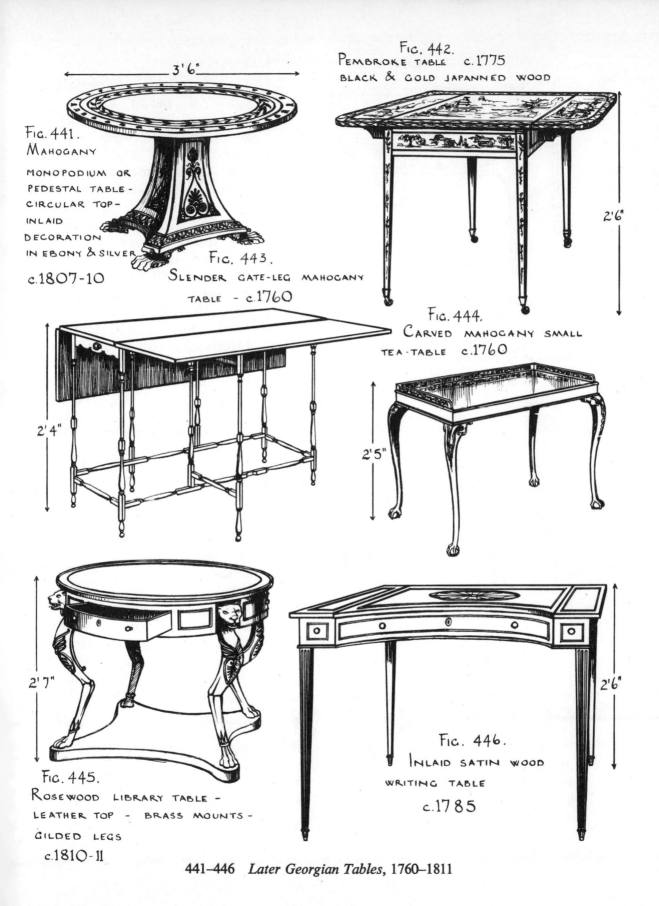

FIG. 441.
MAHOGANY
MONOPODIUM OR
PEDESTAL TABLE -
CIRCULAR TOP -
INLAID
DECORATION
IN EBONY & SILVER
c.1807-10

3'6"

FIG. 442.
PEMBROKE TABLE c.1775
BLACK & GOLD JAPANNED WOOD

2'6"

FIG. 443.
SLENDER GATE-LEG MAHOGANY
TABLE - c.1760

2'4"

FIG. 444.
CARVED MAHOGANY SMALL
TEA-TABLE c.1760

2'5"

FIG. 445.
ROSEWOOD LIBRARY TABLE -
LEATHER TOP - BRASS MOUNTS -
GILDED LEGS
c.1810-11

2'7"

FIG. 446.
INLAID SATIN WOOD
WRITING TABLE
c.1785

2'6"

441–446 *Later Georgian Tables, 1760–1811*

FIG. 447. MAHOGANY SIDEBOARD - INLAID
WITH EBONY LINES - BRASS HANDLES - c. 1795
BRASS GALLERY - CURTAIN

FIG. 448. MAHOGANY SIDEBOARD TABLE WITH
PEDESTAL AT EACH END - SURMOUNTED BY
KNIFE URNS c. 1780-90

447 *and* 448 *Later Georgian Sideboards,*
1760–1811

From the beams hung salted sides of bacon and ham, strings of onions and bunches of herbs. Wooden shelves and a plain wood **dresser** held all the implements and heavy earthenware pots and dishes, while the cupboards below stored linen. **Cooking** was still over huge fires—now generally burning coal—with iron fire-backs, kettle-hangers, chimneycranes and firedogs. The **spit** was turned by clockwork jack or dog turnspit. Ovens were still of brick, and functioned in the same primitive manner as hundreds of years before. The **sink** was usually a shallow earthenware trough, and water (cold) had to be pumped and collected from outside in buckets. A stone-flagged dairy and larder adjoined. In the late 18th and early 19th centuries, cast-iron **kitchen ranges** began to be made, and a few town houses had them. These were, to us, black, coal-consuming monstrosities, but to the housewife of 1800 they must have appeared miracles of efficiency. Some of the more advanced types had an oven, and a boiler on the other side of the fire, with a hot plate on top to keep the kettle on the boil (see Fig. 390). A kitchen is illustrated in Fig. 383, and various utensils in Figs. 396, 397, 399 and 401.

The double-tiered type of massive **chimneypiece** of Palladian style was gradually superseded, during the 1770's, by the one-storeyed type, with an ornamental gift-framed mirror, stucco panel and/or painting over it. At the same time the carved rococo designs were replaced by those introduced by Adam and his contemporaries. These were generally simple and with little projection, consisting of a mantelshelf and entablature supported on classical columns or pilasters. Later these were replaced by simple supports of rectangular shape. The whole chimneypiece became much smaller and more restrained as the century progressed. White marble was the favoured material, particularly for the main rooms, decorated by coloured marble inlay, scagliola or even painted designs. Most of the decoration was on the frieze. Carved wood, painted, was used as a cheaper substitute, for the marble chimneypieces could cost well over £1,000 each. Another type of decoration was supplied by Wedgwood's jasper-ware panels inset into the marble, or by similar plaques. Yet another means of ornament was provided by ormolu or bronze or gilding. In the late 18th century, manufacturers began to make simpler chimneypieces on these lines and sell them to clients, so that the majority of chimneypieces were not designed individually by architects as hitherto. Needless to say, most architects resented this. (Various styles of chimneypieces can be seen in Figs. 377, 378, 381, 382 and 411.)

The fire openings grew smaller in the later 18th century, and almost all **grates** were designed to burn coal, so had cast-iron fire-backs. A fire-basket had replaced the fire-back and andirons, and this varied in shape. The Adam style of **basket grate** was typical, and many were modelled on his designs. The basket was usually semicircular, and the supports of classical design, surmounted by vases or urns. It was usually of polished steel with pierced decoration, and fire tongs, poker, shovel and fender to match (see Figs. 377, 378, 382, 411 and 412). Later in the century, **hob grates** became more usual: these were enclosed and fitted into each side of the fireplace instead of standing separately in the centre of the fire opening as previously. They were made of cast iron and had relief decoration on the side panels; the bars were of wrought iron (see Fig. 381).

The **doorcase** flanked by classical columns or pilasters and surmounted by a pediment was still seen, especially in large homes, until the 1770's, but after this most doors were designed more simply. The Adam doorcase, which most styles followed at this time, was lower in relief, and was surmounted by a frieze and simple cornice. In well-to-do homes the **doors** were of solid, polished mahogany, with ormolu or brass decoration on the six panels. Other doors were of pine or deal and were painted, then decorated by gilded, carved panels. All doors were fairly large and rather taller than a double square (see Figs. 377 and 379). In the early 19th century, panels and decoration were in very low relief, and this was often replaced by ebony inlay to represent panelling.

Sash windows with wood frames were in general use. The glazing bars became narrower, to be about three-quarters of an inch wide by the end of the century, allowing more light into the room. In larger rooms, the top

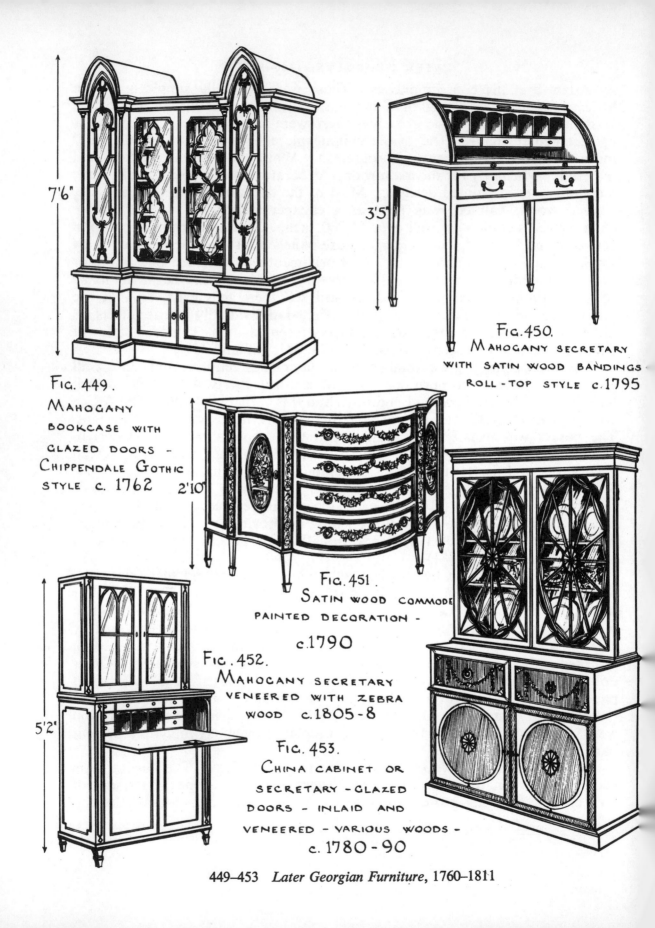

FIG. 449.
MAHOGANY
BOOKCASE WITH
GLAZED DOORS -
CHIPPENDALE GOTHIC
STYLE C. 1762

7'6"

3'5"

FIG. 450.
MAHOGANY SECRETARY
WITH SATIN WOOD BANDINGS
ROLL-TOP STYLE C.1795

2'10"

FIG. 451.
SATIN WOOD COMMODE
PAINTED DECORATION -

C.1790

FIG. 452.
MAHOGANY SECRETARY
VENEERED WITH ZEBRA
WOOD C.1805-8

FIG. 453.
CHINA CABINET OR
SECRETARY - GLAZED
DOORS - INLAID AND
VENEERED - VARIOUS WOODS -
C. 1780-90

5'2"

449–453 *Later Georgian Furniture, 1760–1811*

part of the sash window was generally taller than the bottom part, being three panes deep and three panes wide, to two panes deep in the lower part. In smaller rooms, the two parts would be equal (see Figs. 377, 379, 380 and 383). **Bow windows** were very fashionable in the second half of the century. These were rounded or segmental, and sometimes extended from top to bottom of a house. The frames followed the same bow shape.

The second half of the 18th century is now considered to be the finest period for design and craftsmanship in English **furniture**. Many great cabinet-makers were designing, producing and publishing designs of their work, and several famous architects also designed furniture in keeping with their houses. These designs were copied and used over and over again, and more and more people began to own and use a greater number of pieces of furniture in their homes. Earlier in the century, furniture had been rather massive, gilded and/or carved, decorated by gesso and japanning. Chippendale had introduced more delicate work from about 1755, but it was from 1760 onwards that the more graceful furniture came, with a great variety of woods, methods of ornament and actual designs. **Mahogany** was still the most used wood, both in solid form for carving and as a veneer for polished, plain surfaces, in which case the figured wood was employed. It was ideal for intricate carving, and was thus especially suitable for the styles of 1760–70, though this carving was gradually superseded, as a means of decoration, by painting and inlay. Nevertheless, mahogany was in general use till after the end of the century, especially for the heavier items of furniture in dining rooms and libraries. From about 1785–90, **satinwood** became very fashionable; of golden colour and very hard, it was suitable as a veneer which could be highly polished. Being expensive, it was used chiefly for smaller, more delicate items. It was often inlaid with various woods: ebony, harewood, kingwood, holly, rosewood and tulip-wood. Chestnut and sycamore were also seen a good deal. Inlay and marquetry were both popular as a means of decoration, but were generally found in bands rather than in the complicated floral patterns of the 17th century.

Painted furniture was in vogue from about 1770. This was either decorated in panels or sections painted in floral and festoon patterns, or, less often, painted all over the article. In the former case, the paint was applied to the fine satinwood or mahogany veneer; in the latter, a cheaper wood was employed, either beech or pine. Well-known artists would paint allegorical scenes, like those of Adam ceilings, on panels in ovals or circles on important items of furniture. Such figure compositions were sometimes painted on copper and then sunk into the wood surface. **Gilt** used in conjunction with paint was very popular, especially for mirrors and picture frames, and also for drawing-room furniture. A type of gesso was still employed and, with gilding, provided relief ornament without carving. Other means of decoration

233

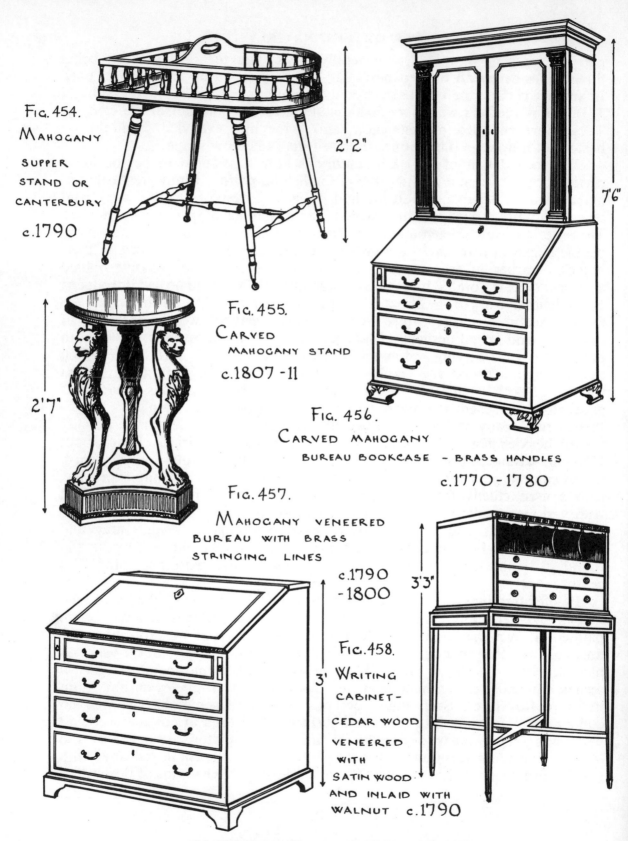

FIG. 454.
MAHOGANY
SUPPER
STAND OR
CANTERBURY
c.1790

2'2"

7'6"

FIG. 455.
CARVED
MAHOGANY STAND
c.1807-11

2'7"

FIG. 456.
CARVED MAHOGANY
BUREAU BOOKCASE - BRASS HANDLES
c.1770-1780

FIG. 457.
MAHOGANY VENEERED
BUREAU WITH BRASS
STRINGING LINES

c.1790
-1800

3'3"

3'

FIG.458.
WRITING
CABINET-
CEDAR WOOD
VENEERED
WITH
SATIN WOOD
AND INLAID WITH
WALNUT c.1790

454–458 *Later Georgian Furniture, 1760–1811*

were provided by scagliola, and Wedgwood jasper-ware panels and medallions inset into the furniture. Lacquered and japanned furniture was seen until about 1765, but tended to go out of fashion after this.

From about 1795 onwards, the French Directoire styles influenced English furniture. Designs became simple, with curved lines. Decoration was by gilding, inlay and carving once more, and motifs were Egyptian as well as Greek, including winged sphinxes—used as leg supports, or with the head alone, as a decorative motif—lions' heads, serpents entwined and hocked animals' legs. Also typical were the Grecian scroll-ended couches and X-framed chairs.

During the first twenty years of this period, two names stand out in the realm of furniture-designing: those of **Robert Adam** and **Thomas Chippendale** (1718–79). It has already been said of Adam that he designed furniture and furnishings for his houses and rooms; he was as eminent in this field as in architecture and interior decoration. His earlier ideas were generally in carved furniture, in mahogany, but

459 *Hepplewhite Style Bedstead—satin hangings lined with silk—carved mahogany posts, cornice and headboard, c. 1794*

he is more especially noted for gilt and painted designs, or those with delicate inlay and marquetry, using satinwood and other fine woods. Drawing-room pieces were usually gilt and/or painted, with slender, tapering legs and, if suitable, silk-covered upholstery. Towards the end of the century, his work was very slender and fragile, being most suitable for feminine use. He introduced the same motifs as in his interior decoration: medallions, oval and circular paterae, the anthemion, the fret, flutings, swags and festoons. In his *Collections of Designs* there are hundreds of furniture designs in engraved plates. **Chippendale** had, as has already been described, made his name before 1760,

235

but from then until his death in 1779, he continued to be one of the most important influences in the furniture of the day. He was primarily a cabinet-maker, not an architect like Adam, but he designed a great deal of furniture also. At other times he carried out other men's ideas and much of this work was for Adam himself. A great deal of his furniture was in mahogany, though he did adapt some of his models to gilt furniture and satinwood. His chairs are particularly noteworthy for their beautiful proportions and crafts-manship. He published the third edition of his *Director* in 1762.

Other designers also established in this period, whose work is sometimes overshadowed by that of Adam and Chippendale, but whose furniture is nevertheless of high standard and whose influence was considerable, were **Thomas Shearer, William Vile, John Cobb, William Ince, Thomas Mayhew** and **Robert Manwaring**. Some of these also published their designs in book form, and all were highly skilled craftsmen in charge of many skilled men.

The two outstanding names in this field in the later period from 1780 onwards are those of **George Hepplewhite**, who died in 1786,[1] and **Thomas Sheraton** (1751–1806). **Hepplewhite's** influence on furniture design was far-reaching, though it is strange that comparatively little is known of the man himself. His *Cabinet Maker's and Upholsterer's Guide* was published post-humously in 1788, with further editions in 1789 and 1794. These publications had a profound influence on other designers and cabinet-makers. He was himself a craftsman as well as designer and had a business in Cripplegate in London from the 1760's. He is famed for his shield-and-oval back chairs, which had a curved section to fit the occupier comfortably. He also designed bow-fronted chests, serpentine-fronted furniture, sideboards, tallboys, book-cases and bedsteads. Much of his furniture was simple and delicate, and he used similar motifs to those of Adam, though he also included his now famous Prince of Wales's feathers. Many items were exquisitely carved, others painted and gilt, or inlaid, whilst legs were gracefully tapered. **Sheraton**—a designer of the late 18th century—was trained in Durham as a cabinet-maker, but when he came to London about 1790, he devoted himself to designing and publishing his work. Among such publications are *The Cabinet Maker's and Upholsterer's Drawing Book*, 1791–94 and 1802, *The Cabinet Dictionary*, 1803, and *General Artists' Encyclopaedia*, 1804–06. His furniture is noted for its apparent fragility, this quality of delicacy tending to extremes at the turn of the century, to become thin and spidery, the legs appearing unable to take the weight of the structure, let alone added stress, but this is illusory. Much of his work resembled that of Adam and Hepplewhite, because he used similar motifs. However, his chair-backs were often rectangular instead of shield or oval, and he had an especial preference for inlaid or refined painting on furniture rather than carving.

[1] Year of birth not known.

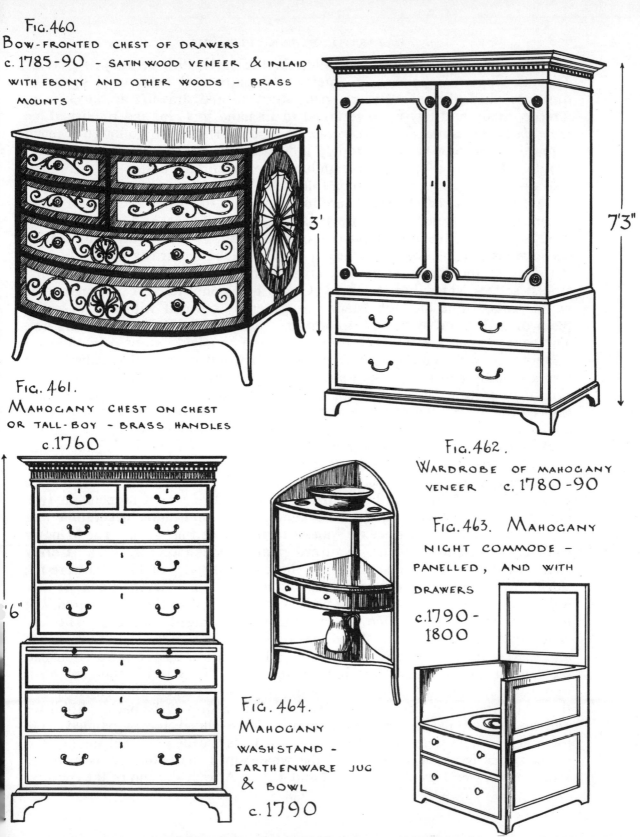

FIG. 460.
BOW-FRONTED CHEST OF DRAWERS
c. 1785-90 - SATIN WOOD VENEER & INLAID
WITH EBONY AND OTHER WOODS - BRASS
MOUNTS

3'

7'3"

FIG. 461.
MAHOGANY CHEST ON CHEST
OR TALL-BOY - BRASS HANDLES
c. 1760

6"

FIG. 462.
WARDROBE OF MAHOGANY
VENEER c. 1780-90

FIG. 463. MAHOGANY
NIGHT COMMODE -
PANELLED, AND WITH
DRAWERS
c. 1790 -
1800

FIG. 464.
MAHOGANY
WASHSTAND -
EARTHENWARE JUG
& BOWL
c. 1790

460–464 *Later Georgian Furniture, 1760–1811*

Another name worthy of mention in the early 19th century is that of **Thomas Hope**. Hope was an interior decorator and amateur designer of furniture, and after some years spent studying and drawing architecture in Greece, Sicily and Egypt, he returned to England in 1796, and published his *Household Furniture and Decoration* in 1807. His work followed French Empire styles, and he was strongly influenced by both Greek and Egyptian motifs. He had a considerable influence on furniture design of this time; also on the Regency period which followed.

Actual items and classes of **furniture** had, by 1760–1811, become far more numerous and varied; therefore it is proposed to deal with such items in groups. One of the most important of these groups is that comprising **seating accommodation**, of which the variety now available contrasts markedly with the days of the Medieval chest. There were now many patterns of chairs, stools, settees, sofas and couches. **Chairs** had upholstered, cane, leather or wood seats, while the upholstery was generally covered with silk or satin, plain or with floral or striped decoration. Some styles had arms, others not. The backs varied greatly, both in carved wood or inlaid and/or painted wood patterns, or with cane or upholstery inside a wood frame. The cabriole leg was gradually superseded by a straight leg, usually tapered, either turned or square in section, and becoming slenderer towards the end of the century. Carved mahogany chairs were popular until 1770, but after this gilt or painted chairs or those with inlaid decoration were more usual, though the carved back remained during the whole period. Among the carved and inlaid wood-backed chairs were the **ladderback style**, as seen from 1750 (see Figs. 377 and 413), the **lyre-back splat type,** where brass stringing was often introduced (see Figs. 418 and 427), and the **carved splat** of mid-century Chippendale type (see Fig. 377). Other splats were carved with **anthemion decoration** (see Figs. 416 and 428) or **Prince of Wales's feathers** (see Fig. 419). The **Windsor chair** continued to be made, in turned pliant woods (see Fig. 417). **Corner chairs** were also still in fashion. The most typical styles of 1775–95 were the **shield**, **oval** and **heart-shaped backs**. These were in carved wood or upholstered in a wood frame. The back was connected to the upholstered seat by some form of decoration, often representing winged sphinxes. The legs were tapering and generally fluted (see Figs. 378, 382, 414, 415, 420, 423, 426 and 428). In the later 18th and early 19th centuries, chairs more often had **rectangular backs**, which were lower after 1800. They were inlaid, painted, upholstered, caned or of carved wood. The back turned over slightly, and the arms often swept down in a long curve from the top of the back. Sphinxes and hocked animal legs became common, often gilded and/or painted. On the whole, chairs were rather smaller and seats less wide now that the hooped skirts under feminine dresses and the whaleboned masculine coats were no longer worn (see Figs. 380, 381, 424 and 425). Also at the end of the century,

238

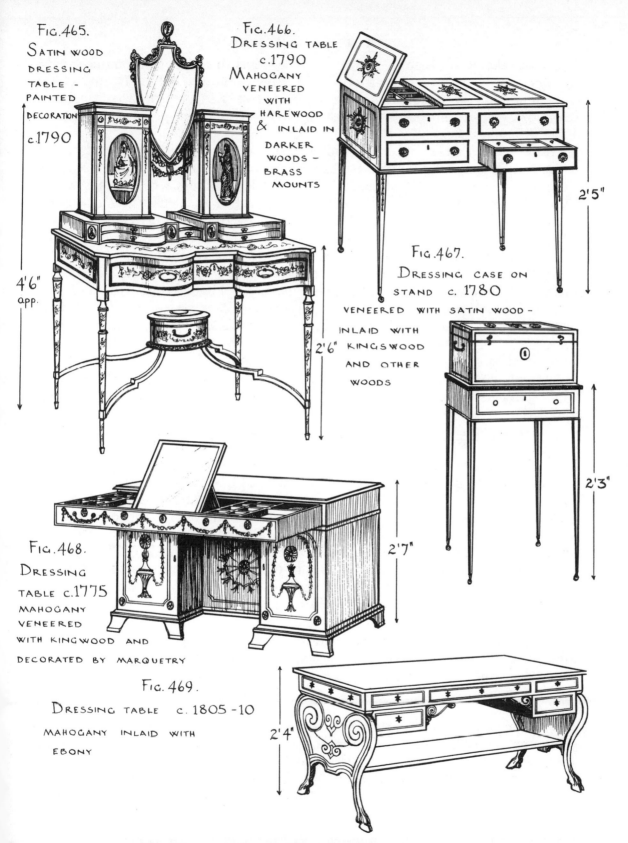

FIG. 465.
SATIN WOOD
DRESSING
TABLE -
PAINTED
DECORATION
c.1790

4'6"
app.

FIG. 466.
DRESSING TABLE
c.1790
MAHOGANY
VENEERED
WITH
HAREWOOD
& INLAID IN
DARKER
WOODS -
BRASS
MOUNTS

2'6"

FIG. 467.
DRESSING CASE ON
STAND c. 1780

VENEERED WITH SATIN WOOD -

INLAID WITH
KINGSWOOD
AND OTHER
WOODS

2'5"

2'3"

FIG. 468.
DRESSING
TABLE c.1775
MAHOGANY
VENEERED
WITH KINGWOOD AND
DECORATED BY MARQUETRY

2'7"

FIG. 469.
DRESSING TABLE c. 1805-10
MAHOGANY INLAID WITH
EBONY

2'4"

465–469   *Later Georgian Dressing Tables, 1760–1811*

japanned chairs of beechwood with cane seats became fashionable again, though in the new prevailing style (see Figs. 421 and 425). Dining chairs were made all the period in sets of six or twelve, with one or two armchairs, while drawing-room chairs were usually in ones or pairs, perhaps making up a set with a settee.

Such **settees** were based on similar designs to the chairs as one style succeeded another; indeed, their backs were frequently made up from multiple chair-backs (see Fig. 432). Some had eight legs, others five. Other settees had long upholstered backs as well as seats, while the legs were in keeping with the prevailing fashions (see Figs. 429 and 430). A lightweight style was produced about 1800, made of japanned or painted beechwood and with a cane back and seat, which would require a squab or cushion.

Sofas, as distinct from settees, were made generally for resting or reclining rather than merely sitting. They were usually upholstered at back and seat, and had developed from the Stuart day-bed. Later styles were in Grecian couch form, with low roll-over back, short curved legs, and a roll cushion at each end. They had frames of carved mahogany or gilded wood, and floral or striped silk covered upholstery (see Figs. 381 and 431). **Stools** had upholstered wood or cane seats, and the legs followed current patterns. Mahogany X-frame stools were seen a great deal from about 1800 (see Figs. 433 and 434).

As with chair design, the number and variety of types of **table** had increased considerably. **Dining tables** were now once more large and long, especially in bigger houses, although, unlike the Jacobean dining tables, they were generally made in sections so that the size could be adjusted to suit the particular occasion. Thus, there was usually a centre table with four legs, and one or more end tables could be attached by hinges or clipped into brass sockets. Double-gate dining tables, with hinged flaps on each end, also existed; side-tables could be added (see Fig. 436). In the late 18th century, sectional tables often had pedestal legs in the required number of sections (see Fig. 380). Some early 19th-century patterns had circular tops on the classical basis, with pedestal or monopodium support (see Figs. 380 and 441). Mahogany was usual for all dining tables.

Pier tables and **side-tables** often had marble, scagliola or mosaic tops and were gilt-framed, with slender legs. The majority were semicircular in plan (see Figs. 378 and 379). In the late 18th century, satinwood, with various woods inlaid to give decoration, replaced the marble tops (see Fig. 437).

Two types of table particularly apposite to the period are the **Pembroke table** and the **sofa table**. The **former** was in common use from 1770, and was generally made of mahogany or satinwood, though japanned versions also were seen. It had a rectangular top with two hinged side-flaps, with delicate

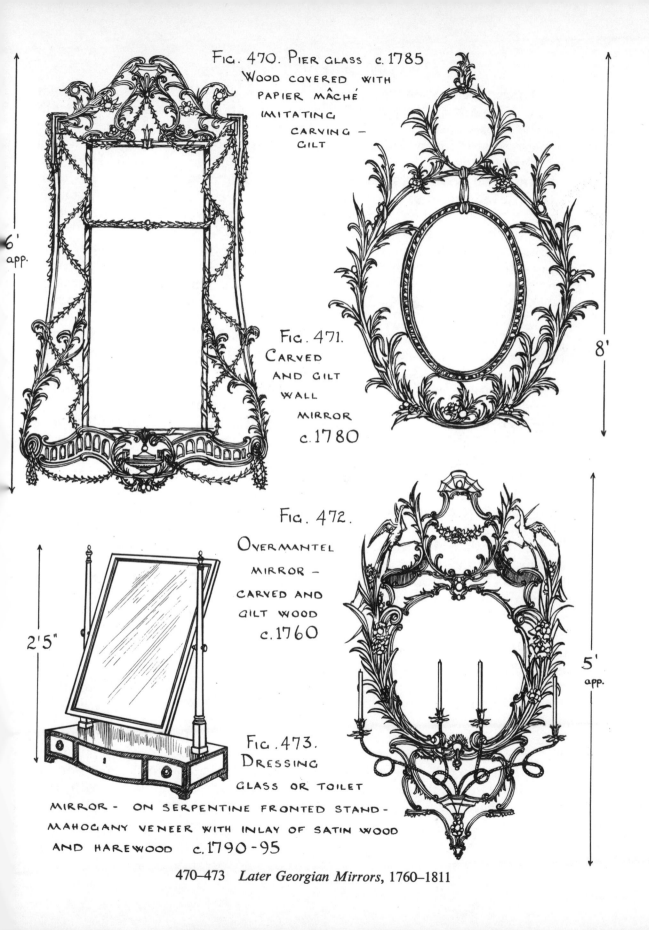

FIG. 470. PIER GLASS c. 1785
WOOD COVERED WITH
PAPIER MÂCHÉ
IMITATING
CARVING —
GILT

6' app.

FIG. 471.
CARVED
AND GILT
WALL
MIRROR
c. 1780

8'

FIG. 472.
OVERMANTEL
MIRROR —
CARVED AND
GILT WOOD
c. 1760

2'5"

5' app.

FIG. 473.
DRESSING
GLASS OR TOILET
MIRROR - ON SERPENTINE FRONTED STAND -
MAHOGANY VENEER WITH INLAY OF SATIN WOOD
AND HAREWOOD c. 1790-95

470–473 *Later Georgian Mirrors, 1760–1811*

tapered legs. A drawer was usual in one side (see Fig. 442). **Sofa tables** were similar but larger; after 1800 they attained about five to six feet in length when the flaps were up. Brackets or trestle ends supported the flaps. Some had sliding panel tops which could be reversed; one side was then inlaid as a chessboard (see Fig. 439).

Library and **pedestal tables** generally had circular tops and were designed to stand in the centre or bay of a room. They were large and solid, usually supported on one pedestal or base, or with four legs, which in the later period were of the hocked pattern (see Figs. 441 and 445).

Allied to such library tables, which had a wealth of drawer space, were **writing tables,** which became very popular with the increased vogue for correspondence, so typical of the late 18th century. These escritoires became smaller and more delicate in design later, but still had adequate drawer space (see Fig. 446).

Among the designs and purposes of small tables were the **tripod pattern** for tea, coffee or chocolate, **work tables**, **card tables** and **reading tables**. The tripod styles still had claw-and-ball feet at first, and the top, which popularly had a "pie-crust" edge, would hinge, to stand flat against a wall when not in use (see Fig. 435). Later versions had plain, tapering tripod legs (see Fig. 377). The tripod stand was used also for other small tables, as in the **reading table** in Fig. 438. **Card tables** were made in varied styles and great numbers, owing to the continuous vogue for gambling. They usually had a hinged top to open and show a baize covering, and were of dainty design. Shapes were rectangular, circular, oval or serpentine (see Fig. 440). **Work tables** and **sewing tables,** like **urn tables**, were small and dainty, and had four tapering legs. The former type would open at the top, displaying a fitted box lined with silk and shaped to take a small drawer, with a pleated silk pouch beneath (see Figs. 378 and 381).

The **sideboard** proper, as distinct from the side-table, is an 18th-century innovation of which the origin is generally attributed to Adam. From 1760 to about 1775, side-tables were used in dining rooms to hold plates of food, napery, silver, etc., and on these were also placed knife boxes and urns. However, Adam designed a side-table to fit between two pedestal cupboards on which were mounted an urn apiece. The urns were metal-lined, and one contained iced water for drinking, the other hot water for washing up the silver. This had to be carried out in the dining room because of the great number of courses and the, as yet, comparative shortage of table silver. One of the pedestals was also used as a plate-warmer and the other as a cellaret. The centre table then had a brass gallery at the back on top for supporting plates, and a knife box and/or urn. Both table and pedestals were of mahogany, though the urns might be of inlaid satinwood mounted with brass or silver (see Figs. 377, 407 and 448). This arrangement developed into a table attached to the two pedestals—in fact a sideboard. Later in the century, sideboards were less massive, and the pedestals were sometimes omitted, drawer space taking their place, for napery and silver. Side-tables were made in sets with the sideboard, and held the urns; all were designed to fit recesses (see Fig. 447).

Other articles of furniture intended to contain or support porcelain, silver ware, napery and food included the **dresser**, the **china cabinet**, the **dumb waiter** and the **canterbury**. **Dressers** had been, by this time, replaced by sideboards in the dining rooms of middle-class and well-to-do homes, and were therefore relegated to the kitchen, where, being capacious, they were laden with crockery, pewter ware and napery (see Fig. 383). However, in smaller homes and farmhouses the dresser remained a dining-room necessity. **China cabinets**, generally with glazed doors, continued to be very popular. They were made in various sizes, and some were of

5'6"

474 *Painted Satinwood Cheval Glass, c.* 1790

hanging style or made to fit a corner (see Figs. 378, 381 and 453). **Canterburies** were designed to hold either plate and cutlery or books and sheet music. The former type was set by the dining table during a meal. It had a wood gallery to prevent articles slipping off the polished surface (see Fig. 454). **Dumb waiters** were introduced in the late 18th century. Most models had a tripod or pedestal base and had two circular shelves or trays on a centre post. Each of these shelves had a metal gallery for safety (see Fig. 381).

There was still a great variety of **cabinets** and cases for other purposes. Among these was a more recent development—the **commode**. This evolved about 1750 from French designs for ornate chests of drawers. Chippendale designed several in rococo style, and after 1760 the commode became a valued piece, and was set against the wall, often under a mirror or picture. Usually made of satinwood, most commodes were bow- or serpentine-fronted and were mounted with ormolu. The tops were decorated with inlaid marble or various woods set in veneer. Often they were painted in designs based on floral or Greek mythological motifs. The doors in front were generally decorated by oval panels, inlaid or painted, and with either drawers or shelves inside (see Figs. 378 and 451). Other **cabinets** followed the styles of the

243

5'

475 *Painted and Gilt Pole Screen—silk-embroidered banner, c. 1775–80*

period, in woods, decoration and designs of legs and ornament. Many had glazed doors. A number still had tops of architectural design in scrolls or a cornice.

Bookcases were now in general use with the increase in the number of books possessed by people of some education. These bookcases were large and solid, made of mahogany, and still rather architectural in design. The upper portion was glazed (see Fig. 449). In the late 18th century, brass trellis work replaced the glazing in the doors; smaller bookcases were designed and greater numbers of them made. From 1808 the revolving bookstand was seen; it had shelves set into a central shaft or column.

Because of the increased interest in correspondence, **bureaux**, **bureau-bookcases** and **writing cabinets** became more numerous, and a new item, the **secretary**, evolved. **Bureaux** still existed with the sloping lid, which let down on to pull-out slides, and had drawers below, but later the roll-top style became more popular, with a tambour which pulled down in side-slots. This tambour operated like a modern roll-top, because it consisted of strips of wood glued to strong canvas. There were also slide-back cylinder tops, but these needed more room at the back for the cylinder when the top was open, compared with the rolled-up tambour. The bureau-bookcase was in two parts as before: a top with glazed or wood doors, enclosing bookshelves, then a let-down or sliding desk top, and either drawers or legs below (see Figs. 381, 450, 452, 456, 457 and 458).

The four-post **bedstead** was still in general use as a prized item of furniture all this period. The cornice or tester and posts were of carved mahogany, now generally uncovered, and the head-board of carved or polished mahogany, though until about 1780 it was still often draped. Posts were plain or fluted, with simple bases and supports. Bed curtains of silk in floral or striped materials gradually replaced the heavy figured velvets and damask, and even these were not always pulled round the bed now, because rooms were warmer and more comfortable. Fringing and tassels still decorated the hangings (see Figs. 382 and 459). Towards the end of the century, beds and hangings became less ornate and massive; carving was reduced, and hangings were less full. Other styles of bedstead made their appearance as alternatives to the four-post type. These included the tent and couch beds. Tent beds were so called because, when the hangings were drawn, they resembled exactly a gable-shaped tent. They were chiefly seen in smaller homes, as they were less expensive; the hangings were only supported on an iron frame.

Couch beds were made as divans or couches, with a wood headboard, footboard and low, curved, wood sides. Of plain and simple design, they generally had roll cushions like the day couches. Mattresses, bed linen and coverlets were similar to those of the previous two hundred years. Mankind had yet to wait for the contribution to comfort provided by the bed spring.

There were rather more and varied items of **bedroom furniture**. By the end of the century, the lady of means would consider a chest of drawers and/or tallboy, a dressing table, a clothes press or wardrobe, a washstand, night commode and several chairs minimum essentials to her comfort. **Chests of drawers** were dignified and elegant pieces of furniture, but still of considerable capacity. They were taller now, with both the top drawers divided in two. Plain and figured veneered mahogany were used in their manufacture all the period, but after 1780 satinwood chests were more popular, inlaid in a decorative manner or painted. Many styles were bow- or serpentine-fronted (see Fig. 460). **Tallboys** were still made, but became redundant in town houses and large country homes when the hanging wardrobes came into favour (see Fig. 461). Until after 1785–90, a **wig stand** was generally placed on a nearby table or chest for easy access from the bed (see Figs. 382, 392 and 395).

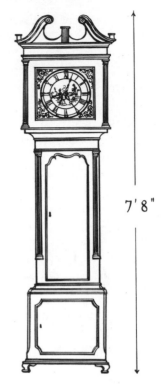

7' 8"

476 *Long-case Clock —mahogany case— brass face, c.* 1780

Dressing tables were considered necessities, whereas previously they had been novelties. Early models were merely chests with a long top drawer divided into many toilet compartments, and containing a mirror which could be raised when the drawer was open. These developed into tables, with a similar mirror and a long drawer (see Figs. 382, 466, 468 and 469). Towards 1800 a more elaborate dressing table was evolved, for the more wealthy homes, of dainty design on tapering legs, and containing small drawers and supporting a hinged mirror on a stand above (see Fig. 465). Mahogany ones were more usual at first, but later types were generally satinwood with painted or inlaid decoration.

Larger items of clothes in the bedroom were generally kept in a **clothes press** until about 1775–80. This was of mahogany, and fitted with shelves inside the top part and large drawers below. In the latter part of the century, **hanging wardrobes** were designed; these were usually after the style of a bachelor wardrobe of to-day. They had a centre portion fitted with shelves, and two side parts for hanging. Large drawers were set below this. Sometimes sliding trays replaced shelves. Mahogany was the usual wood, veneered, and with carved cornice and brass handles. Most wardrobes were large, though refined in proportion and design (see Figs. 382 and 462).

A definite addition to bedroom furniture in this period was the **washstand**. Before this, a ewer and basin had sometimes been kept on a chest or cabinet, but from 1760 a washstand was designed as a special piece of furniture, though later in the century it was sometimes disguised as a cabinet to avoid drawing attention to necessary ablutions. Early washstands were generally supported on a tripod formed by three legs, with a circular rim at the top and a triangular shelf just above the feet. The top rim held the earthenware or porcelain basin. Lower down were fixed small drawers to hold soap and other toilet articles (see Fig. 382). From about 1770–75 a corner style was usual, still with three legs, but having a bow front and three shelves to hold bowl, jug and drawer for toilet necessities. Soap dishes were set by the bowl (see Fig. 464). After 1790 many types were made: some had doors, others were fitted with mirrors, and some just resembled small cabinets. Mahogany, painted pine and inlaid woods were used. A **night commode** or close-chair was general in most bedrooms, and sometimes the former was fitted with drawers and/or a cupboard (see Fig. 463). **Shaving mirrors** were now also becoming fashionable in bedrooms. These had adjustable supports and magnifying lenses (see Fig. 391).

Mirrors of varying kinds were most important in the late-Georgian scheme of decoration; they enhanced the lighting of a room, they ornamented the walls and they were useful. All the famous designers used them in interior decoration: Adam, Chippendale, Hepplewhite and Sheraton mirrors are famous. Some of these, particularly in the years between 1760 and 1790, were very large and quite unsuitable in the average home, but in the large and spacious Georgian drawing rooms were magnificent in effect. Gilt, carved-wood frames were most usual for pier glasses, wall mirrors and chimney glasses, though gilded papier-mâché was used as a substitute. Early patterns from 1760–70 were often still of rococo style, many being designed by Chippendale (see Figs. 471 and 472), but later models, particularly those by Adam, had a rectangular basis, with a decorative top, crested or semicircular (see Figs. 377, 378, 379, 382 and 470). Large mirrors were placed above the chimneypiece or above an elaborate side-table, between window frames on the piers, and were thus called pier glasses (see Fig. 379). Carved motifs included scrolls, swags, urns, paterae and medallions. In the late 18th century, some pier glasses were rectangular, of width greater than the height, and divided into vertical sections by three or four female terminal figures. The convex and concave circular mirrors also became fashionable. Though known as Regency mirrors to-day, many were in use before 1800. Most of these had a gilt, carved frame, decorated by gilt or black balls, and surmounted

246

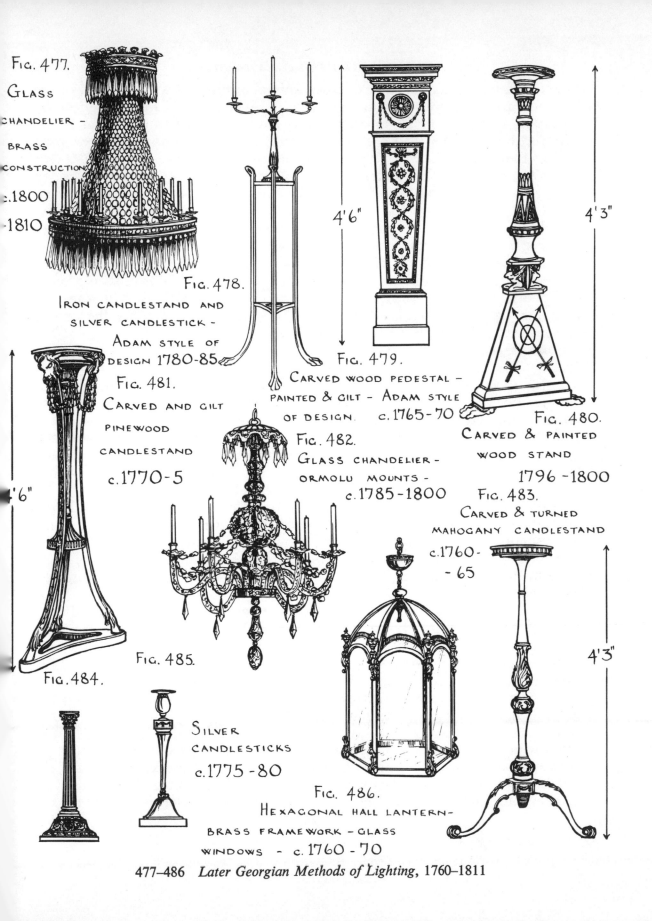

Fig. 477.
Glass chandelier – brass construction c.1800 –1810

Fig. 478.
Iron candlestand and silver candlestick – Adam style of design 1780-85

4'6"

Fig. 479.
Carved wood pedestal – painted & gilt – Adam style of design. c.1765-70

4'3"

Fig. 480.
Carved & painted wood stand 1796 –1800

Fig. 481.
Carved and gilt pinewood candlestand c.1770-5

Fig. 482.
Glass chandelier – ormolu mounts – c.1785-1800

Fig. 483.
Carved & turned mahogany candlestand c.1760- -65

4'6"

Fig. 484.

Fig. 485.
Silver candlesticks c.1775 -80

Fig. 486.
Hexagonal hall lantern – brass framework – glass windows – c.1760 -70

4'3"

477–486 *Later Georgian Methods of Lighting, 1760–1811*

by foliated scrolls and an eagle or other animal or bird. Candlebranches were attached to most wall mirrors in order to increase the lighting effect by reflection (see Fig. 381). Small **dressing glasses**, hinged, and supported by two vertical uprights, and set upon a small box of drawers, had been used during the 17th century. These continued in fashion until about 1790 (see Fig. 473), when the **cheval glass** became more usual for bedroom use, though box types were still made. This cheval or horse glass was of similar design, but much larger, being made to stand on the floor without a box of drawers (see Fig. 474). Their frames were generally rectangular, though in small dressing mirrors oval and circular shapes were common.

There were now more glasshouses than before, and far more glass was made, though it was still costly, because it still had to be blown, then ground and polished by hand. Plates of larger size became available. The Vauxhall manufactory was closed by 1780, but others continued, notably the one at Ravenshead. Some glass was still imported.

Fire-screens were still essential, and provided attractive decoration to the room. The **pole screen** continued to be very popular, though the large rectangular panel of 1760 became much smaller later in the century when oval or circular ones were more fashionable. The mahogany tripod stand was also largely replaced by gilt or painted stands, with slender turned bases or a delicate tripod. There were also cheval screens, which, like the mirrors, consisted of a panel hung between two points on a stand. Both types could be adjusted for height, and had panels of embroidered silk or prints or water-colour paintings (see Figs. 377, 378, 381, 382 and 475).

Long-case clocks continued to be made, but were used only in larger homes until about 1790–1800. Most cases were of mahogany, though some were inlaid (see Fig. 476). Smaller, though highly decorative, mantelpiece and bracket **clocks** were more typical of the late 18th century. Some of these were of gilt and porcelain, and were most ornate, with supporting figures on each side.

There were many types of small, exquisite **boxes** fitted with locks and used to protect valuables. Items of value included jewellery, cosmetics and trinkets, and—surprisingly enough to us—tea; for tea was still a very costly commodity, to be apportioned sparingly by the mistress of the house. **Tea caddies** were generally inlaid and/or painted, or were made of porcelain or earthenware and metals such as silver and pewter. Many designs were octagonal, oval or hexagonal in section (see Fig. 406 and Plate XXVI). Other boxes included **dressing cases** and **work boxes**, lined with velvet or silk and fitted with tiny drawers and compartments (see Figs. 393 and 398).

Papier-mâché work began to be made in the 18th century, although it did not achieve its real popularity until early Victorian times. It was used in England to imitate Far-Eastern lacquer work, and after being made was japanned and decorated with English pictorial scenes or flowers in gold leaf, colour and inlaid mother-of-pearl. The method was invented in Birmingham, and consisted of many layers of wet paper pressed into a metal mould. Each layer was glued to the others, then the whole substance was soaked in linseed oil and tar to make it water-proof. Many small items were made of this material, such as trays, bowls, inkstands and boxes. Metal mounts were added where necessary.

Washing of the person was still considered a somewhat superfluous activity, at least until about 1790–1800, when, after wigs, powdering and cosmetics had gone out of fashion, people attended rather more to personal hygiene. Members of the household washed themselves in their bedrooms at their washstands. **Bathing** was comparatively rare; bathrooms were almost non-existent, and baths, when taken, were from a large bath brought to the bedroom and filled with hot water by the servants. Washing of clothes in the home still took place about once a month, and occupied two or three days.

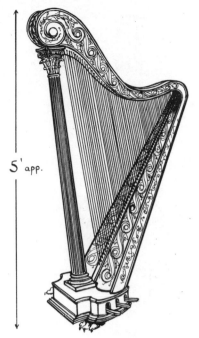

5' app.

487 *Carved and Painted Wood Harp—gilt and blue, late 18th century*

Sanitation had also progressed little. Water closets were invented, and a few were made after 1775. Alexander Cumming took out a patent for a water closet in 1775, and Joseph Bramah produced another method in 1778. Further versions followed, but, apart from the cost of installation, the reason for their limited use was, perhaps, the fact that there was considerable un-pleasantness and even danger from the foul gases attending such appliances, because they were, as yet, fitted with inadequate ventilation. From 1800, closets improved, but were still malodorous. The general method in towns was a privy or closet in the yard at the back of the house, or a larger "bog-house" at the bottom of the garden. These were built over cesspools requiring to be emptied by buckets, which then had to be carried through the house to larger communal cesspools or to the river. In the country, in many cases, these small pits drained through into the drinking-water supply, with fatal results. Sewage disposal was very primitive: night-carts collected from the larger cesspools and emptied their contents into the river. Indoors there were night commodes in bedrooms, and in the dining room there was a set of chamber pots behind a curtain or in the sideboard cupboard, placed for the relief of gentlemen when drinking after dinner and after the ladies had retired into the drawing room.

249

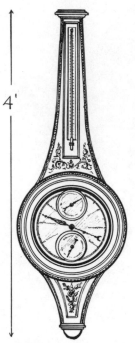

4'

488 *Barometer and*
Thermometer—
mahogany case,
c. 1800

This was a time of overeating and overdrinking by a large section of the community. **Food** was considered to be of great importance in every household budget. A light breakfast was taken of tea or chocolate, with bread and butter, then lunch followed at 11 to 12 noon —a larger meal. The chief repast of the day was dinner at 4 to 5 p.m. This occupied several hours and consisted of many courses, with a great deal of meat of all kinds, vegetables, puddings and fruit. Supper was sometimes taken later. The poor also ate fairly well, at least until the advent of high taxes and cost of living during the Napoleonic Wars at the end of the century, which, unfortunately, coincided with a series of bad harvests. Many then lived at starvation level, and though charity and kindness were shown, the level of wages was altered little. People of means drank imported wines, and also made their own liqueurs and cordials. Spirits were drunk a great deal, especially brandy—which was smuggled in large quantities from France—and gin. Beer was the usual drink of the working man and his family. Soft drinks were popular also, whilst tea, coffee and chocolate were now accepted as necessities, despite their cost. In wealthier households, by 1800, dinner was taken later, and afternoon tea became a pleasant habit with the ladies. Tea still cost up to 25*s.* per pound, and coffee up to 5*s.* per pound, but a great deal of tea was smuggled into the country to avoid payment of the heavy duty on it, enabling many poorer people to obtain it. Sugar was used for sweetening now that adequate quantities were brought in from the West Indies.

Lighting was still by means of candles and rushlights. Good-quality **candles** were bought by the well-to-do; others made their own, as well as rushlights, as before. Lighting was of a better standard now, because more lights were used in a variety of types of support, but, even so, the illumination provided was not what we would consider adequate. The **chandeliers** of the period were very decorative and designed as part of the scheme of the room. Carved wood or ormolu styles existed until nearly 1790, but the glass chandelier gradually ousted these from fashion. Designs generally consisted of S-shaped branches, springing from a centre cut-glass stem, and terminated by cut-glass grease pans. Festoons of cut-glass drops and pendants completed the decorative effect. When the candles were lit in the evening, the result, reflected in the gilt-framed mirrors, was sparkling and romantic (see Figs. 379, 380, 477 and 482 and Plate XXIV). Other types of lighting supports were most varied in

250

form, including wall lights and brackets, vases, girandoles, lanterns and a large number of designs of torchères and stands to hold candlesticks and candelabra. Some of these can be seen illustrated in Figs. 377, 378, 379, 380, 381, 382, 478, 479, 480, 481, 483, 484, 485 and 486, also Plate XXV. From 1800 onwards, colza **oil lamps** began to be used. These had an oil container and burners, and were fitted with a clockwork pump to drive the oil into the wick. Adam's style of Grecian urn lamp was used as a basis for many of these lamp designs. The first gas company was formed in 1809, though gas had been manufactured before 1800. However, gas lighting belongs, in general, to the next period.

This part of the 18th century is renowned as the outstanding time for English **porcelain**. Most of the great factories flourished and many perished in these years. A superb standard of technique, craftsmanship and artistic ability was seen in porcelain ware, as also in the other arts and crafts of the period. Many books have been written on the subject of 19th-century porcelain, and it is therefore only considered necessary to sketch a bare outline here. One of the most famous of the 18th-century factories is that of **Chelsea**, which was at a high level of production and quality of goods in 1760. This continued for another ten years, specialising in great magnificence of colour and gold decoration. Rich coloured grounds were used in turquoise, claret and pea green in particular, with decorative gold borders and central delicately painted panels of flowers, landscapes and figures. Birds, animals and butterflies were also used as painting motifs. In 1770, the factory was bought up by Duesbury of the **Derby** factory, which was also producing in 1760. The

period from 1770 to 1784 is usually referred to as the **Chelsea-Derby** period, when the two factories amalgamated and produced much exquisite work. After 1784, the Chelsea part closed down, but Derby carried on and made porcelain in the late 18th century which echoed the Greek and Egyptian motifs of the day. There were also paintings of Derbyshire landscapes, classical figure compositions and bird, flower and fruit designs. The output was varied indeed.

The **Bow** factory, which was also making fine porcelain in 1760, closed down in 1776,

489 *Rocking Cradle, early* 19*th century—made of turned and joined wood—fitted with clock spring to swing for* 43 *minutes*

490 *Mahogany Hanging Shelves—inlaid decoration, c. 1775*

after the work had dropped in standard and output.

At **Bristol,** Cookworthy set up his factory in 1770, after transferring it from Plymouth, where he had started in 1768. Some good work was done here until the patent rights were sold in 1781 to a firm at New Hall, Staffordshire, where small quantities of the porcelain continued to be made.

Some of the best **Worcester** ware was being made by 1760, in particular dainty tea sets and vases. Transfer printing was used a great deal here. The designs often showed Japanese influence, and much blue-and-white work was produced. In the late 18th century, the standard of product deteriorated to become more commonplace. However, the factory has a fine tradition of craftsmanship and is still functioning to-day.

Smaller amounts of porcelain of less renown—nevertheless of considerable value to us—have come also from the factories at **Liverpool, New Hall, Staffordshire, Longton Hall, Staffordshire,** and **Lowestoft.**

Another famous factory which was functioning in 1760 and still exists to-day is that which started at **Caughley** in Shropshire. In 1760, it was noted for its dark-blue-and-white pottery ware, but did not make porcelain until about 1772. The **Coalport** factory, which had been established about 1790, bought the works in 1799, and since 1814 to the present time it has been known as Coalport ware. This establishment is well known as the originator of the famous Willow Pattern and Broseley Blue Dragon Pattern in the 1780's. It is said that Thomas Minton designed these, but whether their origin was from Oriental legend or European is not fully established. Suffice it to say that the patterns originated here, and, since copied by nearly all other manufactories, still exist to-day as two of the most popular china blue-and-white patterns. Examples of porcelain of this period can be seen in Plates XXII and XXIII.

Salt-glazed **stoneware** was made in Staffordshire all this time in considerable quantities. The white stoneware was often decorated by coloured clays or transfer printing. Some of the work was painted. Salt glaze was also made at Nottingham, but there more generally in brown.

However, all the other **pottery** of the 18th century is eclipsed by the name of **Josiah Wedgwood** (1730–95). He was the first man to produce earthenware of a high standard of design and delicate workmanship which could be sold as a cheap product. Previously, porcelain had been exquisite but costly, pottery had been cheaper but coarser in quality and heavier in design. Wedgwood came from a family of potters in the pottery district—Staffordshire. He was born the thirteenth child of Thomas Wedgwood, potter. When he was nine years old he began to work at Burslem in the family pottery, but at twenty-four he became the partner of Thomas Wheildon, the well-known potter, at Fenton. By 1760 Wedgwood had started his own business at Burslem, and in 1762 was noted for his presentation to Queen Charlotte of a breakfast service of his new cream-coloured earthenware. This was later called "Queensware" and is famous to this day. In 1769, he established a new manufactory which he called "Etruria", after the Etruscans, whose work he used, copied and admired, as Adam did also. "Etruria" is still functioning to-day, and Wedgwood is a household word in the realm of pottery, not only in England, but all over the world. There were six kinds of ware produced at "Etruria", including terracotta, black basalt, white porcelain biscuit and the famous jasper-ware. Jasper-ware is a white porcelain biscuit which can be coloured, with the well-known bas-relief classical figures then left white. These figures were principally designed by Flaxman, the sculptor, for Wedgwood. It can be found in seven colours: blue (the most usual), lilac, sage green, pink, yellow, black and darker green; many of these are still produced to-day.

Wedgwood was an energetic artist and business man. He maintained a high standard of perfection, and would not allow inferior work to leave the factory. His excellent designs were based on the Greek modes of the day, but, like those of Adam, were accurate and beautifully proportioned. Despite this, he catered for the purses of poorer as well as rich people, and so by the end of the century his wares were universally used and praised. A man of foresight, he realised that to be successful in Staffordshire he must improve the transport facilities. Largely owing to his persistence, the canal to connect the Trent and the Mersey was cut. As a result, a shorter route for the conveyance of his clay, salts and flints was made available, enabling costs to be reduced. He had many imitators, but none who reached his standards. His life was devoted to trying to improve earthenwares and make them rank with the fine porcelain of the time. He was elected to the Royal Society in 1783. He

491 *Mahogany Hanging Shelves,*
c. 1770–5

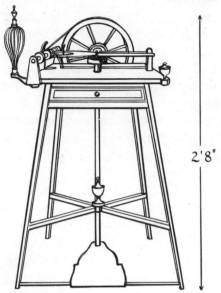

2'8"

492 *Spinning, Wheel, c.* 1790. *Mahogany veneer banded with satinwood*

died in 1795, leaving his family to carry on his work, which they have done until the present day (see Plates XXI and XXII).

A contemporary of Wedgwood, who owed a great deal to his work but who later worked independently in a different way and acquired as much fame, was **Josiah Spode** (the First, 1733–97). He specialised in blue-printed cream earthenware, and, like Wedgwood, he made wares which could be sold cheaply and to all classes. By 1790–95 they were very popular, and created a new fashion in earthenware. Spode had established his factory at Stoke-on-Trent in the 1770's, after having worked also for Wheildon, and the pottery is still working to-day. **William Còpeland** became his partner in 1779, and the combination was a good one: Spode was the potter and Copeland the salesman. When Spode died, his son, **Josiah Spode the Second**, took over the business with Copeland, and began to make porcelain also. He improved on the ware by the addition of bone-ash and felspar, and bone china which we know to-day has evolved from his famous discoveries and experiments of the early 1800's. This ware was durable, and became in great demand in the early 19th century.

Another well-known name in this field is that of **Thomas Minton**, who established a factory at Stoke-on-Trent about 1790, where he made blue-and-white pottery showing Chinese influence. He also made a type of china after 1800.

As with porcelain and pottery, the second half of the 18th century was a time of high standards and fine workmanship in English **glassware**; the technical side of the craft had been mastered, and more varied means of decoration were to hand, while the designs, proportions and artistry were at their best. Wine and spirit glasses were often decorated by white enamel or coloured threads in their plain and twisted stems, especially in red and greens. Opaque white glass was available, and was used in making tea caddies, bottles and vases. A great deal of painting on glass was carried out, using classical, bird, animal and floral motifs. Cut glass was of a very high standard, especially in the late 18th century. Items so treated included chandeliers, wine glasses, candlesticks, bowls and various types of bottles and decanters (see Plate XXIV).

(a) *Tea Urn, Sheffield Plate* (*c*. 1810)

(b) *Cream Jug, Silver-Gilt* (1761–2)

(c) *Silver Jug* (1777–8)

(d) (left) *Silver Candle-stick* (1774)

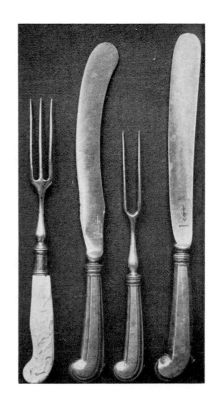

(e) (right) *Knives and Forks with Bone or Silver Handles and Steel Blades* (*18th century*)

(a) *Lamp, Silver-Gilt* (1808)

(d) *Cream Jug, Silver-Gilt*
(1761–2)

(b) *Tea-Caddy, Silver* (1784)

(c) *Tea-Pot, Silver* (1795–6)

(e) *Hot Water Jug and Stand,
Silver* (1805–6)

In **silver ware** also excellent pieces were produced. The rococo designs of mid-century gave place, by 1770, to Adam's influence, and most silver was designed with classical motifs and proportions; as in all other forms of art in this period, the Classic Revival was applied to each different medium as best suited its individual requirements. Far more silver ware was now made and used: even poorer homes boasted one or two highly prized articles in silver, while whole dinner services and tea and coffee sets were used in wealthier establishments. Apart from the adaptation of the classical motifs used in interior decoration and furniture to the silversmith's craft, delicate pierced work was employed a great deal, especially in such articles as trays and sweet-meat baskets. In the early 19th century, the French Empire styles affected silver designs in England, so that the Greek and Egyptian motifs, especially winged sphinxes and lotus leaves, were also seen in this medium. In addition to dinner services and tea and coffee sets, other coveted silver pieces were cruets, centrepieces, candlesticks and candelabra, inkstands, bowls, tankards and tea caddies (see Plates XXV and XXVI). A method of plating was also used, known as "Old Sheffield Plate", after the town of its original manufacture. Employing a silver coating on copper, it was suitable for simpler items (see Plate XXV).

All forms of gambling were still fashionable; bets were placed on almost anything, and lotteries were well supported. Outdoor sports were a source of much pleasure, especially fives, football, horse-racing, golf and the crueller sports of cock-fighting and bull- and bear-baiting. There was also bull-running, where the unfortunate animal was chased through the streets until it was finally exhausted and killed. Hunting continued to be popular, though it was mostly reserved for the well-to-do. Indoors, more books were available, letters written, newspapers read, while dances and visits to the theatre were much appreciated. County cricket matches were established, and by the early 19th century the old game with a curved bat and only two stumps was gradually giving place to the version of the present day.

Music, played by professionals, and as practised by amateurs in the home, was still a predominant means of occupying leisure hours. The **harpsichord** had succeeded the **spinet**, and in this period the **piano** came into our homes to stay. John Broadwood, a Scottish carpenter, was responsible for producing a British "grand harpsichord pianoforte" in the 1780's, aided by Becker and Stodart. He had been working in London for some years, and later evolved the smaller upright pianoforte which became so popular in the early 19th century, to occupy pride of place in many drawing rooms (see Figs. 377 and 381). Other instruments played in the home included the violin, the 'cello, the viol, the double bass, the harp, the guitar lyre, the flute and the trumpet (see Figs. 408 and 487).

NOTES ON ILLUSTRATIONS

Fig. 377. Private Drawing Room. 1760–70

Ceiling, frieze and **walls** of plaster, coloured in different pastel shades. **Stucco** relief decoration on all three in white. Frames to chimneypiece, mirror and pictures also in stucco to match the scheme. **Sash window,** heavy brocade curtains. Polished oak **floor.** Coloured wool **rug. Chimneypiece,** white marble, with carving and inlaid decoration in coloured marble. **Fire grate** and **fender** of burnished steel. **Furniture—Pianoforte,** mahogany case and stand, width 4 ft. approx. **Chair,** carved mahogany, ladderback style, seat velvet-covered. **Armchair,** carved and gilt beechwood, velvet-covered upholstery; height 3 ft. 6 in. **Tripod table,** turned mahogany, height 2 ft. 4 in. **Wall chairs,** carved mahogany, leather seats, height 3 ft. 2 in. **Clock,** inlaid mahogany, height 10 in. **Candlesticks,** brass, adjustable type, height 10 in. when closed. **Pole screen,** carved and turned mahogany, needlework panel, floral pattern, height 4 ft. 9 in.

Fig. 378. Late Georgian Drawing Room. 1770–5

Robert Adam style of decoration and furniture. Plaster **ceiling** and **frieze.** Pastel-shade background and white stucco decoration. Painted panels. Plain plaster **walls,** also in a pastel shade. White-painted dado and wainscot. Polished wood **floor.** Axminster coloured wool **carpet,** design to echo ceiling pattern. White marble **chimneypiece,** plaster decoration on a pale blue background. Steel **grate** and brass **fender.** Carved and gilt pinewood **chimney glass. Wall lights** of carved and gilt pinewood, height 18 in. **Candlestands** of carved and gilt pinewood with **candelabra** on top, total height 8 ft. approx. **Firescreen,** satinwood stand with painted banner, height 5 ft. approx. **Commodes,** mahogany with marquetry decoration, ormolu mounts, height 2 ft. 11 in., width 4 ft. 6 in. **Knife cases,** painted satinwood, height 2 ft. 6 in. approx. **Fireside chairs,** carved and gilt wood, silk-covered upholstery, height 3 ft. 5 in. Two semicircular **side-tables** put together to make a whole circle, painted and gilt wood, height 2 ft. 8 in. Carved mahogany **stand,** height 1 ft. 10 in. Satinwood **urn table,** painted decoration, height 2 ft. 4 in. Silver **coffee-pot,** height 1 ft. 1 in. **Wall chairs,** carved and gilt wood, tapestry-covered upholstery, height 3 ft. 5 in. Mahogany **china cabinet,** inlaid with satinwood, height 7 ft. approx.

Fig. 379. Late Georgian Entrance Hall. 1765–70

Plaster **ceiling** and **frieze.** Low-relief decoration in Adam style. Painted oval and circular panels. Plaster **walls,** simple stucco decoration. Sash **windows,** wood shutters, painted and carved decoration, silk **curtains.** Polished mahogany **doors,** carved decorative panels. Tiled **floor,** black-and-white design to echo ceiling pattern. Brass wall **lights.** Carved and gilt wood **chandelier.** Wall **mirror,** carved and gilt frame. **Table,** carved and gilt decoration. **Pier glass,** carved and gilt frame. **Pier table,** semicircular, inlaid decoration.

Fig. 380. Late Georgian Dining Room. 1795–1800

Plaster **ceiling** and **frieze.** Classical decoration in very low relief. Plaster with painted decoration on **walls.** Alcoves. Polished wood **floor. Carpet** to fit in the scheme with

Temple Newsam, Yorkshire: a room hung about 1806 with Chinese wallpaper (see p. 224)

ceiling design. **Sash windows,** striped silk **curtains** in shades of green, gold cords and tassels, wood curtain **poles.** Glass **chandelier.** Vase **candelabra** in alcoves. Wall **lights,** plaster and gold decoration. Furniture—Mahogany **dining table** in sections with pedestals, brass feet and castors, height 2 ft. 6 in. **Dining chairs,** upholstered seats, decoration by marquetry and brass stringing, height 3 ft. **Chairs** in the bay, japanned beechwood, cane seats, height 2 ft. 9 in. **Table** in bay, circular pedestal breakfast table, mahogany, inlaid top, height 2 ft. 5 in.

Fig. 381. *Late Georgian Private Sitting Room.* 1795–1805

Plaster **ceiling** and **walls.** Simple **cornice** and **dado.** Pale green walls, white stucco work. White marble **chimneypiece** inlaid with coloured marbles, representing ivy leaves in shades of green and brown; height 4 ft. 9 in. approx. Cast-iron **hob grate. Carpet** in coloured wool. **Chimneypiece mirror,** convex type, carved and gilt pinewood frame. **Items on chimney shelf**: Wedgwood vases, earthenware mugs and silver lamp. **Chair** (left), carved mahogany, silk-embroidered seat, height 3 ft. approx. **Chair** (right), painted and gilt beechwood, cane seat. **Dumb waiter,** mahogany tripod, brass galleries and mounts, height 3 ft. 6 in. approx. **Fire screen,** satinwood stand, painted banner, height 5 ft. **Pianoforte,** rosewood and satinwood, inlaid decoration, brass mounts. **Work table,** satinwood, height 2 ft. 6 in. **Silver candlesticks. Sofa,** mahogany frame, upholstery covered in striped silk in gold, red and white. **Bureau-bookcase,** inlaid satinwood, glazed doors, brass mounts, height 7 ft. 2 in. **Hanging cabinet,** mahogany inlaid with brass and various woods.

Fig. 382. *Late Georgian Bedchamber. c.* 1775–80

Decoration and furniture in the style of Robert Adam. Plaster **ceiling** and **frieze** in delicate stucco decoration with painted circular and oval panels. Ground in pale green with white raised ornament. **Walls** covered to dado rail with silk hangings of deep red. **Wainscot** below this level painted white. Polished oak **floor. Carpet,** patterned to imitate ceiling decoration. **Chimneypiece** of statuary marble with green marble inlay. **Basket grate** and **fender,** also **fire-irons,** of burnished steel. **Chimney glass** with carved gilt frame. **Wall mirror,** oval type with carved gilt frame. **Bedstead,** carved wood cornice, posts and headboard, floral patterned silk hangings and coverlet; height 9 ft. 6 in. approx. **Other furniture—Wardrobe,** japanned pinewood. **Chairs,** carved wood and gilt, upholstery-covered in flowered silk; height 3 ft. 3 in. **Fire screen,** carved wood with embroidered silk banner, height 5 ft. **Washstand and towel rail. Mahogany dressing table,** marquetry decoration, mirror attached by hinge to open slide, height 2 ft. 4 in. Semicircular **table,** mahogany, decorated by inlay, height 2 ft. 4 in. **Wig stand, dressing case,** cosmetics, etc. **Candlestand** of carved mahogany and pinewood painted in blue and white, gilt candle-holder, height 4 ft.

Fig. 383. *Late Georgian Kitchen.* 1780–1805

Wood **ceiling** of beams and rafters. Stone-flagged **floor.** Plastered stone **walls. Sash window** with glass—to open. Dog **turnspit.** Iron **chimney crane.** Stone and brick **fireplace.** Dripping tin, spits and rack. Cup dogs. **Oven** at side of fireplace, iron door. **Wood dresser. Stone sink,** cupboards below. Turned wood **chair,** rush seat.

493 *Regency Dining Room, 1811–20 (notes on page 312)*

IX

REGENCY AND EARLY VICTORIAN,
1811–1860

GEORGE III (Regency)	1811–1820	WILLIAM IV	1830–1837
GEORGE IV	1820–1830	QUEEN VICTORIA	1837–1860

IN the 20th century prior to the outbreak of the Second World War, the architecture, arts, interior decoration, furniture and taste of the period from 1811 to 1860 aroused little interest; indeed, the mid- and late-Victorian eras were particularly decried and derided. Latterly, however, interest in the period has revived, and the early Victorian homes are once more beginning to be studied. It is now considered to be modern and informed to be able to see the beauties and charm of early Victorian furniture, wallpapers, carpets, etc., while papier-mâché articles can be seen side by side with Chippendale and Sheraton furniture in antique shops of note. Several fine, often profusely illustrated, books have been written in recent years about Victorian England and its homes, whereas in 1950 it was difficult to find such a work—authors appeared to have lost interest after the year 1830. Recent studies include Mr. Ralph Dutton's *The Victorian Home* and Mr. James Laver's *Victorian Vista.*

From 1811 to 1860 a strong middle class was arising, and with it came an even stronger sense of the importance of both nation and family. The home became a symbol of Victorian stability and prosperity, and the family man strove to occupy as large and expensive a house as possible. In this the family was—willingly or otherwise—united, received friends and callers and gave many dinner parties and receptions.

However, the rising middle class presented only part of the picture of Regency and early Victorian England. At the same time, the **Industrial Revolution** was growing apace, and with it came a steady drift of the increasing population from the country, where unemployment was general, to the already overcrowded towns, where work could be found. Agricultural labourers were very badly paid, uncertain of employment and existed at a poor level of subsistence. The conditions of the poor were aggravated by the war with France, which lasted until 1815.

As a result of the increased demand for labour in the factories, the diminishing employment on the land, and the lack of control of speculative builders and the sale of land, there grew up the first instalment of atrocious housing conditions, particularly in the North of England and the Midlands, which created the bad slums of the present century. The 18th-century slums in London and other large towns had been bad, but this later growth was so rapid that it affected much more extensive areas and a greater number of towns. An attitude of *laissez-faire* on the part of the well-to-do and upper classes contributed not a little to the creation of such living conditions and, later, to their continuance. The face of England altered from being still primarily an agricultural land in 1811, with small factory towns and large country areas, to a considerable encroachment on the countryside by sprawling, smoky industrial towns within fifty years. By 1860 it was becoming difficult to employ and redistribute all the labour flocking to the towns, and emigration to Canada and America increased to a flood, and later in increasing numbers to the settlements in Australia.

There were, however, great benefits from the Industrial Revolution. The railway system was established in the 1830's, and by 1860 far more people were travelling about the country, and even to the Continent, as a result of this new method of locomotion. Road surfaces were improved and travel in stage coaches made easier and more comfortable, so that this means of transport was more patronised.

In Regency England, **prison** conditions were still atrocious, and did not improve until after the passing of the Gaol Acts in 1824. Public hangings still provided a most popular type of entertainment; they were not made illegal until after 1860, although hanging was now only the penalty for severe offences and after 1840 only for murder.

A large number of articles of all kinds were now being produced as a result of the spread of industrialisation combined with new methods of production in quantity. They ranged from furniture to carpets and chair coverings, and from gew-gaws to kitchen ranges. By 1850–55 such articles were, almost without exception, over-ornamented with curling, floral decoration, however ridiculous the result. In the 20th century, we are now apt to refer to this period of mid-Victorianism as the time of the decline or decay of taste. There was, undoubtedly, a lowering of standards of design, but it was one which affected Europe as much, if not more, than England—as can be seen by the foreign contributions to the Great Exhibition of 1851—and should not be blamed, as it so often is, on the Victorians themselves. It was, as has been the case in many centuries, a reaction from the previous hundred years; then rich men could afford the best of design and craftsmanship, and had been educated by long years of training and upbringing to appreciate high standards in this respect. Less well-to-do people could not afford to indulge

494 *Regency Drawing Room, 1811–20 (notes on page 312)*

their tastes in this direction. By 1840–60 the new, large middle class could easily afford the mass-produced article, but, in general, had not been educated to desire and insist upon good design. They received what they liked and what they deserved, and who was to blame, the consumer or the manufacturer who supplied such goods? A parallel case can well be drawn to-day, by anyone who gazes into shop windows containing furniture of inferior workmanship and design, copied—most inaccurately—from earlier styles. A high price indeed has to be paid for the few exceptions.

With the increased importance of family life and the desire for larger homes by the middle classes came a need for more and more **servants**, to make living in such homes comfortable. But, poorly paid though they were, servants were easy to come by, and even those people who were comparatively poor had at least one maid. Wages for servants were about £12 a year, and for this modest sum a woman had to work a very long day, was often fed inadequately, and slept uncomfortably, usually in the attic.

Although the rise to wealth and comfort by many and the sufferings of an even greater number of the poor continued almost unheeded side by side, there were both active and passive reformers at this time. One of the best known of these was Charles Dickens, who, by his writings from 1850 onwards, portrayed the true state of affairs, which the majority of contented middle-class folk did not realise. Another well-known figure who did much to improve living and working conditions was Prince Albert. He was particularly interested in the building of homes, schools and hospitals, and much work was carried out, at this time, on such schemes, as well as on public baths and asylums.

After the rather more frivolous and riotous days of the Regency, the early Victorians settled down to a time of religious revival—a revival symbolised by a Puritan outlook. This was especially apparent on Sundays, which in many homes were passed most literally as a day of rest, and, for the children in particular, were later remembered as interminable days to be endured solemnly without the aid of toys, books, games or work of any kind. The resulting vacuum was only partially filled by Bible readings and prayers.

Although there were as yet most inadequate means for educating the mass of the population, **secondary education** for the sons of the well-to-do, professional and middle classes was now becoming of a higher standard and increasing in scope. This was largely due to the growth and development of public schools. The old-established public schools continued to flourish, but newer ones were growing, and, with the example of such as Rugby—with its famous and enlightened headmaster, Dr. Arnold—were being reformed. The Industrial Revolution gave rise to a desire and need for education at all levels, particularly in science and engineering. To help to meet this need, the Mechanics Institutes spread their successful teaching from Scotland (where

495 *Early Victorian Parlour, 1837–45 (notes on page 312)*

they were established by Dr. Birkbeck) to England. To help supply the growing need for more **university education**, London University was founded in 1827, and students who could not go to Oxford or Cambridge attended.

These advances in education were, in the main, reserved for sons, who were considered to be the important members of a family; a girl's needs in this direction were almost always sacrificed to those of her brothers. The little education granted to daughters still took place at home in most cases, and was on 18th-century lines. A woman's sole purpose in life, as yet, in middle- and upper-class homes, was to marry well and bear a large number of children. It was just too unfortunate if, through no fault of her own, she failed to achieve either aim, and she came to be regarded, as she grew older, as an object of pity and shame. Women of poorer status worked in agriculture if of village stock, or in factories if living in a town. Although they worked very hard, for long hours, under bad conditions and for very little pay, at least they were saved the unutterable boredom of their more fortunate sisters, who had servants to do their housework, and were not allowed to go out to work, and so had to spend their day visiting and paying calls, doing endless and often useless embroidery, or indulging in a little genteel drawing, water-colours or music. On the other side of the picture, due partly to the rigid code of morality of the day, and to the hard line drawn between a code of behaviour for men and one for women, the number of prostitutes was steadily growing. Many girls began this life owing to an unhappy mistake, or an unfair advantage being taken of their ignorance of sex, which, in well-brought up young girls, was generally abysmal.

In addition to the often unfortunate growth of the industrial Midlands and North of England already referred to, other large towns, notably **London,** were expanding quickly. In the capital the population was over one and a half millions, and villages around London which were being developed in Regency times included Hammersmith, Battersea, Wandsworth, Fulham, Bow and Camberwell. By mid-19th century they were becoming suburbs of London itself, and well-to-do homes were being built further out at Richmond and Twickenham. Nearer the centre of the city, many new building projects were planned and completed: in dockland, the West India Dock, London Dock, the Surrey Docks and the East India Dock were all established; Waterloo, Southwark, Hammersmith and Vauxhall bridges were constructed; and in the world of art, the British Museum and the National Gallery were completed, while the Haymarket Theatre represented the field of drama. However, London too had its bad slum areas. Many of these were the same districts which had been slums as far back as the Great Plague of 1665—for example, Bethnal Green and Whitechapel. But others existed also, even dwellings in what is now Mayfair. Tenement houses with very small rooms existed where people lived a family to a room, with only the most primitive

496　*Early Victorian Drawing Room, c. 1840–8 (notes on page 313)*

of cooking and sanitary arrangements and in dirt indescribable. However, many open spaces were reserved and restricted in the capital in this period for the use of Londoners; notable amongst these was the Victoria Park, which was, and still is, an oasis in London's East End.

In general, **Regency architecture** followed on the classical lines, its chief exponents being Sir John Soane and John Nash. A great deal of building was done in London and other towns, also in seaside resorts, where the typical Regency stucco façades could be seen in crescents, terraces and squares. The stucco was painted in shades of stone colour, and this was enhanced by the decorative iron balconies and the bow or bay windows which often extended up three or four storeys. The larger homes were of stone or stucco, detached or in terrace style, in bold, simple, classical architecture, with portico and columns, and steps leading up to the front door. A fine example of this period was Nash's Regent Street, which, unfortunately, apart from the Quadrant plan, remains no longer. Smaller Regency homes were of brick, but still had bow windows and iron balconies. Sir John Soane's influence could be seen in the flatness of the ornament into very low relief, or even inlay, and in the simplification of most forms. In the interior, ornament almost disappeared from walls and ceiling, while cornices were often omitted altogether. The Greek form of decoration was still used, but sparingly and with linear treatment. Frets and reeding were the most usual forms of decoration.

Architecture of the first years of **Victoria's reign** showed little change: much of the work was classical and followed closely on Nash's style. Streets and squares in London and other towns were built mostly in a plain, solid classical style with cube blocks of stucco or yellow brick and slate roofs. Many houses in towns were beginning to be very tall and narrow owing to the increased desire for large homes and to the lack of ground space. Thus we have the classical Victorian basement house with four or five storeys above the ground floor, as seen in Earl's Court and South Kensington. In country areas, considerations of space did not so restrict the plan, and homes were more pleasantly proportioned. In London, much credit is due at this time to the builders Thomas Cubitt and James Burton. In the early Victorian period, Cubitt organised building development in Bayswater, and later Pimlico and South Kensington, making homes for well-to-do and middle-class people who desired spacious, dignified and solid property. He built in the 18th-century tradition, though the result was rather heavier and lacked some of the charm and lightness of the earlier period. However, the good basic design was there and the building construction so good that many of these houses stand to-day, and if they have been adequately kept up, look well and spacious besides their later but more tawdry neighbours. At the same time came the expansion of Belgravia, the surrounding area of Buckingham Palace, which was designed in its now famous squares and streets.

497 *Victorian Bedroom, c. 1850–5 (notes on page 313)*

Although the classical style of architecture continued in use in early Victorian England, the fashion for **Gothic Revivalism** was growing fast. This movement had begun in the 18th century, as referred to in Chapter VIII, but it was from about 1840 that it became a vigorous and, by the mid-Victorian period, a paramount activity. An early example, in Regency times, was Alton Towers, Staffordshire, which showed the Medieval influence, but its interpretation was loose, and the ensemble of flying buttresses, spires and towers was a 19th-century version of Gothicism. From this time onwards, the Revival grew in popularity with both architects and individual members of the public, but the refinement of 15th-century architecture was absent, both proportions and ornament often being faultily reproduced. Unfortunately, as the movement grew in fashion, many well-to-do owners of lovely homes of Tudor and Stuart origin had them altered or developed in the new Gothic mode, generally with unhappy results. By 1850–60 Gothic was the prevailing style of architecture and was adapted for use in homes large and small, though in the former instances, the design was of higher quality. Gothic Revival patterns had now become **Victorian Gothic**, with greater ornamentation. The chief exponents included Sir Charles Barry, Sir George Gilbert Scott and A. W. N. Pugin, although James Wyatt was one of the earlier adherents.

In the **interior** of **Regency homes** there was a feeling of lightness, both in atmosphere and colour, as compared with both the 18th and the later 19th centuries. Windows generally were large and draped with light-coloured silk, linen or chintz curtains, often striped or delicately sprigged to echo the gowns of the day. The curtains were held back from the window to allow the light to enter the room. Wallpaper and upholstery were in sympathy with the scheme. Greater use was now made of papier-mâché, both for cornice and frieze mouldings, as this was less expensive than carving or stucco, also for furniture. Gradually the 18th-century formality of room arrangement gave place to a homelier atmosphere, and articles were placed nearer the centre of the room and at various angles to the walls. The Grecian form of couch and various tables were set in this manner. As the **Victorian period** advanced, more and more furniture was included in a room. Due to the adequacy of servant labour, it was possible to display and keep clean an abundance of china, glass and wood ornaments, so that many items of furniture were made specifically for this purpose. At the same time, the scheme of the room became darker in tone. Ogee-crested Gothic windows were obscured by lace and heavy plush curtains, wallpaper was darker and heavily patterned in sombre hues, while dull chenille coverings and innumerable embroidered cloths and mats draped items of furniture. By 1855–60 the rooms became a heterogeneous mixture of furniture old and new, ornaments, plants and knick-knacks with hardly any floor space between. The same profusion covered the walls, in the form of paintings, engravings and china. The plan

498   *Early Victorian Parlour, 1850–5 (notes on page 314)*

of the house also became more complicated by 1850: there were many passages, rarely straight and unbroken in line, innumerable stairs, due to the increase in height of middle-class and poorer dwellings in towns, and recesses and projections for fireplaces and windows. The introduction of aniline dyes late in this period resulted in more strident colour schemes in the home, seen particularly in upholstery coverings, curtains, carpets and wallpapers. These dyes gradually replaced the earlier more subtle tones of vegetable dyes, and at first were very loud in hue. Particular favourites were Prussian blue and chrome yellow.

The tremendous development in the building of homes for factory workers in the industrial areas of England and Wales from about 1820 onwards was almost unchecked both in direction and quality, and many square miles of country land were soon covered by ugly, mean buildings, row upon row of identical hovels, miserable to look upon and sordid to live in. The **back-to-back homes**, so typical of the Midlands and the industrial North of England, were the worst of these, and their numbers were appallingly great; unfortunately some still exist to-day. Mr. John Gloag in his book *The Englishman's Castle* aptly refers to such homes, saying, "The slave quarters of the Roman villa-house, the wattle-and-daub huts of Saxon serfs and Medieval villeins were better than dank, brick boxes, designed and built by greed." The cheapest of materials were used, and these soon became coal-black from the industrial atmosphere. Once a hundred homes were built on each acre of ground, while the term "back-to-back" meant that the house was one room deep and wide, of about 11 feet square, and each house was built on to the one in front, with a narrow court between each set of streets. There was no yard or garden, and the home was lit only by a small window overlooking the court. Each floor had one room with a staircase opening into it and occupied by a whole family. There were no cupboards or larders, no sinks and no water. The only tap was in the court, and both this and the neighbouring privy were for the use of the whole row of houses. The tenement blocks of the North and in London were little better. Rooms were let at about three shillings a week. Stairs were steep and dangerous, and sanitation was often non-existent. In the country areas, conditions were better, and the light and clean air in themselves alleviated the situation. Some cottages were small but well-built, but others still had no ceilings and an earth floor.

Among the **famous buildings** constructed in this period are such varied edifices as the Palace of Westminster,[1] Buckingham Palace and Balmoral Castle. The Palace of Westminster is a familiar silhouette, and an example of Gothic Revivalism at its best. It was designed by Sir Charles Barry, whose design was accepted in 1836, and the building was generally completed by 1850. It is a fine site and the workmanship is excellent. The exterior

---

[1] Now referred to colloquially as the Houses of Parliament.

(a) *Snuffers and Pan, Silver* (1823–4)

(b) *Salvers, Sheffield Plate* (*c*. 1825)

(c) *Inkstand, Silver* (1823)

(d) *Tea-Pot, Sheffield Plate*
(*c*. 1825)

(e) *Hot-Water Jug, Silver*
(1826)

(f) *Caster, Gilt* (1816–17)

(a) *Oil-Lamp, Brass* (1820–30)

(b) *Candlestick and Candelabrum*
(c. 1810)

(c) *Pocket-Flasks. Nailsea (c.* 1825)

(d) *Glass Paperweight and*
Roundel, both with
Cameos (1820–30)

499 *Kitchen of a Royal Palace—Regency, 1815–20 (notes on page 314)*

silhouette is most impressive, situated on the north bank of the Thames, with its towering pinnacles and delicate tracery rising into the sky and reflected in the flowing river. Much of the credit for the interior is due to Pugin: this is less light-hearted and less exquisite, more sombre and impressive. As Buckingham House, the Buckingham Palace site had been owned by George III since the 1760's. But it was George IV who planned to make it into a palace and to leave Carlton House which had just been replanned and decorated for him. Nash made the designs for the new palace and the work was begun in 1825. These designs incorporated the Marble Arch in the forecourt and an entrance portico of two storeys with Corinthian columns. There was a great deal of criticism of these designs, and complaints that too much money was being spent. The Palace was still uncompleted in 1830 when William IV came to the throne, and a Select Committee took the work out of Nash's hands and commissioned Edward Blore to finish it. By 1837 it was complete and Queen Victoria was the first monarch to occupy it, which she did in the same year. It was enlarged again in the 1840's, and the Marble Arch was later removed to its present site. The Palace was finally altered considerably by Sir Aston Webb in 1913. The Balmoral Estate was bought by Prince Albert in 1852, and he designed the present castle and had it built on the site. It was constructed of granite in the Scottish baronial style with many turrets. Tartan prevailed in the interior decorative scheme, which was comparatively simple in theme. The Royal Family have used the Castle since 1855.

No description of the English home of the Victorian era would be complete without a reference to the **Great Exhibition of 1851**, for this highly successful enterprise, sponsored by Prince Albert, reflected most clearly the numerous articles designed for the domestic sphere, manufactured both in England and abroad. To 20th-century thought and taste, the standard of design, and particularly ornament, is somewhat abhorrent, but, as mentioned earlier in this chapter, opinion is now veering round once more towards such styles of workmanship. There is little doubt that at the time the Exhibition was immensely popular, both with royalty, the well-to-do and the ordinary man and woman, and criticisms were remarkably few. The Exhibition site was in Hyde Park, and great controversy arose over a suitable building to contain it. A competition was held and over two hundred designs were submitted, but the one finally selected was by Joseph Paxton. The formal opening was on May 1st, 1851, by Queen Victoria and Prince Albert. The building was later christened the Crystal Palace by *Punch*—a name which has adhered since then. Paxton was a gardener, and had interested himself in the design of glasshouses since the 1820's. He became head gardener to the Duke of Devonshire and, in 1837, designed the Great Conservatory at Chatsworth. Thus the description by Mr. Nathaniel Lloyd in his book *The English House*

500 *Victorian Kitchen from Middle-class Town House, c. 1850–60 (notes on page 314)*

501   *White Marble Chimneypiece with Carved Decoration—fire opening—black with gilt ornament—steel grate, 1811–25*

of "Paxton's big greenhouse" is an apt one when referring to the Crystal Palace. It was an amazing structure, 1,851 feet in length and about 450 in width, comprising a tremendous area of glass in large panes set into an iron framework. It required over six hundred columns to support it, and elm trees from the Park continued to grow and flourish inside it as a part of the scheme. By an incredible feat it was erected in Hyde Park in seventeen weeks, and later dismantled and re-erected at Sydenham, where it provided a familiar landmark to Londoners until its spectacular destruction by fire in 1936. There was a good deal of criticism of this original use of materials in architecture, but also great popular acclaim, and it was hailed as the dawn of a great new era in architectural design. Our evidence of the Exhibition itself is contained for us to-day in the Illustrated Catalogue, which, rather unfortunately, was illustrated by hard, line drawings which do not show the exhibits at their best. It is a pity that the first-class photography of to-day was not then available.

Apart from the Exhibition building and various conservatories and glass-houses, there were arising many new uses for **cast iron**, even by Regency times. For example, the new Royal Pavilion at Brighton has much cast-iron work inside and outside; the interior has several iron columns and an iron staircase

274

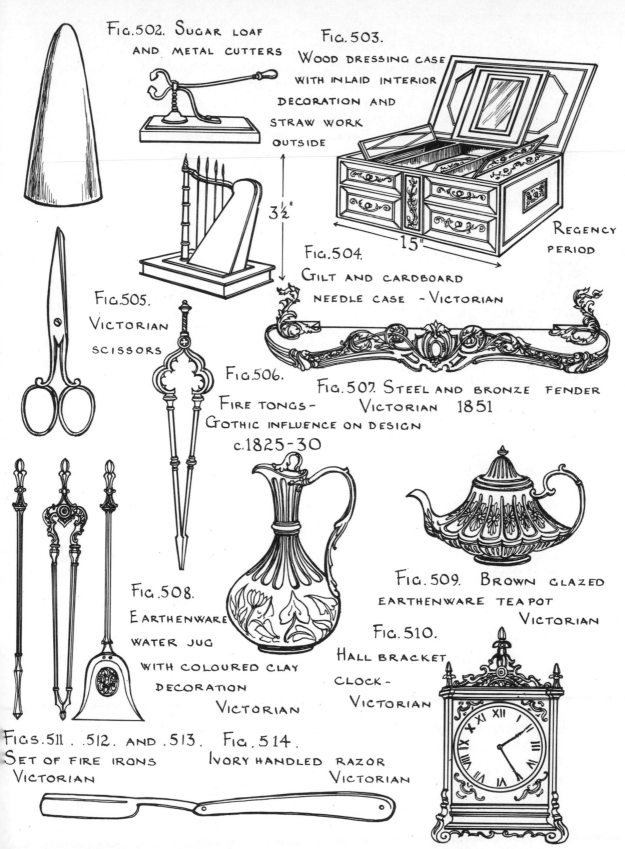

FIG. 502. SUGAR LOAF AND METAL CUTTERS

FIG. 503. WOOD DRESSING CASE WITH INLAID INTERIOR DECORATION AND STRAW WORK OUTSIDE

REGENCY PERIOD

15"

3½"

FIG. 504. GILT AND CARDBOARD NEEDLE CASE - VICTORIAN

FIG. 505. VICTORIAN SCISSORS

FIG. 506. FIRE TONGS - GOTHIC INFLUENCE ON DESIGN c.1825-30

FIG. 507. STEEL AND BRONZE FENDER VICTORIAN 1851

FIG. 508. EARTHENWARE WATER JUG WITH COLOURED CLAY DECORATION VICTORIAN

FIG. 509. BROWN GLAZED EARTHENWARE TEA POT VICTORIAN

FIG. 510. HALL BRACKET CLOCK - VICTORIAN

FIGS. 511. 512. AND 513. SET OF FIRE IRONS VICTORIAN

FIG. 514. IVORY HANDLED RAZOR VICTORIAN

502–514   *Miscellaneous Items, Regency and early Victorian, 1811–60*

and balustrade. Balconies, staircase balustrades and railings were commonly made from cast iron. By 1850–60 there tended to be a misuse of the medium, and the highly decorated lamp standards and park benches are present reminders of such misuse, over-ornamented as they are with floral motifs. It became a very common medium, as it was inexpensive, easy to manufacture and most durable, but it was often employed for articles which would have been much preferable in other materials—in general, wood.

The **garden**, by the Victorian period, was essential to most homes, and not merely confined to the well-to-do house or the country cottage. The formalised 18th-century gardens had now given way to naturalistic free gardens, whatever the scale, with winding paths, odd-shaped lawns and, those plants so dear to Victorian hearts, evergreens in the shape of privet and laurel. With a preponderance of these, there was apt to be a sombre air to the garden as well as in the house by 1860—a predominance of dark green outside and dark red inside.

The chief contributors to **Regency architecture** were **Sir John Soane** (1755–1837), James Wyatt (1764–1813) and **John Nash** (1752–1835). **Sir John Soane** continued his late 18th-century work, and his designs became simpler and more and more linear. His use of decoration was severely restricted and in very low relief or even inlay. Two of his best-known works of this time are his own house in London, now the Soane Museum, built in 1812–14, and the Art Gallery and Mausoleum at Dulwich, 1811–14. **Wyatt** continued his work on the Gothic Revival theme, but this was abruptly terminated by his death in a carriage accident in 1813, and his work in hand was completed by his nephew, Jeffrey Wyattville. **Nash** became architect to the Prince Regent in this period, and continued working for him later when the Prince became George IV in 1820. Nash was thus given a great opportunity of designing large areas of London and parts of other towns. He was an exponent of classicism in stucco, and his façades in the Regent's Park area are justly famous. He published his designs for Regent's Park in 1812, and the original scheme, later curtailed as too costly, was to build a great thoroughfare to link the Regent's House in Carlton Terrace with the Regent's Park. Nash's Regent's Park terraces and crescents, which were completed by 1827, are of high renown. These include Park Crescent, York Terrace, Cumberland Terrace and Cambridge Terrace. Regent Street itself was designed by Nash to sweep in one unit of design from Portland Place to Piccadilly Circus, and most of the work was done between 1817 and 1823, while Nash did excellent work in overcoming the objections and difficulties produced by the various occupants of sites on this route. The result was a great success and a tribute to the architect, but sad to say, its qualities of unity and fine proportion and design are not possessed by the present thoroughfare. All that is now left of the original work is All Souls' Church at one end and the Quadrant layout at

515 *Regency Palace Kitchen Fireplace—steel spits turned with chains by power of chimney draught—revolving fan can be seen in opening—iron bars and construction supports—bronze smoke canopy* (1815)

Drawn from the kitchen at the Royal Pavilion, Brighton, by kind permission of the Director, Mr. Clifford Musgrave

the other. Nash also designed the new Brighton Pavilion for the Regent, and carried out some of the alterations and replanning of Carlton House for him. Later Nash made the first designs for the new Buckingham Palace. A well-known architect and builder of this period was **James Burton**, who assisted Nash in his Regent Street scheme and was responsible for much development in the area of Bloomsbury.

Amongst the principal architects of the **early Victorian period** can be numbered **Sir Charles Barry** (1795–1860), **Sir Robert Smirke** (1781–1867), **George Basevi** (1794–1845), **Charles R. Cockerell** (1788–1863), **William Wilkins** (1778–1839), **John B. Papworth** (1775–1847) and **Decimus Burton** (1800–81). **Sir Charles Barry** worked in both classical and Gothic styles, and though he is perhaps most famous for his Palace of Westminster, of Gothic design, and his Manchester Art Gallery, in Greek classicism, much of his best work was in Italian classical vein. He toured Italy in his youth, and later Greece and Egypt and parts of Western Europe. Barry became a Royal Academician and was later knighted in 1852. **Sir Robert Smirke** was a strong classicist, and though his work is often considered solid and uninspired, it is well proportioned and of sound design. He made a tour of Italy and Greece in the early 1800's, and became a Royal Academician in 1811. He worked with Nash on the London schemes, and later his best-known works included Covent Garden Theatre, 1809, his G.P.O. in St. Martins-le-Grand, 1823 (both later destroyed), and the British Museum, on which work was begun in 1823 but was not completed until 1847. **George Basevi**—a cousin of Benjamin Disraeli—was primarily a classicist, whose best-known work is in Belgravia and South Kensington in London and the Fitzwilliam Museum in Cambridge. **Charles R. Cockerell** was a strong classicist, and after a seven years' tour of Greece and Sicily later became architect to the Bank of England in 1832. He was a Royal Academician by 1836, a Professor of the Royal Academy in 1840, and became the first President of the Royal Institute of British Architects. His most famous work is the Ashmolean-Taylorian Museum at Oxford, dated 1845. **William Wilkins** was also a staunch classicist of the Greek school and also became a Royal Academician, and later, in 1837, a Professor of the Royal Academy. His best-known work, which, however, received considerable criticism, is the National Gallery in London, 1832–38. Prior to this he designed St. George's Hospital at Hyde Park Corner. **John B. Papworth** is best known for his domestic building on the outskirts of London, particularly the Dulwich Estate at Brockwell Park, also for areas of Cheltenham. He too favoured the classical style. **Decimus Burton** was the son of James Burton, the builder already referred to; he did a great deal of work in South Coast towns, and in London he designed the Charing Cross Hospital in 1831, and prior to this the famous arch and screen now positioned at the top of Constitution Hill at Hyde Park Corner, and called the Quadriga, from the

FIG. 516.
EARLY VICTORIAN
PAPIER MÂCHÉ
CHAIR — GOLD AND
MOTHER OF PEARL
DECORATION ON
BLACK — CANE
SEAT

FIG. 517.
BENTWOOD
CHAIR — PAINTED
BLACK —
CANE SEAT.
c. 1855-60

FIG. 518.
PRIE DIEU
CHAIR —
MAHOGANY —
TAPESTRY
COVERED
UPHOLSTERY —
FAWN BACKGROUND
EARLY
VICTORIAN

FIG. 519.
c. 1855-60

CANE SEAT
TURNED
WALNUT

FIG. 520.
VICTORIAN PIANO
CHAIR WITH
ADJUSTABLE SEAT-
TAPESTRY COVERED
CUSHION IN
FAWN AND
COLOURS

FIG. 521.
CHILD'S CHAIR —
TURNED WOOD —
PAINTED BLACK —
CRIMSON VELVET
SEAT — GOLD BRAID
TRIMMING

FIG. 522.
1850-60
MAHOGANY
CHAIR —
HORSEHAIR
COVERED
BUTTONED
SEAT

FIG. 523.
CARVED
MAHOGANY
CHAIR —
ROCOCO STYLE-
CRIMSON SILK
COVERED UPHOLSTERY
c. 1855-60

FIG. 524.
CARVED, PAINTED & GILT
ARMCHAIR - REGENCY PERIOD-
CANE SIDES AND
SEAT — CUSHION

FIG. 525.
CARVED MAHOGANY
CHAIR — GREEN
VELVET SEAT —
VICTORIAN
1855-60

FIG. 526.
RED SILK
COVERED
UPHOLSTERY -
GILT
MAHOGANY
FRAME-
REGENCY
PERIOD

FIG. 527.
REGENCY MAHOGANY
CHAIR - BRASS INLAY -
CANE SEAT.

FIG. 531.
IRON,
ADJUSTABLE MUSIC
STOOL -UPHOLSTERED
SEAT
AND
BACK
1851-
60

FIG. 528.
CARVED WALNUT CHAIR—
UPHOLSTERY COVERED IN
CRIMSON AND GOLD
DAMASK —
VICTORIAN —
1855

FIG. 529.
REGENCY
ROSEWOOD
CHAIR - BRASS
STRINGING —
STRIPED SILK
SEAT COVERING

FIG. 530.
BLACK PAINTED
WOOD CHAIR -
CANE SEAT-
EARLY
VICTORIAN

516–531 *Regency and early Victorian Chairs, 1811–60*

532 *Regency Stool—of mahogany with brass mounts and stringing*

sculpture group surmounting it. This was the work of the sculptor Adrian Jones, and was erected in the early years of the 20th century. A famous builder of this period who carried on the work of James Burton was **Thomas Cubitt**. Cubitt did a good deal of work in Bloomsbury, then turned to Belgravia and, later, Pimlico. After this he worked at Clapham, and also built Osborne House on the Isle of Wight for Queen Victoria. Cubitt's work was sound and efficient; his houses were well built and adequately drained, and he set a high standard by his example—an example badly needed in ordinary domestic building at this time.

Most of the architects so far referred to have been primarily classicists. In turning to the adherents of the Gothic Revival one name stands out as being unique, and that is **Augustus Welby Northmore Pugin**. Pugin was a strange man with a fierce, burning spirit of fervour for everything Medieval. He so wore himself out by this fervour and overwork that he died in 1852 at the age of forty, insane in Bedlam. He was the leader of the Gothic style at this time, and fervently believed that all architecture, and indeed the whole way of life, since the Reformation, had been useless and beneath contempt. A strong anti-classicist, therefore, he scorned all the great classic achievements from Wren to Adam, and concentrated only on the Gothic Revival. Much of his work was ecclesiastical, amongst it the Roman Catholic cathedral at Southwark. In domestic architecture he closely followed the work of the 15th century in design, and his larger houses have sombre Great Halls with screen and gallery, stone chimneypieces and mahogany panelled ceilings. He used narrow, winding stairs, and dull, heavy wallpapers on the living-room walls. One of his last commissions was the arrangement of the Medieval Court at the Great Exhibition, but perhaps his finest achievement was the interior work in the Palace of Westminster, which he did for Barry. Pugin published several books, among which *Contrasts, or a Parallel between the Noble Edifices of the Middle Ages and Corresponding Buildings of the Present Day; showing the Present Decay of Taste*, published in 1836, is best known and shows his extreme views clearly.

The architect who followed on Pugin's work and became the leader of the Gothic movement in England was the man whose work, until recently, it was the fashion to scorn and deride above all other Victorian architects—the grandfather of the present architect of the same name—**Sir George Gilbert Scott, R.A.** (1811–78). Scott, however, though a contemporary and great admirer of Pugin, was a different type of man. He worked very hard and had a tremendous output; he dedicated his life to his appreciation of the

Gothic style, but did not become unbalanced because of it. He was more constructive, and spread the popularity of the style by his standard and volume of work. Although so derided in the first half of the 20th century, his work was immensely popular in his time with all classes. By 1850–60 he had built up a very large practice, but most of his better-known achievements came after this date. Another Gothic Revivalist of this time was **William Butterfield**, whose work is familiar because of its coloured materials in black and yellow, and red brickwork.

Although hangings and tapestry were still in use, the most common wall covering of this period was now **wallpaper**. Regency papers were light and gay, either to match the chintz chair or curtain materials, or plainer versions with floral borders. Many striped papers were used, often satin-grounded, also flock papers, and those in imitation of marble, which replaced the former stucco (see Figs. 493 and 494). Early Victorian papers were still light and fresh in colour, though generally floral in design, with stripes still as a favourite wall design (see Figs. 495 and 496). From 1850–60 the walls echoed the over-decoration and crowding of the remainder of the room, and wallpaper designs were busier and more sombre in tone, though, with the introduction

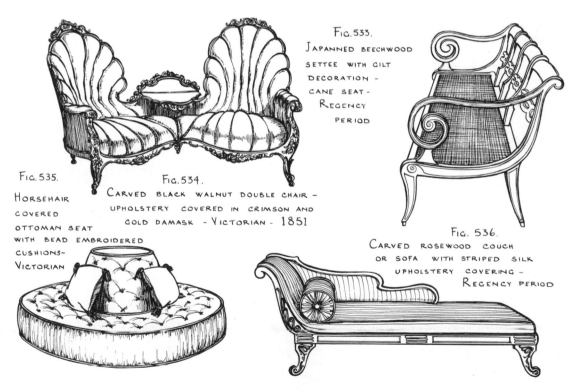

533–536 *Regency and early Victorian Resting and Seating Furniture*, 1811–60

281

FIG. 537. VICTORIAN GAMES TABLE - PAPIER MÂCHÉ TOP INLAID WITH MOTHER OF PEARL c.1850

FIG. 538. VICTORIAN CARVED MAHOGANY PEDEST DINING TABLE c.1851-5

FIG. 539. TULIP WOOD AND KING WOOD JEWEL CASE AND STAND - ORMOLU AND PORCELAIN DECORATION - VICTORIAN c.1855

FIG. 540. VICTORIAN SATINWOOD ESCRITOIRE INLAID WIT TULIP WOOD - ROCOCO STY c.1855-60

FIG. 541. REGENCY PERIOD SOFA TABLE OF MAHOGANY - INLAID WITH EBONY - c.1820

4'

2'4"

2'9"

FIG. 542. VICTORIAN PAPIER MÂCHÉ TEA-POY WITH GILT AND INLAID MOTHER OF PEARL DECORATION ON BLACK - LID HINGED TO OPE c.1850

537–542   *Regency and early Victorian Tables, 1811–60*

of aniline dyes, strident colours were also blended in, but the subtle shades of earlier days were seldom seen. Motifs followed the general Gothic trend, also the rococo designs as typified at the Great Exhibition. There were heraldic insignia, scrolls, acanthus leaves and formal floral patterns reminiscent of Medieval Italian velvets but now less refined in design. Purple, crimson and bottle green predominated, with gilt and black decoration. Despite the profusion of pattern on the walls, the area up to and just above the eye level was also largely covered by pictures of all kinds—oils, watercolours (often home-produced), drawings, engravings, silhouettes and daguerrotypes of friends and relations (see Figs. 497 and 498). Hand-printed papers were still imported from China, depicting Chinese scenes and flowers and birds in delicate designs. Such papers were still usually affixed to canvas on a wood frame as before. Many patents for early types of wallpaper-printing machines were taken out in the 1830's, but it was after 1841 that successful results were obtained and machine-printed wallpapers began to replace the hand-printed ones. The demand for such papers was tremendous and mass production was soon established, though hand-printed papers continued to be made for those with money and discrimination. Wallpaper generally covered the wall from wainscot to picture rail, while woodwork was painted —in light shades and white in the Regency period, and in grained or darkbrown hues by mid-century.

Floors were of polished wood, and were covered by rugs and carpets, though kitchen and hall were often tiled. Many **carpets** were now made in England, by Axminster, Kidderminster and Wilton in particular, also in Scotland at Glasgow, Hawick and Kilmarnock. Designs were generally floral, with a centrepiece and outer border, though by the Victorian period geometrical or floral repeat patterns were more usual. By this time also production had increased considerably owing to the introduction of steam power to the looms and also the adaption of the Jacquard system. Some embroidered carpets and rugs were still made at home by devoted souls, whilst, for cheaper use, painted felt sufficed (see Figs. 494, 497 and 498).

Ceilings were now much plainer, and decorated white or a light colour in plaster. There might be a central decoration from which to suspend the means of lighting, and a simply moulded cornice and plain frieze would finish the ceiling (see Figs. 493, 495 and 496).

The majority of **staircases** of this time were of iron balustrading, with mahogany handrails, while the stairs might be of stone or wood. Regency styles were fairly simple, with plain vertical balusters or S-shaped ones, or, alternatively, simple scrollwork. The Gothic influence on design could be seen later. Victorian styles of 1850–60 were more elaborate, with curves and floral ornament. Some turned and painted wood balusters were also in use at this time. Stair carpets were more generally used now, while the stair

Fig. 543. REGENCY LIBRARY TABLE OF CARVED MAHOGANY

2'7"

2'6"

Fig. 544. ROSEWOOD AND WALNUT TABLE - INLAID TOP WITH BRASS STRINGING - BENTWOOD LEGS - REMOVABLE TOP - c. 1851-5

2'4"

Fig. 545. ROSEWOOD WORK TABLE WITH PINK SILK POUCHES - ALSO FITTE WITH GAMES BOARD - REGENC PERIOD

2'4

Fig. 546. PAPIER MÂCHÉ WORK TABLE DECORATED WITH PAINTINGS AND GILT 1855-60

2'1"

Fig. 547. EARLY VICTORIAN PEDESTAL SIDE TABLE - CARVED WALNUT WITH DELICATE FLORAL PATTERN INLAID IN THE TOP c. 1840-50

2'8"

2'6"

Fig. 548. VICTORIAN PAPIER MÂCHÉ TEA TABLE INLAID WITH MOTHER OF PEARL AND DECORATED WITH GILT - c. 1840-50

543–548   *Regency and early Victorian Tables, 1811–60*

treads were often painted in dark tones of brown (see Figs. 551, 552, 553, 554 and 555).

Regency **chimneypieces** were generally of white marble in a simple, dignified form of carved decoration with gilt, painted or inlaid marble ornament. There was a mantelshelf of small projection, a decorated frieze and side pilasters or carved figures. **Grates** were of the **hob** type still or, alternatively, **sarcophagus grates**, which stood on paw feet with Egyptian motifs in decoration. **Fenders** and fire-irons were of brass or steel, while the grate was of steel and cast iron (see Figs. 493, 501 and 506). Until about 1845, simple marble chimneypieces and **basket grates** were most popular, but after this the highly ornamented styles became fashionable; these were a mass of scrolls and curves and floral tendrils and forms. Grates were in keeping, and cast iron predominated as a material. Brass, iron, marble and stone were used for the chimneypieces, also painted iron or wood (see Figs. 495 and 497). A fender and fire-irons of about 1851 can be seen in Figs. 507, 511, 512 and 513. After 1850, grates were generally fitted rather than of the basket type, and a pelmet board was often attached to the mantelshelf, with curtains of crimson or green plush draped on it, usually with tassel or fringe edging (see Fig. 498). An ornamental mirror over the chimneypiece helped to lighten the rather gloomy rooms.

Sash windows were in use all this period: Regency types were large, with narrow glazing bars, and, on the lower storeys, often reached from the picture rail nearly to the floor. Panes were rectangular, with each window section usually having two in the width and two or three in the depth. Many windows were of bay style or were bow-fronted in section. **Curtains** were draped most decoratively over a large pole, and were either striped in silk or satin, or patterned florally in a delicate design (see Figs. 493 and 494). In the 1840's, with the introduction of **plate glass**, large panes became fashionable and glazing bars were often abandoned. **By 1850–60, curtains** had become very dark and heavy, made of velvet or rep, and were hung by brass rings on a massive mahogany pole. Nottingham lace curtains were hung all over the remainder of the window so that little light could enter; sunlight was greatly deprecated, as it might fade the furnishings and was thought to age the occupants. A large plant, of evergreen type, was usually set on a table in front of the window, and this also helped to obscure any remaining light (see Fig. 498). **French windows** were introduced in this period and became very popular.

Regency doors were plain and had panels in low relief, usually six in number. The architrave was generally simply reeded (see Fig. 494). **Victorian doors** were usually four-panelled, with plain *cyma reversa* mouldings and, later, were covered by dark paint, which replaced the white or light tones (see Fig. 498).

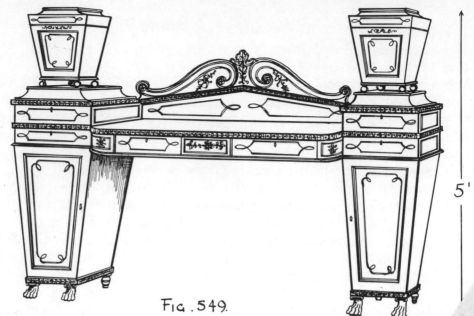

5'

FIG. 549.

REGENCY ROSEWOOD SIDEBOARD DECORATED BY BRASS INL
TWO PEDESTAL CUPBOARDS FITTED AS PLATE WARMER AND CE   E -
KNIFE BOXES ABOVE -

FIG. 550. VICTORIAN CHIFFONIER OF CARVED MAHOGANY WITH MIRROR
BACK AND GLAZED SIDE DOORS - ELECTRO-GILT METAL DECORATION -
c. 1855 - 60

549 and 550   *Regency and early Victorian Dining-room Furniture, 1811–60*

Three **Regency rooms** are illustrated: a **drawing room** in Fig. 494, a **dining room** in Fig. 493 and a **kitchen** in Fig. 499, also a Regency palace kitchen fireplace in Fig. 515. There is an **early Victorian parlour** in Fig. 495, and a **drawing room** in Fig. 496, while a **Victorian bedroom** can be seen in Fig. 497. A **Victorian parlour of 1850–55** is shown in Fig 498, and a **kitchen** of the same date in Fig. 500.

Fabulous quantities of **needlework** and embroidery were produced by the ladies of Victorian homes, much of it either useless or ugly, but some which had a utilitarian purpose. Every possible item of furniture was covered in this way. Cushions, chairs, mantelpieces, tables, footstools and sofas all received their share and more. The work was in petit point, satin stitch or beadwork, and the usual motifs were flowers, in particular cabbage roses. Victorian samplers are, of course, familiar to most of us; although samplers had been made, usually by unwilling children and young ladies, in both the 17th and 18th centuries, far more were produced in the 19th. The results spoke of hours, months, even years of toil, patience and tears, and the proud effort was then framed and hung on the wall in a place of honour. Many pictures were reproduced in embroidery—Windsor Castle, of course, and Landseer's animal scenes, and the inevitable "Stag at Bay". Patchwork was employed a great deal, usually for quilts or cushion covers (see Figs. 495 and 496).

Among the designers of **Regency furniture** should be mentioned **Thomas Hope** and **George Smith**. **Hope**, as referred to in Chapter VIII, had already made some designs in the late Georgian period. His great penchant was for Egyptian form and decoration, and his chairs and tables show this feature most clearly. His sofas and chairs had low seats, and he designed numerous circular-topped tables. He advocated the use of bronze and silver in marquetry designs. His work was purely theoretical—he did not make furniture. **George Smith** was, on the other hand, primarily a cabinet-maker, though he designed a good deal of furniture, and among his published work is *A Collection of Designs for Household Furniture and Interior Decoration*, published in 1808, and *The Cabinet Makers' and Upholsterers' Guide*, published in 1826. His designs were drawn from Greek, Egyptian and Roman sources, with also a touch of Gothic. Among his best-known features of design are his monopods, usually with winged paw foot, low seats, circular dining tables with pedestal support of a plinth set on the paws, brilliantly coloured upholstery, and ivy and lotus leaf motifs. Also at this time was published Ackermann's *Repository of Arts*, brought out monthly from 1809 to 1828, and including designs of interior decoration and furniture which were prevalent at the time.

Furniture in **Regency** times continued to be made with a high standard of craftsmanship, although cabinet-making was also beginning to be affected by the industrialisation of the day. Some of the processes such as sawing and

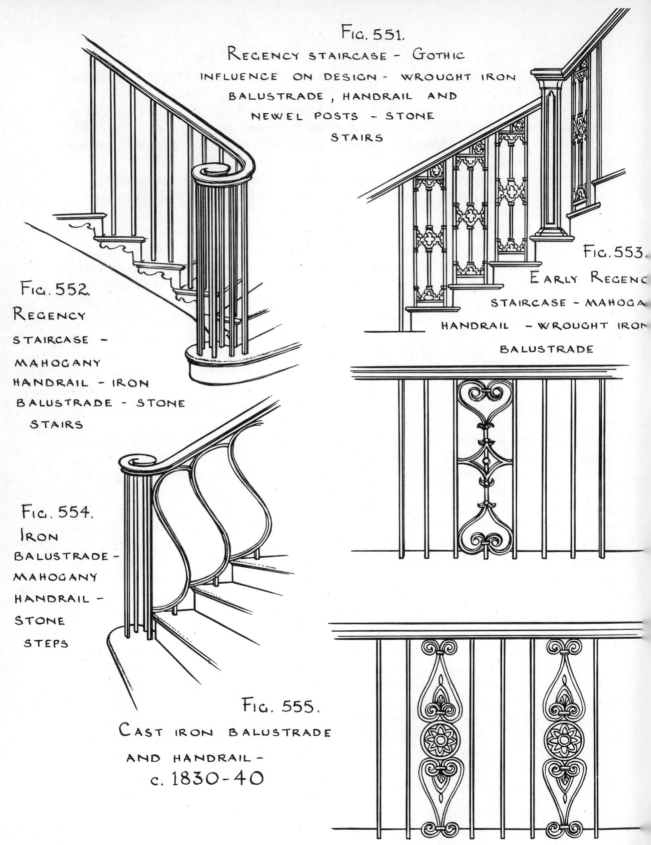

FIG. 551.
REGENCY STAIRCASE - GOTHIC
INFLUENCE ON DESIGN - WROUGHT IRON
BALUSTRADE, HANDRAIL AND
NEWEL POSTS - STONE
STAIRS

FIG. 552.
REGENCY
STAIRCASE -
MAHOGANY
HANDRAIL - IRON
BALUSTRADE - STONE
STAIRS

FIG. 553.
EARLY REGENC...
STAIRCASE - MAHOGA...
HANDRAIL - WROUGHT IRON...
BALUSTRADE

FIG. 554.
IRON
BALUSTRADE -
MAHOGANY
HANDRAIL -
STONE
STEPS

FIG. 555.
CAST IRON BALUSTRADE
AND HANDRAIL -
c. 1830-40

551–555   *Regency and early Victorian Staircases, 1811–60*

planing were now carried out by machine, at least by the large firms. This resulted in a greater amount of furniture being made. The inspiration of the designs was still Greek and Egyptian, and a rather formal appearance was now usual. Many items were rectangular in silhouette, and a certain heaviness of members could be seen by 1820. The chief characteristics of furniture of the period included spiral or vertical reeding; round-sectioned tapering legs; stringing lines of inlay in wood or brass; paw feet, generally of lion origin, alternatively scroll feet; monopod supports, that is, a leg or support made from a human or animal head, body and leg all in one piece; dolphin, eagle and lion motifs and scrolled ends to chair arms. A good deal of furniture was painted or gilded, while inlay and carving were also in use for decorative means. Rosewood was a very popular wood, and with increased imports of satinwood more of this was now used. Mahogany was retained for more massive items of furniture such as dining tables and bookcases. For cheaper furniture, or for use as a carcase for a veneer, pine, deal, oak and beech were employed. The latter wood was particularly suitable when the furniture was to be painted or japanned. Elm was in general use for country and farmhouse furniture. Veneered furniture was most fashionable, either in a plain surface or in simple patterns of woods—complicated marquetry designs were unusual. Satinwood was in great demand as a veneer, as also was rosewood. In inlay decoration, ebony, holly, satinwood, brass, silver and ivory were all in general use. Ormolu was still seen, but much less frequently than in French furniture. It was later processed by a less expensive method wherein the brass was covered by a lacquer gilt. Japanned furniture remained popular on a beech basis, with gilt decoration; much bedroom furniture was made in this way. Upholstered furniture was generally covered by silk or damask, and sometimes by brocade. Plain, striped and gay floral patterns were usual: the latter were generally in spray or sprig form. Greek motifs were very popular, particularly the key pattern. Chintz and cotton were also employed, printed or embroidered with motifs of flowers, birds or scenes from the period.

Among the new items of furniture introduced about the Regency time were the upright pianoforte, the chiffonier, the circular bookstand, the whatnot and the davenport. Canterburies were now in much more general use.

Early Victorian furniture up to about 1845 continued in the same vein to a large extent. Rosewood continued to be the popular wood, with mahogany reserved for the larger items of furniture, particularly in dining rooms. Satinwood was kept for the important, valued pieces. However, the desire for a greater number of items of furniture was beginning to be seen, and with more furniture available, at a lower price due to part machine production, the arrangements of rooms became less selective and the available floor space smaller. By 1837 the classical style of furniture and classical motifs were giving way to the Gothic influence and also to the rococo. Straight lines were being replaced by curves, although some of the Gothic-styled work was rather severe. French polish was now used on furniture, though some furniture was painted, and other cheaper articles, of pinewood, were merely varnished.

By 1845–50 the transitional early Victorian period in furniture was ended, and the change-over from Regency to Victorian styles of furniture and room arrangement was complete. The **Victorian rooms** of **1850–60** were well upholstered, amazingly overcrowded and almost every possible surface was decorated in some way. The craftsmanship was excellent, despite the fact that machine-made furniture meant that production was greater than ever before, and the woods employed were of high quality, but, in general, the style and design of the items themselves were a conglomeration of past styles, with rococo and Gothic predominating. Many Chippendale and Manwaring rococo patterns were reintroduced, but with less refined curves and scrolls and far more decoration than was originally intended; hence the dignity of conception was lost. Mahogany, carved in solid form, became the typical material, and many pieces were heavy and massive, rather sombre and excessively over-decorated. The Great Exhibition Catalogue shows such designs in abundance: there is solidity and good workmanship but there is also vulgarity and ostentation. The lightness and delicacy of late 18th-century work had vanished completely, and the dignity and simplicity of earlier 17th- and 18th-century designs were also absent. The decoration was provided in the form of cornucopiae, scrolls, curves, foliage and fruit in profusion.

All rooms were impossibly overcrowded: the typical **Victorian dining room** had a massive mahogany dining table and chairs, one or more enormous sideboards or chiffoniers, and numbers of smaller tables, chairs and other items. The **drawing room**, to the present-day idea of arrangement, was in chaotic confusion. It included a grand or upright pianoforte, or both, a horsehair sofa, innumerable small tables and work tables, chairs, stools, china cabinets and such prized items as stuffed birds or wax fruit and flowers under glass domes, crystal paper weights, photograph albums, china and glass ornaments and boxes of all sizes and shapes. There were also fire-screens and mirrors, pictures and photographs. Every available surface was covered by a mat or cloth, of lace, wool, silk or bead embroidery, generally home-made. *Anti*macassars draped the chair-backs, made in lurid shades of wool and silk, to protect the upholstery from the masculine head, sleek with macassar oil. The **bedrooms** were equally overcrowded, with the great double bed, massive wardrobe, chairs, bedside cupboards, chests-of-drawers, toilet table and mirror—and that Victorian monstrosity, a marble-topped washstand, complete with floral basin and jug.

Iron was used a good deal in Victorian furniture, particularly for garden equipment, but also for chair and table legs and for beds. It was sometimes

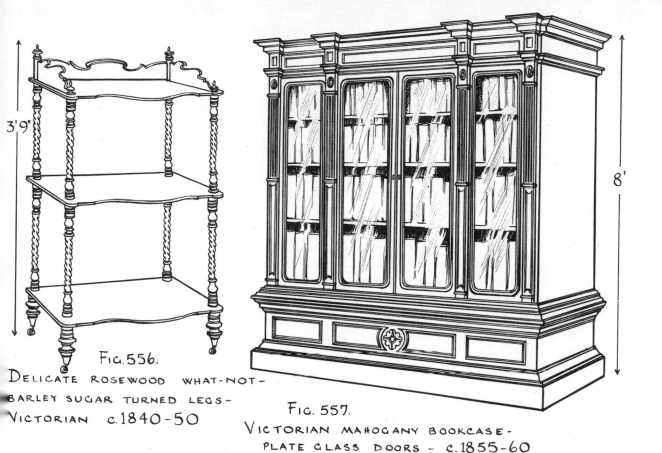

3'9"

8'

FIG. 556.
DELICATE ROSEWOOD WHAT-NOT-
BARLEY SUGAR TURNED LEGS-
VICTORIAN c.1840-50

FIG. 557.
VICTORIAN MAHOGANY BOOKCASE-
PLATE GLASS DOORS - c.1855-60

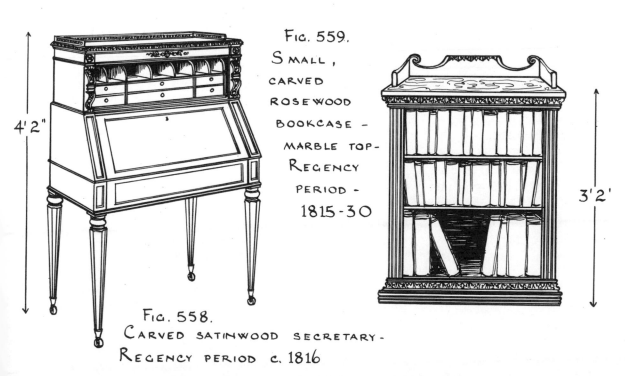

4'2"

FIG. 559.
SMALL,
CARVED
ROSEWOOD
BOOKCASE -
MARBLE TOP-
REGENCY
PERIOD -
1815-30

3'2'

FIG. 558.
CARVED SATINWOOD SECRETARY-
REGENCY PERIOD c. 1816

556–559 *Regency and early Victorian Furniture, 1811–60*

gilded or painted. **Marble** was very popular for table tops and for the tops of sideboards, washstands and chiffoniers. **Mosaic** was also often seen in this context.

Upholstery was covered by velvet, plush, silk or horsehair, also by petit-point needlework and other forms of embroidery. It was either of dark crimson or green, or patterned in a floral design, commonly of cabbage roses. Paisley shawls were also used for chair and sofa coverings, while in the bedroom, white muslin or silk predominated in dressing-table hangings and toilet covers, decorated by embroidery and large bows.

Contrasting strangely with the massive mahogany furniture of the time was the dainty **papier-mâché work** and **Tunbridge ware** also so typical of the period. A large number of articles of furniture were now made in **papier-mâché**: chairs, tables, work tables, cabinets, boxes and even beds. The work was decorated by gilt and inlaid with mother-of-pearl or shell, and painted in panels depicting scenes and buildings of the age, notably Windsor Castle, also flower designs in garlands and all-over patterns, including birds and scrolls. The height of popularity for papier-mâché furniture was reached from 1850 to 1860, when nearly every home would boast at least one or two pieces. The furniture was light but most surprisingly durable. Birmingham was the principal centre of manufacture at this time. **Tunbridge ware**—so called because of its earlier manufacture at Tunbridge Wells among other places— was really a reintroduction of a 17th-century method. It had continued to be made in the 18th century, but it reached a peak of fashion from 1840 to 1860. Very small strips of wood in different colours were glued together to make a pattern, and the whole was applied as a block veneer, which could be cut off in layers as required. Such decoration was used on smaller items such as boxes, trays, table tops, tea-poys, etc., and was in the form of geometrical designs, flowers and birds, also views of castles and abbeys.

Seating accommodation was most varied by this time, and in Victoria's reign upholstery was much more common than hitherto. **Regency chairs** were influenced by a mixture of styles and origins: Greek, Roman, Egyptian, Chinese and Gothic; particularly the Greek and Egyptian. The French Directoire and Empire influence on English design of the time was also marked. The chief characteristics of Regency chairs were the curved and tapering front legs, the arms which were set high on the back, then rounded forward in scroll effect, the curved back rail to accommodate the sitter, and the gaily striped or patterned upholstery covering in silk or satin, in delicate tones and refined designs. Common motifs for decoration included lion's-paw feet and lion's-head terminals for arms, also gryphons and sphinxes. Seats were of cane or wood, usually with a cushion, or upholstered. Painting and gilding were common, also carved decoration and inlay of brass or contrasting coloured wood in stringing lines or simple pattern. Mahogany and

FIG. 560. REGENCY DRESSING AND WRITING CABINET – WOOD, COVERED IN LEATHER – BRASS MOUNTS – INTERIOR OF BLUE SILK WITH DECORATIVE GOLD BORDERS – c.1813

1'6"

4'

FIG. 561. REGENCY MAHOGANY WINE COOLER – BRASS MOUNTS

1'6"

FIG. 562. VICTORIAN PAPIER MÂCHÉ CABINET DECORATED BY MOTHER OF PEARL, PICTURES OF WINDSOR CASTLE AND GILT SCROLL WORK – COMPRISES DESK, DRAWERS AND MIRROR – c.1840-50

FIG. 564. MAHOGANY CHEST OF DRAWERS – VICTORIAN – c.1850

FIG. 563. ATLAS CANTERBURY MADE OF WOOD – SIDE SUPPORTS ACT AS LEAVES AND CAN BE LET DOWN TO THE HORIZONTAL AS REQUIRED BY PULLING CORDS WHICH ARE OPERATED BY RATCHET – VICTORIAN – c.1840-50

3'6"

3'6"

560–564   *Regency and early Victorian Furniture, 1811–60*

rosewood were usual materials, with beechwood for japanned treatment (see Figs. 493, 494, 524, 526, 527 and 529).

After 1840, **Victorian chairs** became most varied in design, but completely different from the Regency types. Gothic and rococo were the chief sources of inspiration, but the Victorian version of both of these was only distantly related to the original conception. The majority of chairs were upholstered, either with buttoned upholstery all over the seat, arms and back, or with a back panel which had a carved rococo frame, oval or kidney-shaped, and buttoned upholstery within it. The upholstery was covered with leather or velvet (generally deep red), or, most commonly, horsehair, or if for drawing-room use, needlework in petit-point or beadwork, with floral or scenic design. The chair-backs had a small waist and fuller top, while the seats echoed this shape. Legs were short and curved, in rococo vein, and castors were usual on all chair-legs (see Figs. 495, 496, 498, 522, 523, 525 and 528). Lighter-weight chairs had cane seats and wood backs, while cheaper chairs, which were produced in large quantities for shops, bedrooms, servants' quarters, etc., were entirely of wood. The balloon back and double C back were most common after 1850 in this type of chair, and by 1860 the bentwood chair in this style, with cane or wood seat, was most prevalent. Legs of such chairs were tapering, turned and splayed slightly outwards (see Figs. 495, 498, 517, 519 and 530). Papier-mâché was most popular for chair-making from 1840 to 1860, especially for bedroom use, and seats were generally of cane, with a cushion added if required (see Figs. 495, 497 and 516). Some Windsor chairs were still made, and many chairs were produced for special purposes—children's chairs, music chairs, reading, sketching and writing chairs and prie-dieu chairs, etc. (see Figs. 496, 518, 520, 521 and 531).

Stools were still in use: Regency types were generally of the X-frame design, of mahogany or rosewood with brass stringing, and leather, cane or upholstered seats (see Fig. 532), while Victorian stools were either piano stools or stools for children (see Fig. 498), or were long, low footstools of carved mahogany with needlework tops (see Figs. 495 and 498).

Settees were still popular in **Regency times**, and were usually of a light-weight design with cane seat and squab cushions, and with a frame of japanned beechwood or painted wood (see Fig. 533). Rather more typical of the period is the **Grecian couch** of carved mahogany or rosewood, with curved, rolled ends and back, and short, outwardly curving legs in the form of lion's paws on castors. The upholstery was silk-covered in stripes or floral design, and there was a matching roll bolster at each end (see Figs. 494 and 536). In the **Victorian period, sofas** were the most usual form of this type of seating accommodation, and the graceful line of the curving Grecian couch had been lost. It had given place to a massive carved mahogany-framed sofa, highly over-ornamented, and usually possessing upholstery covered in black, shiny,

FIG. 565.
CONVEX,
REGENCY
MIRROR –
CARVED, GILT
PINEWOOD
FRAME

FIG. 566.
CARVED
AND GILT
WOOD
OVERMANTEL
2'3" MIRROR –
BLACK KEY
PATTERN
DECORATION –
REGENCY
PERIOD

3'7"

FIG. 567.
SILVER FRAMED
TOILET GLASS WITH
CANDLE
BRANCHES –
ROCOCO
STYLE –
VICTORIAN –
1851

FIG. 569.
CARVED MAHOGANY
OVAL TOILET GLASS –
VICTORIAN –
1850-60

FIG. 568. CARVED ROSEWOOD
BOX TOILET GLASS – 1825-30

565–569   *Regency and early Victorian Mirrors, 1811–60*

prickly horsehair. Beaded and tasselled cushions then completed the picture (see Fig. 496). With the Great Exhibition came the **double chair**, curved in rococo design, and with a little table-rest between (see Fig. 534), and at this time the Victorian **ottoman** also became popular. This item of furniture had originated during the Regency as a backless upholstered seat, but by 1850 it became a centrepiece for the drawing room, often designed in circular form and having a central back support so that people could sit all round it. The upholstery was buttoned and covered in velvet, cretonne, damask or horsehair. Cushions were added for comfort. In the centre would probably be set some greenery of the palm family (see Fig. 535).

The circular-topped **dining table** with the central pillar support, introduced in the late Georgian era, continued in use through both Regency and Victorian times. The Regency version had a plinth, and legs ending in paw terminals, or was of pedestal type with four legs curved outwards, each having brass mounts and castors (see Fig. 494). In Victorian days, the support grew bulbous and much heavier, while the legs were lavishly carved and had paw or plain terminals (see Figs. 498 and 538). The rectangular **dining table** also continued in use from 1811 to 1860 as an alternative design, chiefly in larger homes where a good deal of entertaining was done. This table was still in sections, with pedestal supports during the Regency (see Fig. 493), while Victorian versions were more massive, and had heavy legs to support the top, generally obscured by a chenille cloth.

There were many other types of table large and small, made for various specific purposes. **Sofa tables** were still in use during the Regency, with extending leaves and drawers in front (see Fig. 541), while dainty **work tables** on tripod or four-legged stands had pleated silk pouches beneath and fitted drawers above (see Fig. 545). Rather massive **library tables**, carved with pedestal figures, were still made for large houses (see Fig. 543). Among **Victorian tables**, small **papier-mâché** types, with pedestal or tripod stands, were very common as **tea tables, work tables, chess tables,** etc. (see Figs. 495, 496, 497, 498, 537, 542, 546 and 548). So also were rococo-styled, cabriole-legged tables in daintier design, made as **stands** or **writing tables** (see Figs. 539 and 540). **Side-tables** of pedestal style were also made, generally to stand under the window and support a potted fern (see Figs. 495 and 547). Bentwood and cast iron were used for table legs after 1850, and an example of the former can be seen in Fig. 544. **Gate-leg tables** continued to be made all the period, both in large and small editions (see Fig. 498). The **tea-poy** became a fashionable item of furniture from Regency times. It was a small table containing equipment for making tea, and was used in addition to the tea tables (see Fig. 494). Various materials were used for all these tables: mahogany was usual for dining tables, but among other types Regency tables favoured rosewood, mahogany and satinwood with brass and wood inlay,

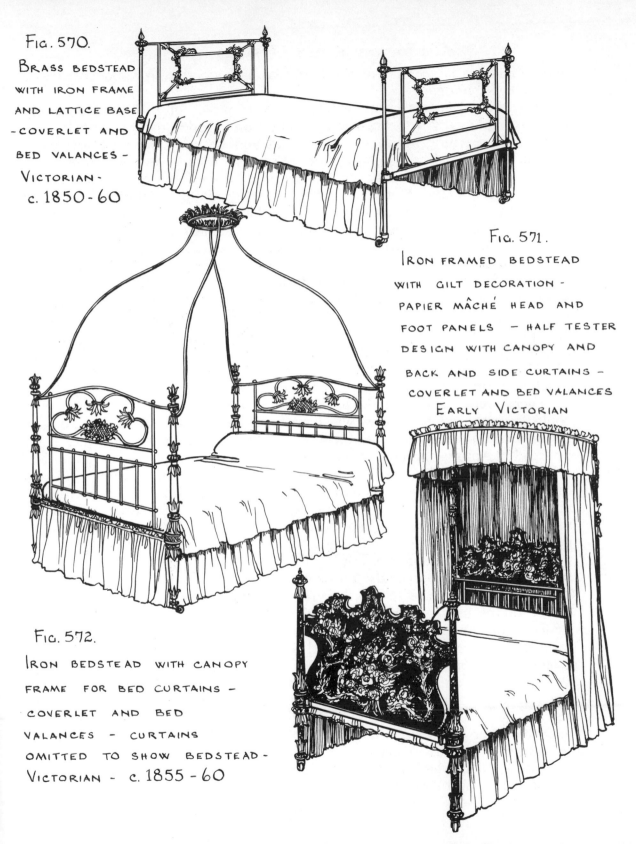

Fig. 570.
Brass bedstead
with iron frame
and lattice base
-coverlet and
bed valances -
Victorian -
c. 1850-60

Fig. 571.
Iron framed bedstead
with gilt decoration -
papier mâché head and
foot panels - half tester
design with canopy and
back and side curtains -
coverlet and bed valances
Early Victorian

Fig. 572.
Iron bedstead with canopy
frame for bed curtains -
coverlet and bed
valances - curtains
omitted to show bedstead -
Victorian - c. 1855-60

570-572   *Regency and early Victorian Bedsteads, 1811-60*

while Victorian tables were of papier-mâché, satinwood, tulipwood, rosewood, walnut and mahogany.

Regency sideboards continued to be large pieces of furniture, generally made of mahogany with brass inlay decoration. Pedestals were attached on either side reaching nearly to the ground and standing on paw feet; these pedestals possessed considerable storage space. Usually one was fitted as a plate-warmer with a metal lining and the other as a cellarette. On them were placed knife boxes or urns, as before (see Fig. 549). **Victorian sideboards** were even more massive and became, by 1850, a riot of carving representing fruit and flowers; they had several shelves and capacious cupboards. Many later sideboards had a mirror at the back with an elaborately carved mahogany frame. **The chiffonier** of this period is very like the sideboard, and the one is often taken for the other. The chiffonier originated during the Regency, when the top part consisted of receding shelves for displaying porcelain, and the lower part was a cupboard with doors, fronted with brass diamond lattice and pleated pink silk backing (see Fig. 493). Later, Victorian types had marble tops, ornately carved cupboard doors below, some of which were glazed, and a mirror back with carved mahogany frame. They were colossal articles of furniture and, in general, rather ugly (see Figs. 495 and 550).

There were various methods of housing books in Regency times: they could be arranged on **shelves** which were set fairly low on the wall so that pictures could be hung above them, or contained in a **bookcase**, either large or small. Among the latter types were the circular and revolving bookcase, and also a rectangular style (see Fig. 559). Bookcases could be open in front or had doors with brass trellis instead of glazing. Although the Victorians also used bookshelves their bookcases were generally very large, almost invariably of mahogany, and had glazed doors with cupboards, wood-fronted, below. The majority of such bookcases had an architectural flavour, usually Gothic in interpretation (see Fig. 557).

Cabinets of various kinds continued to be made, among which were china cabinets, writing cabinets and others for no specific use other than the personal choice of the user. **China cabinets** generally had glazed doors and/or brass trellis in the lower part (see Figs. 494 and 496). A small Regency writing cabinet can be seen in Fig. 560, and a most ornate papier-mâché **Victorian cabinet** in Fig. 562, with an abundance of scrolls and ogee curves. **Secretaries** were still seen, chiefly in the Regency period, and these had dainty tapering legs (see Fig. 558). The **what-not** made its appearance about the same time, and was later beloved of the Victorian housewife as an ideal article on which to display her treasured ornaments such as wax flowers under glass domes, ships in bottles, glass paperweights, china and glass figures and ornaments of all kinds. The what-not was a dainty stand, about three to four feet in height, with several shelves and delicate turned legs, often in barley-sugar-twist style (see Fig. 556). **Canterburies** had various uses now: as a dining-table server, to hold music, or to contain and support atlases. The music canterburies were placed at the side of the piano to hold a variety of books and sheet music (see Figs. 496 and 563).

In Regency times, the convex wall **mirror** reached a height of popularity; it was generally hung over the chimney-piece, and had a circular, gilt, carved frame with gold or black balls set in the mouldings. It was crested by floral decoration, an eagle or other bird or animal (see Figs. 493 and 565). Rectangular mirrors were also used, as pier glasses or chimney glasses. These were generally divided into sections by four carved female figures. Many such mirrors had a Greek or Egyptian basis in design (see Fig. 566). For the bedroom, the tall

573 *Iron Child's Cot with wool fringe and basket lining—Victorian, c.* 1851–5

cheval mirrors and swinging **toilet glasses** on box supports were still in use (see Fig. 568). **Victorian mirrors** were generally placed over the chimney-piece, and frequently had highly over-decorated carved gilt frames, in rococo mood. Some had candle-branches attached. These mirrors did help to light otherwise very gloomy rooms (see Figs. 497 and 498). **Victorian toilet glasses** ranged from the simple (see Fig. 569) to the highly ornate (see Fig. 567), and could have a toilet box attached; some also had candle-branches. Plates of glass were still blown and hand-ground and polished until 1830, so the size of mirror plate was still limited.

In Victorian **bedstead** design, the four-post type with full canopy had, to a certain extent, though not entirely, been abandoned. Instead the half-tester was becoming popular. This was generally a massive double bed, made of carved mahogany, later very ornate, with a mahogany half-tester and two mahogany posts. Curtains hung at the head and sides (see Fig. 497). Papier-mâché versions of these beds were also made, with semicircular metal-framed testers (see Fig. 571). Alternatively there was the coronet or tent design, with metal supports for the draped curtains (see Fig. 572). Some bedsteads, particularly those of the Regency, followed French Empire fashions and were designed as couches, with curved wooden ends and sides and without any curtains, but this was comparatively rare in England as yet. After 1850 iron or brass bedsteads were becoming fashionable, and these

299

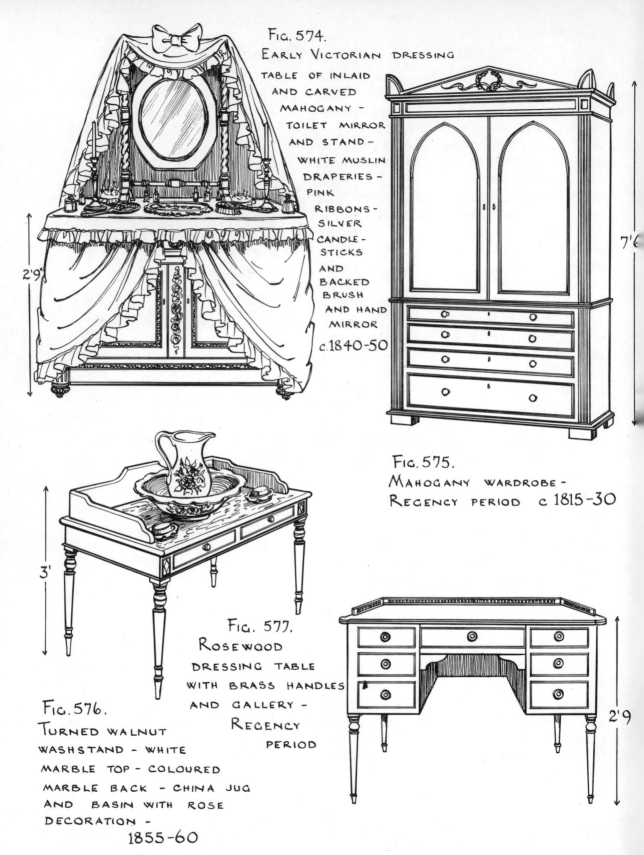

FIG. 574.
EARLY VICTORIAN DRESSING
TABLE OF INLAID
AND CARVED
MAHOGANY -
TOILET MIRROR
AND STAND -
WHITE MUSLIN
DRAPERIES -
PINK
RIBBONS -
SILVER
CANDLE -
STICKS
AND
BACKED
BRUSH
AND HAND
MIRROR
c. 1840-50

FIG. 575.
MAHOGANY WARDROBE -
REGENCY PERIOD c 1815-30

FIG. 577.
ROSEWOOD
DRESSING TABLE
WITH BRASS HANDLES
AND GALLERY -
REGENCY
PERIOD

FIG. 576.
TURNED WALNUT
WASHSTAND - WHITE
MARBLE TOP - COLOURED
MARBLE BACK - CHINA JUG
AND BASIN WITH ROSE
DECORATION -
1855-60

574–577   *Regency and early Victorian Bedroom Furniture, 1811–60*

were made both with and without a half-tester or coronet canopy. The metal frame was ornately decorated with Gothic and floral designs (see Figs. 570 and 572). The bed basis was still of rope mesh or, later, metal mesh in wide diamond pattern. Feather beds were placed on top, with adequate supplies of sheets, blankets, etc., and finishing with a decorative quilt or coverlet, usually embroidered and often of patchwork. Bed valances were attached to the bed frame to hide the bed legs, also the inevitable china article under the bed.

Children's **cots** were oval or boat-shaped and swung from a frame. A scroll at the head was devised to support a curtain and frill. Cots were of wood, brass or iron (see Fig. 573).

Among the essential items of **bedroom furniture**, in addition to the bedstead, were included a dressing table, a wardrobe, a chest of drawers, a toilet mirror, a bedside cabinet, a chair and a washstand. **Regency dressing tables** were simple, dignified pieces of furniture, made from rosewood or mahogany, and containing several drawers. Legs were tapering and delicate, and the top was often fitted with a brass gallery. A **toilet mirror** would usually be set on top (see Fig. 577). **Victorian dressing tables** varied: they might be merely tables without drawers, or might have cupboards and/or drawers below. Both the dressing table and **toilet mirror** were frequently draped with muslin with flounced edges and ribbon bow decoration (see Fig. 574). **Regency wardrobes** were still commonly of the press type, with large drawers in the bottom part, and doors in the top section concealing shelves (see Fig. 575). By 1820–30, however, **hanging wardrobes** were beginning to take their place, and the typical **Victorian wardrobe** was of mahogany in massive design with plate mirror in the central door. Below the hanging space was a large drawer, and above was a heavy cornice (see Fig. 497). The **bedside cabinet** was a small piece of furniture, and its wood or marble top was used for holding a candlestick and toilet articles, while in the cupboard below the essential article(s) was housed (see Fig. 497). **Chests of drawers** were of mahogany and often bow or serpentine fronted. They were fairly plain in design but large and capacious. Some stood on four turned feet (see Fig. 564). The **washstand**, which had originated in late Georgian times as a dainty tripod to hold a small basin and soap, etc., became a slender though larger piece of furniture by Regency days, but by 1850 had developed into that ugly but unfortunately necessary item of furniture so beloved of landladies of to-day where the tariff is inexpensive and the conveniences not so modern. Such washstands were large and rectangular, and had a marble top with one or two circular holes into which were set large, florally decorated basins with jugs to match. A mirror back was common, with carved mahogany frame, while below were drawers and/or cupboards. Pseudo-Gothic designs were very popular; alternatively carved mahogany rococo scrolls and fruit (see Figs. 497 and 576).

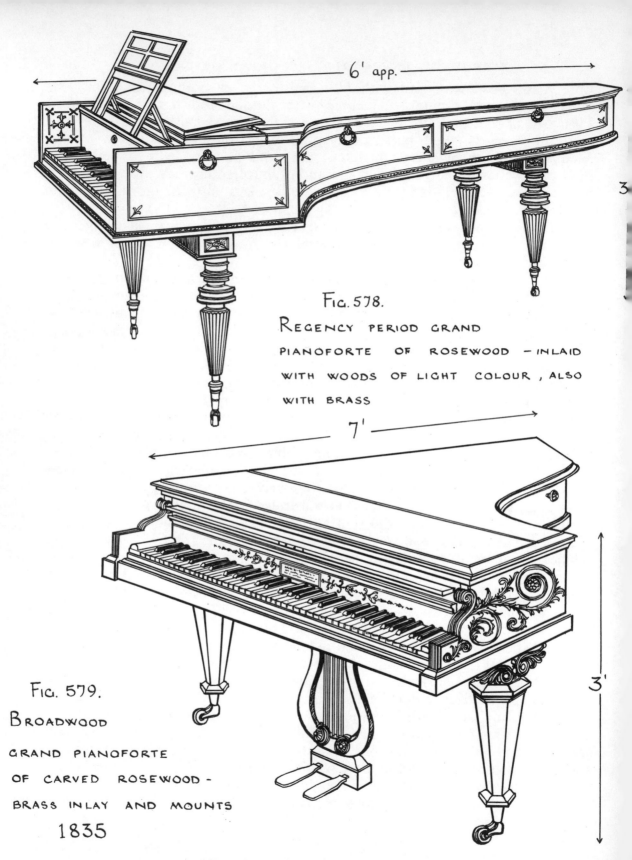

6' app.

Fig. 578.

REGENCY PERIOD GRAND
PIANOFORTE OF ROSEWOOD — INLAID
WITH WOODS OF LIGHT COLOUR, ALSO
WITH BRASS

7'

3'

Fig. 579.

BROADWOOD

GRAND PIANOFORTE

OF CARVED ROSEWOOD —

BRASS INLAY AND MOUNTS

1835

578, 579 *Early 19th-century Pianofortes*

The **pianoforte** had begun to be a most important piece of furniture during the Regency, and was replacing the harp and the harpsichord. In Victorian homes, the piano had become an essential mark of respectability, and even small houses had at least one such prized possession. There were grand and upright designs, at first in rosewood and later mahogany. The earlier pianofortes were sparing in decoration—generally in the form of brass inlay—but were beautifully proportioned pieces of furniture (see Figs. 578 and 579), but mid-Victorian versions were becoming ornate and beginning to lose dignity of design. Early Victorian upright pianofortes generally had pleated pink silk panels (see Figs. 496 and 498).

Fire-screens were still in general use, designed in three chief types: the pole screen, the cheval screen and the hanging banner screen. **Pole screens** followed 18th-century tripod designs but were now heavier in ornament. Banners were of petit-point needlework or a painted material (see Figs. 498, 580 and 581). **Cheval screens** were hung between two pillars, and could be swung at various angles, while **banner screens** were of heavy material hung from a pole and cross-bar.

580 *Victorian Fire Screen of mahogany with banner of petit-point roses on black background*

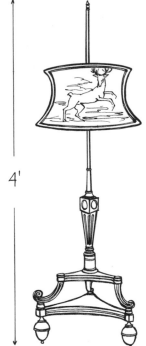

581 *Regency Pole Screen of mahogany with ebony decoration —painted velvet banner*

The long-case **clock** had almost disappeared by Regency times and its place was taken by wall clocks with pendulums below, or bracket or shelf clocks. The designs were classical, and often very ornate and decorative, being supported by mythological figures. They were gilded and made of marble and porcelain (see Fig. 493). Victorian clocks were also ornate but more in rococo vein, and were of carved wood, perhaps gilt, or of papier-mâché or china (see Figs. 498 and 510). They were set on a bracket or the chimney-piece mantelshelf.

Among the numerous types of small **box** of this period were dressing cases, work-boxes and tea-caddies.

FIG. 583.
PARIAN WATER
JUG WITH
HIGH RELIEF
DECORATION
VICTORIAN

FIG. 582.
SILVER
BOTTLE
STAND -
VICTORIAN

FIG. 584.
GILT CHASED TOILET
MIRROR FRAME -
VICTORIAN

FIG. 585.
SILVER TEA
SPOON -
VICTORIAN

FIG. 586. VICTORIAN
SILVER CAKE BASKET

FIG. 587.
PAINTED WOOD
WORK BOX - VICTORIAN

FIG. 588.
PEARL
FISH KNIFE

FIG. 589.
PEARL HANDLED
DESSERT
KNIFE

FIG. 590.
STEEL SCISSORS -
VICTORIAN

FIG. 591.
BELLOWS -
GOTHIC DESIGN
c. 1830

582–591   *Miscellaneous Items, Regency and early Victorian, 1811–60*

These were made of various materials: papier-mâché, Tunbridge ware, carved wood, needlework or metal. Victorian boxes were highly decorated, and often had carved pictures of views or buildings. After 1851, the Crystal Palace was a popular subject (see Figs. 498, 503 and 587).

One or two **sewing machines** found their way into the Victorian home by 1860. Singer had patented his first machine in 1851, while an earlier type had been produced in the 1840's. However, they were not in general use as yet.

Floral decoration had become of great importance to the well-to-do and middle-class home by the Victorian period. Flowers as decoration for the table had been seen during the Regency, but the passion for growing plants indoors was a Victorian one, and particularly so after 1850. Many homes possessed a conservatory adjoining the reception room, in which plants of all kinds were nurtured; all houses contained plant pots, bowls and jardinières. These latter creations were placed in the hall or drawing room and were tall metal or wood erections containing a plant and pot. They usually stood on three paw or claw feet and were decorated by climbing plants in the same medium. Evergreens were very popular with the Victorians, the best known amongst such plants being the famous aspidistra. This plant had been introduced earlier from the Far East, but it was after 1850 tha' me ubiquitous. This was partly due to the fact that aspidistras gh indestructible, so that while a more delicate plant would have f in the stuffy, airtight, darkened mid-Victorian drawing room, tra grew apace and produced more and more dark, shiny leave ed lovingly day by day.

Although by this period **candles** and **rushlights** we ans of lighting for homes, candles continued in use th' ing the Regency, they were in common use ssed costly glass **chandeliers** cut- plement ate XXVIII). available to them, but still candle, especially in country areas where gas was not provided. Dinner tables were also often lit by soft candlelight. Designs of candleholders varied considerably: some were simple, others very ornate, while brass, silver, bronze, iron, wood and porcelain were used in manufacture (see Figs. 495, 496, 497, 595 and 597). Until about 1840–50, the chief fuel for **oil lamps** was still colza oil, though this gave only a dull light. As the oil was so heavy it had to drain downwards from a container to the wick, which could be regulated by a lever. This type of lamp was designed to stand on a table, to be attached to a wall, or as a hanging lamp, wherein the oil drained from a central container into three or four wickholders. In all cases,

FIG. 593. REGENCY CUT GLASS CHANDELIER WITH EIGHTEEN LIGHTS

6'

FIG. 592. BRASS GAS LAMP OR CHANDELIER c.1855

FIG. 594. BRONZE GAS PILLAR VICTORIAN 1850-60

FIG. 595. VICTORIAN SILVER CANDLESTAND c.1855

FIG. 596. BRONZE AND BRASS WALL OIL LAMP VICTORIAN c.1855-60

FIG. 597. BRONZE GIRANDOLE VICTORIAN c.1851

FIG. 598. BRASS CANDLE LAMP COLOURED IN PARTS - VICTORIAN c.1851-60

592–598 *Lighting in Regency and early Victorian England, 1811–60*

the flame was enclosed in a white glass bowl, and a tray was placed beneath the lamp to collect the dripping oil (see Plate XXVIII). About 1840–45, camphine lamps were introduced, but although these gave a better light, they were inclined to be explosive owing to the volatility of the spirit. The result was exciting if not convenient (see Figs. 498 and 596). However, to town dwellers the greatest invention in the field of illumination at this time was the new carburetted hydrogen or **gas lighting**. The experiment had been tried in some factories in the early 1800's, and in London Pall Mall was the first street to be lit by it in 1807. It was not until about 1840 that gas lighting in town houses became fairly general, when the Gas Light and Coke Company was well established. The gas pipes in each room were brought to a central plaster rosette in the ceiling, from which could be hung a three- or four-light brass or bronze chandelier, also to S-shaped brackets on either side of the chimneybreast. The flame was enclosed in a frosted globe and gently popped and purred as the gas escaped. The light was quite pleasant and, compared with candles, it was most efficient, providing a good standard of illumination. Gas fittings can be seen in Figs. 496, 497, 498, 499, 592 and 594.

In general, there was very little improvement in the standards of **sanitation** until after 1850. In London and other large towns, the 18th-century system of draining from the houses into cesspools continued. Where a large river was available, as in London, the sewage was drained through to it to make it a large cesspool; and in view of the fact that the Thames was also the chief source of water for the capital, the reason for recurrent epidemics of unpleasant diseases was not far to seek. In tenement blocks, the situation was worse: most inadequate means of sanitation were provided, often with the cesspools immediately under the floorboards of a living room. It was not until after a severe outbreak of cholera in the 1840's that much action was taken, but main drainage followed, and cesspools gradually disappeared. In many town houses there was now a water closet, generally placed in the yard or garden outside or in a cellar or basement; large houses might have more than one. In country areas, however, such amenities were still rarely seen. Full-length **baths** were also somewhat rare until after 1860, though some well-to-do homes did possess them, sometimes with a shower and hand water pump attached (see Fig. 599). In general, the majority of the population used basins and hip baths, or even just a pail.

More care and thought was now given to the planning of **kitchens** and their function in a house. The 18th-century custom of banishing the kitchen, with its attendant odours, as far from the dining room as possible was regarded with less favour in Regency days, and greater convenience and easier access were established, although in the early Victorian times of large staffs of servants, it was not necessary to study the problem too thoroughly. The cooking facilities were revolutionised in this period by the emergence of the

599 *Bath and Shower with curtains —hand pump for water—Victorian, 1855–60*

range or **kitchener** as an essential installation. These ugly cast-iron monsters were commonly in use by 1860; while consuming large quantities of coal, and pumping smoke into the atmosphere to aggravate the acute Victorian problem of "smog", they were labour-saving compared with the earlier methods, despite the fact that they were difficult to keep clean and that the boiler had to be filled by hand with water—indeed, it was considered miraculous to possess such a thing as a boiler. Most kitcheners were made with an open fire grate flanked on each side by ovens and also had a boiler. Later types possessed a hot-plate on top, and the fire was more enclosed (see Fig. 500). A **stove grate** is illustrated in Fig. 600. A Regency kitchen can be seen in Fig. 499, and a Victorian one in Fig. 500.

During the first part of the 19th century, most of the remaining original **porcelain** factories closed down, leaving only Worcester and Derby, while the latter had also closed by 1850. The bone china which Josiah Spode II had perfected at this time began to replace the earlier soft-paste porcelain and, in the Victorian period, came into general use. It was made cheaply and mass-produced, so that it ousted both the earlier porcelain and pottery from their former place, and was established as the medium for both well-to-do and poorer homes. The cost only varied according to design and the amount of decoration involved. The principal name in pottery design and manufacture continued to be that of Wedgwood, and due to his efforts pottery still kept a place in both the mass-production race and in good design. Other famous makers of this period include the names of Minton and Coalport. Little stoneware was made.

Designs in the Regency period were influenced strongly by the French Empire motifs, while colour became stronger and gilding more lavish. By Victorian days the over-ornamentation which had affected other crafts so greatly was most apparent in the design and decoration of china. Gilding was even more lavishly applied and colours were bright and vivid. Ground colours were popular, particularly in red or gold, yellow, apple-green and dark blue. Patterns included Chinese designs, rococo motifs, Gothic or classical ideas, and by 1850–60 the picture motif was very common, generally in the form of views of Windsor Castle and others. Flower designs were ubiquitous, especially roses or peonies; white birds with rich plumage often intruded. Many articles were made in strange shapes most unsuited to the medium, and over-decoration was later so great that it was sometimes quite difficult to distinguish the use or purpose of the article. The process of lithography was adapted for the use of ceramic decoration in the early 1840's; at first in one colour only—a shade of blue—but later six colours were available, including black.

The **Staffordshire ceramic industry** grew apace in this period and by 1850–60 productions from there were seen in great quantities in many parts of the world. These particularly included the blue printed ware and bone china ware.

The **Derby** factory continued in production until 1848. The Derby work of the Regency was distinctly Empire in conception, particularly notable in the coloured grounds. Derbyshire landscapes were still painted on the ware, also bird, flower, fruit and figure subjects. Other coloured grounds included black, claret, dark blue and pink. This factory should not be confused with the Royal Crown Derby Factory, which commenced production in the 1870's.

The manufactory of **Worcester** made some fine ware during the Regency; coloured grounds were used a good deal, particularly in orange, crimson and blue. Gilding was employed, often in Greek border motifs, and subjects for painting included Japanese designs, flowers, shells and landscapes. In the Victorian period, the work became over-decorated and coarser in design; gilding was heavily applied.

Rockingham ware is typical of this time; the factory—situated in Yorkshire—was founded about 1820 and closed in the early 1840's. Tea services were usual items of ware from this factory, also dessert pieces, and the designs showed a strong rococo influence, with curved and scrolled edges and gilding used in abundance. Much of the ware was over-decorated with fruit and flower patterns, but the earlier work was often of very fine quality.

Other well-known factories included those at **Sunderland**, **Nantgarw** and **Swansea**, all founded about the Regency period.

It has been described in Chapter VIII how **Josiah Spode II** took over his father's factory in the late 1790's, and how soon afterwards he perfected his method of making bone china. In the first twenty years of the 19th century, this ware came into general use both at home and overseas. Josiah died in 1827, but during his lifetime the work of the factory was much influenced by Empire fashions, so that lavish gilding and Empire motifs such as lion's-paw feet, plinth bases, and Egyptian- and Greek-styled handles were used a great deal. The work was of fine quality and made, in general, for the well-to-do homes. **Josiah Spode III**, a cousin to the second Josiah, succeeded to the factory in 1827 and continued in charge until his death in 1833, when the factory was bought by **William Copeland II** and came to be known as Copeland's. The Victorian work of this factory, like that of other contemporary works, was over-decorated. It specialised in floral designs and painted landscapes of castles, famous views and familiar architectural piles. Gold was used in excess, and relief work was common. The ware was sold all over the world, including a somewhat new but large American market. Coloured grounds, particularly in turquoise and dark green, were employed as a means of decoration all the period. The blue-and-white pottery ware made popular by Josiah Spode I continued to be made in large quantities. Designs still included the Willow Pattern and allied patterns, which were much in demand.

600   *Iron Stove Grate—Victorian, c. 1855*

The firm of **Thomas Minton** were in a sense rivals to that of Spode, as both factories were in Stoke-on-Trent and produced a great deal of similar work. Thomas Minton died in 1836, but his son **Herbert** (1793–1858) took over the factory at his father's death. Minton had made blue-and-white pottery from the late 1790's but, in this period, is noted particularly for his bone china, which by 1830 was of fine quality. He employed coloured grounds in turquoise, green and blue, and used much gilding. Like Spode, he also used transfer prints to decorate his wares with pictures of landscapes and buildings.

Coalport ware became very famous from the early 1820's. It specialised in a rococo style of work, using relief mouldings, gilded and painted. Coloured grounds in claret, turquoise and rose were popular, and so also were floral designs. Much of the early Victorian work was in imitation of the famous 18th-century wares from Dresden and Sèvres. The firm was particularly known for its ornamented dinner services.

In the field of pottery, the **Wedgwood** firm, led by Josiah Wedgwood and, after his death, other members of his family, continued to make fine ware of good design. With the success of bone china, it became necessary to re-organise pottery manufacture in order to compete, and Wedgwood attained

(a) *Porcelain from the Potteries of New Hall, Spode and Longport* (1820–30)

(b) *Rockingham, Derby, Coalport and Spode Porcelain* (1815–30)

(a) *Earthenware Plate. Burslem* (*c.* 1835)

(b) *Cup and Saucer. Rockingham* (*c.* 1840)

(c) (left) *Artificial Flower Ornament* (*mid-Victorian*)

(d) (right) *Decorated Glass Jug* (*mid-Victorian*)

(e) *A Group of "Summerly's Art Manufactures"* (*c.* 1847)

XXX EARLY AND MID-VICTORIAN DECORATION

a high level of mass-production output in his factory. The work suffered a temporary set-back in the 1850's but revived again afterwards. Examples of porcelain and pottery can be seen in Plates XXIX and XXX.

The most usual method of decorating the **glassware** of this period was by cutting. In Regency times, the cuts were still fairly shallow, but after 1820 deeper-cut designs were made. Moulded glass was also produced in imitation of cut glass, for the less expensive markets. Glass was engraved from about 1830, giving coloured designs in the form of hunting scenes or views. Towards 1860, etching was employed on glass as a shallower but cheaper method than engraving. Coloured glass was very popular, generally seen in blue, green, purple and amber. Items particularly suited to this medium included cruet bottles, smelling bottles and drinking glasses. Opaque white glass was also in vogue, and from 1850–60 gilded glassware became fashionable. As with other industries, glassware received certain mechanical advantages from the Industrial Revolution, such as the use of steam power for driving the cutter's wheel. From Regency times a novelty process was in use called *crystallo* ceramic ware, in which low-relief white-clay models of figure compositions or flowers were set into molten glass, and these were later made up into articles such as vases or paperweights. They were particularly fashionable from the 1840's. The principal centres in Britain for cut glass and other glassware were Birmingham, Newcastle, Stourbridge and Bristol. Examples of glassware are illustrated in Plate XXVIII.

Regency **silverware** was, on the whole, simple and dignified in design; decoration included predominantly beadwork, reeding, fluting and gadrooning. Classical motifs were still seen, in particular acanthus and vine leaves, while the Egyptian lotus was also used. In more costly work, caryatid candlesticks were fashionable, also relief ornament in the form of friezes decorated by Greek mythological scenes. After 1820, work in the classical vein continued to be produced, but other revivals were also seen; these included the Chinese method of decoration and the rococo. Victorian silverware was in many and varying styles, generally over-decorated, but rococo and Gothic versions predominated. As in other crafts, there was a profusion of flowers, fruit, scrolls, animals and figures, all thrown together in a riot of decoration. The most common items in general use included tea- and coffee-pots, tea sets, dinner ware and salt cellars (see Plate XXVII).

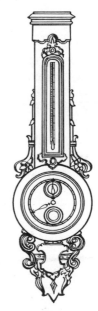

601 *Victorian Barometer*

Large quantities of **Sheffield plate** were still produced until about 1850, but by that time electro-plating, which had been introduced about 1840, was in general use, and superseded the former process (see Plate XXVII).

Pewter ware was still made and was popular for kitchen use and for less well-to-do homes, despite the new electro-plate ware; it kept its place in the home, particularly in the form of tankards, candlesticks and inkwells.

NOTES ON ILLUSTRATIONS

Fig. 493. Regency Dining Room. 1811–20

Plaster **ceiling, cornice** and **frieze**. **Wallpaper** in vertical lengths, delicate colouring and design, classical basis. Sash **window**, narrow frames. Panelled recess. **Curtains,** of striped silk in green and cream. Green cords and tassels. Gilded wood pole and ornament. Polished wood **floor**. Plain wool **carpet**. Glass crystal **chandelier**, with metal framework. White marble carved **chimneypiece**. Steel **grate**. Cast-iron fireback. Steel fire-irons. Brass **candelabra**. Gilt, porcelain and ormolu **clock.** Gilded wood frame to convex **mirror**, carved eagle and decoration. **Furniture**—Rosewood **chiffonier**, mirror backs to shelves, porcelain displayed and reflected; brass lattice to cupboard doors, backed by pleated pink silk; height 5 ft. 8 in. approx. **Pole screen,** of mahogany with ebony inlay, painted velvet banner; height 4 ft. Occasional **table**, rosewood with decorative top of brass inlay and coloured woods; height 2 ft. 4 in. Window **chair**, rosewood, brass inlay, cane seat; height 2 ft. 10 in. Dining **table**, mahogany, pedestal supports, brass mounts; height 2 ft. 6 in. Dining **chairs**, mahogany, striped silk-upholstered seats. **Sideboard**, rosewood inlaid with brass; height 5 ft. approx.

Fig. 494. Regency Drawing Room. 1811–20

Striped **wallpaper** in shades of green. Polished oak **floor**. **Woodwork** painted white. Wool **carpet**, octagonal and floral design in beige and shades of green, pink and blue. Bay **window**. Gold satin **curtains**, green cords and tassels. Glass **chandelier**. Silver **candelabrum**. Carved and painted gilt **stand**. Porcelain **vase**. **Furniture**—Circular **table**, mahogany; height 2 ft. 6 in. **Writing cabinet** on top, wood covered in blue and gilt leather; height 1 ft. 6 in. **Chair,** carved and gilded mahogany, cane seat. **Cabinet,** rosewood, brass lattice doors, lined with pleated pink silk; height 4 ft. 9 in. **Work table,** rosewood, brass mounts and stringing, pink silk pouch bag; height 2 ft. 3 in. **Grecian sofa,** carved mahogany, brass inlay, gold-striped upholstery. **Tea-poy,** rosewood.

Fig. 495. Early Victorian Parlour. 1837–45

White plaster **ceiling, cornice** and **frieze**. **Woodwork** of picture rail, wainscot, window frames and chimney-piece painted white. **Wallpaper,** striped lilac and white. **Sash window,** plain dark-green wool **curtains**. Brass curtain rail round bay. Polished oak **floor**. Wool carpet, strong, dark shades of reds and blues. **Chimneypiece,** gilt decoration on white paint, pink silk curtain. Brass **fender**. Coloured glass and china ornaments on shelf. Ornate gilt **picture frames**, oils, water-colours and black **silhouettes**. Framed sampler over chimneypiece. **Crystal chandelier,** metal fittings. Wall **sconce,** carved and painted wood. **Furniture**—Long **fireside stool,** mahogany, needlework top, rose design. **Fireside chair,** imitation rococo carving in mahogany, flowered-silk-covered upholstery, embroidered cushion, rose design. **Fireside table,** papier-mâché, black and gilt design; height 2 ft. 6 in. **Chiffonier,** carved mahogany, mirror back and doors marble top; height 2 ft. 9 in. Brass **candlesticks,** glass dome on wood case containing wax flowers. **Fire-screen,** mahogany, petit-point panel, black background, rose design; height 4 ft. **Small table,** papier-mâché, inlaid with shell, gilt decoration; height 2 ft. 1 in. **Large table,** mahogany; height 2 ft. 6 in., length 4 ft. Carved wood **candlesticks,** height 1 ft. 4 in. **Chair** by table, wood painted black, cane seat. **Child's chair,** bobbin turned, wood painted black, cane seat; height 2 ft. 4 in. **Chair** in bay, papier-mâché, cane seat, butterflies in shell pattern. **Semicircular table,** carved walnut, inlaid top; height 2 ft. 6 in.

Fig. 496. *Early Victorian Drawing Room. c. 1840–8*

White plaster **ceiling, cornice** and **frieze.** Wooden **window** frames. Doors to open on to garden. Crimson velvet **curtains. Wallpaper,** silver and dark-red stripes. Polished oak **floor. Carpet,** plain, dark-blue centre, border in red, black, fawn and grey. Brass hanging **gas fitting. Furniture**—Mahogany **sofa** with horsehair upholstery; length 7 ft. Cushions in bright colours, embroidered with beads and decorated with tassels. **Prie-dieu,** carved mahogany, tapestry-covered upholstery in fawn and colours. **Chair,** carved mahogany, red-velvet-covered seat. **Work table,** papier-mâché, gold design on black, pictures of Windsor Castle on top and sides, pleated pink silk pouch; height 2 ft. 8 in. **Tripod table,** mahogany; height 2 ft. 5 in. Glass dome containing wax fruit on top. **Cabinet,** rosewood, glazed doors in top part, brass lattice in lower part, inlaid decoration, also brass stringing; height 7 ft. Broadwood upright **pianoforte,** carved rosewood, brass inlay and mounts, top section covered by pink silk; height 6 ft. 6 in. **Candlesticks,** carved rosewood, attached to piano. Gilt **candleholders** on top of piano, decorated by turquoise and gilt porcelain. **Vase** on top of piano, red glass with gilt holder. **Piano stool,** mahogany, adjustable type, tapestry-covered top in rose design. **Music canterbury,** carved mahogany, rococo style; height 1 ft. 4 in.

Fig. 497. *Victorian Bedroom. c. 1850–5*

Plaster **walls** and **ceiling.** Floral **wallpaper** in silver, reds, greens and several other shades. **Woodwork** painted brown. Polished oak **floor.** Wool **hearth rug,** red and white roses on dark maroon-coloured ground. Carved marble **chimneypiece.** Cast-iron fire opening. Wrought-iron **grate** and brass **fender. Chimney glass,** carved pinewood and gilt in imitation rococo style. **Ornaments,** glass vases. **Gas lighting,** brass and decorated glass. **Wall pictures,** mahogany and gilt frames, landscapes and photographs. **Furniture**—**Bed,** mahogany carved frame, half-canopy style; height 7 ft. 6 in. Hangings of crimson silk, with cords and tassels. Silk embroidered coverlet. **Washstand,** carved mahogany, marble top, mirror back; height 2 ft. 6 in. Floral painted decoration on china jugs and basins, also soap dishes. **Bedside cupboard,** mahogany, brass candlestick. **Wardrobe,** mahogany, mirror on door; height 7 ft. 9 in. **Chairs,** papier-mâché, cane seat. **Table,** papier-mâché, tripod stand; height 2 ft. 5 in.

Fig. 498. Early Victorian Parlour. 1850–5

Typical dark, overcrowded room with sombre, rich colour scheme. Wallpaper, floral design in various colours on crimson background. **Carpet,** fitted all over floor, patterned in reds, greens and blues. **Sash window.** White lace **curtains** and longer crimson velvet **curtains** hung from mahogany pole with mahogany rings. All **woodwork** painted dark brown. White marble **chimneypiece,** top part covered in green plush with tassels. **Fireplace, grate, fender, trivet** and **irons** all of cast iron. Iron **coalbox** painted black. **Mantelpiece ornaments,** coloured glassware and porcelain. **Clock,** japanned and decorated with mother-of-pearl and gilt. **Pictures,** sampler, water-colours and prints. **Mirror,** gilt frame. **Lighting,** gas lighting on each side of chimneybreast, oil lamp on pianoforte, porcelain support. **Furniture**—Mahogany **pianoforte,** brass mounts. **Music stool,** mahogany, tapestry-covered upholstered top. **Gate-leg table,** mahogany, embroidered cover, floral pattern. Ornaments and large pot and aspidistra on top. **Centre table,** mahogany. Ornaments, mahogany box, silver box, and flowers under glass dome. **Screen,** embroidered panel showing Crystal Palace, stand carved and turned, painted and gilt wood. **Work table,** papier-mâché, gilt decoration. **Chairs,** mahogany, cane and red-velvet seats. **Footstool,** carved mahogany, needlework top in rose design. **Tripod table,** papier-mâché, inlaid box on top.

Fig. 499. Kitchen of a Regency Royal Palace. 1815–20

Plastered stone **walls.** Sash **windows** with glass, wood frames. Lower part of walls **tiled** with white Dutch tiles. Stone-flagged **floor.** Cast-iron painted **columns,** copper palm leaves. Glass and metal **lanterns,** gas lighting. Bronze smoke **canopies** over ovens and fireplace. Wood-panelled **doors.** Cast-iron **ovens,** hot-air draught for cooking and boiling water. **Kitchen range** as part of oven design. Wood **tables** and shelves. **Utensils** of copper and iron.

Fig. 500. Victorian Kitchen from a Middle-class Town House. c. 1850–60

Green painted **walls.** Dark-brown painted **woodwork.** Stone-flagged **floor. Gas lighting,** central iron gasolier. Painted iron **chimneypiece.** Cast-iron **range** and **boiler.** Stone **hearth.** Iron **poker** and **shovel.** Copper **kettle.** Painted wood **dresser,** in dark brown. Wood **shelves,** scrubbed. Stone **sink,** wood cupboards below. Wood **roller towel fitting. Pans** and other **utensils,** iron and copper.

X

LATE VICTORIAN AND EDWARDIAN, 1860–1914

QUEEN VICTORIA 1860–1901   EDWARD VII 1901–1910
GEORGE V 1910–(1935)

THE **population** of England and Wales doubled during the reign of Victoria, a tremendous increase that occurred largely in the years 1860–90. After 1890, birth control was practised more often, but only by the well-to-do and middle classes, who had begun to find the cost of raising and educating their large families to "the standard to which they were accustomed" a strain on their incomes; the working people continued to live and increase as before. Because of this rise in population, a large percentage of the nation lived at, or below, subsistence level from 1860 to 1900, despite the fact that this was a highly prosperous time for the country as a whole. Unemployment resulted because the increased labour force was not absorbed as quickly as it arose. Moreover, most women of the working classes, also children over ten, and, later, eleven years, had to go out to work, thus aggravating adult male unemployment, but of necessity, because a man's wages were quite inadequate to keep his family from starvation. The conditions of work and pay for women were very bad: hours were long; the work in factory, mill and home was hard, and men workers and foremen took advantage of their superior strength by exacting their "rightful entertainment" from the more attractive workers. Babies and young children were left with a "minder" who frequently ill-treated them. Homes were insanitary slums—a legacy from early Victorian mass building enterprises—food putrid and inadequate and clothes were rags.

In the middle and upper classes the scene was very different. The home was inviolate; there the wife and children spent their lives, joined by the husband during most of his non-working hours. The man was the head of his small gathering, and his wife, though she had little or no housework to do, used her energies as best she might in endless (and often useless) needlework of incredible variety. Her main *raison d'être* was to reproduce, so that most of her life from the age of eighteen to forty-five was spent in pregnancies.

315

600. *Mid-Victorian Parlour, 1860–70 (notes on page 373)*

She did not have to look after the children, and had ample servants and nursery assistance, but this did not compensate for the excessive strain on her body, which, in only too many instances, rebelled in, or after, childbed, and the sorrowing widower with large family was comforted—after a suitable interval—by a second, or even third, wife. Remarriage was not difficult, despite the presence of probably fourteen or fifteen step-children, as until 1880–90 the only career open to middle-class women was marriage, and most of them accepted it without question.

However, by 1890, great strides were being made both in the relief of the poor and in the emancipation of women from their long service as inferior beings. The public conscience was being stirred over the question of poverty, an important beginning, for it had been the apathy and ignorance of the mid-Victorian middle class which had allowed bad conditions to continue for so long. Well-to-do and influential people began to organise schemes to assist the poor. There was more than a hint of patronage in these, but in many instances it was quite unintentional. District visits were organised and relief given; parks were open to public use as owners gave up land for such purpose in crowded towns; and the Salvation Army was beginning its work. Towards the end of the century, the **Fabian Society** under Mr. and Mrs. Sidney Webb propounded its Socialist creed and the first two Labour members were admitted to Parliament. By 1900, wages had improved a good deal; **trade unions** were organising, and learning the power of concerted strike action, particularly in the docks and the mines, where alleviation of the abominable conditions resulted.

Among the more intelligent and well-to-do early Victorian women dissatisfaction with the limitations of their lives was awakening a feeling of restlessness: child-bearing, embroidery, needlework, interminable social calls, parties and entertainments were becoming to be regarded as inadequate recompense for a well-to-do husband. But it was not until the late Victorian period that opportunity was given to such women to escape into a fuller and more interesting life. They had had little or no chance of education, and without this they could not fit themselves for any useful work, however intelligent they might be. Paradoxically the greatest opponents to women's emancipation were women and the fiercest opposition of all came from Queen Victoria. Though of dominating personality herself, she upheld that other women should be submissive, meek and gentle, and be guided in all things by their men. Victoria appeared to see no irony in this, though her attitude to Prince Albert had apparently been the reverse of submissive. Eventually, step by step, came the openings, forced upon an unwilling society by a few brave and intelligent women and by a changing social structure. The need of hundreds of women began to be realised, and with the opportunities came a greater need, developing in a tide of public opinion. It was not until the

Late Victorian Drawing Room, 1870–85 (notes on page 373)

604 *Mid-Victorian Bedroom, c. 1865–75 (notes on page 374)*

605 *Late Victorian Dining Room, c. 1890–5 (notes on page 374)*

606 *Edwardian Drawing Room, 1901–14 (notes on page 374)*

Great War of 1914–18 that it was realised how necessary and useful women could be outside the home, but prior to 1914 came university education and girls' public schools, also wider educational facilities in secondary schools for girls and openings in the professions such as medicine, nursing, teaching and journalism.

Towards the end of the century, **servants** also began to rebel against their position. For years they had worked at hard and monotonous tasks for very long hours and very little pay. The Victorian home was anything but labour-saving; there had been no need to consider conserving labour when it had been cheap and plentiful. Homes were large, with many flights of stairs between cellar and attic, children numerous—fifteen was an average family—and the home was overflowing with furniture, ornaments, pictures, photographs and knick-knacks of all kinds. Polishing was a full-time job, as both essential fittings and ornaments were commonly of brass or copper, and stainless cutlery was not yet known. All washing was done at home, including bed-linen and the many layers of underwear in the form of panta-lettes, corset covers, petticoats, etc., with many flounces to starch and iron. Baking also was a home production, especially in the north of England, and on an "improved kitchener" was a hot and wearisome business. Gas was in use in towns, but chiefly for lighting until after 1900, whilst electric lighting was a 20th-century innovation. Coal had therefore to be carried up to all floors for bedroom fires and for water heating. Carpets had to be swept, as vacuum cleaners were not available until the 20th century, so that the resulting dust on all surfaces can be imagined. Labour-saving devices had been introduced into factories more and more, but it was not until after 1900 that they were adapted for use in the home, when the formerly willing servants began to find other occupations open to them due to the emancipation of their sex. The middle- and upper-class housewives demanded mechanical assistance. In fact it was not until they had something else to do outside the home that the home required their full attention.

Holidays away from home in the summer were now enjoyed. These had previously been restricted to the well-to-do, but, by 1900, large numbers of people flocked to the seaside and country. Devon and Cornwall became popular with the improved railway services, while the north-country folk migrated to Blackpool. More energetic holidaymakers began to walk and climb the fells in the Lake District and North Wales. More people went abroad and climbing in the Alps became a pursuit of the young and the hardy.

In the realm of **education**, a universal state-organised system of primary schooling was established, which meant that children of poorer working-class families, who had formerly worked in mine and factory, were now forbidden to do so, and received some, if not adequate, education. Nevertheless, secondary education was reserved for those who could pay fees. Girls now

(a) *Tankard (Doultons), Vases and Pottery Owl* (c. 1875)

(b) *Late Victorian and Edwardian Glass*

(c) *Pottery designed by William de Morgan* (1882–98)

XXXI   LATER VICTORIAN CERAMICS

(a) *Embroidered Linen Cushion Cover* (1899)

(b) *Wallpaper designed by William Morris* (1876)

(c) *"Art Nouveau" Chafing Dish, Silver* (c. 1905)

(d) *Bronze Stove, designed by Alfred Stevens* (1851)

607 *Late Victorian Entrance Hall and Staircase, 1895–1900 (notes on page 375)*

began to have educational opportunities, but not by any means on equal terms with boys.

From the 1870's onwards more and more people began to take part in, and watch, various forms of **sport**. Previously most games had been played at public schools and universities by the sons of well-to-do families, and, in a small way, on the village green. But with the enormous increase of population, and the consequently enlarged wealthy Victorian middle class, far more children were educated at secondary schools, and later, colleges, so that, as communications and transport facilities improved, enthusiasm for sport became more widespread. The costume was most unsuitable, especially that of the ladies, but, towards 1900, even this was gradually altered so that greater physical prowess at games could be developed. **Cricket** became a national sport: county clubs were formed and matches organised, and the Test Matches[1] against Australia date from 1877. It was at one of these, in 1882 at the Oval, that the expression "The Ashes" originated. England was defeated and historic words were written "To the memory of English Cricket", "the body will be cremated and the ashes taken to Australia"—ashes which we have fought to recover and retain with varying success ever since. The most famous cricketer of this period was, of course, Dr. W. G. Grace, that bearded immortal and hero of the 1890's. **Football** also grew in popularity and, although still rather rough and boisterous at this stage, was developing steadily on club and international level, and acquiring increasing support from its fans. In the realm of **athletics**, the Y.M.C.A. and The Polytechnic gave facilities and gained much support, while the Olympic Games were held on an international scale. However, the most popular sports for increasing numbers of average men and women included **golf**, **tennis**, **crocquet** and **swimming**. **Tennis**, in particular, became almost a craze by 1890. The All England Croquet and Lawn Tennis Club were holding championships regularly, and these were attended with great enthusiasm, though the play was slow compared to that of to-day. The most popular outdoor entertainment of all in the 1890's was provided by the **bicycle**, as epitomised in that old song "Daisy, Daisy". Both young men and women were equally energetic on their two wheels, or even three, and, despite a lack of springs and an excess of petticoats, enjoyed themselves immensely. Altogether the outdoor life was claiming more and more town dwellers in their leisure time, so that the fresh-air bogey of the earlier Victorians was retreating fast.

Among the other forms of amusement and entertainment could be numbered whist drives, church social activities and, at home, gardening and the playing of and listening to music performed by family and friends. Leisure time was still limited, as hours of work were long, and, until 1900, most people, as yet, had to make their own forms of entertainment. A new interest

[1] Not called Test Matches until after 1894.

608   *Late Victorian Kitchen and Scullery, c. 1880–95 (notes on page 375)*

was opening up for women in the form of afternoon tea parties. Formerly these had always been held in the homes of various friends, but, towards the end of the century, it became the fashion for women to meet their friends in tea-shops, first in London, later in provincial towns. Men had done this from the coffee-house days of the 17th century, but for women it was an exciting and daring departure from the normal, and more and more stores and tea-shops opened to serve tea and cakes and meet the new demand, while "afternoon shopping in Oxford Street" became an adventure and an outing. Concert halls, pantomimes and opera were well attended, so also was the theatre, while more people were now patronising the growing number of art galleries. **Entertaining in the home** was still indulged in on a large scale and provided the most usual way of meeting one's friends, particularly for those over thirty, who did not support the new sports and clubs to a great extent. Guests were invited to all meals: even breakfast parties were given, though lunch, tea and dinner parties were more common. Tea was served at five o'clock, which was regarded as the suitable hour for informal calls, indoors in the winter and in the garden in good summer weather. Dinner parties were long, formal affairs with enormous quantities of food in numerous courses, accompanied by suitable wines. The ladies still retired to the drawing room while the gentlemen enjoyed their port, and until 1880–90 tobacco smoke was considered offensive to delicate feminine nostrils, and smoking was confined to a specific masculine room and attire. The average dinner menu would include oysters—if in season—soups, several types of fish, three or four entrées, red meats and game, substantial puddings—hot, then cold versions—biscuits and cheese, ices, dessert, liqueurs, port and coffee. Guests were entertained by numerous games, amongst which charades were most favoured, but also enjoyed were instructive games with paper and pencil and music in various forms.

1860–1914 was an extremely fertile period for inventions. Scientific work, in the various fields which had been progressing in Europe and America for many years, crystallised into new forms of communications, heating, lighting, motion and entertainment. We take these for granted to-day, but our forebears of the 19th century regarded them as miraculous. They only saw the crude beginnings of many of these

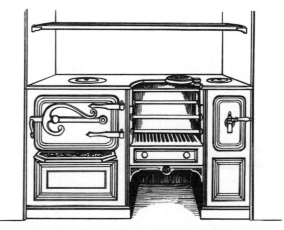

610   *Iron Cooking Range, cottage type— Victorian*

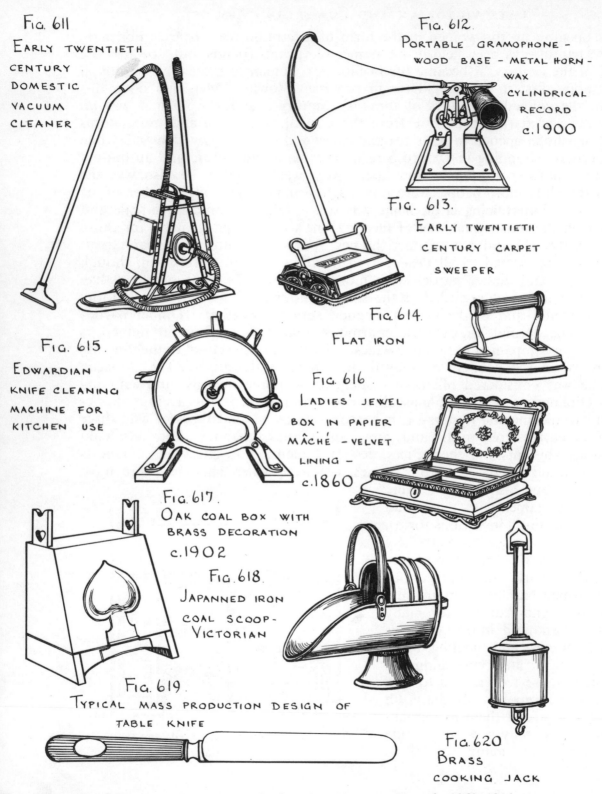

Fig. 611
EARLY TWENTIETH
CENTURY
DOMESTIC
VACUUM
CLEANER

Fig. 612.
PORTABLE GRAMOPHONE —
WOOD BASE — METAL HORN —
WAX
CYLINDRICAL
RECORD
c.1900

Fig. 613.
EARLY TWENTIETH
CENTURY CARPET
SWEEPER

Fig. 614.
FLAT IRON

Fig. 615.
EDWARDIAN
KNIFE CLEANING
MACHINE FOR
KITCHEN USE

Fig. 616.
LADIES' JEWEL
BOX IN PAPIER
MÂCHÉ — VELVET
LINING —
c.1860

Fig. 617.
OAK COAL BOX WITH
BRASS DECORATION
c.1902

Fig. 618.
JAPANNED IRON
COAL SCOOP-
VICTORIAN

Fig. 619.
TYPICAL MASS PRODUCTION DESIGN OF
TABLE KNIFE

Fig. 620.
BRASS
COOKING JACK

611–620   *Later Victorian and Edwardian Domestic Utensils, 1860–1914*

services which we have nowadays seen come into full use, and the effect on life in the home and outside it has been far-reaching for all strata of society. Among such 19th-century "miracles" came the telephone, the cinematograph, electricity, the internal-combustion engine and the propagation of radio waves.

Alexander Graham Bell developed and produced a **telephone** which he exhibited in 1876. Bell was of Scottish birth, but from 1871 had been employed as a Professor of Vocal Physiology in Boston, U.S.A. In his work on the telephone he employed the carbon microphone produced by **Thomas Edison**; the combination of their work enabled the telephone experiment to be made. In Britain, progress towards general use of the telephone was slow, but the National Telephone Company was formed in 1889, and London was gradually linked to other towns, first Brighton, then further afield. By 1900–10, numbers of homes had telephones, and after the G.P.O. took over the service in 1911, it was enlarged to a national scale (see Fig. 632).

The **cinematograph** was developed in this period to become a highly popular form of inexpensive entertainment. Our present term "cinema" is an abbreviation of cinematograph or kinematograph, which, in turn, is derived from the Greek words meaning "motion" and "I write". Early work in the 19th century, which formed a basis for later film shows, was done by **P. Mark Roget** in 1824 in England, later by **Dr. Joseph A. Planteau** in Ghent and **Dr. Simon R. von Stampfer** in Vienna, also **Coleman Sellers** and **Dr. Wellman** in the U.S.A. The credit for developing sensitised celluloid film for use instead of glass plates, and for the experiments on a new shutter device in 1889, must go to the pioneer **William Friese-Green,** an Englishman, while

Thomas Edison produced the Kinetoscope in New York in 1894. This was a peep-show film, fifty feet long, running for approximately thirteen seconds. **Thomas Armat's** Vitascope followed in 1895, and in America the first motion-picture theatre, called the Nickelodeon, was opened in Pittsburgh in 1905, showing stories in film medium. Public exhibition in France was given by the **Lumière Bros.,** and in England by **Robert Paul.** The Frenchman **Méliès** produced story films from 1899 such as "Cinderella", and in 1902 "Trip to the Moon". More ambitious films followed, such as Italy's "Rape of the Sabines" and "Last Days of Pompeii", 1912–14, and, in 1913, the famous "Quo Vadis", fore-runner of the mid-20th century's "mighty

621   *Cast Iron and Steel Gas Cooking Range—early 20th century*

spectacle". Despite many sneers and wet-blanket predictions, the attraction of the early cinematograph grew, and the public in London and other towns flocked to sit on their wooden benches for a penny or twopence a time and stare enthralled at the jumpy moving pictures with spirited piano accompaniment. In London, regular public shows began in 1905, and by 1914 every large town in Britain had at least one cinema, now with velvet-covered seats and often with an organ to replace the upright piano. The stars followed after this, though the great Charles Chaplin made his first film appearance in 1914.

In general, the benefit of **electricity**, from the commercial standpoint, was not felt in the home until the 20th century, but early examples of electric lighting and power could be seen before this. Despite objections from the gas enterprises, most large towns had electric power by 1900, and in London, trains and trams were running on it, the tube system had begun, and famous buildings and streets such as the House of Commons, main-line railway stations, the British Museum and Pall Mall were lit by it.

The development of the **motor-car** with its internal-combustion engine, known to the late Victorians and Edwardians as a "horseless carriage", was severely held up in England by the fierce opposition of horse owners and riders who wished to ban it from the road. They succeeded in rousing public opinion to the extent that British law would only permit a four miles per hour speed limit[1] and each car had to be manned by three persons, one of whom preceded it walking with a red flag. On the Continent, no such restrictions existed, and from 1885, cars with such famous names as Benz, Daimler and Mercedes took the road in increasing numbers. After the repeal of the "Red Flag Act" in 1896,[2] when the speed limit was raised to fourteen miles per hour, cars became immensely popular, and to possess a "horseless carriage" was a great thrill. There was, of course, no protection against the English climate, so motoring attire of caps, hats, veils, goggles and overcoats, seemingly for Arctic use, was adopted. Horseless 'buses gradually replaced the more romantic and decorative horse 'buses in London streets, but these still had no "tops" as yet.

A Scottish physicist, **James Clark Maxwell,** first propounded a general theory of the propagation of radio waves in the 1860's. After this, in Germany, experiments on radio waves were carried out by **Heinrich R. Hertz.** Following on from this work, in England, **Marchese G. Marconi,** an Italian who had worked under Hertz, was the first man to produce apparatus to send messages by radio on a commercial scale. In 1896 he sent messages up to nine miles distant in England, and in 1897 founded the Marconi Wireless

[1] Dated from the Act of 1865 when the speed limit was reduced to 4 m.p.h. and 2 m.p.h. in towns.

[2] A celebration of the repeal was held in 1896 by a car rally from London to Brighton in which 54 cars took part. This rally is now an annual event as the 'Old Crocks' Race.'

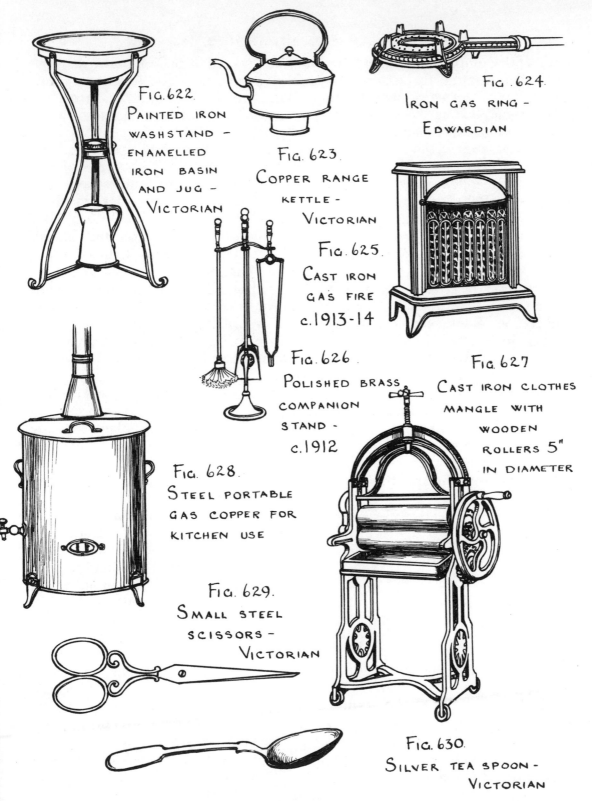

FIG. 622.
PAINTED IRON
WASHSTAND –
ENAMELLED
IRON BASIN
AND JUG –
VICTORIAN

FIG. 623.
COPPER RANGE
KETTLE –
VICTORIAN

FIG. 624.
IRON GAS RING –
EDWARDIAN

FIG. 625.
CAST IRON
GAS FIRE
c. 1913-14

FIG. 626.
POLISHED BRASS
COMPANION
STAND –
c. 1912

FIG. 627
CAST IRON CLOTHES
MANGLE WITH
WOODEN
ROLLERS 5"
IN DIAMETER

FIG. 628.
STEEL PORTABLE
GAS COPPER FOR
KITCHEN USE

FIG. 629.
SMALL STEEL
SCISSORS –
VICTORIAN

FIG. 630.
SILVER TEA SPOON –
VICTORIAN

622–630   *Later Victorian and Edwardian Domestic Articles, 1860–1914*

Telegraph Company Limited. In 1901, he succeeded in sending a message across the Atlantic from Cornwall to Newfoundland. The furtherance and adaptation of this work, which led to general broadcasting and radio receivers in the home, belong to the post-1914–18 period, but the beginnings had been made in Victorian England.

A beginning was also made at this time in man's conquest of the air. **Gliders** were known and used by the Victorians, and the early types of **aircraft** which endeavoured to imitate the flight of a bird, and which were developed after the Wright Brothers' successful attempt to make a short flight in a heavier-than-air craft, were made in Edwardian days. On July 25th, 1909, the Frenchman **Louis Blériot** became the first man to cross the English Channel by air; he landed in a monoplane at Dover after a flight of about half an hour in a plane with a 24-horsepower engine.

A further discovery which greatly affected and assisted mankind, though not in the realm of the home or entertainment, was that of **X-rays** by **Professor Wilhelm K. Röntgen** at the University of Würzburg in Germany in 1895. Within three months these rays were used in medical diagnosis and therapy in Vienna, and by 1896 **Sir Joseph J. Thomson,** the famous British physicist, was engaged in further research on X-rays.

The tremendous increase of population between 1860 and 1914 was accompanied by an equally great expansion of domestic, public and ecclesiastical **building**: towns spread into the surrounding countryside and villages became towns. The scope of industry was extended and often moved to another part of the country, causing new urban areas to spring up on hitherto open land. The great bulk of this building, at least until 1900, was in the **Victorian Gothic style**, although some heavily classical work was carried out at the same time. For public and ecclesiastical building, stone was employed, but in the domestic field, and for some of the public work, yellow and dark-red brick were used. It is a period of architecture which is still completely out of favour in our own time, and we can, generally speaking, have little good to say of it. To us, it appears fussy, over-ornamented, lacking in dignity and simple precept: it seems to take the worst of Gothic design and re-adapt it to Victorian use. However, it is, as yet, too near to

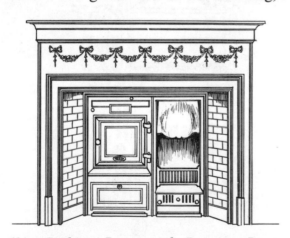

631 *Cooking Range and Drawing Room Grate combined, of cast iron and steel—tiled surround and hearth—painted iron chimney-piece and mantelshelf, c. 1910–14*

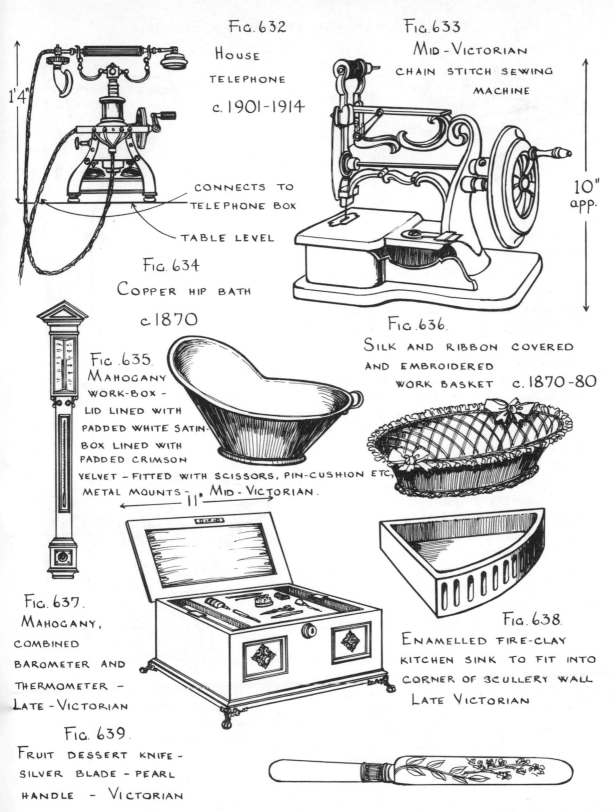

Fɪɢ. 632
House
ᴛᴇʟᴇᴘʜᴏɴᴇ
c. 1901–1914

Fɪɢ. 633
Mɪᴅ-Vɪᴄᴛᴏʀɪᴀɴ
ᴄʜᴀɪɴ ѕᴛɪᴛᴄʜ ѕᴇᴡɪɴɢ
ᴍᴀᴄʜɪɴᴇ

1' 4"

10"
app.

ᴄᴏɴɴᴇᴄᴛѕ ᴛᴏ
ᴛᴇʟᴇᴘʜᴏɴᴇ ʙᴏx

ᴛᴀʙʟᴇ ʟᴇᴠᴇʟ

Fɪɢ. 634
Cᴏᴘᴘᴇʀ ʜɪᴘ ʙᴀᴛʜ
c 1870

Fɪɢ. 635.
Mᴀʜᴏɢᴀɴʏ
ᴡᴏʀᴋ-ʙᴏx –
ʟɪᴅ ʟɪɴᴇᴅ ᴡɪᴛʜ
ᴘᴀᴅᴅᴇᴅ ᴡʜɪᴛᴇ ѕᴀᴛɪɴ–
ʙᴏx ʟɪɴᴇᴅ ᴡɪᴛʜ
ᴘᴀᴅᴅᴇᴅ ᴄʀɪᴍѕᴏɴ
ᴠᴇʟᴠᴇᴛ – ꜰɪᴛᴛᴇᴅ ᴡɪᴛʜ ѕᴄɪѕѕᴏʀѕ, ᴘɪɴ-ᴄᴜѕʜɪᴏɴ ᴇᴛᴄ,
ᴍᴇᴛᴀʟ ᴍᴏᴜɴᴛѕ – 11" Mɪᴅ-Vɪᴄᴛᴏʀɪᴀɴ.

Fɪɢ. 636.
Sɪʟᴋ ᴀɴᴅ ʀɪʙʙᴏɴ ᴄᴏᴠᴇʀᴇᴅ
ᴀɴᴅ ᴇᴍʙʀᴏɪᴅᴇʀᴇᴅ
ᴡᴏʀᴋ ʙᴀѕᴋᴇᴛ c. 1870–80

Fɪɢ. 637.
Mᴀʜᴏɢᴀɴʏ,
ᴄᴏᴍʙɪɴᴇᴅ
ʙᴀʀᴏᴍᴇᴛᴇʀ ᴀɴᴅ
ᴛʜᴇʀᴍᴏᴍᴇᴛᴇʀ –
Lᴀᴛᴇ-Vɪᴄᴛᴏʀɪᴀɴ

Fɪɢ. 638.
Eɴᴀᴍᴇʟʟᴇᴅ ꜰɪʀᴇ-ᴄʟᴀʏ
ᴋɪᴛᴄʜᴇɴ ѕɪɴᴋ ᴛᴏ ꜰɪᴛ ɪɴᴛᴏ
ᴄᴏʀɴᴇʀ ᴏꜰ 3ᴄᴜʟʟᴇʀʏ ᴡᴀʟʟ
Lᴀᴛᴇ Vɪᴄᴛᴏʀɪᴀɴ

Fɪɢ. 639.
Fʀᴜɪᴛ ᴅᴇѕѕᴇʀᴛ ᴋɴɪꜰᴇ –
ѕɪʟᴠᴇʀ ʙʟᴀᴅᴇ – ᴘᴇᴀʀʟ
ʜᴀɴᴅʟᴇ – Vɪᴄᴛᴏʀɪᴀɴ

632–639 *Later Victorian and Edwardian Domestic Articles, 1860–1914*

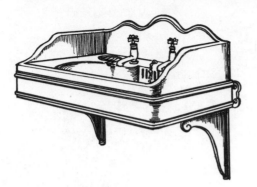

640   *Wall Bracket Wash Basin—*
painted iron bracket—brass taps—
Edwardian

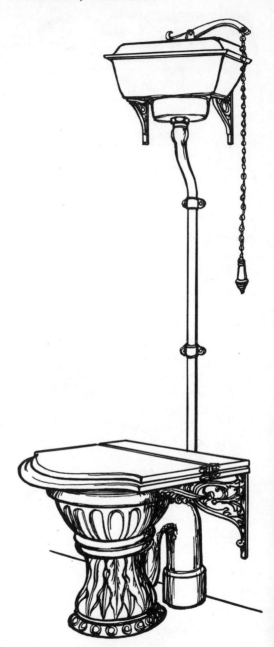

our own time—which is in reaction to
it—to judge fairly, and in another fifty
years it may well be appreciated again.
One thing may certainly be said in its
defence: except for the poorer dwellings,
the work was well done. Modern conveniences may be lacking, and modern
methods of building, but the foundations,
bricklaying and general construction were
good and have, in most cases, where not
utterly neglected, survived two world
wars and the English climate very well.
It is very doubtful that the same may be
said of mid-20th-century work.

The homes of 1860–90 were generally
rather dark still; rooms were large and
high but not always well lit and the style
of furnishing accentuated the darkness.
The narrow, tall house predominated in
towns, due to the lack of space, and with
large families to house, extension had to
be made vertically; terrace houses were
common in this style. Numbers of books
and papers were available now on how
to furnish and decorate the home, and
many of these advocated less curved,
flamboyant furniture than had been

641   *Water Closet, c. 1890–1900—*
painted iron brackets—fawn and white
pedestal closet—polished mahogany seat
and lid—painted cistern—china grip

334

popular at the Great Exhibition of 1851, and a simpler arrangement of rooms, but still adhered to the dark, sombre wallpapers and over-decorated ceilings and friezes. However, most people still heavily over-furnished their houses, and the drawing room in particular was still crammed to capacity with small and large items, ornaments, covers, wax fruit, papier-mâché, photographs, etc. One cannot help admiring the skill with which the ladies must have negotiated all this with, first, crinoline skirts and, later, bustle draperies. Despite the great quantity of furniture and ornaments, there appeared to be no definite arrangement: items were placed here and there at different angles to each other and to the walls, where the only aim appeared to be that it was desirable to cover all the floor space, if possible. Some fine old furniture was mixed up with cheap bamboo, painted beechwood or cane and the whole was stirred up together in a glorious mixture. This applied equally to all homes, poor or wealthy. In general, architects no longer designed furniture to go with their houses, so the furniture had little or no connection with the house plan (see Figs. 602, 603 and 604).

Towards 1890, a lightness began slowly to invade the well-to-do home, though the middle class clung solidly to its velvets, crimson and bottle green, and its over-furnishing. The heavy curtain fabrics were replaced by cottons, silks and cretonne, in gayer, floral patterns, and the lace curtains were drawn back to let in a little daylight. The dark-brown and grained paintwork was changed to cream or white, and the wallpaper was of a lighter design and colour scheme, while the frieze often assumed decorative supremacy. Carpets were softer in tone and less busily patterned. By 1900, classical designs and motifs were becoming fashionable again, though of Adam and Classic Revival style, not the Palladian; the latter was considered heavy and vulgar by the Victorians. Pseudo-Adam decoration was applied to friezes, doorways and chimneypieces, and pseudo-Sheraton furniture was designed to be in keeping. Both these styles had a Victorian flavour, but did at least give a greater simplicity and lightness to the design of the room (see Figs. 605 and 607). The drawing room was generally decorated in white and pale colours now, while the dining room was still in the dark browns of leather, oak and mahogany. Palms were everywhere, in drawing rooms, halls, parlours and sitting rooms. Greenery was supposed to be elegant, flowing and springing in tall jardinières and short pots alike (see Figs. 602, 603, 605, 606 and 607). Also at this

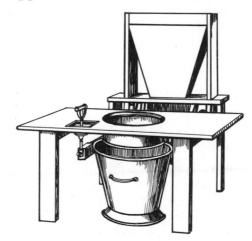

642 *Earth Closet—late 19th century*

335

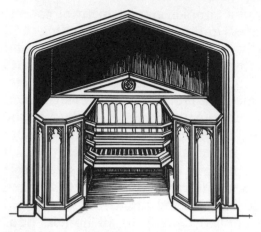

643 *Cast-iron Grate—Victorian Gothic design, c. 1870–5*

time, due to the beginning of the servant shortage problem, houses were built to be more labour-saving. Stairs were designed with a better tread and to be less steep; the kitchen was placed near to the dining room, and food lifts were installed in larger homes.

The **period 1900–14** produced homes of greater simplicity; Georgian designs were reintroduced for larger homes, but most houses had large sash windows, good-sized rooms and simpler exterior decoration. The stucco, pseudo-Gothic panels, swags and sprays tended to disappear, and dignified silhouettes were seen in red and yellow brick, with slate or tiled roof. Houses had fewer storeys as families were smaller and less servant accommodation was needed. Attics and cellars tended to be left out and two-storey houses became popular. The complicated arrangement of the 1860–70 house, with three reception rooms, breakfast room, kitchen, larder and pantries, smoking room, study and innumerable bedrooms and attics, gave place to three reception rooms, kitchen on the ground floor, three or four bedrooms and a bathroom on the first floor. One or two toilets were now considered necessary. Ceilings were plain or simply ribbed, woodwork white or cream, and wall and frieze papered in a fairly simple design. Carpets were plain or bordered and often fitting (see Fig. 606).

Needless to say, although the desire of well-to-do and educated people was changing towards 1914 away from the over-crowding, darkness and over-decoration, this does not mean that everyone's home changed in the same way. Older people, in particular, rarely like change from what they have been used to when younger, and, on the whole, the average middle-class home in 1914 was still over-burdened with furniture and ornaments, still had dark-

644 *Cast-iron Grate—blue tiles—carved oak chimneypiece and mantelshelf—centre mirror—side panels—Edwardian*

336

brown paint, a whitewashed over-decorated plaster ceiling, and a fierce carpet in blues, reds, greens and purples in a complicated all-over pattern. The mantelpiece would still be surmounted by a massive and intricate erection of cupboards, shelves and mirrors, hung with velvet drapery, fringe and tassels, and decorated with innumerable photographs and ornaments, and, in general, the whole room would still look like that in Fig. 602 or Fig. 603. Indeed, who is there among us who does not know of some rooms, even in 1956, which have changed little from this?

On the other side of the picture, and working in the direction towards simplicity of design and functional craftsmanship in the Victorian period, there were a group of people, chiefly artists, designers, architects and craftsmen, who followed William Morris and his friends in their work. Prominent among this group were Morris himself, Philip Webb, Dante Gabriel Rossetti and Edward Burne-Jones. The company formed in the 1860's, **Morris and Co.,** produced glassware, tiles, wallpaper, ironwork and, later, furniture. Webb

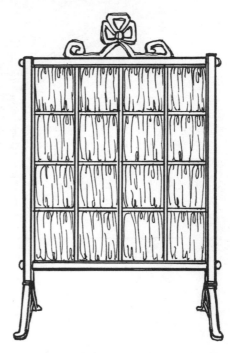

645—*Brass Fire Screen—pink silk curtain backing—Edwardian*

designed homes among which was the Red House, built for Morris himself, near Bexley Heath. These men were in a minority in their lifetime, and appeared to have had but a small effect on the general art, design and architecture of the period, but the effect has been lasting, and much of the early 20th-century work has something of their ideals and effort in it.

Another minority viewpoint in architecture and interior decorative design and furniture was expressed by the exponents of the **Art Nouveau** style in the Edwardian period. The British version of this was rather more solemn and dignified than the Continental, and its chief characteristics were extreme simplicity of line, and the

646　*Cast-iron Stove—Victorian*

337

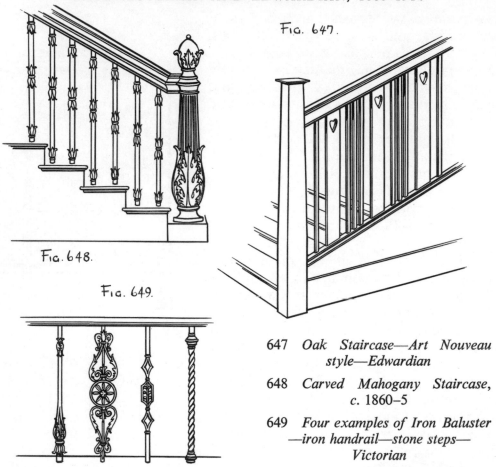

FIG. 647.

FIG. 648.

FIG. 649.

647 *Oak Staircase—Art Nouveau style—Edwardian*

648 *Carved Mahogany Staircase, c. 1860–5*

649 *Four examples of Iron Baluster —iron handrail—stone steps— Victorian*

tallness of its furniture and decorative features. Voysey and Mackintosh were two of its primary exponents in Britain, also Gimson and Walton. The architecture was simple and austere, with casement windows, plain roofs and low buildings. Inside, wainscot covered much of the wall up to four or five feet, and friezes were decorated with floral patterns as important features of the room design. Woodwork was painted white or left unpainted, floors polished and with plain rugs or carpet, and furniture was tall, thin and singularly uncomfortable. Vine, hearts and flowers were typical motifs, used indiscriminately but sparingly on furniture, walls, carpets, stained glass in windows and fire accessories. Again, this minority viewpoint had a small effect only in its period, but a greater following in later years. To-day it is generally extolled by the art critic and intellectual, perhaps largely because it stood out so clearly and strangely in its own time.

Examples of Art Nouveau furniture and decoration can be seen in Figs. 606, 647, 650, 659, 665, 671, 677, 695 and 728, and Plate XXXIIc.

From 1860 onwards, **photographs** were becoming increasingly popular in the Victorian home, both professional studio portraits and those carried out by amateur photographers. The likenesses of innumerable sons, daughters, uncles, aunts, cousins and grandparents were set in array on the piano and sideboard, while photograph albums were cherished and provided dubious entertainment for the unwary guest. As time passed, more people took up this fascinating hobby; societies were formed, and by the end of the century seaside snapshots were all the rage.

The leading **Victorian architects** who supported and fostered the paramount Gothic style of architecture between 1860 and 1900 were **Sir George Gilbert Scott, 1811–78**, **George E. Street, 1824–81**, **William Butterfield, 1814–1900**, and **Alfred Waterhouse, 1830–1905**. **Sir George Gilbert Scott** was continuing his practice which had been flourishing in the mid-Victorian period and was, by 1870, at the height of his fame as the leading Gothic architect of his day. He was very hard-working and prolific, and was responsible for many buildings some of which were partly carried out by others. Such buildings included churches, railway stations, public buildings and memorials. He remained an ardent Gothicist in ideal, and most of his work was in this vein. The notable exception is his Foreign Office, completed in 1867; the original designs were extremely Gothic in conception, but after governmental pressure was put upon him, Scott redesigned a classical building, and later used the scorned design as the basis for St. Pancras Station, after winning the competition for this work. His Albert Memorial (1872) was intended as a medieval shrine and was very popular at the time, though in the 20th century it has become the subject for great controversy, scorn and derision being poured upon it and its author by the intellectual and younger members of society. Now, public opinion is beginning to veer round once more and it is more fashionable to say that it is perhaps not so ugly after all, and not in such bad taste as it was once thought to be. Needless to say, considerable exaggeration has been shown on both sides of this argument. His son, also **George Gilbert Scott,** continued work in his father's tradition. **George E. Street** worked under Scott in his office for some years, and was an equally strong Gothicist. His work was also largely concerned with ecclesiastical and public buildings, the best known of which are the Law Courts in the Strand in London. **William Butterfield**, a Londoner, also designed many churches in the Gothic theme. His work is not appreciated greatly to-day, being too harsh and solemn. Among his most famous achievements is Keble College, Oxford. **Alfred Waterhouse** was, like Scott, a highly successful and industrious Gothic architect of this period. His work was solid and strong, often in yellow and red brick or stone, and based on Decorated Gothic and Tudor styles. In general, it is unpopular at the present time, and amongst examples quoted in this respect are the National History Museum at South Kensington, built

Fig. 650.
Oak chair with cane seat - Art Nouveau style 1899-1900

Fig. 651.
Mahogany chair with horsehair seat 1870-80

Fig. 652
Oak adjustable chair - buttoned upholstery 1870-5

Fig. 653.
Horsehair upholstered arm-chair - mahogany frame - 1875

Fig. 654.
Plain wood chair 1890

Fig. 655.
Mahogany corner chair with leather seat 1880-5

Fig. 656.
Cast iron garden chair - 1860-80

Fig. 657.
Basketwork chair with chintz covered cushion 1880-90

Fig. 658.
Mahogany dining chair with velvet covered seat 1901-5

Fig. 659.
Child's chair of inlaid oak - leather seat - Edwardian

Fig. 660.
Mahogany chair with horsehair buttoned seat 1860-70

Fig. 661.
Mahogany dining chair with velvet seat 1880-5

Fig. 662.
Mahogany chair horsehair seat 1875-80

Fig. 663 Bentwood and cane rocking chair 1870-80

Fig. 664.
Birch chair with rush seat - 1880-5

Fig. 665
Oak chair - velvet seat Art Nouveau style 1897-1900

650–665 *Later Victorian and Edwardian Chairs, 1860–1914*

1879, and the Prudential Assurance Building in Holborn. Two other well-known examples of his work are St. Paul's School, London, and the University College Hospital.

Three architects who began in this period by working as Gothicists under George Street were **R. Norman Shaw, 1831–1912, W. Eden Nesfield** and **Philip Webb, 1831–1915. Norman Shaw** was a Scot who came to work with Street in 1858. After four years, he set up in independent practice, and later broke away from the Gothic tradition and tried various styles: Tudor, Stuart and, eventually, 18th-century classic. He designed some fine houses in London, also in the country, and is noted for his New Scotland Yard (1888) and the Piccadilly Hotel (1905). **Nesfield** continued in the Gothic theme, but **Philip Webb**, after leaving Street's office, broke away completely from Gothic and traditional styles. He met Morris in 1856, and from 1861 onwards collaborated with the firm Morris and Co., just established. He was not prolific and much of his work was on a small domestic scale. He used Tudor, Georgian and Gothic ideas, but his own work was original and none of these. He is best known for the house he designed and built for Morris himself, "The Red House" at Upton, Bexley Heath, in the 1880's.

Among the famous **architects** of Edwardian and early 20th-century renown are three outstanding names: **Sir Aston Webb, 1849–1930, Sir Giles Gilbert Scott, 1880–   ,** and **Sir Edwin Lutyens, 1869–1944. Sir Aston Webb's** work was predominantly classical and chiefly concerned with public buildings and memorials. These include such famous work as the extensive alterations and new front to the Victoria and Albert Museum (1909), the Admiralty Arch, Trafalgar Square (1910), the Victoria Memorial (1911)—also a bone of contention to-day—and the new and present front to Buckingham Palace (1913). **Sir Giles Gilbert Scott** is the third in line of the famous architects of this family, being the grandson of the redoubtable Sir George. Among his well-known work of this period can be counted his Liverpool Cathedral (1910), for which he won the competition in 1903 at the youthful age of twenty-three years. Since then he has been almost as prolific and as well known in his profession as his grandfather, though his work is of more varying style to meet modern needs and requirements. Later works, which bring us more up to date, include the University Library at Cambridge, the new Bodleian Library at Oxford, the new Waterloo Bridge and the new Commons Chamber at Westminster. **Sir Edwin Lutyens** is named by many as the greatest British architect which the 20th century has produced so far, and this claim is not without justification. He commenced his architectural work in the 1890's, and before long had established a great reputation. Much of his work was in the Renaissance style, soundly and well designed and constructed, having dignity and taste. He designed country houses, large and small, farmhouses, town houses and public buildings and memorials. One example, showing typical dignity

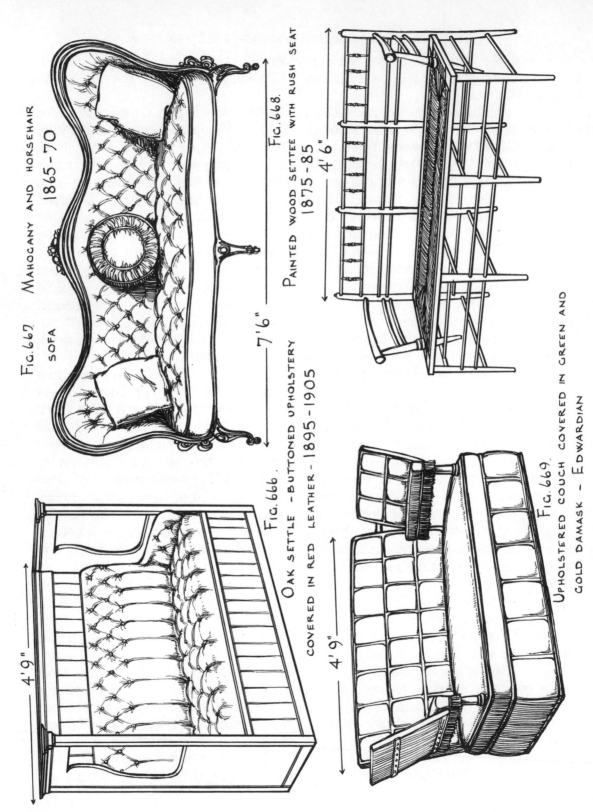

FIG. 667. MAHOGANY AND HORSEHAIR 1865-70 SOFA

7'6"

FIG. 668. PAINTED WOOD SETTEE WITH RUSH SEAT 1875-85

4'6"

FIG. 666. OAK SETTLE – BUTTONED UPHOLSTERY COVERED IN RED LEATHER – 1895-1905

4'9"

FIG. 669. UPHOLSTERED COUCH COVERED IN GREEN AND GOLD DAMASK – EDWARDIAN

4'9"

666–669 *Later Victorian and Edwardian Furniture for seating purposes, 1860–1914*

and simplicity, is the Cenotaph in Whitehall, also the Roman Catholic Cathedral at Liverpool. Lutyens was President of the Royal Academy of Arts from 1938 to 1943.

There was another school of **architects** of the late Victorian and Edwardian period, designing homes and public buildings from 1890 to 1910, who kept away from the traditional styles of architecture, and tried to found a new approach. Two outstanding contributors of this faction were **C. F. A. Voysey** and **C. R. Mackintosh.** **Voysey** designed principally houses of medium size in brick. They were simple in construction and plan and were furnished in the Art Nouveau manner. Like the 18th-century architects, he usually designed the furniture and furnishings to be in keeping with the house as a whole. **Charles R. Mackintosh, 1868–1928** was, as his name suggests, a Scot, and most of his architectural work was for Scotland, in particular in Glasgow, and thus his effect on English architecture is less strong. When still a young man he designed the new Glasgow School of Art, also the Daily Record Office in that city. His work was highly original, and like that of Voysey, has had a greater impact on later generations than it had at the time.

The reference to **William Morris, 1834–96,** has been left to a separate paragraph because, although he studied with Webb in Street's office as an architect from 1856, he soon discovered that his interests and talents lay in other directions. Morris was a single-minded man, and his overriding interest was in Medievalism, not as the Victorian Gothic Revivalists saw it, but in a simpler, more austere form. Like his predecessor, Pugin, he held extreme views on the subject and saw no merit at all in Renaissance and post-Reformation art, architecture and decoration. The work of the 17th- and 18th-century classicists left him unmoved. At the same time, he was determined to establish better forms of design and art than his contemporaries were producing in Gothic Revival form. He had studied at Oxford from 1853, and after his sojourn in an architect's office, he studied painting. He was very friendly and in accord with the pre-Raphaelite painters of the day, notably Rossetti and Burne-Jones, and much of the furniture, wallpapers and decorative schemes that he later designed had that same melancholy quality. In 1861, Morris, Marshall, Faulkner and Company was formed, and after a few years, steadily produced and sold furniture, wallpapers, glassware, ironwork and various other forms of decorative art. Some of Morris's furniture was very large, though less ornamented than was common at the time, but it is his wallpapers which are perhaps best known and remembered, and even to-day form a basis for some of our designs. At the time, he and his friends represented a very small minority of opinion, but their work has lived and has had a profound effect on later productions (see Plate XXXIIb).

The use of **cast iron** in architecture and building in both exterior and interior use increased enormously from 1860 onwards. It was employed on

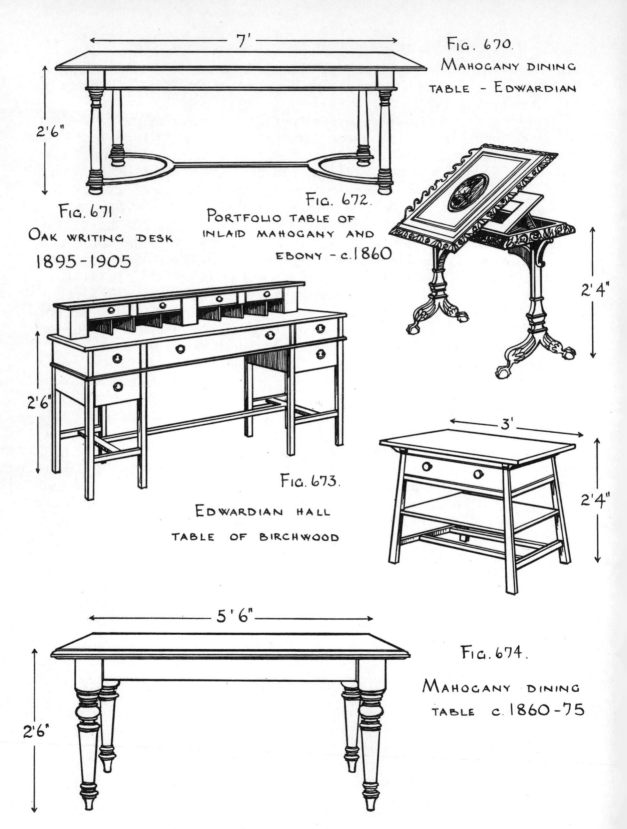

7'

FIG. 670.
MAHOGANY DINING
TABLE - EDWARDIAN

2'6"

FIG. 671.
OAK WRITING DESK
1895-1905

FIG. 672.
PORTFOLIO TABLE OF
INLAID MAHOGANY AND
EBONY - c.1860

2'4"

2'6"

FIG. 673.
EDWARDIAN HALL
TABLE OF BIRCHWOOD

3'

2'4"

5'6"

FIG. 674.
MAHOGANY DINING
TABLE c.1860-75

2'6"

670–674   *Later Victorian and Edwardian Tables, 1860–1914*

a large scale for erections such as seaside piers, bandstands, railway stations and, also at the seaside, in constructing the Winter Gardens so popular in the 'eighties and 'nineties. In smaller items, it could be seen in the form of park seats, garden chairs, lamp standards, post boxes, balconies, balustrades and staircases, while in the home itself, there were a myriad uses for it, ranging from umbrella stands and chimneypieces to kitcheners and coal grates. It was frequently painted, or, in the home, black-leaded, to prevent rusting. In design, much was still left to be desired. Until 1900 at least, most designs were over-ornamented and unsuited to the medium, with twirls and foliates of leaf and stem giving a busyness to the whole conception, and acting as a dust-trap. In the 20th century, steel began to replace cast iron in building construction, but iron was still used for items such as post and telephone boxes, at least until concrete began to be employed more and more. Typical examples of domestic cast ironwork can be seen in Figs. 603, 605, 606, 607, 608, 610, 614, 618, 621, 622, 624, 625, 627, 631, 633, 641, 643, 644, 646, 649, 656, 705 and 719.

The Victorian **garden** was usually well tended, neat and controlled; there was adequate cheap labour to assist in this as yet. The gardens were laid out with lawns, gravel paths and flower beds, but the evergreen shrubs were at their height of popularity till 1900, and an excess of privet hedge and laurel bushes (the two most ubiquitous varieties) gave an air of damp, shiny gloom to the garden. Towards the end of the century, gardening became more and more popular as a hobby; innumerable books were written and illustrated and great pride was taken in growing flowers and shrubs. There was a conservatism in planning borders, however, which often had a patriotic tinge in summer, with geraniums, lobelia and alyssum laid out in neat geometrical patterns. At the same time, the passion for jardinières, pots, window boxes and hanging baskets of plants—evergreens chiefly—was growing apace. Large houses had conservatories and greenhouses for this activity, and the products were then displayed in the hall and drawing room.

The Victorian **entrance hall** was, in many houses, particularly in towns, dark, long, tall and narrow, terminating in a flight of stairs, ascending directly in line with the front door to three or four upper floors. In large homes and in the country, a squarer, more spacious hall was sometimes encountered, with perhaps an entrance porch divided from the entrance hall by a stained-glass and wood partition. Until 1890–1900, the furnishing and interior decoration of a hall contributed greatly to its gloom. Woodwork was painted in dark brown, black or grained varnished paint; walls were painted, wall-papered or covered with lincrusta paper of a dark, heavily patterned type, also varnished, and in crimson, green or grey. The ceiling and frieze were distempered, painted or papered, also patterned, and in dull tones. The hall was then over-filled with furniture, including jardinières and pots of ferns,

345

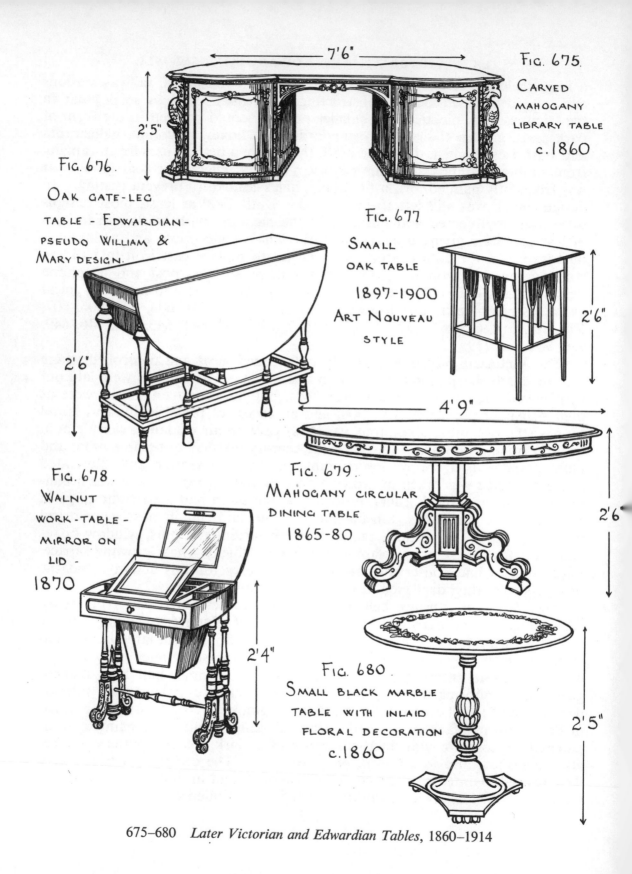

Fig. 675.
Carved mahogany library table
c.1860

7'6"

2'5"

Fig. 676.
Oak gate-leg table - Edwardian - pseudo William & Mary design.

2'6"

Fig. 677
Small oak table
1897-1900
Art Nouveau style

2'6"

4'9"

Fig. 678.
Walnut work-table - mirror on lid -
1870

2'4"

Fig. 679.
Mahogany circular dining table
1865-80

2'6"

Fig. 680.
Small black marble table with inlaid floral decoration
c.1860

2'5"

675–680 *Later Victorian and Edwardian Tables, 1860–1914*

palms and the prized aspidistra, a cast-iron and/or wood hall stand—a veritable colossus of complicated design—several chairs, a dinner gong, a barometer, a wood settle, and various large cupboards. Lighting was by gas, oil lamps or even candles. Large and solemn pictures obscured most of the remaining wall space. The floor was tiled or of stone, but was later covered with execrable designs in crude colours in oilcloth. Many halls in houses of this age have changed little to-day and give the impression of entering a mausoleum. By 1890–1900, however, various reputable books and periodicals on interior decoration and furnishing were recommending a dark, stained oak floor or polished tiles with Oriental rugs, a light distempered ceiling and rich red tapestry wallpaper, still with dark-brown varnish paint, rather fewer and smaller items of furniture, prints on the walls to replace large pictures, and more adequate artificial lighting. This was as far as the better furnished and decorated houses advanced by 1914, a version of which can be seen illustrated in Fig. 607.

The **drawing room** or **parlour** was a feminine room in most Victorian homes, and, until about 1895, was impossibly overcrowded. As with the hall, the paintwork was dark, usually brown, and the ceiling white or light-coloured, in plaster or covered with lincrusta paper. The dado was often left out in the drawing room, and walls from frieze to wainscot were papered with a large-patterned, gloomy wallpaper. Lighting was by gas or oil lamps, and daylight was barely permitted to enter, despite large windows, owing to long white lace curtains completely covering the window, with heavier velvet or satin dark-patterned curtains on top, supported by brass rings on a thick mahogany pole. The chimneypiece was of cast iron or marble, very ornate, and surmounted by an elaborate erection of numerous cupboards and shelves on which were placed countless ornaments and articles. The room was greatly over-furnished with a grand and/or upright piano, tables, chairs, a couch, workboxes, a jardinière, stools and screens, and each was littered with mats, cloths, antimacassars, glass-domed wax fruit displays and birds, plants and ornaments. Examples of such rooms can be seen in Figs. 602 and 603. By the turn of the century, well-to-do homes were still over-furnished, but their decorative schemes were lighter and less overpowering: white or cream paint replaced the dark brown, ceilings were light and wallpaper and frieze gayer and simpler. Carpets were often plain, with a fur hearthrug. A simple mirror replaced the chimneypiece erection, and wood or marble mantelpieces were also more dignified. The furniture was based on Adam, Sheraton or Art Nouveau designs, and was delicate to the point of being thin and spindly. Gayer cretonne curtains and loose covers on the upholstery gave colour and lightness to the decorative scheme. Electric lighting began to replace gas in larger homes, and was cleaner and gave better illumination. An Edwardian room of this type is illustrated in Fig. 606.

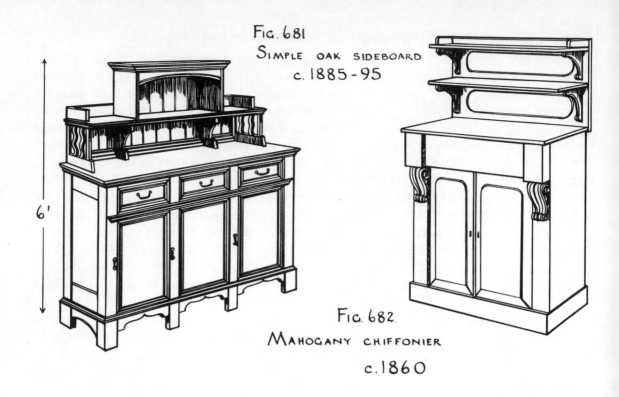

FIG. 681
SIMPLE OAK SIDEBOARD
c. 1885-95

6'

FIG. 682.
MAHOGANY CHIFFONIER

c. 1860

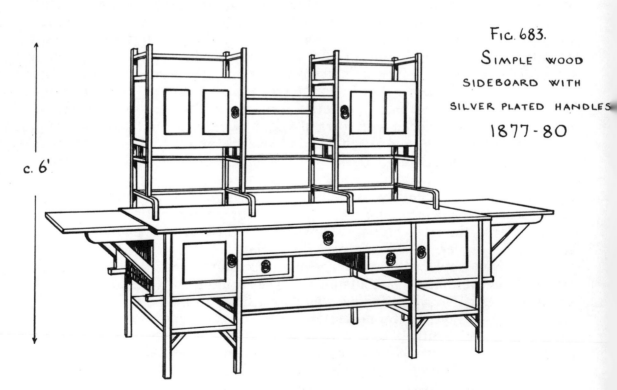

FIG. 683.
SIMPLE WOOD
SIDEBOARD WITH
SILVER PLATED HANDLES
1877-80

c. 6'

681–683   *Later Victorian and Edwardian Sideboards, 1860–1914*

684   *Oak Sideboard, c. 1875*

The **dining room** all through this period was kept in a darker, warmer scheme. Until about 1890, it was very sombre, with a papered lincrusta ceiling, varnished and coloured a deep stone hue, a two-foot deep patterned papered frieze and a strong red patterned wallpaper to the dado rail. The latter was about three feet six inches from the floor, and the wall between dado and wainscot was covered with dark-brown varnished, patterned lincrusta paper. All paintwork was dark brown, grained and varnished. The floor was of polished oak, with dark, strongly patterned carpet and rugs. The chimneypiece and window decoration were like that of the drawing room of this period, but the furniture, though less abundant, was more massive in design. It usually consisted of an enormous dining table in the centre of the room, with six or more dining chairs, one or two sideboards, a china and other cabinets, a screen, other chairs and tables, and numerous large pictures on the walls. From about 1890 onwards, lighter paintwork and ceilings often prevailed, while carpets were less loud in design. The heavy mahogany furniture tended to be replaced by oak or walnut in Sheraton, Adam, Chippendale or Jacobean styles; leather covering was popular for upholstery and dining-chair seats. Marble chimneypieces in pseudo-Adam design were very fashionable, with a cast-iron dog or hob grate to match. Velvet or damask curtains prevailed in dark colours and formal, floral patterns, but the lace curtains were thinner, and drawn back to let in a little light. However, in general, the dining room remained a dark sombre room until 1914, with its owners under the firm impression that unless it was decorated in this way, it could not be considered "furnished", or "warm and home-like". In the 1920's, fashions reacted to the exactly opposite viewpoint, the appearance of a bare and hygienic hospital ward being achieved. At the present time, at last, we appear to be

685   *Edwardian Sideboard in Oak*

beginning to achieve a compromise between the two extremes. A dining room of 1890–5 can be seen in Fig. 605.

Larger houses often had a **study** or **library**, of which the scheme was sombre like that of the dining room. Walls were often panelled in oak, or papered in brown lincrusta to imitate panelling. The frieze was deep and decorated in dark red, green or old-gold paper, while the ceiling was panelled, or ribbed in cream plaster. The floor was of stained and polished oak, with carpet or rugs in dark red or grey. The woodwork was painted dark brown, grained and varnished, while bookcases and other furniture were in oak with dark-green leather seating. Curtains would be in keeping, in dull, dark brocade or velvet.

Victorian **bedrooms**, from 1860–90, were furnished and decorated in a similar manner to the drawing rooms, with light and air excluded as far as possible, the windows being kept tightly closed. Subsequently, decorative schemes were lighter and less furniture was in use. White paintwork and chintz curtains were seen, and the enormous mahogany wardrobes often replaced by built-in cupboards, painted white with the scheme of the room. Earlier bedrooms generally had fitted carpets, but later this was considered unhygienic, as it was difficult to clean under the furniture, and rugs or smaller carpets were set on polished floors. Essential bedroom furniture included the large double bed, a dressing table draped in muslin and lace, wardrobe, bedside table, chairs, a small table and washstand with china set. Wall mirrors, bookshelves and a box ottoman were often added. For extra comfort, stone hot-water bottles were now in use, and closets were available in more homes on bedroom floors, though the inevitable china article was still kept in the bedside cabinet. A bedroom of 1865–75 is illustrated in Fig. 604.

The Victorian **kitchen** was generally large and capacious, and had a **scullery** built adjacent to it. These rooms were in the basement in basement-type town houses, or on the ground floor in others. Servants lived and ate in the kitchen, though they slept at the top of the house in attics. As 1900 approached, kitchens were rather smaller, and placed nearer to the dining room to save labour, in view of the smaller families and shortage of servant assistance. A typical kitchen with scullery opening out of it of the period 1880–95 can be seen in Fig. 608. The colour scheme is still dark brown and green, though the red quarry tiles on the scullery floor strike a gayer note of colour. Lighting is by gas, but water heating and cooking by coal. It was usual to cook on a **kitchener** or kitchen range until the 20th century. These ranges, as illustrated in Figs. 608 and 610, were large, coal-consuming affairs, made in cast iron and steel, and requiring very hard work to use, refuel and keep clean. In general, the oven was on one side, then the fire in the centre, with the boiler—which still had to be filled by hand—on the other side. Some versions had two ovens instead of a boiler. Pans and kettles could be boiled

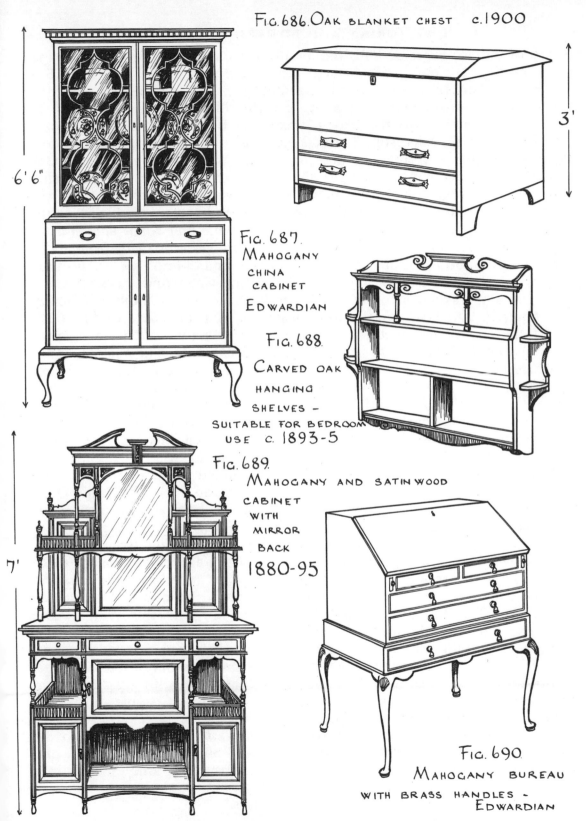

FIG. 686. OAK BLANKET CHEST   c. 1900

3'

6'6"

FIG. 687.
MAHOGANY
CHINA
CABINET
EDWARDIAN

FIG. 688.
CARVED OAK
HANGING
SHELVES –
SUITABLE FOR BEDROOM
USE c. 1893-5

FIG. 689.
MAHOGANY AND SATINWOOD
CABINET
WITH
MIRROR
BACK
1880-95

7'

FIG. 690.
MAHOGANY BUREAU
WITH BRASS HANDLES –
EDWARDIAN

686–690   *Later Victorian and Edwardian Furniture, 1860–1914*

on top of the hot plates or hob, and an airing rail was fixed above for heating plates or drying cloths. Mechanical jacks were still in use (see Figs. 608 and 620). Kitcheners were temperamental monsters, and could refuse to heat or over-heat if the coal was poor, or if the chimney needed sweeping, or even if the wind was in the wrong direction. In summer, domestic work must have been an exhausting business, especially in view of the fact that all cooking, baking, jam making and preserving were done at home. **Gas cookers**, or gas cooking ranges as they were termed, were slow in being developed. A version had been shown at the Great Exhibition of 1851, but it was not until about 1900 that they were in use in homes. Such early 20th-century models were of cast iron, very cumbersome and solid, and difficult to keep clean (see Fig. 621). **Electric cookers** or ranges were made from about 1890, but they had many defects of manufacture, and did not become popular until after 1918. A **copper** was used for heating water and washing where either a boiler was not incorporated in the kitchener or an additional facility was required. At first, coppers were heated by coal or coke (see Fig. 608), but at the end of the century, gas coppers were made, and were in great demand (see Fig. 628). By 1910, a **sitting-room grate** and **cooking range combined** could be obtained—a boon to those who had only limited accommodation. Pots and kettles were hung over the fire or put on a trivet (see Fig. 631). Another useful Edwardian device was the cast-iron **gas ring** which could be used in the parlour or sitting room to boil a kettle, or in the kitchen to supplement the range (see Fig. 624). The **kitchen sink** was now more frequently supplied with running water, at least in towns. It was made of earthenware, and was large and shallow with fluted sides, and either rectangular or made to fit into a corner (see Figs. 608 and 638). **Kitchen utensils** and gadgets were now very numerous; a number of them, though often made of different materials, were similar to those in use to-day. New articles introduced in this period included **knife-cleaning machines** (see Fig. 615), **mincing machines**, new-style **flat irons** (see Fig. 614), and **clothes mangles** (see Fig. 627). Early **vacuum cleaners**, known as carpet sweepers, were found in well-to-do homes after 1908; they were worked with bellows and brush (see Fig. 611). The Hoover Company took out a patent in this year. There were also what we should term **carpet sweepers** (see Fig. 613), and early versions of washing and washing-up machines, though these were rare as yet.

Until 1900–10, **bathrooms** and full-length **baths** were only found in large, well-to-do homes. The baths were of painted cast iron, with brass taps, and were set in a deep mahogany surround. The majority of people still used a basin or hip bath of iron or copper, or later, the rather larger size bath (see Fig. 634). Water still had to be heated in the kitchen and carried to the bathroom or bath. By 1910, houses were being built with bathrooms, and older houses altered to take them. A typical example of one of these in a

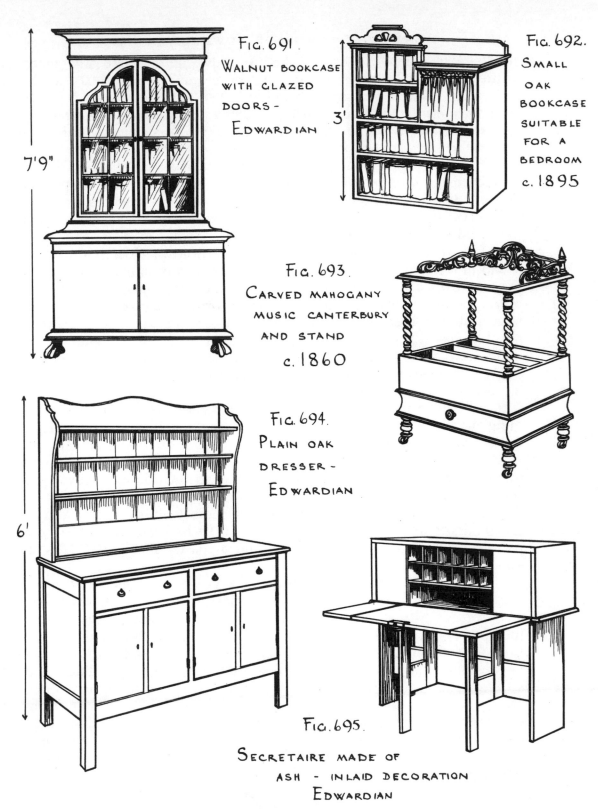

Fig. 691.
Walnut bookcase
with glazed
doors —
Edwardian

7'9"

3'

Fig. 692.
Small
oak
bookcase
suitable
for a
bedroom
c. 1895

Fig. 693.
Carved mahogany
music canterbury
and stand
c. 1860

Fig. 694.
Plain oak
dresser —
Edwardian

6'

Fig. 695.
Secretaire made of
ash — inlaid decoration
Edwardian

691–695 *Later Victorian and Edwardian Furniture, 1860–1914*

middle-class home can be seen in Fig. 609. Baths were still generally of painted cast iron, with brass taps, but porcelain baths did exist at this time. Hot running water was slowly being installed, but many baths were still filled by hand. Rather ornate copper **gas geysers** appeared and were regarded as dangerous but useful articles (see Fig. 609). **Wash basins**, called lavatory basins, were becoming more usual; they were supported on painted iron legs or highly decorated, painted iron wall brackets (see Figs. 609 and 640). Curtained-off **showers** were in use also; early versions were operated by a chain. By 1914, various bathroom fittings were coming into use: bath seats and trays, shaving cabinets and mirrors, bathroom scales, towel rails, soap trays and toothbrush holders (see Fig. 609).

After 1890, **water closets**, known as wash-down closets, previously only found in large houses, were becoming a more common installation. Even so, they were placed in the basement or in the yard outside the house. Like other Victorian designs, they were more ornate than our present versions, with cast-iron brackets and moulded earthenware pans (see Fig. 641). Far more homes still sufficed with an **earth closet**, especially in country areas, but these were very hygienic in comparison with earlier types (see Fig. 642). **Night commodes** were still commonly used in bedrooms until after 1900.

The majority of **ceilings** in Victorian homes were now of plain plaster with an ornate plaster cornice and central "rose" from the middle of which hung the chief lighting feature, whether candles, oil, gas or electricity. The ceiling was whitewashed, distempered or painted in white, or various shades of cream or stone colour, or perhaps even pastel shades. In larger houses, lincrusta wallpaper was used on the ceiling to provide an all-over pattern in low relief in imitation of 18th-century plasterwork, but these designs were of floral or formal geometrical all-over type, most unlike 18th-century stucco. Other larger homes of the period 1890–1910 had simple ribbed ceilings or pseudo-Adam plasterwork, in white and/or pastel shades (see Figs. 605, 606 and 607).

From 1860–90, the interior **walls** of a house were generally divided into frieze, wall, dado and wainscot. The **frieze** was deep, extending about two feet from cornice to picture rail; the **wainscot** was about nine inches to one foot in height, and the dado rail was set at about three feet six inches to four feet six inches from the ground. Both frieze and wall were generally papered in a dark, strongly patterned **wallpaper**, but in two different designs, although, in some cases, the frieze was painted or whitewashed to match the ceiling. These wallpapers had large-motif designs, in a formal arrangement of flowers, fruit and birds; colours were strong and heavy, crimson, gold and dark blue and green being especially favoured. In downstairs rooms, papers were expensive and thick, and were expected to last for many years. As the pattern was so dark, and the sunlight always excluded from the room, this was

Fig. 696.
MAHOGANY
DRESSING TABLE
AND TOILET
MIRROR –
1890-1901

Fig. 697.
MAHOGANY WASHSTAND
WITH REP CURTAINS AND
WHITE MARBLE TOP – WHITE
TILES AND CHINA SET –
1890-5

Fig. 698.
OAK WASHSTAND
WITH BLACK AND WHITE
MARBLE TOP AND COLOURED
SPLASH TILES – COLOURED
CHINA SET –
EDWARDIAN

Fig. 699.
MAHOGANY INLAID
WITH SATINWOOD
DUMB WAITER –
BRASS GALLERIES
1895-1900

Fig. 700.
SERVING TABLE OR
DUMB WAITER FOR TEA
TIME USE – MAHOGANY
1890-5

696–700 *Later Victorian and Edwardian Furniture, 1860–1914*

a reasonable anticipation. Bedroom wallpapers were thinner and lighter, but were equally strongly patterned in a riot of flowers and fruit (see Figs. 602, 603, 604 and Plate XXXII). The part of the wall between dado rail and wainscot was either panelled or left plain plaster, and in both instances was painted to match the rest of the room, in a dark-brown varnished paint, grained with a comb to imitate wood markings. Alternatively, it was papered with a heavy, varnished lincrusta paper, also generally in dark brown and washable. The wallpapers designed by Morris and Company were also in dark tones and rather formal in design, but were of a far better standard of work than the general commercial product of the period. The "Pomegranate design" is one well-known instance, and the "Daisy" is another. Considerable influence on later wallpaper designs resulted from such examples. By 1890–1900, lighter wallpapers were used, both in colour, pattern and actual weight of paper; friezes often dominated the scheme and were sometimes in the form of decorative landscapes, or alternatively, floral designs with a formal approach. In some cases, walls were **distempered** or **painted** in a plain shade, often light in tone, while in others, **stucco** work, after the Adam style, was employed. **Wood panelling** was reintroduced, also tapestry and leather wall covering (see Figs. 605, 606 and 607). Until 1900 at least, Victorian walls were decorated by a lavish display of **paintings**, either originals or prints. Among the former works, many were by well-known professional artists of the day, for costs were lower at this time than to-day, and the rising middle class was well-to-do and could afford to patronise artists. As a result, the Victorian artists of 1860–1900 were in a better position financially than ever before or since, and many of them were honoured and recognised by the Queen and by the public. As many rooms were lofty, quite large paintings were bought even by an average householder. Without competition from first-class reproductions and little from the camera, artists were in a paradise indeed. Most of such paintings were sentimental in feeling and told a story or set a problem to the beholder—narrative and problem pictures as we now term them—and many such paintings illustrated pathos, grief and agony. Famous artists of the day included Lord Leighton, Sir John Millais, William Holman Hunt, Dante Gabriel Rossetti, George Frederick Watts, Sir Edwin Landseer and Sir Edward Burne-Jones, and most of us are now familiar with either the originals or reproductions of such typical paintings as "Diana of the Uplands", "Two Strings to her Bow", "The Vigil", "When Did You Last See Your Father?", "The Bath of Psyche", "The Boyhood of Raleigh", "Hope" and "The Light of the World". In addition to such paintings there would be on display an abundance of prints and photographs. Among the former, the most popular subjects were the Queen, Prince Albert and members of the Royal Family, while photographs were generally of members of the family at home. Amateur water-colours were frequently hung also,

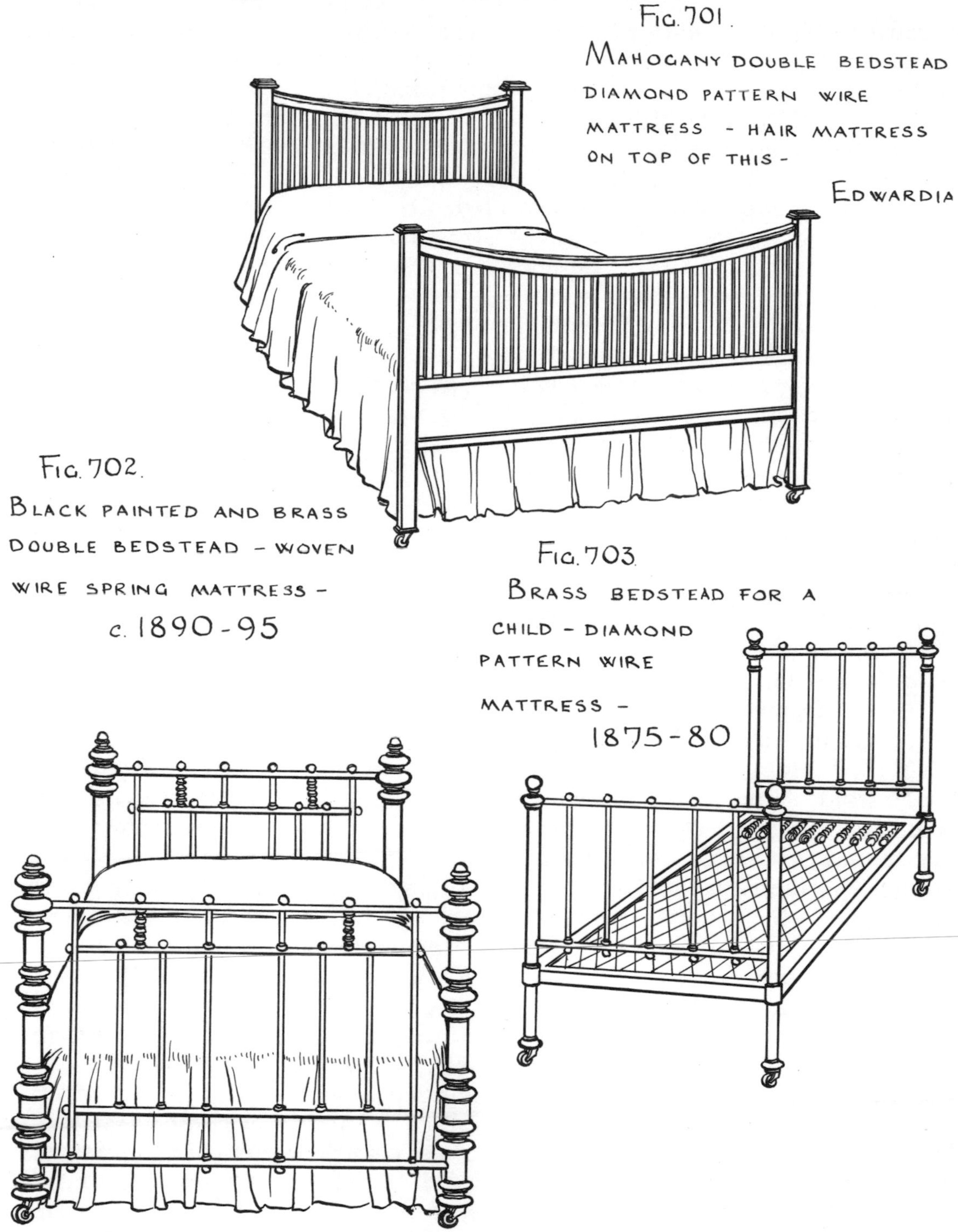

Fic. 701.

MAHOGANY DOUBLE BEDSTEAD
DIAMOND PATTERN WIRE
MATTRESS - HAIR MATTRESS
ON TOP OF THIS -

EDWARDIA

Fic. 702.

BLACK PAINTED AND BRASS
DOUBLE BEDSTEAD - WOVEN
WIRE SPRING MATTRESS -

c. 1890-95

Fic. 703.

BRASS BEDSTEAD FOR A
CHILD - DIAMOND
PATTERN WIRE
MATTRESS -

1875-80

701–703   *Later Victorian and Edwardian Bedsteads, 1860–1914*

as most young ladies at home were expected to become reasonably proficient at this art, though their subject matter was rather limited, generally consisting of flowers or fruit studies, or tentative landscapes.

Floors were of oak boarding except in the hall, bathroom and scullery, where tiles, stone or brick were more usual. Until 1880–90, close carpeting was general in reception rooms, but after this, a square or rectangular carpet with polished oak surround was favoured. Hearthrugs were in general use, and in bedrooms, large and small rugs were set on the polished boards. Stair-carpets were now general. Carpets and rugs were patterned all over in Oriental designs or English versions of these, in rich colours, and formal, complicated patterns. Later versions were plainer, often with just a decorative border. **Linoleum** and **oilcloth** were made now, and became very popular by the end of the century, especially for halls, kitchens and bathrooms. Early designs were loud and crude, but an improvement was seen by 1900. In wealthy homes, parquet flooring was very fashionable after 1890 (see Figs. 602, 603, 604, 605, 606, 607 and 609).

Interior **doors** were painted wood in keeping with the scheme of the room: while six-panelled doors were still fitted into larger homes and the chief reception rooms, the four-panelled version, with two larger panels at the top, was the most typical Victorian design. Front doors had more panels, often set with patterned glass (see Figs. 603, 607 and 608). To keep out draughts, reception-room doors were generally fitted with a velvet or chenille curtain on a brass pole. French windows or doors had lace curtains.

Most **windows** of this period were **sash** type with large plate-glass panes. Often the top half of the window was set in six or more rectangular panes, while the bottom part was plain. Windows were large, usually of bay design in the front of the house, and with French windows and doors in the sitting room at the rear, which could be opened into the garden or conservatory. A few homes of the Edwardian period returned to smaller **casement** windows. Until 1890, the large window area did nothing to assist in lighting or airing the room, as the window was always kept tightly shut, and heavy curtains, also lace curtains, obscured the light. Massive mahogany poles supported these, with brass fittings. By the turn of the century, rather more light and air was admitted, curtains were thinner, and lighter and gayer in colour and pattern, but the Victorian habit of drawing curtains across the windows to ensure privacy died very hard (see Figs. 602, 604, 605, 606, 607 and 609).

The **chimneypiece** was regarded as the dominant decorative feature of the room: it was designed to attract attention and be the focal point of interest. Until 1890, the design was very elaborate: the **mantelpiece** was of black-leaded or painted cast iron, marble or polished wood; the whole surface was decorated with scrolls, foliates, flowers and fruit, or, from 1870–90, drew its inspiration from Gothic sources with a four-centre arch fire opening, and decorated in the

704 *Brass and Iron Child's Cot with drop side, c. 1880–90*

form of cusps and arches. Above the mantelshelf was an amazing erection of shelves, mirrors and cupboards, culminating in a pediment or cornice. All horizontal surfaces were occupied by ornaments, clocks, vases and plates, and the whole was draped with tasselled and fringed velvet to match curtains and covers (see Fig. 603). After 1890, mantelpieces were simpler in design: Adam ornament prevailed, with classical mouldings and decoration. Polished wood, cast iron and marble were all used, but the surround and hearth were tiled. The chimneypiece erection was also less elaborate, and hangings were seen less often (see Figs. 605, 606, 631, 643 and 644). **Fire openings** were circular, rectangular or four-centre arches, and **grates** generally of cast iron. These latter were most varied in design, but often based on earlier styles: thus the hob and dog grates of the 18th and early 19th centuries were revived (see Figs. 605 and 643). Others were of basket form, and later versions were much simpler and had a metal smoke canopy overhead (see Figs. 603, 606, 631 and 644). **Fenders, companion stands, coal boxes** and **scuttles, fire guards** and **curb suites** were in keeping with the grate and period, while various metals were used, including brass, copper and iron. **Firescreens** were made of metal with glass or fabric (see Figs. 603, 605, 606, 617, 618, 626 and 645). In the early 20th century, cast-iron **stoves** were becoming popular, designed with a back boiler to heat the water, and burning coal or coke. They often had a door with mica panels to open as required and warm the room. Many people used them in kitchen and breakfast room, also in the nursery (see Fig. 646 and Plate XXXIId).

The **staircases** of Victorian homes were dark, gloomy places, not well lit,

705 *Folding Iron Baby's Cot covered and decorated with muslin ribbons and flouncing, 1870–5*

as the windows were heavily curtained, and artificial lighting was by gas, oil or perhaps only a candle carried in the hand. Woodwork was painted dark brown, wallpaper was dark and fiercely patterned in crimson or green, while the staircarpet echoed this in sombre hues. Staircases themselves were of oak, mahogany or cast iron. Dark-brown, grained, varnished paint was used on the woods, alternatively they were polished and unpainted. Balusters were turned in bulging mouldings; newel posts were heavy and substantial. Cast-iron blausters were set into stone or wood stairs and had a mahogany handrail. Their design followed the fashion of the day, ranging from barley-sugar twists to complicated floral entanglements. Edwardian staircases were simpler, often having plain, straight, wooden balusters and newel posts in square section. Various styles of staircase can be seen in Figs. 607, 647, 648 and 649).

Victorian **furniture** from 1860–80 continued to be massive and over-decorated. Mahogany was used in both solid and veneer forms, and was seen primarily in dining-room and bedroom furniture. For the drawing room a variety of materials were in use: papier-mâché still, japanned beech, painted furniture, oak, walnut and mahogany. Most designs were based on Rococo and Gothic ideas, but were far removed from the original forms; carving was profuse with flower, leaf and fruit motifs, and most pieces were ungainly and lacking in dignity and charm. All rooms were overcrowded and packed to capacity. After 1880, past styles became fashionable again: much imitation Sheraton, Chippendale, Hepplewhite and Adam furniture was made. Well-to-do, educated people began to collect actual antiques. For everyone else, more and more copies were made, but they were copies "improved upon" by Victorian craftsmen. The craftwork was good, but the "improvements" doubtful; more inlay and carving were added and pieces became spindly and thin. A tremendous variety of woods came into use, including fumed oak, walnut, satinwood, rosewood, ebony and some mahogany. Inlay was even more varied, providing many colours and types of graining. By 1900, nearly all furniture was based on or copied from an earlier style, Jacobean and Stuart now being added to the 18th-century designs. A minority of men designed furniture which aimed at being original, and which was made of older English woods, particularly oak, elm and yew. **Morris** was one of the earliest of these; his furniture was styled after the English cottage and farmhouse work of the 15th and 16th centuries, and he tried to re-establish craftsmen's work as opposed to machine- and mass-produced articles. **Ernest Gimson** and **Sidney Barnsley** followed later, working on similar lines and producing original furniture designs which were simple and unpretentious. In the 'nineties, **Sir Ambrose Heal** began to design oak and walnut furniture in a simple, dignified and pleasing style for ordinary homes. His work provided a basis for further designs and became very popular. The Edwardian period saw the Art

Nouveau designers producing original furniture also, but this style was angular, tall, and uncomfortable in appearance. It was certainly original, and not based on past styles, but owing to a lack of elegance and charm, it has not lived as a basic principle of design. All these designers of original furniture contributed towards their period, and produced a foundation for 20th-century work which has now culminated in the Scandinavian forms of design and use of woods and polishes popular to-day, but, at the time, they were in a small minority, and as much of their furniture was craftsmen-produced, there is only a small quantity of it left. The furniture of the majority of homes until 1914 was a copy of, or based upon, a past style of the 17th, 18th and 19th centuries; some of it was badly designed, some excellent, but almost all of it was soundly made and constructed. We may abhor a piece of Victorian furniture which we possess and think it ugly, but we find it almost impossible to break it or wear it out.

Seating accommodation had become immensely varied in design and function by 1860, and included chairs, stools, couches, sofas, ottomans, settles, settees and chesterfields. **Chairs** were made in numerous materials for different purposes, rooms and homes. Tremendous quantities of plain **wooden** chairs were produced for shops and offices as well as for the home, where they were chiefly used in the kitchen, nursery and hall. Some were of bent-wood, others more solid in construction; some had plain wood seats, others were of cane (see Figs. 604, 608, 654 and 664). A typical Victorian chair had a **balloon back** and cane or upholstered seat (see Figs. 604 and 660), while others had **buttoned-upholstered seats** and backs and were with or without arms (see Figs. 602, 603, 652, 653 and 662). **Papier-mâché chairs** were still made (see Fig. 602), as also were Rococo designed armchairs (see Fig. 603). Both adjustable-backed chairs and **rocking chairs** were very popular in the late Victorian period, usually set by the fireside and draped with an anti-macassar (see Figs. 603, 652 and 663). **Basketwork** and cane chairs also enjoyed great popularity, especially as they were cheap to make; with a chintz-covered cushion they were very comfortable, though rather squeaky (see Fig. 657). In the early 20th century, **upholstered armchairs** were made, based on the old grandfather wing chair design, with cretonne covers, often of removable type; these were the forerunners of our easy chairs of to-day (see Figs. 605 and 606). Art Nouveau styles of chair can be seen in Figs. 606, 650 and 665. **Couches, sofas** and **ottomans** were made in large numbers, and every home had one or more. They were massively designed until 1890, usually of mahogany frame with buttoned horsehair upholstery, sometimes covered in plush or damask, and decorated by several embroidered, beaded and tasselled cushions. Some versions had a back and arms, some were more like a Grecian sofa, with a roll back and one side supported, while the ottoman was circular or made to fit into a corner, with no arms, only a central

6' 6"

Fig. 706
Bedside
cabinet
of inlaid
mahogany
c. 1875

2' 9"

Fig. 707.
Carved mahogany
dressing table
1875-80

Fig. 708.
Mahogany wardrobe
with plate glass
mirror on door
1895-1905

Fig 709
Painted beech towel
rail for bedroom use
1870-4

Fig. 710
Carved mahogany chest
of drawers
c. 1860-75

3' 3"

706–710   *Later Victorian and Edwardian Bedroom Furniture, 1860–1914*

back-rest (see Figs. 602 and 667). Later styles often had let-down or adjustable ends and were of less rounded and massive design (see Fig. 669). The **settle** was generally of wood with buttoned upholstery or squab cushion. It was set in a corner or by the fireside, and was generally soundly constructed and attractively designed on simple, dignified lines (see Fig. 666). **Settees** varied greatly in type, but the majority were made in the form of two or three chair backs put together, often with cane seats (see Fig. 668).

The Victorian **dining table** was almost invariably massive, solid and made of mahogany. There were two chief styles, one with four legs and the other of pedestal design. The four-legged type had a solid top and heavy, turned legs (see Fig. 674), or, later in the period, slender straight or turned legs with or without stretchers (see Figs. 605 and 670). The top was rectangular or polygonal. The pedestal design was less common but equally massive, with a tripod pedestal support (see Fig. 679). **Gate-leg tables** remained fashionable and were generally made of oak (see Fig. 676), while **smaller pedestal tables** of mahogany, oak or papier-mâché could be found in drawing and dining rooms, also bedrooms (see Figs, 602, 603, 607 and 680). **Kitchen tables** were strong and solid, and had four turned or straight legs, a drawer and a scrubbed white top (see Fig. 608). Among the small tables were many varied designs: there were **work-tables** of walnut, rosewood or papier-mâché (see Figs. 602, 603 and 678), small **tea tables** on pedestal or four-legged support (see Figs. 602, 605, 606 and 677), and **many-sided tables** of slender construction with numerous legs (see Fig. 604). In addition, there were tables for specific purposes as **library tables** (see Fig. 675), **writing desks** (see Fig. 671), portfolio and **drawing tables** (see Fig. 672), and **hall tables** (see Fig. 673).

The **sideboard** or **chiffonier** was the most important item of dining-room furniture apart from the dining table. Until about 1880–90, it was based on Rococo designs or was architectural in feature. It was a very large piece of furniture, generally built up in two or more stages, containing cupboards and shelves for display and storage of crockery and cutlery. Chiffoniers often had a rounded mirror back with carved wood frame. Mahogany was the usual material, alternatively walnut (see Figs. 603, 682 and 684). Smaller, less elaborate oak sideboards were made for country areas and for small homes (see Fig. 681). At the turn of the century, daintier sideboards based on Jacobean and late Stuart side-table designs were made; these were in oak or walnut and stood on four turned legs (see Fig. 685). Large sideboards with cupboards, mirror, shelves and drawers were also still made for larger homes, but in simpler design, based more on rectangular lines (see Figs. 605 and 683).

There were many varieties of **cabinet** and **cupboard** for different purposes, some very large, some quite small, but, in general, the designs from 1860–90 were elaborate and over-decorated. Mahogany was in general use for larger

FIG. 711

COTTAGE PIANOFORTE HARMONIUM CARVED IN
MAHOGANY — c. 1860

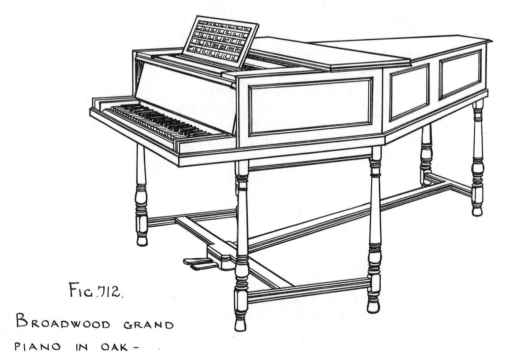

FIG. 712.

BROADWOOD GRAND

PIANO IN OAK —

EDWARDIAN

711 and 712   *Later Victorian and Edwardian Pianofortes, 1860–1914*

cabinets, while papier-mâché, walnut and satinwood were more typical for smaller ones. Towards 1900, designs were simpler and generally based on 17th- and 18th-century work, particularly the William and Mary, Queen Anne, Jacobean and Sheraton periods (see Figs. 606 and 689). **China cabinets** were still in general use and most homes had one or more, with glazed doors in the top part to display the best china (see Figs. 603, 605 and 687).

Bookcases were possessed by most homes now. They were either very large and cumbersome, designed on architectural lines, with cornice or pediment, plinth and base (see Fig. 691), or were in the form of a small, movable or fixed bookcase. Book-shelves were also erected: these were often placed fairly high on the wall, especially in bedrooms (see Figs. 604, 688 and 692).

Among furniture designed for writing purposes were large **library desks** (see Fig. 675), various styles of **bureaux** (see Fig. 690), and, alternatively, a **secretaire** (see Fig. 695). Again, in general principle, the earlier models were large, cumbersome and ornately decorated in mahogany or walnut, and later versions were of more varied woods and much simpler in style, usually based on 17th- or 18th-century design.

Numerous **canterburies** and **stands** were still in popular use, including those for music and books (see Fig. 693), and those for serving food and acting as dumb waiters (see Figs. 699 and 700). The later versions of these were also often based on Sheraton and Adam patterns, as in Fig. 699.

The plain, solid oak **dresser** was a fixture in Victorian kitchens (see Fig. 608). Since it was usually painted to conform to the scheme of the room, it could be washed easily. It was very large and capacious in order to accommodate all the everyday crockery, cutlery and linen for a large family and servants. By 1900, polished oak and walnut dressers were revived for dining-room use as alternatives, or additions, to sideboards, and were generally based on Jacobean or country Tudor designs (see Fig. 694).

Hall stands and cupboards were in general use for accommodating hats, coats, umbrellas and sticks. They were either small with a drawer, and a potted palm on top as in Fig. 607 (right), or in two or more stages with cupboards at the bottom and hat and coat pegs with mirror in the top part as in Fig. 607 (left). Some versions were in wood, others of cast iron.

Until about 1880–90, the Victorian **bedstead** was commonly of the half-tester variety with tall, upright posts at the head supporting a curtain rail from which the hangings and valance depended. Most bedsteads were of brass or iron, often partly painted. They were elaborately designed with a multiplicity of knobs and scrolls on which the person making the bed caught both the bedclothes and her own attire. Feather mattresses were placed on a wood or iron lattice (see Fig, 604). Subsequently, the half-tester was rarer, though brass bedsteads were made in large numbers throughout the period (see Figs. 702 and 703). From 1900, some plainer, wooden bedsteads were

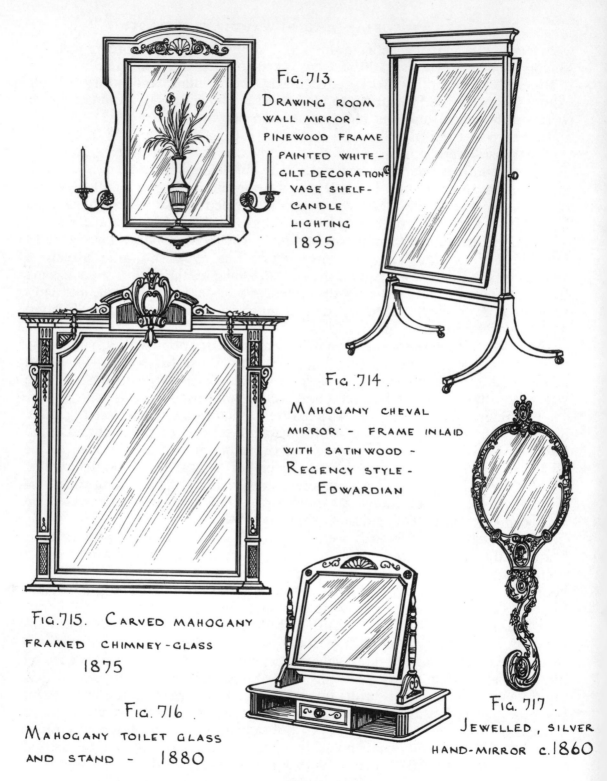

FIG. 713.
DRAWING ROOM
WALL MIRROR -
PINEWOOD FRAME
PAINTED WHITE -
GILT DECORATION
VASE SHELF -
CANDLE
LIGHTING
1895

FIG. 714.
MAHOGANY CHEVAL
MIRROR - FRAME INLAID
WITH SATINWOOD -
REGENCY STYLE -
EDWARDIAN

FIG. 715. CARVED MAHOGANY
FRAMED CHIMNEY-GLASS
1875

FIG. 716.
MAHOGANY TOILET GLASS
AND STAND - 1880

FIG. 717.
JEWELLED, SILVER
HAND-MIRROR c. 1860

713–717   *Later Victorian and Edwardian Mirrors, 1860–1914*

made, with an iron bed frame, but these were by no means general as yet (see Fig. 701). A lattice work spring on an iron frame, or a woven spring mattress was usual from about 1880, on which either a feather, flock or hair mattress would be placed. A very few box spring mattresses were being made by the end of this period. Pillows and bolsters were filled with feathers, flock or hair. Double beds were in general use for married couples till after 1914, though twin beds did come in by the Edwardian period. The latter were considered most improper, however, and were tacitly referred to as "twin French beds". Children's **cots** were made of brass in a simplified version of brass bedsteads, with a rail all round which let down on one side. Like the bedsteads, all four feet were fitted with castors (see Fig. 704). Cots for babies were made with a wood or iron framework; they were decorated by yards of flouncing, lace and ribbons and surmounted by a canopy of hanging draperies and ribbon bows (see Fig. 705). Though very pretty, a full-time launderer was required.

The remaining **bedroom furniture** was generally designed as a suite now. This included a wardrobe, chest-of-drawers, a washstand, dressing table and mirror, bedside cabinet, towel rail and chairs. Mahogany was the most popular wood for these, at least until after 1895, when oak and walnut became more fashionable. Wardrobes were very large, fitted with two or more doors, often with plate-glass mirrors on the outside (or inside) and having two or more deep drawers at the bottom. A cornice surmounted the top member. Despite their size, Victorian wardrobes are rarely high enough to hang dresses properly, because so much of the height is taken up by the drawers; this is surprising considering that the dresses of the time were much longer than ours are to-day. However, they did possess one virtue lacking in many present-day wardrobes: they were deep enough in projection to accommodate a coat-hanger at right angles to the door (see Figs. 604 and 708). **Chests-of-drawers** were also massive and capacious, usually with two small drawers at the top and the others of full width (see Fig. 710). The toilet table or **dressing table** was, until 1890–1900, draped with muslin and lace, and decorated with flouncing and ribbons. This was a dangerous custom in view of the candles flickering in their fitted sockets, and it must also have obscured the mirror considerably (see Fig. 604). Later styles were generally of Sheraton design (see Figs. 696 and 707). The **washstand** was made to match the dressing table but had a marble top with splash tiles at the back and/or a curtain hung from a brass rail. A set of bowls, jugs and appropriate jars and soap dishes would be included (see Figs. 604, 697 and 698). The bedside or **night cabinet**, later called the pedestal, generally had a marble top, suitable for placing hot drinks upon, and contained a cupboard to house the necessary china article(s) (see Figs. 604 and 706).

The **pianoforte** was an essential item of furniture for every home—a grand

718 *Banner Screen —black silk banner with gold fringing and coloured silk embroidered design —mahogany stand, c. 1860*

piano was desirable, but if the family was less well-to-do, an upright or cottage version was valued. Often there would be more than one in the home. The piano acted as a central feature to the house: in the winter evenings, family and friends would gather round it to sing, play and listen. Most pianos were very ornate with carved decoration; silk inset pleated panels were still usual, and carved wood or wrought-iron candleholders sprang out on each side (see Figs. 602, 603 and 711). Edwardian instruments were plainer, with simple, turned legs, and panelled sides (see Fig. 712). **Piano stools** were adjustable in height, and generally had velvet or leather-covered seats (see Fig. 602).

Wall mirrors of various kinds were used a great deal to decorate and light different rooms. A **chimney glass** of some kind was usual in the principal rooms, either as a focal feature or incorporated into an elaborate chimney overmantel scheme. Some of these mirrors were very large, with ornately carved frames which were often gilded. Other frames were of polished mahogany, oak, papier-mâché or had inlaid wood decoration (see Figs. 603, 605, 606 and 715). **Wall mirrors** were also hung, particularly in halls, drawing rooms and bedrooms. These often had a shelf for a flower vase and fittings for candlebranches see (Figs. 604 and 713). In the bedroom, **cheval mirrors** were still in use, but more particularly during the Regency revival period about 1900–10 (see Fig. 714), while **toilet mirrors** were used in conjunction with dressing tables in all bedrooms (see Figs. 604, 696 and 716). **Hand mirrors** were also essential items for the dressing table (see Fig. 717). In the bathroom, a decoratively framed mirror was usual over the washbasin, and special **shaving mirrors** were hung in convenient places there (see Fig. 609).

Banner screens were seen more than pole screens from 1860–90 (see Figs. 602

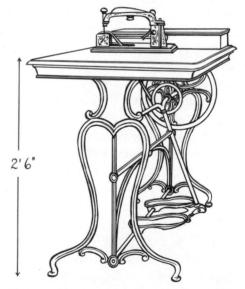

719 *Treadle Sewing Machine, c. 1860 —cast iron frame in black and gilt— also steel—mahogany table top and box, also lid to place on top when machine not in use (not shown)*

368

and 718), but after this, **fire screens** such as that in Fig. 645 were used during the summer, when there was no fire in the grate. An alternative method was the popular Victorian one of drawing curtains across the empty fireplace.

A useful and important item of furniture in the home was provided, after 1860, by the **sewing machine**. These became fairly common by the 1890's: most houses possessed a small or full-sized one. The most typical were the treadle type, made with cast-iron support and treadle, and a wood table on to which the machine was set. A lid was closed down on to the machine when it was not in use (see Fig. 719). Smaller table models to make various stitches had to be turned by hand (see Fig. 633). The cast-iron parts of these machines were usually painted black, with gilt decoration in the form of ornate scrolls and twists; the design was somewhat ugly, and required considerable work to keep it dusted. Singer provided the most popular models.

Coal was used as the most common method of **heating** until 1914. Coal grates were fitted into almost all rooms, and were kept burning all day in cold weather in the reception rooms. Fires were also lit in bedrooms in well-to-do homes and for illness (see Figs. 603, 605, 606, 608, 631, 643, 644 and 646). This excessive use of coal, as opposed to smokeless fuels, in wasteful but often cheery grates, helped to account for the heavy "smogs" which afflicted all Victorian cities, especially London, each winter. **Gas fires** existed in the 'nineties, but were not often used until Edwardian days, owing to the smell of fumes caused by inadequate flue ventilation. When it was learned how to fit the apparatus properly, gas fires became very popular (see Fig. 625). Electric fires were rare in this period.

Lighting, from 1860 to 1914, was provided by four different means: gas, oil, candles and electricity. From 1860 onwards, **gas lighting** was brought within reach of more and more homes; in the 1870's it was in general use in towns, and by 1900, only the more remote country areas were without it. However, it was common, until the 20th century, to find gas laid on only in the ground floor of a house, while the upstairs rooms and landings were lit by oil and candles. The gas enterprises were very slow to improve the fittings and equipment for their product, and, despite the fact that gas had been in use since Regency days, it was not until competition from electric lighting was imminent, at the turn of the century, that much progress was made. The gas light was provided by a flat flame until the invention of the incandescent mantle, which was not perfected to a safe and usable condition until the 1890's. The inverted burner was in use early in the 20th century—a great improvement on the early forms of gas lighting. Gas fittings were varied: large rooms had a central pendant with two, three or four burners, called a gasolier (see Figs, 602, 603, 607 and 721), while wall brackets were used to supplement these, also to light smaller rooms (see Figs. 605, 609 and 720). In the 'nineties, a circular metal band with hanging silk curtain gathered into the rim was fashionable (see Fig. 605), and in kitchens, sculleries and bathrooms, a single burner with a simple shade was in general use (see Fig. 608). Fittings were of metal, chiefly brass or copper with shades of glass, either transparent or white, and often engraved and painted. **Oil lamps** were used in country areas until after 1914, also in towns for extra lighting and for upstairs rooms. Some of these were designed as hanging lamps (see Fig. 724), and others to stand on a table or pianoforte (see Figs. 603 and 604). **Candles** were also in use all the period, as sole or additional lighting, whilst some people, towards the end of the century, preferred this form of lighting for dining and because of its restfulness. Candles were set in candlesticks, wall brackets, mirror and piano brackets and candelabra stands. Metals such as brass, silver, pewter and iron were used for these, also china and wood (see Figs. 602, 604, 608, 725 and 728).

Electric lighting in the form of arc lamps had been available in the mid-19th century, but it was after **Sir Joseph W. Swan**[1] invented a carbon-filament[2] lamp in 1860 in England that domestic use could be made of this means of lighting. By the 1890's, streets and large buildings were being lit by electricity, and current had become available to homes in towns. However, it was not common until after 1914, owing to the cost of cable laying and installation, so the change-over from gas to electricity was, perforce, a slow process. At this time, electric-light fittings were very similar to gas-fitting designs, especially as seen in hanging, central pendants, called electroliers, and wall brackets (see Figs. 606, 727, 729 and 730), but in the Edwardian period, table lamps and standard lamps were designed; these had fringed and flounced shades which were more modern in form (see Figs. 606 and 726). Simpler hanging fittings also came out, such as the alabaster bowl shown in Fig. 723.

As in other forms of art and decoration, **pottery** and **porcelain** suffered in this period from a tendency to over-ornateness and from a heterogeneous mixture of styles and influences. Among such influences were Greek and Roman, Japanese and Indian, also, towards the end of the century, the Art Nouveau theme, ostensibly on a nature basis, but actually artificial and rather anaemic. There was no definite style of the period, and most designs suffered from an excess of ornament and feeling of busyness. Some of the best work came from the sound, often inexpensive, but good-quality **Wedgwood** pottery, also from the **Minton** factory. **William Morris's** factory was producing some more original work. **William de Morgan,** whose name stands out at this time as a man working away from the over-elaboration of the period, was in sympathy with Morris, and also produced some pleasant and

---

[1] The discovery of the carbon-filament lamp is often accredited to Thomas Edison in America, but Swan's lamp was a prototype of Edison's, which did not appear until 1879.

[2] The tungsten-filament lamp came later; this metal is still used in modern bulbs.

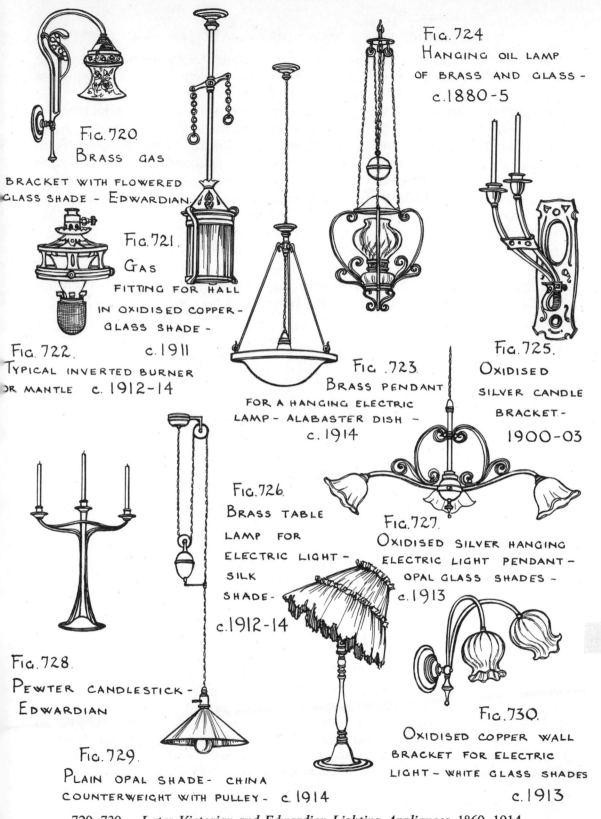

Fig. 720.
Brass gas
bracket with flowered
glass shade - Edwardian.

Fig. 721.
Gas
fitting for hall
in oxidised copper-
glass shade -
c. 1911

Fig. 722.
Typical inverted burner
or mantle   c. 1912-14

Fig. 724.
Hanging oil lamp
of brass and glass -
c. 1880-5

Fig. 723.
Brass pendant
for a hanging electric
lamp - alabaster dish -
c. 1914

Fig. 725.
Oxidised
silver candle
bracket -
1900-03

Fig. 726.
Brass table
lamp for
electric light -
silk
shade -
c. 1912-14

Fig. 727.
Oxidised silver hanging
electric light pendant -
opal glass shades -
c. 1913

Fig. 728.
Pewter candlestick -
Edwardian

Fig. 729.
Plain opal shade - china
counterweight with pulley - c. 1914

Fig. 730.
Oxidised copper wall
bracket for electric
light - white glass shades
c. 1913

720-730   *Later Victorian and Edwardian Lighting Appliances, 1860-1914*

delicate work. The firm of **Doulton** were making stoneware at Lambeth at the end of the century: much of this was good-quality ware. Examples of ware from this period can be seen in Plate XXXI.

A similar pattern is evident in the **glassware** of this time: a mixture of styles, over-ornamentation of nearly all work, and an abundant use of painting on glass in the form of landscapes, flowers and figure subjects. Deeply cut decoration was also used profusely. The Japanese influence was also apparent in this field after 1870, past styles of work being revived and Victorianised. Again, efforts were made to imitate 16th-century Venetian work, but it was largely over-decorated. Gilt was used a good deal, in addition to the other forms of ornament. Large quantities of cheaper pressed glass were produced to imitate the cut glass, as is so to-day, and this work found its way into many homes. Small amounts of blown glass were produced by individuals and small factories, such as William Morris and his associates; some of this work was of high quality. Glassware of the period can be seen in Plate XXXI.

731   *Mahogany Frame and Stand for Embroidery Panel, c.* 1860

NOTES ON ILLUSTRATIONS

Fig. 602.   Mid-Victorian Parlour.   1860–70

Wallpaper—cornice to dado. Vine pattern in strong but sombre shades of purple, green and grey. **Woodwork** of wainscot, window frame, etc., painted in dark-brown graining. Fitted **carpet**—wool, multicoloured in fawn, blue, crimson, yellow and grey. **Picture frames** gilded or plain wood. White mounts. **Lighting**—Brass gas **chandelier** in centre. Brass wall **sconce**. **Wall shelves** to hold pottery—covered in crimson velvet with white embroidery, beads and tasselling. **Window curtains**—patterned brocade in green and gold. White lace curtains over whole window. **Furniture—Jardinière** with fern, brass vase and holder, mahogany support, height 3 ft. 6 in. **Brass gong,** wrought-iron stand, height 2 ft. 4 in. **Chair,** mahogany, red velvet seat. Small **table,** wood inlaid with shell and mother of pearl all over, height 1 ft. 10 in.; glass dome on top filled with stuffed birds; on black wood base. Carved wood **pianoforte.** Adjustable mahogany **stool** with green velvet seat. Papier-mâché **chair** (centre), chintz-covered buttoned seat. **Banner screen** of black silk, embroidered in colour in Gothic design; gold cords, tassels and fringing; mahogany stand, height 3 ft. **Armchair,** carved mahogany, buttoned upholstery covered in brocade; embroidered petit-point cushion. Papier-mâché **work table,** height 2 ft. **Pole screen,** mahogany—banner of petit-point embroidery. **Table** (under window), mahogany, pedestal style, height 2 ft. 6 in.; covered by dark-green plush cloth embroidered in red and white silk roses; lace mat under ornamental dark-blue and coloured pot containing earthenware flower pot and aspidistra. **Chair,** mahogany, red velvet seat. **Sofa,** mahogany, horsehair upholstery; wool and silk antimacassar in cyclamen, yellow and green, tasselled; bead-embroidered cushion in red and white.

Fig. 603. *Late Victorian Drawing Room.* 1870–85

Plain plaster **frieze.** **Woodwork** painted in dark brown. **Wallpaper**—flock in dark green, gold and red. Fitted **carpet**—plain dull red with patterned border in black, grey, dark blue and pink. Fur skin **hearthrug.** Cast-iron **mantelpiece, fireplace** and **grate.** Brass **fender** and **fire irons.** Carved mahogany **chimneypiece** above with mirror on both tiers. Crimson velvet hangings, tassels and fringe. Numerous vases and ornaments on shelves and in niches. Carved and inlaid decorative clock. Porcelain clock on lower shelf. Gilt wood and mahogany **picture frames.** **Lighting.** Central **gasolier** of brass. **Oil lamp** on piano, of glass and bronze. **Furniture—Jardinière** of carved mahogany with gilt decoration, earthenware pot with palm. Carved mahogany **grand pianoforte.** **Chiffonier** of carved walnut inlaid with ebony and tortoiseshell; statuary marble top, mirror back; glass domes containing wax flowers and fruit. Fireside **chair** (left), carved mahogany, upholstery buttoned and covered in green velvet; petit-point embroidered cushion, roses on black background, gold tassels. **Work table,** carved mahogany, lid lined with baize. **Table,** mahogany, covered by dark-red silk cloth with fringe and coloured silk embroidery. China tea service and tray. **Cabinet,** mahogany inlaid with ebony (to contain china and books). Fireside **chair** (right), wood frame, painted black; green-felt-covered upholstery with gold fringe and cording; white crochet antimacassar. Ladderback **chair,** cane seat.

Fig. 604. *Mid-Victorian Bedroom.* c. 1865–75

Wallpaper—dark-grey background. Formal design in reds, blues and silver. **Floor**—polished oak. **Rugs**—wool, strong colours. **Sash window**—plate glass. Long lace white curtains and dark-blue velvet curtains and frill with black fringing. **Woodwork** painted dark brown. **Lighting**—candles in brass candleholders and bronze candlelamp. **Bedstead** of brass and iron. Half-tester with metal rails. Curtains of chintz with velvet band borders and fringed edges. Multicoloured patchwork quilt. Bed valances to match hangings. **Furniture—Bedside cabinet, chairs, washstand, dressing table** and **wardrobe** of mahogany with incised and inlaid decoration. **Chairs** have cane seats. **Dressing table** draped in white muslin with blue satin bows and white lace edging. **China toilet set** on washstand with purple and green floral decoration. **Hanging bookshelves—** mahogany. **Mirror,** gilt, wood frame. Poly-sided **table** of walnut with castors. **Towel rack,** mahogany. Gilt wood **picture frames**.

Fig. 605. *Late Victorian Dining Room.* *c.* 1890–5

Room decorated after the style of Adam. Ribbed plaster **ceiling** and moulded **cornice—** distempered in cream. Plaster **frieze—**distempered white. Olive-green plain painted **walls. Woodwork** of window frames, dado rail and wainscot painted white. Polished oak **floor.** Dark-green **carpet** with maroon borders. Fawn woollen **hearth rug.** White marble **chimneypiece.** Shelves with mirror backs above—fire opening of coloured marble, oatmeal tone. Cast-iron **hob grate—**copper curb, dogs and fire irons. **Window curtains—**dark-green rep lined with fawn poplin, brass rail. **Lighting—by gas. Central pendant burner—**brass fitting with green silk shade. **Wall brackets** on chimneybreast— brass with glass shades. **Furniture—**Mahogany **screen** with silk panel. Mahogany **sideboard** with painted panels and circular mirror, silk curtain; height 6 ft. 6 in. Brass **lamp** with pleated pink shades. Mahogany **dining table** and **chairs**; table, height 2 ft. 6 in.; chairs, upholstered seats covered in gold-coloured leather. Brightly coloured wool table runner. Window **table** of teak—inlaid decoration with walnut, sycamore and rosewood; height 2 ft. 4 in. Window **chairs,** mahogany, similarly inlaid, leather-covered seats. **Cabinet,** oak inlaid with ebony, glass-panelled doors; height 5 ft. 9 in. Mahogany longcase **clock,** brass mounts. Upholstered **wing armchair,** chintz covering.

Fig. 606. *Edwardian Drawing Room.* 1901–14

Cream-painted ribbed **ceiling** and **cornice. Woodwork** of window, picture rail, wainscot and door painted white. White marble **chimneypiece.** Cast-iron **fire opening, hood** and **grate—**all decorated. White side tiles—blue hearth tiles. Brass **fender, fire irons** and **coal box.** Papered **frieze** in white, pink, blue and pale green. **Wallpaper** in grey, rose and white. **Curtains** and pelmet in dark-blue silk, lined with cream and cream fringing. **Carpet—**grey and blue. Black sheepskin **hearthrug. Lighting—by electricity. Central pendant light—**brass counter-weight type with pink silk flounce. **Wall brackets** —polished brass on wood block—glass shade. **Standard lamp—**brass with pink silk shade—grey fringe and blue embroidered decoration. **Chimney glass—**carved oak frame. **On mantelshelf—**porcelain and wood clock, pewter plates, china vases. China **vase** in ingle nook by window, with palm. Oak **wall stand. Furniture—Chair,** mahogany, leather seat. **Occasional table,** mahogany, height 2 ft. 4 in. On top, **portable gramophone** with wax cylindrical record, metal horn, wood base, width 1 ft. 11 in. **Cabinet on stand,** ebony inlaid with mother of pearl, height 3 ft. 10 in.; Vase. **Easy chair,** covered in chintz with satin cushion, gay colours. **Footstool,** walnut, embroidered top.

Fig. 607. *Late Victorian Entrance Hall and Staircase.* 1895–1900

Hall and staircase well **ceiling**—papered in lincrusta paper of deep cream colour. **Walls** wallpapered—floral pattern in gold, greens and browns. **Between dado and wainscot**—lincrusta paper in dark brown. Polished mahogany **staircase**—turned newel post and balusters—patterned staircarpet. **Woodwork** of stair panelling, door, door-case, dado, wainscot and window frame painted in grained brown varnish paint. **Window** sash type —brown velvet curtains. Polished oak **floor**. **Hall carpet**—floral pattern in wools— gold, green and dark blue. Polished oak **picture frames,** white mounts. **Gas lighting**— brass pendant with glass shades. **Furniture**—**Hall stand** (right), mahogany, metal lining to umbrella rest; pot and palm. **Hat and umbrella stand** (left), mahogany, inlaid. **Umbrella stand,** cast iron, painted black. **Jardinière,** mahogany stand with brass mounts.

Fig. 608. *Late Victorian Kitchen and Scullery.* c. 1880–95

Whitewashed plaster **ceiling**. Painted **walls**—dark green. **Floor** covered with dark-brown oilcloth. Coconut **mat** in front of fender. **Woodwork** of dresser, cupboards, doors and chimneypiece painted dark brown. **Gas lighting**—brass fitting—glass shade. In **scullery** through doorway—floor tiled with red quarry tiles. Woodwork, ceiling and walls to match kitchen. Iron washing **copper** to burn coal or coke with iron smoke pipe. **Sink**—enamelled fireclay. Galvanised **dustbin** and **pail**. Wood **plate-rack**. Wood roller **towel rail**. **Brooms**. Wood **chairs**. Wood **kitchen table**. Wood clothes horse. Iron double oven **kitchener** to burn coal. Iron and copper **utensils**. Iron **shovel, poker** and **coal hod**. Iron **fender**. Wall **clock**.

Fig. 609. *Edwardian Bathroom.* 1901–10

Ceiling—painted green. **Walls**—tiled. Coloured, flower-decorated frieze. Plain white tiles above dado rail, and white and green tiles below dado. **Floor**—tiled black and white. Black and white **mats**, also cork mat. Metal **towel rails**. **Woodwork** of door, window, wainscot, cupboard and dado painted white. (Curtains omitted to show the window.) Porcelain enamelled iron **bath**. Copper **gas geyser**—iron and wood stand. Brass **gas wall bracket**. Porcelain enamelled **lavatory basin**—metal supports. Floral back **splash tiles**. **Mirror** with brass frame—wood shelf. Metal **shaving cabinet** and mirror.

BIBLIOGRAPHY

For reasons of space this bibliography cannot be comprehensive; these books and catalogues have been of assistance to the author and are recommended for further study by the reader as required.

BOOKS

Social History

VON BOEHN, M., *Modes and Manners* (4 vols.), Harrap, London, 1935.

BOTT, A., *Our Fathers* (*1870–1900*), Heinemann Ltd., London, 1931.

BOTT, A., and CLEPHANE, I., *Our Mothers* (*1870–1900*), Gollancz Ltd., London, 1932.

BOURCHIER, J., Translated. Ed., G. C. Macauley, *The Chronicles of Froissart*, Macmillan and Co., Ltd., London, 1924.

CUTTS, The Rev., E. L., *Scenes and Characters of the Middle Ages*, De La Mare Press, London, 1911.

DAVIS, H. W. C., *Medieval England*, Clarendon Press, Oxford, 1924.

FRANCIS, R., *Looking for Georgian England*, Macdonald, London, 1952.

HARTLEY, D., and ELLIOT, M. M., *Life and Work of the People of England* (4 vols.), Batsford, London.

HARVEY, J., *Gothic England 1300–1550*, Batsford, London.

KNIGHT, C. (Ed.), *Old England* (several vols.), Sangster and Co., London.

LACROIX, P., *Manners, Customs and Dress during the Middle Ages*, Chapman and Hall, London, 1874.

LAVER, J., *Victoria Vista*, Hulton Press, London, 1954.

LEES-MILNE, J., *Tudor Renaissance*, Batsford, London, 1951.

PHILLIPS, A. H., *Georgian Scrapbook*, T. Werner Laurie Ltd., London, 1949.

QUENNELL, M., and C. H. B., *Everyday Life in Roman and Anglo-Saxon Times*, Batsford, London, 1959.

QUENNELL, M., and C. H. B., *A History of Everyday Things in England* (4 vols.), Batsford, London, 1958.

RICHARDSON, A. E., *Georgian England*, Batsford Ltd., London, 1931.

ROSCOE, E. S., *The English Scene in the Eighteenth Century*, Constable and Co., Ltd., London, 1912.

Shakespeare's England, Clarendon Press, Oxford, 1916.

TAPPAN, E. M., *In Feudal Times*, Harrap, London, 1913.

TRAILL, H. D., and MANN, J. S. (Ed.), *Social England* (several vols.), Cassell and Co., Ltd., London.

TREVELYAN, G. M., *Illustrated Social History* (4 vols.), Longmans, London, 1950.

TURBERVILLE, A. S., *Johnson's England* (2 vols.), Clarendon Press, Oxford, 1933.

VINOGRADOFF, P., *English Society in the Eleventh Century*, Clarendon Press, Oxford, 1908.

WEIGALL, A., *The Grand Tour of Norman England*, Hodder and Stoughton Ltd., London.

BIBLIOGRAPHY

Art, Architecture and Interior Decoration in the Home

ALLEN, A., *The Story of Your Home*, Faber and Faber Ltd., London, 1949.

AYRTON, M., and SILCOCK, A., *Wrought Iron and its Decorative Use*, Country Life Ltd., London, 1929.

BERTRAM, A., *The House*, A. and C. Black, London, 1945.

BIRNSTINGL, H. J., *Sir John Soane*, Ernest Benn Ltd., London, 1925.

BRIGGS, R. A., *Homes for the Country*, Batsford, 1909.

BROWN, G. B., *The Arts in Early England*, John Murray, London, 1915.

CESCINSKY, H., *The Old-World House* (2 vols.), A. and C. Black Ltd., London, 1924.

CLARK, K., *The Gothic Revival*, Constable, London, 1928.

CONNOISSEUR, THE, *The Concise Encyclopedia of Antiques*, London, 1956–8.

CONNOISSEUR, THE, *Period Guides*, 6 vols., London, 1956–8.

DUTTON, R., *The English Interior (1500–1900)*, Batsford, London, 1948.

DUTTON, R., *The Victorian Home*, Batsford, London, 1954.

DUTTON, R., *London Homes*, Allan Wingate, London.

EDIS, R. W., *Decoration and Furniture of Town Houses*, C. Kegan Paul and Co., London, 1881.

GIBBERD, F., *The Architecture of England*, The Architectural Press, 1947.

GIEDION, S., *Mechanisation Takes Command*, Oxford University Press, New York, 1948.

GLAZIER, R., *A Manual of Historic Ornament*, Batsford Ltd., London, 1933.

GLOAG, J., *Georgian Grace, 1660–1830*, A. and C. Black, London, 1956.

GLOAG, J., *The Englishman's Castle*, Eyre and Spottiswoode, 1949.

GLOAG, J., and BRIDGWATER, D., *A History of Cast Iron in Architecture*, Allen and Unwin Ltd., London, 1948.

GOODHART-RENDEL, H. S., *English Architecture since the Regency*, Constable, London, 1953.

HAMLIN, A. D. F., *A History of Ornament, Ancient and Medieval*, Batsford, London, 1916.

HAMLIN, A. D. F., *A History of Ornament, Renaissance and Modern*, Batsford, London, 1923.

HARLING, R., *Home: A Victorian Vignette*, Constable, London, 1938.

HOLE, C., *English Home Life, 1500–1800*, Batsford, 1947.

HOLME, C. (Ed.), *Modern Domestic Architecture and Decoration*, The Studio, London, 1901.

HUSSEY, C., *English Country Houses Open to the Public*, Country Life Ltd., London, 1951.

JEKYLL, G., and JONES, S. R., *Old English Household Life*, Batsford, London, 1944–45.

JONES, S. R., *English Village Homes*, Batsford, London, 1936.

JOURDAIN, M., *English Interior Decoration, 1500–1830*, Batsford, London, 1950.

JOURDAIN, M., *English Interiors in Smaller Houses, 1660–1830*, Batsford, London, 1933.

JOURDAIN, M., *English Decoration and Furniture of the Later Eighteenth Century, 1760–1820*, Batsford, London, 1922.

JOURDAIN, M., *English Decoration and Furniture of the Early Renaissance, 1500–1650*, Batsford, London, 1924.

KNIGHT, E., *Taste and Economy in Decoration and Furniture*, Batsford, London, 1893.

LANCASTER, O., *Homes Sweet Homes*, John Murray, London, 1939.

LEES-MILNE, J., *The Age of Adam*, Batsford, London, 1947.

BIBLIOGRAPHY

LENYGON, F., *Decoration in England, 1660–1760*, Batsford, London, 1914.

LENYGON, F., *The Decoration and Furniture of English Mansions during the Seventeenth and Eighteenth Centuries*, T. Werner Laurie, London, 1909.

LLOYD, N., *A History of the English Home (from Primitive Times to the Victorian Period)*, The Architectural Press, London, 1931.

London Interiors, Joseph Mead, London, 1841.

MUSGRAVE, C., *Royal Pavilion*, Bredon and Heginbothom Ltd., Brighton, 1951.

NASH, J., *The Mansions of England in Olden Time*, The Studio, London, 1906.

NAVES, G., *Royal Homes*, Country Life Ltd., London, 1953.

PEVSNER, N., *High Victorian Design*, Architectural Press, London, 1951.

PILCHER, D., *The Regency Style 1800–1830*, Batsford, London, 1947.

REDMAYNE, P., *The Changing Shape of Things*, John Murray, 1945.

REILLY, P., *An Introduction to Regency Architecture*, Art and Technics Ltd., London, 1948.

ROGERS, H. MORDAUNT, *The Making of a Connoisseur*, The Estates Gazette, London, 1949.

SACKVILLE-WEST, V., *English Country Houses*, Collins, London, 1945.

SITWELL, S., *British Architects and Craftsmen, A Survey of Taste, Design, and Style during Three Centuries, 1600–1830*, Batsford, London, 1945.

STEEGMAN, J., *The Rule of Taste, from George I to George IV*, Macmillan and Co., Ltd., London, 1936.

STRANGE, T. A., *English Furniture, Decoration, Woodwork and Allied Arts, Last half of seventeenth century, eighteenth century and early part of nineteenth century*, McCorquodale and Co., Ltd., London, 1950.

STRATTON, A., *The Styles of English Architecture* (2 parts), Batsford, London.

SUMMERSON, J., *Georgian London*, Pleiades, 1945.

TIPPING, H. A., *English Homes* (4 vols.), Country Life Ltd., London, 1929.

TURNER, L., *Decorative Plasterwork in Great Britain*, Country Life Ltd., London, 1927.

TURNOR, R., *Nineteenth Century Architecture in Britain*, Batsford, 1950.

WARREN, C. H., *English Cottages and Farmhouses*, Collins, London, 1948.

WHIFFEN, M., *Elizabethan and Jacobean Architecture*, Art and Technics Ltd., London, 1952.

Furniture

BLAKE, J. P., and REVEIRS-HOPKINS, A. E., *Old English Furniture for the Small Collector, Mediaeval to Victorian Times*, Batsford, London, 1948.

BRACKETT, O., *English Furniture Illustrated*, Ernest Benn Ltd., London, 1950.

BRACKETT, O., *Thomas Chippendale*, Hodder and Stoughton Ltd., London.

CESCINSKY, H., *English Furniture of the Eighteenth Century*.

CESCINSKY, H., and GRIBBLE, E. R., *Early English Furniture and Woodwork* (2 vols.), George Routledge and Sons Ltd., London, 1922.

COTCHETT, L. E., *The Evolution of Furniture*, Batsford, London, 1938.

DAVIS, FRANK, *A Picture Book of English Furniture*, Edward Hulton, London, 1958.

EBERLEIN, H. D., and MCCLURE, A., *The Practical Book of Period Furniture*, J. B. Lippincott Co., Philadelphia and London, 1914.

FENN, F., and WYLLIE, B., *Old English Furniture*, George Newnes Ltd., London, 1905.

BIBLIOGRAPHY

GLOAG, J., *British Furniture Makers*, Collins, London, 1945.

GLOAG, J., *English Furniture*, A. and C. Black, London, 1934.

GLOAG, J., *A Short Dictionary of Furniture*, Allen and Unwin Ltd., London, 1952.

GORDON, H., *Old English Furniture*, John Murray, London, 1948.

HARRIS, M., *The English Chair—its History and Evolution*, M. Harris and Sons, London, 1946.

HAYDEN, A., *Chats on Cottage and Farmhouse Furniture*, T. Fisher Unwin, London, 1912.

HAYWARD, C. H., *English Period Furniture, 1500–1800*, Evans Bros. Ltd., London, 1936.

Hepplewhite Furniture Designs from the Cabinet-Maker and Upholsterer's Guide 1794, A. Tiranti, London, 1947.

HUGHES, B. and T., *After the Regency, 1820–1860*, Lutterworth Press, London, 1952.

JONES, B., *English Furniture at a Glance*, The Architectural Press, 1954.

LENYGON, F., *Furniture in England 1660–1760*, Batsford, London, 1914.

MANWARING, R., *The Cabinet and Chair Maker's Real Friend and Companion, 1765*, John Tiranti, London, 1937.

READE, B., *Regency Antiques*, Batsford, London, 1953.

REEVES, D., *Furniture—an explanatory history*, Faber and Faber Ltd., London, 1947.

ROE, F., *Ancient Coffers and Cupboards*, Methuen and Co., London, 1902.

ROE, F. G., *Victorian Furniture*, Phoenix House Ltd., London, 1952.

ROGERS, J. C., *English Furniture*, Country Life Ltd., London, 1923.

SHERATON, T., *Sheraton Furniture Designs from the Cabinet Maker's and Upholsterer's Drawing Book, 1791–4*, John Tiranti Ltd., London, 1945.

SMITH, D., *Old Furniture and Woodwork*, Batsford, London, 1945.

STANLEY-BARRETT, H., *The A.B.C. History of Antique English Furniture*, The Old-World Galleries Ltd., London.

The Art Journal Illustrated Catalogue of the Great Exhibition of 1851, George Virtue, 1851.

WENHAM, E., *Old Furniture for Modern Rooms from the Restoration to the Regency*, G. Bell and Sons Ltd., 1948.

Ceramics

BARRETT, F. A., *Worcester Porcelain*, Faber and Faber, London, 1952.

DIXON, J. L., *English Porcelain of the Eighteenth Century*, Faber and Faber, London, 1952.

HAYDEN, A., *Chats on English China*, Ernest Benn Ltd., London, 1947.

HAYDEN, A., *Chats on English Earthenware*, T. Fisher Unwin, 1919.

HONEY, W. B., *English Pottery and Porcelain*, A. and C. Black, London, 1945.

HUGHES, G. BERNARD AND THERLE, *The Collectors' Encyclopedia of English Ceramics*, Lutterworth Press, London, 1956.

HURLBUTT, F., *Old Derby Porcelain*, T. Werner Laurie, London, 1928.

MANKOWITZ, WOLF, *Wedgwood*, Batsford, London, 1953.

MOORE, N. H., *The Old China Book*, Tudor Publishing Co., New York, 1903.

RACKHAM, B., *A Key to Pottery and Glass*, Blackie and Son Ltd., London, 1945.

SEMPILL, C., *English Pottery and China*, Collins, London, 1944.

WEDGWOOD, J. C., *Staffordshire Pottery and its History*, Sampson Low, Marston and Co., Ltd., London.

WILLIAMS, S. B., *Antique Blue and White Spode*, Batsford, London, 1945.

Silverware and Other Metals

BURGESS, F. W., *Chats on Old Copper and Brass*, T. Fisher Unwin, Ltd., London, 1914.

HAYDEN, A., *Chats on Old Sheffield Plate*, T. Fisher Unwin Ltd., London, 1920.

HAYDEN, A., *Chats on Old Silver*, T. Fisher Unwin Ltd., London.

HUGHES, B. & T., *Three Centuries of Domestic Silver*, *1500–1820*, Lutterworth Press, London, 1952.

HUGHES, G. B., *Collecting Antiques*, Country Life Ltd., London, 1949.

HUGHES, G. B., *Small Antique Silverware*, Batsford, London, 1957.

OMAN, C., *English Domestic Silver*, A. and C. Black, London, 1947.

WILDING, P., *An Introduction to English Silver*, Art and Technics Ltd., London, 1950.

Glass

HUGHES, G. B., *English, Scottish and Irish Table Glass*, Batsford, London, 1956.

THORPE, W. A., *English Glass*, A. and C. Black, London, 1949.

Textiles and Wallpaper

ENTWHISTLE, E. A., *The Book of Wallpaper*, Arthur Barker, London, 1954.

GLAZIER, R., *Historic Textile Fabrics*, Batsford, London, 1923.

KENDRICK, A. F., *English Decorative Fabrics of the Sixteenth to Eighteenth Centuries*, F. Lewis, Essex, 1934.

Cutlery

HIMSWORTH, J. B., *The Story of Cutlery*, Ernest Benn Ltd., London, 1953.

Food

DRUMMOND, J. C., and WILBRAHAM, A., *The Englishman's Food*, Jonathan Cape, London, 1939.

CATALOGUES

Published by Victoria and Albert Museum, London

50 *Masterpieces of Textiles.*
50 *Masterpieces of Pottery and Glass.*
Flowers in Embroidery.
Mid-Georgian Domestic Silver.
Georgian Furniture.
English Chairs.
Tea-pots.
The Panelled Rooms (several vols.).
Glass (W. B. Honey).
Glass.

BIBLIOGRAPHY

English Medieval Silver.
Masterpieces in the Victoria and Albert Museum.
Tudor Domestic Silver.
Early Stuart Silver.
Charles II Domestic Silver.
Queen Anne Domestic Silver.
Catalogue of an Exhibition of Victorian and Edwardian Decorative Arts (illustrated).
Adam Silver.
Regency Domestic Silver.
English Wrought Iron Work.

Published by the Geffrye Museum, London

Geffrye Museum Handbook.

Published by the London Museum, London

Medieval Catalogue.

Published by the British Museum, London

The Sutton Hoo Ship Burial.

Published by Horniman's Museum, London

Musical Wind Instruments.

Journals

The Furniture Gazette 1873–6.
The Building News 1874–5.
Punch from 1848.
Illustrated London News.
The Studio.

INDEX

Page references are printed in ordinary type; figure references in **heavy type**.